Golf Course Design

Golf Course Design

Robert Muir Graves
and
Geoffrey S. Cornish

John Wiley & Sons, Inc.
New York Chichester Weinheim Brisbane Singapore Toronto

Designations used by companies to distinguish their products are often claimed as trademarks. In all instances where John Wiley & Sons, Inc. is aware of a claim, the product names appear in initial capital or all capital letters. Readers, however, should contact the appropriate companies for more complete information regarding trademarks and registration.

This book is printed on acid-free paper. ∞

Copyright © 1998 by John Wiley & Sons, Inc. All rights reserved.

Published simultaneously in Canada.

No part of this publication may be reproduced, stored in a retrieval system or transmitted in any form or by any means, electronic, mechanical, photocopying, recording, scanning or otherwise, except as permitted under Sections 107 or 108 of the 1976 United States Copyright Act, without either the prior written permission of the Publisher, or authorization through payment of the appropriate per-copy fee to the Copyright Clearance Center, 222 Rosewood Drive, Danvers, MA 01923, (508) 750-8400, fax (508) 750-4744. Requests to the Publisher for permission should be addressed to the Permissions Department, John Wiley & Sons, Inc., 605 Third Avenue, New York, NY 10158-0012, (212) 850-6011, fax (212) 850-6008, E-Mail: PERMREQ @ WILEY.COM.

This publication is designed to provide accurate and authoritative information in regard to the subject matter covered. It is sold with the understanding that the publisher is not engaged in rendering professional services. If professional advice or other expert assistance is required, the services of a competent professional person should be sought.

Library of Congress Cataloging-in-Publication Data:
Golf course design / [edited by] Robert Muir Graves and Geoffrey S.
    Cornish.
        p.   cm.
    Includes bibliographical references (p.) and index.
    ISBN 0-471-13784-7 (cloth : alk. paper)
    1. Golf courses—Design and construction.   I. Graves, Robert
Muir.   II. Cornish, Geoffrey S.
    GV975.G586 1998
    712'.5—dc21   97-37559

Printed in the United States of America.

10 9 8 7 6 5 4 3 2 1

Contents

Part I

The Game and the Course

Part II

Construction and Grow-In

Part III

The Business of Golf Course Design

Foreword

There's one secret of golf course architecture you won't learn from this fine book by my good friends Geoff Cornish and Bob Graves.

It's the longevity of these designers.

These two have been designing courses forever, or so it seems to us youngsters. Geoff has been at it longer than Jack Nicklaus has been winning tournaments, longer than Paul Newman has been making movies, longer even than Alaska and Hawaii have been states. Bob Graves started back when a ten spot bought you a round of golf at Pebble Beach, Augusta National still had a rough, and Jack Kennedy's set of clubs was worth only retail.

Cornish and Graves offer just about everything we would want to know about golf architecture in this book, except how to make nice, long, successful careers at it.

Of course, it's their wealth of experience that makes them perfect teachers of golf design. They've seen and done it all.

Geoff, a Canadian, started under the tutelage of the magnificent Stanley Thompson. In the early 1950s, Geoff detected a golf course void in New England and systematically filled it with every type of course imaginable. He's produced one of the truly great short courses in America, Blue Rock Par 3 on Cape Cod, as well as the absolute longest one in the nation, the 8,300-yard International in Bolton, Massachusetts. He's built entry-level courses with rock bottom prices and pricey courses out of rocky bottoms. Everywhere he's gone, he's preached playability.

Bob, from Michigan, studied landscape architecture at Michigan State and Berkeley a good decade ahead of the civil unrest experienced there, then settled in Walnut Creek where the whole West Coast (and even the Pacific Rim) lay at his feet. He's built on ocean bluffs and Malaysian swamps, chopped Douglas firs for some fairways, transplanted oaks along others, and created one of the country's prettiest courses, Quail Lodge, and one of its toughest, La Purisima. Everywhere he's gone, Bob has preached pulchritude, a landscape architect's five-dollar term for beauty.

These two have never worked together on a course design, but their careers brought them together 30 years ago. Both were accepted for membership in the American Society of Golf Course Architects in the same year, 1967. Never back-benchers, Bob assumed the presidency of the Society in 1974 and Geoff succeeded him the following year.

Between them, Cornish and Graves have encouraged, trained, promoted, or sponsored more aspiring course architects than anyone is able to count. And that's not factoring in their traveling road show, those two-day seminars that have roamed from the halls of Harvard to the Strip in Las Vegas for nearly two decades, attracting superintendents, club pros, green chairpersons, writers, and even cardiologists, and instilling in every one of them the notion that golf architecture is the most fascinating, creative experience of any sport.

This book, in fact, is a by-product of those seminars. Like the lively Cornish and Graves classroom repartee, it educates us and teaches us to examine golf design in new and different ways. It tells us nearly everything we want to know about course architecture as an art, a science, and a lifetime study. It even makes us dream of being golf course architects.

This a book worth reading, even if it doesn't teach us how to last as long as Geoff Cornish and Bob Graves.

Ron Whitten

Preface

This book introduces the context and parameters of golf course architecture. Its narrative and illustrations outline what is involved in creating an exciting, memorable, and maintainable golf course of integrity—one that is an asset to the environment and the community.

In golf, there are no rigid dimensions and no standard playing fields. Everyone who has ever designed a golf course (indeed, anyone who plays the game) has had his or her own ideas about how it should be done. The resulting variety of courses is one of many reasons that golf is such a fascinating and durable pastime and that its architecture is one of the most intriguing of all professions.

The contemporary golf course architect practices in an era of vast technological advances and an expanding global economy. Change, unprecedented since the Renaissance and the Industrial Revolution, is occurring in all aspects of our lives. The Royal and Ancient Game of Golf and its playing fields are providing some stability—and respite—during this whirlwind of transition.

Of course, some elements of the game have changed as well. Technological improvements in equipment and concern for environmental quality pose distinct challenges for golf course design. We introduce both topics in Part I and integrate them throughout the book.

We recognize that there is talent—even genius—involved in producing layouts, whether of outstanding design or merely functional. Nevertheless, with a combined total of almost a century of practice, we have observed that talent and genius in our profession arise from persistence, hard work, experience, and judicious use of knowledge and available resources, rather than something inherent in the architect's makeup—unless that "something" is determination and the ability to apply oneself.

There is no substitute for on-the-ground study before a designer puts pencil to paper. Nevertheless hands-on exercises are part of the learning process, as we have discovered in seminars presented at Harvard University and to the Golf Course Superintendents Association of America. Background plans for these exercises are outlined in Appendix B of this book. We urge that the reader accept the challenge and undertake them.

A golf architect's knowledge must be infinitely broader than course design. Still, we have limited this book to an in-depth treatment of the discipline itself and merely introduce collateral but important fields such as turfgrasses, irrigation, planning surrounding real estate, finance, construction and development of courses as wildlife habitats. A number of acclaimed experts have contributed chapters and appendices covering these subjects.

Moreover, we recognize that the enduring greatness of an architect's creation lies in the hands of the dedicated course superintendents but have refrained from discussing their field beyond establishment of the greensward.

We treat environmental issues somewhat similarly, recognizing that the environment is the background for creation of the playing fields of golf. There are now excellent texts available on environmental planning, as there are on the aforementioned collateral issues.

The impressive qualifications of our contributing editors, a glossary of design terms—perhaps the most complete ever presented on this subject—and an up-to-date bibliography follow the appendices. Appendix A includes guidelines prepared by three persons influential in our art form. Once known as the *design codes*, they remain basic and eternal.

Renowned golf architect Robert Trent Jones has pointed out that members of our profession have created an art form on a very broad canvas and in doing so have produced the playing fields that constitute the cornerstone of the game. Golf architects attempt to express their deepest values in their creations, although they are constantly forced to weigh one important consideration against another. The integrity of what they say (Ronald Whitten) in exercising their freedom (Thomas Fazio) depends largely on their vision (Thomas Doak) and their judgment. The end result is a work of art by an artist who, when he or she deems it best, overlooks rules of thumb, such as those presented in this book, and takes responsibility for doing so.

A half century has come and gone since a handful of visionaries met to form the American Society of Golf Course Architects in 1947, a meeting that followed the Depression and World War II, in which our art form could have become a lost art. Decades since have seen an explosion in the apparently limitless expansion of golf and its playing fields, together with creation of the most impressive layouts since golf spread from Scotland.

Keys to the future lie in dedication to education, research, and excellence, together with the profession's responsibilities to the environment, society, and its dominant role to provide the cornerstone of golf. Surely the decades of the new millennium will provide opportunities for golf course architects greater than any in the history of the profession and art form.

Robert Muir Graves
Geoffrey S. Cornish

Acknowledgments

This book is drawn from 13 years of seminars presented annually at Harvard University, part of the Professional Development Summer Continuing Education Program under the directorship of William S. Saunders, assistant dean of External Relations. It is also based on a similar 14-year series of lectures conducted under the auspices of the Golf Course Superintendents Association of America.

In addition to our distinguished contributing authors, we acknowledge the good-will and assistance provided by all members of the American Society of Golf Course Architects, together with that society's productive executive secretary, Paul Fullmer, and his wife, Sandra. We also acknowledge the help of Chad Ritterbusch, assistant to Paul, who lends his enthusiasm to all ventures related to the ASGCA. In fact, the good-will of members of the ASGCA made this book possible, and we feel deeply that their combined experience of several thousand years is reflected herein.

We have been enriched by our ongoing association with the British Institute of Golf Course Architects, where we have listened to presentations by notaries such as Fred Hawtree and his son Martin Hawtree (the third generation of Hawtrees in course design), Don Steel, architect and author, and Howard Swan, who practices in the tradition of globetrotters Mackenzie and Alison.

Two writers helped to bring our work to fruition. Without Valerie Faith, a part-time professional writer of Amherst, Massachusetts, who went far beyond the call of duty in preparing the book despite a very full schedule, we could not have completed this work. Bob Labbance of Stockbridge, Vermont, a superb writer and editor-in-chief of *Vermont Golf*, *New Hampshire Golf*, and *New York Golf* magazines, and *New England Golf Atlas* series enabled us to meet a deadline with Dan Sayre, the understanding senior editor who originally conceived this book). Along the way we encountered Twyla Webb of the Scott Seed Company of Marysville, Ohio. We thank her for finding two eminent scientists within her organization to review and edit technical information related to specifying and purchasing seed and fertilizer.

We also thank Damian Pascuzzo, partner in the firm of Graves and Pascuzzo of Walnut Creek, California, who took over Graves' load so that he could work on this text. We also thank Mahan CADesign of Wilton, California, for assistance in finalizing sketches. Both Charlie Mahan and Damian Pascuzzo contributed greatly to the coverage of CADD and its influence on the golf course design process.

Joseph Beditz, president and CEO of the National Golf Foundation, cooperated with our many requests for assistance. It was he who recommended Richard L. Norton and Catherine Suddarth, both of the Foundation, to prepare a chapter and an appendix, respectively.

Finally, we acknowledge Theodore Kozlowski, renowned plant physiologist, who has authored some 25 textbooks and is presently a visiting scholar at the College of Natural Resources, University of California, Berkeley. We respect the example he has set in providing textbooks for ours and future generations, and we thank him for the encouragement and friendship given over the years, long before and during the critical path of this work.

The Game
and
the Course

The History of Golf and Golf Course Design

The courses of Great Britain abound in classic and notable holes, and one has to study them and adopt their best and boldest features. Yet in most of their best holes there is always room for improvement.

Adapted from *Scotland's Gift GOLF,* 1928, by Charles Blair Macdonald (1856–1939)

Golf evolved on the links of Scotland, undulating land sparsely covered with grazed fescues, broom, and other links plants found along the coastlines of the British Isles. Over a period of five hundred or more years golf has endured, growing into the worldwide pastime that is now part of so many people's way of life.

Pastimes resembling golf, with similar playing equipment, were pursued in Europe as early as the days of the Roman Empire, when the game of paganica was played. Other early European games resembling golf include pall mall in Italy, chole in Belgium and France, and kolven in the Netherlands, where some say golf originated. All but the Scottish game have virtually disappeared.

The Early Scottish Links

Wind and weather contributed to the development of golf, as did the Scottish way of life. Characteristics of the links that influence contemporary golf course architecture include:

- The vegetation, with broom, gorse, heather, and coarse grasses interspersed, with areas of grazed bent grass and fescues predominant.
- The commons: links land was publicly owned, allowing free play.
- The landscape, was devoid of trees and freshwater ponds that could have made the game discouraging rather than exciting.
- The climate: blades of grazed grass standing stiff and erect, as a result of the salt air, supported the leather-covered feather ball (or "featherie") used during the early centuries of the game. Boxwood balls had been in use prior to the featherie.
- The soil, sandy and well drained, provided the mystical link between sand, golf, and drainage that continues to this day.
- The winds, often gale force, drove livestock to seek shelter behind hillocks, where they trampled grass into sandy scars that Scottish farmers called "bunkers." These added challenge and excitement for those hitting balls across the links.
- The bunkers: high winds scoured these bunkers ever deeper, as did the recovery shots of those whose balls had come to rest in them. Still other scars were created by local residents quarrying seashells for their gardens.
- The northern latitude, where long daylight hours in summer made it possible to start play early in the morning and extend it well into the evening.

3

The Spread of Golf
Throughout the British Isles

From its beginnings in the fifteenth century, golf evolved on the Scottish links with no known designers. Then in the mid-nineteenth century the gutta percha ball, or "gutty" replaced the featherie. Fairways on the Old Course at St. Andrews were widened to accommodate increased play arising from the use of the livelier, less expensive, and more durable gutty. At the same time, rapid expansion of the British railway system made it possible for people from as far away as London to reach the links in a day or less to watch prominent professional golfers play in matches.

In the British Isles, golf had been played as early as the seventeenth-century near London by Scottish expatriates as well as on the plantations of Ireland as far south as Dublin. Yet none of these early golfing grounds survive. Really golf spread from Scotland to England in the last half of the nineteenth century. At first it followed the linksland of the English coast but soon spread inland, where players encountered heavy soils unsuitable for golf in an era when agronomy, the science of soil management and crop production, and equipment for modifying these conditions were relatively unknown.

Professional golfers who were successful in staking out courses that provided exciting play were soon recognized and sought out for their ability as designers. Three of the earliest known designers in the British Isles were Allan Robertson, Tom Morris, and Tom Dunn. All claimed the title "Greenkeeper and Professional."

Allan Robertson (1815–1859) of St. Andrews is the earliest known golf course designer. His first projects were the Road Hole, the 17th on the Old Course at St. Andrews, his home course, and early efforts to create the huge double greens at that ancient links together with the first widening of its fairways. Robertson laid out several links elsewhere in Scotland, including holes at Barry Angus that eventually became Carnoustie.

Robertson's protégé, Tom Morris (1821–1908), still known in the world of golf as "Old Tom," far exceeded his mentor in the number of golfing grounds he staked in Scotland, England, Wales, and Ireland. He concurrently continued the improvement initiated at St. Andrews by Robertson, notably the double greens and widening of the fairways. Morris's layouts include, but are by no means limited to, Muirfield, Royal County Down, Dornoch (now Royal), and Pwllheli in Wales, together with the New and Jubilee courses at St. Andrews.

Tom Dunn (1849–1902) was probably the most active designer in the last decades of the nineteenth century, although Old Tom Morris was the more renowned. Dunn's contribution was the creation of an abundance of functional layouts, mostly inland, for the tidal wave of newcomers taking up the game.

Still, until the turn of the twentieth century many English golfers felt that truly enjoyable golf could be found only on the coastline links. Then the heathlands near London, with their sandy soils, were discovered to be ideal for golf.

Dunn had already created several functional layouts on the heaths, but the heathland era was only dawning. The brilliant school of architects who started their practices on the heaths heralded the inception of modern golf course architecture in which earth was moved and features were constructed.

Willie Park Jr., who had already laid out several links courses in Scotland, H. S. Colt, W. H. Fowler, and J. F. Abercromby are the four best-known designers of this era. Their work elsewhere led to methods for converting fields of clay to satisfactory playing fields for golf.

Golf Spreads to North America

All these designers except Abercromby crossed the ocean to mingle with Scottish professionals who had preceded them in planning courses in the New World, where golf had spread to Canada as early as 1872 and to the United States a decade or so later. By the turn of the twentieth century, when the Haskell rubber-cored ball was introduced, courses in the United States outnumbered those in the British Isles.

Although the American courses had been designed by Scottish professionals and greenkeepers, no American course at that time could compare in playing interest and enjoyment to those on the links of Scotland and on the heaths of England. It was left to American and British designers to create the landmark North American golf courses that were soon to emerge.

By the early 1890s, Charles Blair Macdonald was designing golf courses in the Chicago area. He laid out the first nine holes of the Chicago Golf Club at Belmont in 1892, and the second nine a year later.

Born in Canada, reared in Chicago, and graduated from Scotland's University of St. Andrews, Macdonald coined the term "golf architect" and became known as the father of American golf course architecture. By 1911 his National Golf Links of America had opened on Long Island. Its excellence led to the rebuilding of existing layouts throughout North America—and probably in the British Isles—and its quality inspired that of courses yet to be built.

In 1913, when young American amateur Francis Ouimet defeated renowned British professionals Vardon and Ray to win the U.S. Open Championship at the Country Club in Brookline, Massachusetts, America went wild over golf. Until then golf had followed the path of the British Empire and was played wherever the British settled. Beginning in 1913, it rapidly became an American game, with the fortunes of golf following the fluctuations of the American economy and its social trends.

In the Roaring Twenties, golf expanded; superb layouts came into play worldwide, most notably in the United States. Funds were available, real estate costs were relatively low, and ideal land was open for development. Prominent North American golf architects, including A. W. Tillinghast, Stanley Thompson, Donald Ross, and William Flynn, along with Britishers Harry Colt, Charles Alison, and Alister Mackenzie produced masterpieces on both sides of the Atlantic and on other continents.

However, the Depression of the 1930s followed by World War II curtailed the expansion of the game. Although, according to the National Golf Foundation, about 1,000 new courses were opened for play in the United States from 1930 until the end of World War II, this figure was offset by closings of others, so that in 1953 there were fewer courses in the United States than in 1929.

The Era of Expansion: The 1950s to the Present

Following the Korean War, golf expanded in yet another era of growth, often referred to as the age of Robert Trent Jones. Jones designed more than 400 courses around the world and is regarded as having influenced course design and golf more than any other golf architect in history.

This postwar expansion has continued to the present, with the exception of a downturn between 1974 and 1982, when unfavorable economic conditions resulted in inadequate financing for golf course construction. Yet by 1982 golf was again expanding rapidly in North America, Europe, Japan, and other parts of the world. With more adequate funding available, spectacular courses emerged with ever-increasing quality in both construction and maintenance.

The history of golf architecture is related to course openings (Table 1.1). Catherine Suddarth, Senior Research Associate of the National Golf Foundation, compiled these statistics on the numbers of new facilities opened by decade and year in the U.S. Records are not available for the opening year of all of the nation's 15,000 plus courses, and tables do not include expansions as provided to the media. For example, course openings plus expansions for the years 1990 through 1994 are 289, 351, 354, 358, and 381, respectively, according to the National Golf Foundation. Almost 500 new courses opened in 1995.

The 1980s and 1990s yielded courses of immense visual impact. However, the importance of environmental concerns was increasingly recognized, and permit requirements, frequently involving wetland issues, ruled out many sites for golf (Figure 1.1). Architects accepted these challenges. In the 1980s, many integrated golf-residential communities were designed and built, mostly in the United States. While the residential community was not always successful, the golf course almost invariably was.

Under the influence of the husband-and-wife team of Paul "Pete" and Alice Dye, whose work was receiving increased attention by the 1970s, golf course design turned back to the links, yet with a North American flair. The Dyes' style required moving immense quantities of earth. Architects had long modified terrain and soils to emulate the naturally occurring, exciting, and pleasurable conditions of the Scottish links, but none to the extent and with the artistry of the Dyes. Their practice of creating land forms contrasted with that of Donald Ross, the grand master of the art form during the 1920s, who observed, "God created golf holes. It is the duty of the architect to discover them" (Figure 1.2).

Table 1.1
Course Openings

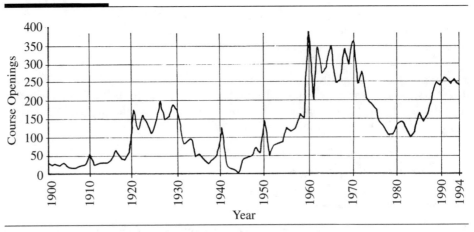

Notes: Records are not available for opening years of all the nation's courses.

These data do not include expansions of existing facilities. For example, course openings plus expansions for the years 1990 through 1994 are 289, 351, 354, 358, and 381, respectively, with 468 new courses and expansions opening in 1995 and 442 in 1996.

Approximately 1,000 facilities do not have a recorded opening date.

Source: Catherine Suddarth, Senior Research Associate, National Golf Foundation.

FIGURE 1.1   This par 3 green in a hollow was carefully interspersed among hills, valleys, forest vegetation, and wildlife wetlands at Port Ludlow Golf Course in Washington State.

FIGURE 1.2   This green at Widgi Creek Golf Course in Bend, Oregon, was sculpted from relatively flat ground by borrowing a minimum amount of fill from an adjacent area.

Nevertheless, the spectacular Dye style was eminently successful, attracting many newcomers to the game. Its visual impact became the order of the day, involving giant mounds, pot bunkers, wooden bulkheads, and other features of the Scottish links. Golf courses continued to enhance surrounding real estate values, the quality of life for those living nearby, and as open spaces provided habitat for innumerable other species. Not surprisingly, design professionals often refer to this era of spectacular golfing grounds with increasing perfection in construction and maintenance as the age of Pete Dye, even though it overlaps the age of Robert Trent Jones.

By the 1990s a return to the natural style, using terrain as it existed and reducing the quantity of earth to be moved, was apparent in the links and courses of several architects, notably Thomas Doak and William Coore, the latter working with the eminent professional golfer Ben Crenshaw. This trend also became apparent in the writings of Ronald Whitten, the celebrated author on the subject of golf architecture. Also in the early 1990s, architects such as Richard Phelps and Dennis Griffiths pioneered designs in an effort to accommodate disabled persons, while architects Michael Hurdzan and William Love were leaders in adapting golf to wetlands and addressing other environmental issues.

Emergence of a Team Approach

As in the earliest years of course design in Great Britain, a number of professional golfers established practices in the United States. Backed by staffs of trained planners, these renowned touring players, with their comprehension of the game, added another dimension to the art form. Of equal importance, their large staffs provided more opportunities for young designers who were well prepared, academically and in the field, to enter the profession.

Increasingly in the 1980s and 1990s specialists joined the architect in bringing a project to a successful conclusion. Teams of environmental, development, management, and other consultants left architects freer to practice their own art form, namely, design. The National Golf Foundation helped significantly by gradually taking over or assisting others in feasibility and impact studies.

Similarly, as golf course construction expanded, more experienced contractors specialized in the field, lightening, but by no means diminishing, the architect's responsibility in overseeing site construction. Moreover, the number of "design and build" firms practicing in this area increased as well. As a result, by the last decade of the twen-

FIGURE 1.3   *This green bunker at Seven Oaks Country Club in Bakersfield, California exemplifies the use of capes (protrusions) and bays (indentations) in modern bunker design. With a "feathered" edge, it would be reminicient of the old bunkers that evolved on early Scottish golf courses.*

tieth century, golf architects became true specialists in their own field, in contrast to the 1950s and 1960s, when they were called upon for assistance in a variety of related fields.

Throughout the evolution of golf, so closely tied to the increasing quality of its playing fields, golf architects have kept to a precept attributed to Sir Guy Campbell (1885–1960), architect, author, and soldier: "Lessons learned long ago on the links must never be forgotten." Like Sir Guy, contemporary designers, contractors, superintendents, and many golfers are keenly aware of that mystical bond between sand and golf inherent to the links (Figure 1.3).

The spectacularly beautiful golf courses—and their special features—that have emerged and are in play today would not have been possible without the nation's turfgrass scientists and engineers, who have provided architects, builders, and superintendents with knowledge and a diversity of products.

The impact of golf and its playing fields on the environment cannot yet be defined. Still, the effect of these large open spaces, in the United States alone equaling the total land area of Delaware and Rhode Island combined and managed by trained superintendents, is, we feel, positive, with architects, builders, superintendents, and ruling bodies repeatedly demonstrating their dedication to the "high road" by sponsoring independent research and taking action as problems become manifest.

Evolution of Golf Course Features

Golf is a game of enduring tradition, its appeal due in part to the lore of the links and to the style of its playing fields. Yet style fluctuates. To grow, a tree puts forth branches; similarly, a healthy art form also must branch out in order to grow.

The two main schools of golf architecture design, and many combinations, coexist. One school adapts the course to existing terrain, and the other creates spectacular layouts regardless of existing contours. The early Scottish links and their anonymous designers are as the roots of the art, while the courses of mainstream designers comprise its trunk. We might consider designers' use of archetypal symbols on the landscape as the branches.

Consider the symbolism employed by Desmond Muirhead at Aberdeen Golf and Country Club in Florida, Stone Harbour in New Jersey, and other courses overseas. Robert Cupp's Palmetto Hall Plantation in South Carolina is another example, and some would include architect Robert Berthet's extensive but controversial efforts in France.

There is no doubt that symbolistic layouts contribute to interesting golf. Landscape architect Kenneth L. Helphand of the University of Oregon recognized them in his authoritative "Learning from Linksland."[2] Yet his doing so is not inconsistent with his statement, "Golf is a landscape game where golfers compete with terrain. . . ."

Women have participated enthusiastically in golf since Mary Queen of Scots played in the sixteenth century. It is surprising that little was done architecturally to accommodate their game until after World War II, although several "Ladies Only" clubs had been established and two women practiced golf course architecture in the 1920s, namely, Mary Gourlay in England and May Hupfel,* daughter of Tom Dunn, in America. In the 1950s increasing attention was given to siting women's tees in relation to haz-

---

* Around 1892, Morris County Golf Club in Convent Station, New Jersey, was founded by ladies as a Ladies Only club. The ladies couldn't keep it up financially and in the early 1900s invited their husbands to become members in order to keep the club running. Within a few years, the ladies were pushed out, and it became a men's club.

ards and other features, and by the 1980s golf architect Alice Dye was championing the rights of women players.

With men and women of nearly all ages playing golf today, it can be concluded that in an age of rapid and constant change the traditions of the game contribute to its enduring popularity. Just as its growth depends on economic and societal trends, so the future of its architecture depends on these trends and belongs to those who prepare themselves thoroughly.

Greens, Tees, and Bunkers

Magnificently sculptured, contemporary greens evolved from links land closely grazed by sheep and rabbits, while the earliest fairways were "swards," or grass-covered land, resulting from less close grazing by cattle. Today's gently undulating greens evolved from putting areas built up from decades of top dressing, spreading sand over naturally raised areas (plateau greens) or on those areas nestled in hollows.

The introduction of greens rollers enhanced this smoothness as did heavy play, while continued top dressing year after year on an expanding area contributed to the heights and sizes of existing greens on the ancient links that we find so exciting to play today (Figures 1.4 through 1.8).

FIGURE 1.4   One can imagine how this flattish hilltop could be worn flat by the wear and tear of golf play combined with the elements.

FIGURE 1.5   Judging from the surrounding terrain, this north coast Scottish green appears to be a simulation of the classic plateau green, sometimes referred to as "gun platform" greens.

FIGURE 1.6   *This relatively modern green at Orinda Country Club in California is obviously a simulation of the classic plateau green.*

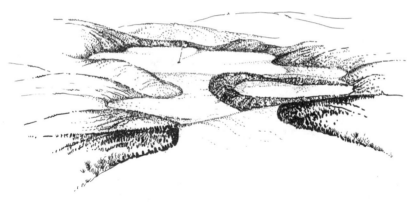

FIGURE 1.7   *This inviting little glen would be a natural destination or site for an early golf hole.*

FIGURE 1.8   *The 18th green on the Old Course at St. Andrews is barely discernable from the adjacent fairway, all of which is puttable. The renowned "Valley of Sin," at the right side of the photo, requires the reading of multiple breaks to get to the hole.*

Until about 1875 a player teed the ball on the green using a handful of earth from a hole that at that time had no metal cup. Small but level teeing areas were then provided adjacent to the green (Figure 1.9). These teeing grounds gradually became larger, while their shapes became increasingly more interesting. But many greenkeepers continued to resort to nonturf surfaces until, in the 1920s, it was realized that size was the key to maintaining turf (Figure 1.10). This size was most often achieved by a single large tee, geometric or free-form in shape, although there were instances of multiple tees on a single hole (Figures 1.11 through 1.13).

Scars created on the links where livestock trampled the turf challenged golfers and thus contributed to playing interest (Figures 1.14 and 1.15). Soon developers modified these natural "bunkers," using wooden bulkheads, railroad ties, or sod revetments to stabilize them and reduce the drifting of sand (Figures 1.16 and 1.17). Dramatic bunkering, introduced by Willie Park Jr. and developed further by H. S. Colt with his protégés C. H. Alison and Alister Mackenzie, became increasingly common. Stanley Thompson and his young protégé Robert Trent Jones later enhanced this bunker style. Links-style pot bunkers were also introduced around the world as the popularity of golf spread. Except in the British Isles they almost disappeared for several decades but emerged again with Pete Dye's creations.

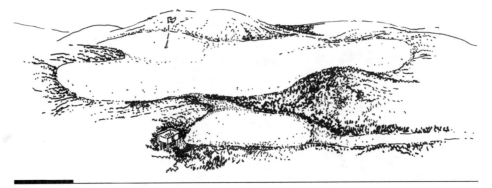

FIGURE 1.9 *By today's standards, the closeness of tee to green is unsafe. In the early days, it was a great improvement and allowed the art of greens maintenance to develop.*

FIGURE 1.10 *This artificial tee at a practice range is similar to the type of artificial surface sometimes used for regular golf play when the grass tee is too small or otherwise too worn.*

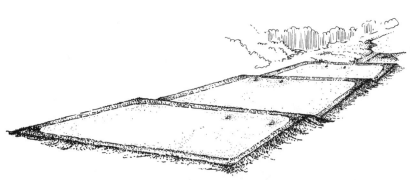

FIGURE 1.11   This tee could be fit to a sloping site and still offer plenty of teeing area. It repeats the rectangular shape often found in older tees.

FIGURE 1.12   This large tee, a mix of geometric and free-form, is part of the golf course at La Purisima near Santa Barbara, California.

FIGURE 1.13   A prime example of the modern-day free-form tee is located at Innisbrook Golf Club and is further enhanced by the juxtaposition of dormant Bermuda grass alongside the cool season grass tee surface.

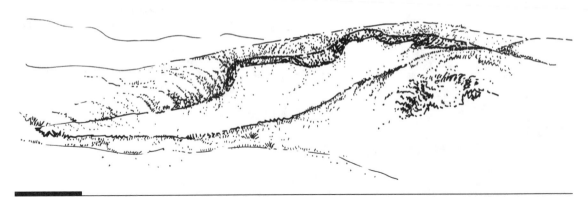

FIGURE 1.14   *This area, protected from the winds, would attract herds of sheep, goats, or cattle, thereby disturbing the area enough to expose the sand beneath the turf cover. Thus, a future bunker is born.*

FIGURE 1.15   *On this Irish links course, the front U-shaped bunker has been maintained to develop a refined shape. To its right, we can see sand being exposed by wear and weather, likely the genesis of its more polished neighbor.*

FIGURE 1.16   *Where the sand banks continually collapsed, turf sections, or sod, were cut from the outlying areas and placed in layers like bricks to hold the bank in place. Also see Fig. 1.16.*

FIGURE 1.17   *Here, along the north coast of Scotland, the sod embankment was tried and later replaced with the wooden bulkhead. Placement of the wood at an angle helps to prevent a ricocheted ball causing damage or injury.*

The Greensward

The impact of golf and its playing fields is interwoven with the greensward, or turfgrass covering, and its development.

Putting Surfaces

Turfgrass science is a discipline overlapping and integrated in many respects with the art form of golf architecture. As noted previously, golf course turf was first kept short by grazing animals. Later on, top dressing and rolling became the common practices for smoothing putting surfaces.

By the late nineteenth century greens were mowed regularly with lawnmowers, first invented by Edwin Budding in England in 1835. From the 1880s until after World War I, greenkeepers experienced in both construction and maintenance continued to arrive in North America from Scotland and other parts of the British Isles.

Seedsman Martin Sutton established Sutton's Grass Station, a commercial research and development center in Reading, England in 1863. Soon British seed companies expanded their services and provided products to other parts of the British Empire and to the United States. During the 1920s the multibladed greens mower was introduced. Its greater frequency of cut contributed to still smoother putting surfaces.

In the United States, several land grant colleges instituted turfgrass research in the last decades of the nineteenth century. Before World War I, C. V. Piper*, turfgrass scientist of the United States Department of Agriculture (USDA), consulted on establishment of turf at the National Golf Links of America, then under construction. This is believed to be the first time an agrostologist (a botanist who specializes in grasses) contributed directly to the establishment of a golf course in the United States. In 1917, Piper collaborated with R. A. Oakley on the seminal text *Turf for Golf Courses*.

By 1912 an association of British greenkeepers had been formed, and in 1920 the Green Section of the USGA was established. It became a major force in turfgrass research and management. In 1926 greenkeepers in the United States and Canada formed a professional society that soon became the Golf Course Superintendents Association of America (GCSAA). In 1927 Lawrence S. Dickinson established a school for greenkeepers at the Stockbridge School of Massachusetts Agriculture College. It was followed by others, and many undertook extensive turfgrass research.

Following World War II, scientific turfgrass management, sophisticated automatic irrigation systems, and technological advances in maintenance equipment contributed to many changes, not the least of which was the change to aerial golf, "playing the ball through the air as contrasted to 'bumping' it along the ground."

The USGA method for putting green construction developed by turfgrass scientist Marvin Ferguson, who later became a golf course architect, was introduced in 1960. Still later in that decade a growing number of contractors were specializing in golf course construction, and in 1970 they formed a professional group, the Golf Course Builders Association of America.

In 1978 the stimpmeter, invented in 1936 by Edward S. Stimpson to measure the speed of greens, was remodeled by the Green Section. This led to intense competition among courses for ever-faster putting surfaces, which in turn called for less steep grades. By the early 1980s, course superintendents with increasing budgets were downgrading the use of triplex mowers for their greens and returning to "walk behinds." This further enhanced putting green trueness.

Fairways

During the 1980s, lightweight mowing of fairways became popular. That was accompanied by contour mowing, characterized by undulating rather than straight lines between fairway and rough. These lines enhanced eye appeal and playing interest and intentionally reduced the area mowed to fairway.

Many new cultivars (species) of bent grass, bluegrass, ryegrass and fescues were developed, with Penncross creeping bent grass and Merion Kentucky bluegrass released by H. Burton Musser in the 1950s among the first. Fine-bladed bermudagrass also appeared, owing to the efforts of Glen W. Burton at the Tifton Georgia Coastal Plains Experiment Station.

In addition to its turf advisory service, the Green Section developed many programs, including financial grants for research into the impact of golf courses on people and the environment and a cooperative program with the Audubon Society of New York State on the relationship of wildlife and golf courses.

Turf for golf courses continues to be scientifically managed by superintendents, with many holding college degrees. Their training in stewardship of the land combined with modifications in design are leading to golf courses that are in all ways compatible with the environment.

Ruling Bodies, Playing Equipment, and Ball Technology

Golf had been played for three centuries on the links of Scotland before its first golf club was established. Then, in 1747, the Honourable Company of Edinburgh Golfers was formed for play on the links of Leith. It issued 13 articles, the earliest known rules of the game. Formation of that first club and its articles led to improvements in the "green" a hundred years later and the first instances of golf course design. The catalyst was the rivalry that arose among clubs.

The Society of St. Andrews, a club formed in 1754, adopted the Rules of the Honourable Company. In 1834, with the permission of King William IV, this Society became the Royal and Ancient Golf Club of St. Andrews (the R & A). In 1897 the R & A agreed to become the governing authority on the rules of golf in Britain.

Three years earlier, in 1894, the Ruling Body for Golf in the United States had been formed. It eventually became the United States Golf Association. In 1951 a joint committee of the R & A and USGA convened to adopt universal rules. The R & A and the USGA now work together on matters regarding rules and playing equipment.

Early golf balls made from leather and feathers—the "featheries"—had long replaced wooden balls by the time the gutta percha, or "gutty," was introduced. Acceptance of the livelier gutty in the 1840s resulted in replacement of hard thorn clubs with durable fruitwoods. Drivers, spoons, irons, and putters were soon in use.

Iron-headed clubs beat down the heather, which was therefore replaced with bent grass and fescues. These grasses, along with intentional widening of fairways, contributed to more enjoyable golf. With the advent of the livelier and less costly gutty and the rapid spread of the British railway system, the links became more crowded with golfers, the game soon spreading beyond Scotland.

In 1900 the even livelier rubber-cored Haskell ball was introduced, requiring still lengthier golf holes. In 1904 center-shafted putters appeared. Fearing these innovations and others that might occur, the R & A and the USGA adopted regulations concerning balls and equipment, but with standards differing somewhat on each side of the Atlantic.

The 1920s witnessed the introduction of matched sets of clubs, and clubs with steel shafts were legalized. In the Depression years, professional Gene Sarazen introduced a straight-faced sand wedge, causing the ruling bodies to establish a limit of 14 clubs. Ball velocity was also limited. These limits were achieved, but with a difference in the ball for several years.

Improving technology and new playing equipment continues to expand the parameters of the game. In 1994, the American Society of Golf Course Architects (ASGCA) authorized a study by its golf equipment committee. The findings of this committee are reported in the following question-and-answer format, authored by its chairman.

Findings of the Golf Equipment Committee

by Thomas A. Marzolf
GOLF COURSE ARCHITECT
FAZIO GOLF COURSE DESIGNERS, INC.
CHAIRMAN, ASGCA EQUIPMENT COMMITTEE

Q: **Has the game of golf changed due to advancements in course maintenance, club design, and ball technology?**

A: Yes and no. Yes, if you are a tour player, golf architect, or course superintendent. No, if you are an average golfer of average strength. Yes, if you are a dues-paying member at a golf club. No, if you are a dues-paying member of USGA. Yes, if you happen to work for a golf equipment manufacturer. No, if you work for the USGA. Yes, if you have ever walk-mowed a green. No, if you don't pay attention to how a golf course is maintained these days. Yes, if you play golf at any course that hosts a professional golf tournament. No, if you don't play golf.

Q: **Has golf been impacted by improved balls and clubs? Has the American quest for perfectly maintained golf courses changed the way we play the game?**

A: It depends on whom you ask. Some say yes, definitely. Some say no, not at all; it is just the normal evolution of the sport. What we're talking about when we list the impacts on the game of golf are really facts. Or is it merely opinion?

Everything changes. Things evolve. It is only natural for golf to adjust and keep pace with trends. Golf has done a great job of expanding and growing. The USGA has done an excellent job of steering golf through the fast-paced growth of the last 30 years. But most golf architects and superintendents are very much aware of the real changes in how courses are designed and maintained today.

Maintenance of courses has gotten expensive, and turf conditions are improving. Most golfers in America want perfect turf and are willing to pay for it. Most golf architects in America are aware of the turf improvements and have had to change the way they design greens, tees, bunkers, and fairways. Irrigation has softened courses and reduced the amount of roll. Smoother, faster greens must have less pitch or you can't make putts. Today's golf balls and clubs allow top players to add more distance and accuracy. Golf course architecture has changed dramatically to keep pace with these advancements in turf and equipment.

The purpose of this report is to draw attention to changes radical and otherwise that have evolved in golf architecture. Mostly, this has been a long, slow evolution. Let's review, in detail, just how golf has changed.

Q: **How has greens maintenance changed golf architecture?**

A: The early 1900s putting surface was designed to challenge golfers relative to the maintenance practices of the period. Early greens mowers were crude at best when compared to the contemporary arsenal of equipment, mostly because they could not cut turf as closely as today's precision instruments. Consequently, the actual putting surface had longer blades of grass and did not approach the smoothness and uniformity of present greens.

Early greens were indeed slow by today's standards. How much slower? It is difficult to say exactly because the stimpmeter, although invented in the 1930s, did not become popular until 1976.[1] Furthermore, greens at one time were rolled repeatedly with heavy rollers, perhaps weighing a half ton or more. For several days following, the greens remained extraordinarily fast.

However, we can say with some degree of certainty that early 1900s greens were designed with steeper surface pitches (or percentage of slope) than today's greens. Obviously, the steepness of the slope was a reaction by golf architects to achieve exciting and challenging putting in relation to the slower surface condition of the grass. In other words, a green's contouring is designed around the intended level of maintenance.

Early 1900s greens averaged slopes of 5 to 8% (5 ft to 8 ft of fall in a 100 ft distance). This steep pitch was considered fair in view of the prevailing heights of cut in those years.

Modern greens are designed with much less pitch. Why? Because today's greens mowers and improved grasses allow for extremely low heights of cut in comparison with earlier greens. This low cut, along with improved turf varieties, has produced very smooth, uniform turf conditions. The ball rolls farther and faster on this smoother surface due to reduced turf friction. Green design was forced to change from the earlier 1900s pitches.

The pitches of today's greens average 1.0 to 3.75% slopes. These slopes are implemented to provide fun by creating fair challenges that match intended maintenance practices. If golf architects had continued to build greens with 5 to 8% slopes, putting would be ridiculously difficult.

In summary, golf course design has changed to keep up with the evolution of putting greens.

Q: **How has greens maintenance changed golf equipment design?**

A: Steep slopes helped to slow or stop the forward movement of incoming shots and hold the ball on the green. On the other hand, incoming shots to modern greens, with their flatter contours and smoother surfaces, are not slowed to the same extent.

Today's perimeter-weighted clubs produce a higher-trajectory shot that lands and stops more quickly; thus, there is less forward roll.

Moreover, contemporary golf balls are designed with higher backspin ratios that help stop them when they land. This change in ball design is in direct response to a green designed with less pitch, which in turn is a direct response to a change in maintenance practices.

Golf continues to change:

- The target for a green is flatter because grades on contemporary greens are gentler.
- The grass on the putting surface is often a new and improved variety, cut much lower and with a technologically advanced machine.
- The club hits the ball higher.
- The ball has more spin than ever before.[2]

These are major changes to a game that is little more than 100 years old in the United States. Americans have Americanized golf, while changing maintenance practices have been the driving force behind playing equipment changes by manufacturers and changes in design.

Q: **How have changes in balls and clubs contributed to golfers' opinions?**

A: Golf architects have seen similar changes before and have listened to comments from great players and other influential people in the game. Many truly believe that the advancements in the game's implements have resulted in real changes.

Opinions differ regarding this statement: "Players with excellent swings and real talent can get more out of equipment improvements than average or poor players."

—— **Opinion 1:** The average player does not gain much from improvements to balls and clubs.

Only excellent golfers have the ability to consistently take advantage of improved balls and clubs.

—— **Opinion 2:** All players benefit from improvements to balls and clubs.

Famous players—Ray Floyd, Sam Snead, Jack Nicklaus, and Lee Trevino among them—have said, in one form or another, "I hit the ball today farther than I did twenty, thirty years ago. I know I'm not any stronger today than I was in my twenties. It has to be the ball."

Key figures in golf on this topic: "The ball goes farther, it flies straighter, more accurately today. The lower flex point shafts and the improved flight path of the ball make it easier to be accurate" (A. Murray, 1994 Green Committee chairman, Augusta National).

"Our research indicates the ball travels 8 to 12 yards farther in 1996 than in 1960" (Reid McKenzie, 1994 chairman of the Implements and Ball Committee, USGA).

—— **Opinion 3:** Changes in equipment affect the game, but not always in a positive way.

Prominent golf architects render their opinions:

"Let's slow down the ball" (Jay Morrish).
"Pros now are swinging at 125 mph" (Pete Dye).
"The ball, in general, is out of control" (Bobby Weed).
"A 160-acre golf course in 1960 now requires 176 acres [because of increased distance]" (Bob Cupp).
"Golf architects have lengthened the distance from the tee to the dogleg point [because of new equipment]" (Clyde Johnson).
"Movement in greens must now be very gentle [because of maintenance practices]" (Ron Kirby).

Golf architects summarize their thinking in light of the foregoing as follows. Increased distance by the game's best players is a combination of better technique, stronger athletes, and an improved golf ball. These factors have not resulted in substantially lower scores in four-day tournaments.

The real change has been in what club is hit on the second shot into par 4s and 5s. Obviously, the game is easier if you're using a club with more loft on your second shot. This extra loft has made it more difficult to challenge the game's best players.

Golf architects are aware of this and are adding features to ensure that better players continue to be challenged. Bunkers are placed in different locations in landing areas to test new length shots. We architects are seeing a resurgence of closely mowed turf adjacent to the green to bring back chipping and to let the ball roll farther away from the green on miss-hit shots to add challenge to the short game and help protect par.

Q: **How has better club construction allowed tour players to swing faster and get away with it?**

A: Titanium, graphite, boron graphite, lightweight steel: these materials are now the norm for golf shafts used on the PGA tour. The great Bobby Jones played the game with hickory shafts. Flex points in shafts (high, low, medium, and two-step) can now be custom fitted to match a player's height, arm strength, and swing path to the ball. This high-tech advantage has allowed expert players a consistency that wasn't there in earlier shafts. Because today's pros have a shaft that performs more consistently, they can swing harder and get away with it.

Obviously, if a player gets a club in his hand made specifically to match his particular swing, that's an advantage. Combine that shaft with a forgiving clubhead with perimeter weighting that reduces the penalty for off-center hits, and golfers can unleash their power.

In summary, new metal woods and hi-tech shafts with their predictable consistency have allowed swing changes that can produce more clubhead speed. Several tour players have adapted their swings as a reaction to this new equipment (for example, Davis Love and John Daly). Obviously, the advanced equipment provides a definite advantage to professionals.

Bobby Jones had a slight pause at the top of his swing so that the hickory shaft could catch up to his hands. Whereas today Davis Love has an extremely late release of his hands, which allows him to generate enormous clubhead speed.

Q: **Has technology changed tournament golf?**

A: For better or for worse, equipment technology is affecting the game of leading golfers. For example, the contemporary ball cuts through the wind whereas older balls, if mishit, kept curving. The advantage for the master golfer who seldom makes a bad shot is therefore reduced. New equipment is creating parity. Some say that is not fair.

Q: **What are the impacts of golf maintenance?**

A:
1. The greens mower has changed dramatically in the 1990s. The latest makes can be equipped with attachments that allow for a much lower height of cut.
2. Newly introduced turf grasses have upright growth habits that may help to reduce grain and certainly have the potential to increase speed.
3. The stimpmeter, popularized in the mid-1970s, was intended to promote consistency of green speed. However, the outcome has been that green speeds are forced to be immeasurably faster due to competition among courses for ever-faster greens.
4. The reemergence of the roller is noteworthy. Here again, the original intent was to give the superintendent a tool to allow for smoother, faster greens at a higher, healthier height of cut. But this too has gone the way of the stimpmeter; that is, the roller is being misused to allow even faster greens at a lower height of cut.
5. Wall-to-wall sophisticated irrigation has softened playing surfaces. While turfgrass appearance and overall conditioning have improved, the gap between high handicap players and the plus players has widened as a result of less roll on softer courses. Irrigation has helped switch the emphasis from a game that is still played on the ground in Scotland to an aerial Americanized game.

Q: **What is the impact of televised golf tournaments?**

A: Every week, American golfers turn on TV and see professional golf. TV has definitely helped the game grow; there is no question about its positive impacts. But in most cases the tournament course has been groomed to be in or near perfect condition for the cameras. This high level of maintenance has spread across America and around the world. The golfer's yearning for perfect turf has grown along with the game. Turf conditions have been improved by televised golf, and maintenance costs go up as players demand ever more perfection.

ASGCA Equipment
Report 1996 Update

Since the ASGCA report and survey was released in 1994, the United States Golf Association has twice adjusted the wording in the rule book regarding golf ball testing. Both revisions have been outlined for future implementation, within the testing procedures currently in place, to regulate golf balls for compliance with the overall distance standards. The adjustments are

1. Maximum distance a ball can travel was adjusted from 280 yards +/– 6% tolerance to 280 yards +/– 4% tolerance.

    The 2% reduction in tolerance was added because of the ability to perform that test more accurately than in the past. This sets the stage for a possible 2% reduction in tolerance in the best balls manufactured today.

    Note: This adjustment applies to balls hit at the USGA testing lab by "The Iron Byron" set at 109 degrees swing speed. The golf club used in this machine has a steel shaft and a laminated wood head. The USGA currently does not test combinations of new technologies (new shafts and heads) when testing golf balls for distance compliance.

2. Beginning in 1997, each brand of golf ball is now tested under its own "optimum launch angle." This is determined by new machinery developed for the USGA lab. This may, or may not, have an impact on golf balls that are currently approved and in play. The new 1997 testing may result in a challenge of the USGA authority to implement new standards to previously approved equipment. Current manufacturing technology is improving at a fast rate with space age materials and, unless new rules are added by the USGA, new technology "loopholes" are difficult to regulate.

3. Recent golf club advances include

    1970: First cavity back iron, by Solheim
    1972: Graphite shaft
    1980: First metal wood, by Gary Adams
    1985: Improved quality of graphite shaft, by David Pell
    1990: First oversized club, by Eli Calloway
    1995: Titanium club head.

Conclusion of the Marzolf Committee

Everyone connected with the game of golf should applaud the efforts of the R & A and the USGA to protect the game during rapid advancements in club and ball production techniques.

Notes

1. Kenneth L. Helphand, "Learning from Linksland," *Landscape Journal* (Spring 1995): 74–85.
2. Bradley S. Klein, former tour caddy, now a golf writer and college professor (Government), has put forward a controversial statement that the problem with the modern ball is not overall distance, but that distance is achieved largely through the air rather than along the ground.

    Dr. Klein says the contemporary ball flies much farther than earlier balls. Yet it does not roll as far because its trajectory is loftier. He concludes that professionals hit the ball farther and average golfers achieve less distance because their shots do not roll as far with watered fairways (Bradley S. Klein, *Golfweek,* March 18, 1995).

Planning the Course

There can be no really first-class golf course without good material to work with. The best material is a sandy loam in gentle undulation, breaking into hillocks in a few places. Securing such land is really more than half the battle. Having such material at hand to work upon, the completion of an ideal course becomes a matter of experience, gardening, and mathematics.

Adapted from *Scotland's Gift GOLF,* 1928, by Charles Blair Macdonald (1856–1939)

Robert Trent Jones said that golf architects have created an art form on a broad canvas, adding, "Golf today, in all honesty, is what the architects have made it—a game of relaxed recreation and limitless enjoyment for millions and a demanding examination of exacting standards for those few who would seek to excel, depending on the requirements of the moment".[1] Robert Trent Jones Jr. states, "Golf has a playing field like no other."[2]

Together these statements by father and son are starting points for outlining the basic considerations of course design. Persons in other design fields have observed that a golf course is equivalent to an art gallery with 18 huge compositions created by the designer. Yet architects acknowledge that the enduring greatness of their creations also lies with the superintendents who maintain and enhance them.

General Principles

Designers seek to create golf courses so that most players feel better following a round, regardless of scores. Playing this absorbing game in the fresh air is a major source of this sense of well-being. In turn, the feeling is enhanced by the magnificence of the course, the perfection of the greensward, and the strategy, interest, and excitement incorporated into each hole together with continuity and balance throughout the round.

In designing a golf course, or any of its features, there are three basic considerations:

- The game itself
- Aesthetics
- Future maintainability

These are sometimes referred to as the three *P*'s—*P*layability, *P*ulchritude, and *P*racticality—and are depicted in Figure 2.1 as an equilateral triangle, with each side representing one of the considerations and the interspace representing the environment, a word we use in its broadest sense throughout this book to emphasize that the background of course design is nature in the context of societal and economic issues.

The canvas for the 18 compositions is the tract of land upon which the holes are delineated. Yet, designers also embrace distant vistas, the sky, the horizon, and day-long changes in light and shade. For example, one of the many charms of the Old Course at St. Andrews is the differences caused by the change in light as the day advances, while at Banff Springs in the Canadian Rockies the snow-capped peaks impress the most

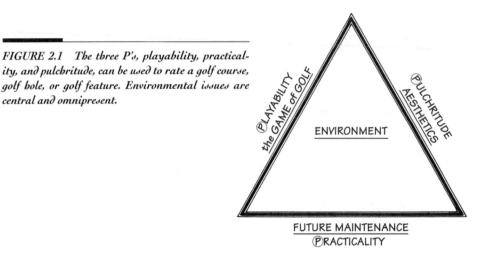

FIGURE 2.1   *The three P's, playability, practicality, and pulchritude, can be used to rate a golf course,
golf hole, or golf feature. Environmental issues are
central and omnipresent.*

absorbed golfer. Conversely, on some sites, often those in urban areas, the designer may
want to block out views of roadways, structures, or unsightly surroundings.

The architect's design media, or "paints," are earth, grass, trees, sand, and water. His
or her objective is to use these media to create a work of art, art that is a product of vision and
freedom but conforms to the basic triangle of the game, aesthetics, and future maintainability. Although the architect as an artist may not always follow them, the guidelines following
enable the architect to paint the picture that is to become a functioning composition.

Design Factors

Length is the most critical factor in golf difficulty. Yet, if the challenge depended on
sheer length, the layout would be exceedingly dull and scorned by golfers.

Advances in equipment technology are making golf an increasingly aerial game in
North America, and to a lesser extent on other continents. The bump-and-run shot over
the ground is fast disappearing. This profound change in the player's game largely par-
allels developments in turfgrass science attributable to agronomists and other scientists,
the increasing sophistication of automatic irrigation, and the perfection of the
greensward arising from superintendents' skill and dedication.

When a professional golfer or accomplished amateur plans a course or a feature of a
course, he or she is apt to emphasize playing aspects at the expense of the two other sides
of the triangle, whereas a landscape architect may favor eye appeal and a superintendent
maintainability. Yet no course or any feature on it will be a true and lasting success unless
its design embodies the three basic considerations. Golf architecture, therefore, involves
judicious balance of the three: the game, aesthetics, and maintainability.

The designer's discernment in achieving such balance becomes the mark of his or
her design integrity. Furthermore, in creating shapes of individual features on the
course, such as greens and bunkers, the axiom "Form follows function" is as much a part
of golf architecture as it is for other forms of design. For example, the longer the
approach shot, the larger the green; and the closer the bunker to the green, the deeper it
is and the steeper its face.

Design for Play

Contemporary design is essentially *strategic* as contrasted to *penal*. The latter punishes
poor shots and tends to discourage those who are out to relax (Figure 2.2). On the other

hand, *strategic* design provides a layout interesting for the accomplished but not a monster for those who already have troubles enough.

Strategic holes require players to think. They provide alternative routes from tee to green, with safer but longer routes for those not capable of maximum distance and accuracy (Figure 2.3). In accomplishing this, many an architect places hazards so they come into play less often so as not to discourage the short hitter unduly. Yet such placement still forces the long hitter to think and to play accurately (Figure 2.4).

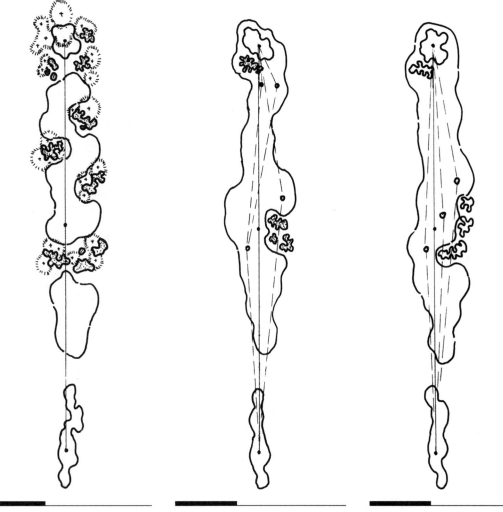

FIGURE 2.2 You could consider penal design the predecessor of target golf. Old-fashioned penal hazards appear either to have been used as nature provided or to have been purposely placed where they would create the most havoc. Today, more thought and effort goes into creating targets in relation to average shot lengths and degree of accuracy.

FIGURE 2.3 Play of a strategic-design golf hole definitely requires the thought process along with the shot process. The green bunker suggests that a right-to-left shot would be most successful. The golfer must survey the situation, select the most practical route, and go to work. Playing safe will likely add a stroke.

FIGURE 2.4 The green bunker on this hole suggests a right-to-left shot might be most productive. Staying right off the tee means deciding how much of the fairway bunkers you dare to carry. The more you carry, the better the position for your approach shot.

One design philosophy, that the farther a player hits the ball the more accurate he or she must be, is inherent to both the strategic and penal concepts. While contemporary design is essentially strategic, a designer may include one or more penal holes in the routing. The designer may also employ a few holes using still a third type of design, termed *heroic,* or *bite-off.* Features on these holes allow players to attempt to carry what they think they can. The more players carry, the shorter their approach to the green or to the second landing area (Figure 2.5).

At this point, you may conclude that a golf hole is invariably strategic, penal, or heroic. But an architect may include holes with these design styles barely perceptible. In practice, holes that do not fit one of the three design concepts may be included to accent those that do. Often, such holes provide a "breather" where the golfer may relax (Figure 2.6).

Strategic design embraces the contemporary concept "The greater the risk involved, the greater the reward." Before the risk-reward term was coined, architect George C. Thomas said, "The strategy of the golf course is the heart of the game. The

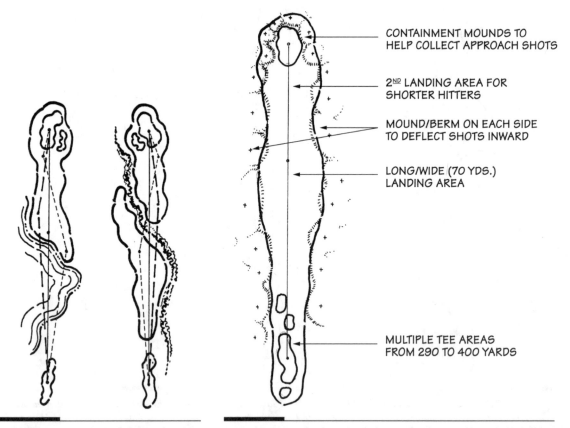

CONTAINMENT MOUNDS TO HELP COLLECT APPROACH SHOTS

2ND LANDING AREA FOR SHORTER HITTERS

MOUND/BERM ON EACH SIDE TO DEFLECT SHOTS INWARD

LONG/WIDE (70 YDS.) LANDING AREA

MULTIPLE TEE AREAS FROM 290 TO 400 YARDS

FIGURE 2.5 With the lake in play, this classic bite-off hole requires you to decide how much you can safely carry to attain the left-most approach shot available. With the creek crossing, simply carrying the creek allows a right-to-left approach shot. Staying short and left is safer but may obligate two shots to reach the green.

FIGURE 2.6 This breather hole accommodates golfers of all skill levels with its variation in length and wide landing areas (a second one for shorter hitters). Mounding on each side of the fairway and around the green will tend to collect and retain in play all but the most wayward shots.

spirit of golf is to dare a hazard, and negotiating it, reap a reward, while he who fears or declines the issue of the carry has a longer and harder shot for his next" (Figures 2.7 and 2.8).[3]

Whatever the problem, it is, ideally, visible or known to the player so that he or she can solve it.

Classic Golf Holes As golf evolved on the links, a number of memorable holes developed by accident or by design and became widely known as "classics," a word now used in reference to any hole renowned in the world of golf. However, golf architects still use the word to describe holes that have been widely adapted around the world, or even copied. Three examples are the Redan, the Alps, and the Cape.

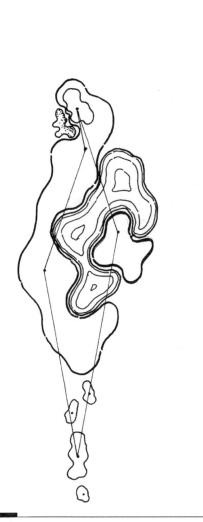

FIGURE 2.7 The green bunker indicates that an approach from the right could be most successful. The risk taker can shoot for the target fairway area, setting up a right-to-left shot into the green. Those less daring (or less skilled) can play safe along the left-hand route, but likely will add a stroke to their score.

FIGURE 2.8 On this strategic hole, the shorter hitter can blast away with relative abandon, but the longer hitter must carefully place the shot into an ever-narrowing landing area. A bunkered shot will add at least one stroke and perhaps more.

REDAN
NORTH BERWICK NO. 15

FIGURE 2.9 The Redan is probably the most copied of the classic holes. This type of bite-off hole personifies risk-reward at its best. Playing safe to the right-front of the green leaves a long and testing putt. For each segment of the gaping left side bunker that is carried successfully, and the longer in length the shot, the more makeable the remaining putt becomes.

The Redan: The 15th at North Berwick in Scotland This is a medium-length par 3, with the green on a diagonal to the shot and a frightening greenside hazard on the left requiring players to carry its entire length if they play directly for the pin (Figure 2.9). On the other hand, if they play for the front of the green, they are faced with an exceptionally difficult putt, which on the original Redan is downhill (Figure 2.10). The Redan concept may also be used for approach shots on par 4s and 5s, and it can be reversed with the hazard, sand or water, on the right.

FIGURE 2.10   This is the original Redan. The depth and difficulty the bunker presents is accentuated by a green obviously falling away from the shot.

The Alps: The 17th at Prestwick in Scotland The green at Prestwick is not visible from the approach. In adaptations the flag is often visible but behind a mound (Figure 2.11), yet the player must still carry the mound to reach the green. If the ball strikes the mound, it may come to rest in a hazard or other problem area (Figures 2.12, 2.13, 2.14). The 3rd at the National Golf Links of America is one example of an adapted Alps (see again Figure 2.11).

The Cape. This is a Charles Blair Macdonald original—not a links hole but nevertheless a classic (Figure 2.15). It is most often a par 4 dogleg left or right with a "heroic" carry required from the tee if the golfer is to reach a green perched on a cape within the regulation number of strokes. An excellent example is the 5th at the Mid-Ocean in Bermuda (Figure 2.16 and also Figure 2.15).).

In creating the National Golf Links of America, Charles Macdonald set out to adapt British classics to his masterpiece. With protégés Seth Raynor and Charles Banks, Macdonald adapted these classics and his own originals to many other layouts which that trio later developed together or separately.

ALPS
NATIONAL NO. 3

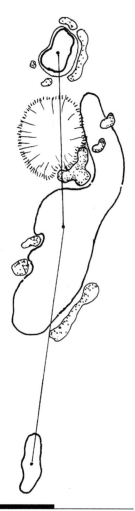

FIGURE 2.12   This is the original Alps hole at Prestwick in Scotland. The golfer faces a long walk to locate the ball's position and contemplate how to play the approach shot. See also Figure 2.13 below.

FIGURE 2.11   This diagram of an Alps hole, the No. 3 at National Golf Links, cannot begin to suggest the bewilderment a golfer can experience facing the huge mound screening any chance of a look at the green or the current pin position.

FIGURE 2.13   If you have not already peeked or consulted with your caddy, climbing the hill affords the long awaited confirmation that you did indeed play it right, or that you have another problem to solve before holing out.

FIGURE 2.14 Here, the original Alps, a gaping bunker lies at the base of the ridge that obscures the green. A rolling green, just past the bunker, completes the components of a puzzling hole where par is most gratifying.

FIGURE 2.15 Reminiscent of the famous 18th hole at Pebble Beach, the problem at the 5th, or "Cape," at the Mid-Ocean in Bermuda is the same: How much water, ocean, or bay do you feel you can cut off?

There are many other classic golf holes that abound, including the "Hogs Back" (Figure 2.17), "Valley" (Figures 2.18, 2.19, 2.20) and "Dell" (Figures 2.21, 2.22, 2.23). In addition, golfers may also discover a "Long," "Short," "Dyke," "Burn," "Road," etc.

We have already referred to classic greens—the "Plateau," or "Gun Platform," and "Punch Bowl." Again, there are many others of varying degrees of authenticity.

It is noteworthy that several architects have designed classic holes not knowing that they were modeling an original. Such fortuity arises from the architect's following the axiom "Form follows function."

The argument over whether courses should be designed for the low or the high handicap player, for the short or the long hitter, for championship or regular play is a constant. In practice, with adequate thought the course can be planned for golfers at all levels.

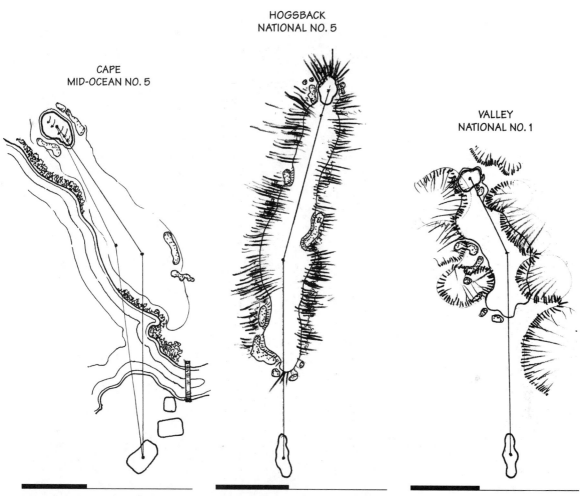

CAPE
MID-OCEAN NO. 5

HOGSBACK
NATIONAL NO. 5

VALLEY
NATIONAL NO. 1

FIGURE 2.16 At Mid-Ocean's classic cape hole, for every degree you shift your line-of-flight to the left, you shorten the required approach shot.

FIGURE 2.17 Playing along a ridge can conjure up all sorts of bad thoughts. Any appreciable deviation to either side means possibly flying and/or rolling off to the side into potential trouble.

FIGURE 2.18 As opposed to the hog-back hole, the valley hole (here it is the 1st at National Golf Links) can look relatively comfortable, for a missed shot just might be deflected back into the short grass.

FIGURE 2.19 A good example of a valley hole is the 12th at La Purisima, Santa Barbara County, California. From in front of the forward tee it looks almost inviting once you carry the lake—unless you stray it far to either side. The side slopes are perfect for spectator viewing. See Chapter 4 regarding spectator mounds.

FIGURE 2.20   *Looking back to the tee from above the green on the 12th at La Purisima, you can easily replay the hole in your mind, contemplating how to challenge it the next time out.*

DELL
LA HINCH NO. 6

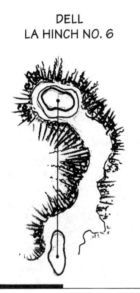

FIGURE 2.21   *Similar to the problem posed by the classic Alps hole, again the golfer is prevented from seeing the target. This one-shot hole, the Dell at Lahinch in Ireland, offers only a painted rock and your caddy's gestures to determine your best line of flight.*

FIGURE 2.22   *This side view into the Dell hole at Lahinch is much more descriptive of the shot problem than the view from the regular tee.*

Because of the crowded conditions on today's courses resulting from the popularity of golf, planners must devote additional attention to safety factors, including protection of players, abuttors, and passing motorists. This is one reason that contemporary layouts require more acreage than those built before World War II. Skillful placement of hazards, tees, and trees, together with interesting mowing patterns, have helped reduce the need for more acreage arising from technological improvements. Yet architects fear still more advances.

FIGURE 2.23 *Blind shots, particularly on one-shot holes, are to be avoided. However, here on the Oregon coast is a modern-day version of the Dell hole. One-third of the green is visible, but the rest remains a mystery until you reach the green and discover whether you have hit the appropriate shot.*

Design for Aesthetics

Golf courses rank among the most beautiful of landscape creations. Immaculate grooming and perfection of the greensward are two important contributions to eye appeal, while magnificent trees and flowering shrubs together with light, shade, color, and texture present an effect so striking that even the most absorbed golfer is aware of it.

Beauty is further increased by dramatically designed greens, tees, bunkers, and ponds. A green sculptured and raised above fairway level, set among trees and guarded by white sand, is breathtaking in its eye appeal. And even tees, for so long monotonous rectangles, are now designed in a sculptured or free-form fashion (Figure 2.24). Gracefully shaped ponds with capes and bays also contribute to beauty as they heighten playing interest (Figure 2.25). Indeed, water can be the most dramatic, exciting, and memorable hazard on a course.

Principles of Art Contemporary golf course architects consciously or unconsciously compete to provide the most impressive golfing grounds. Increasingly, a round of golf has become a visual and memorable experience. To achieve this effect, an architect must remain aware of the principles of art and use them when appropriate in creating compositions. These principles are

- Harmony (Figure 2.26)
- Proportion (Figure 2.27)
- Balance (Figures 2.28, 2.29)
- Rhythm (Figure 2.30)
- Emphasis (Figure 2.31)

FIGURE 2.24 A curvilinear tee such as this one at the Atlantic Golf Course looks more natural than a geometric shape and blends comfortably with the rolling hillocks in the background.

FIGURE 2.25 A lake covers the entry and left side of this par 3 hole on the Golf Club at Quail Lodge, Carmel, California. The Monterey Peninsula, one of the nation's golf capitals, features water hazards ranging from tiny ponds to the vast Pacific Ocean.

FIGURE 2.26 The native rock wall, with a pond in the foreground, green contour, and adjacent mounding all repeat and strengthen the rolling, tapered shape of the distant mountains, each in harmony with the other. (Lightening "W". Ranch Golf Club in Nevada)

FIGURE 2.27 *The view at eye level is more important to the golfer than continued views from elevated platforms. These green bunkers and mounds are all sized, shaped, and configured in proportion to one another. (Widgi Creek Golf Club in Bend, Oregon)*

FIGURE 2.28 *This green at Port Ludlow in Washington demonstrates asymmetrical balance. The golf course features, concentrated on the left, are offset by the massive trees and their dark shadows on the right.*

FIGURE 2.29 *Nearly symmetrical balance appears at this camera location, but the symmetry changes radically as the observer moves from one side of the tee or fairway to the other. A rather symmetrical mountain in the distance is always aiming to distract the golfer's view and concentration on the job at hand. (Big Meadow Golf Club at Black Butte Ranch, Oregon)*

FIGURE 2.30 The shape and contour of the bunker against the green edge and collar sets up a repetitive, rhythmic sequence of curvilinear patterns that is quite pleasant to see and be around. (Sonoma Golf Club in Sonoma, California) (Courtesy of Robert Holmes)

FIGURE 2.31 There is little question that this 7th green at Pebble Beach is the emphatic center of attention when contemplating winds that can vary a shot from a wedge to a 3 iron.

The golfer may seldom consciously recognize that these aesthetic principles are embodied in a course layout. Nevertheless, the player probably senses the correctness or incorrectness of the hole as an art composition. This, along with the play of the game, becomes a major dimension in the golfer's sense of well-being, as does playing on an unblemished greensward.

The many acres on which golf is played provide an enduring contribution to beautifying the landscape and surroundings. Through immense efforts of their superintendents, together with dedicated chairpersons and committees, the playing fields of the game become even more beautiful as they mature. This adds to the pleasures of a golf round and is another reason why golf is so successful a game.

Design for Maintenance

Golfers expect the greensward to be perfect. In fact, one of the earliest impressions of a course that a visiting golfer receives is the quality of its turf. Design helps or hinders the superintendent in achieving this perfection.

One general way for the golf course architect to help is by creating mowable slopes if steep ones are not called for by the strategy of the hole's play. Another is by providing surface drainage on all areas and subsurface drainage where needed.

Written specifications for course construction have a profound bearing on maintenance. For example, specifications include, but are by no means limited to, clearing widths and the avoidance of traffic patterns that result in worn areas. Moreover, the contract documents and the architect's inspection visits to the site to consult with the contractor lead to painstaking construction, which in turn leads to a more maintainable golf course. This maintainability can be enhanced further if the future superintendent is on-site during construction, for example, to insist on smooth, mowable surfaces.

Design for the Environment and the Community

Just as golf is more than mastering its mechanics, golf courses are more than playing fields for this ancient and intriguing game. In the last decade of the twentieth century, more than 15,000 golf courses in the United States occupy acreage equivalent to the land area of Rhode Island and Delaware combined. Those who design, build, and maintain these courses bear an immense responsibility to the environment.

Golf course ecosystems yield innumerable benefits, according to James C. Balogh and William C. Walker, editors of the United States Golf Association's (USGA) definitive *Golf Course Management and Construction—Environmental Issues*. Yet there are also negative environmental aspects. The game's ruling bodies are providing huge sums to research these issues. When problems are found, architects, superintendents, and others are taking steps to correct them.

Balogh and Walker list beneficial and adverse effects of turfgrass systems.[4]

Beneficial

1. Recreational value
2. Aesthetic value
3. Erosion control
4. Adsorption of atmospheric pollutants
5. Mitigation of water pollution
6. Dust control
7. Cooling effect
8. Reduction of noise
9. Enhancement of real estate values
10. Provision for wildlife habitat

Adverse

1. Leaching and runoff losses of nutrients and pesticides from established turfgrass sites
2. Soil erosion and runoff losses of sediment and nutrients during construction and losses from disturbed riparian zones
3. Exposure of beneficial nontarget soil organisms, wildlife, and aquatic systems to pesticides
4. Development and resurgence of insect and disease populations resistant to current chemical management strategies
5. Excessive use of water resources for irrigation during drought conditions and in semiarid and arid climatic zones

6. Degradation of stream and lake quality resulting from sediment, chemical, and thermal pollution
7. Disturbance or loss of wetlands, which is a serious public concern especially in regard to the development of new golf courses
8. Disturbance and toxicity impacts on wildlife

Golf architects and superintendents, turfgrass scientists, and ruling bodies have been leaders in environmental responsibility since before the current era of environmental awareness. They have long been engaged in identifying grasses that require less water. Today, wastewater is being more widely used on golf courses, particularly in the Southwest, and contemporary irrigation systems are more efficient in the use of water. Indeed, each of the adverse effects listed by Balogh and Walker is being addressed. In this regard it is noteworthy that a healthy greensward is extremely efficient in reducing leaching, runoff, and loss of nutrients as contrasted with a field that is cultivated regularly.

Balogh and Walker also emphasize that Integrated Pest Management (IPM) is a significant but not a singular component of integrated management systems for turfgrass. They point out that the goal of the integrated systems approach is to manage the golf course and turfgrass while balancing the quality of the course with the cost, benefits, public health issues and environmental qualities of importance to the larger community.

The Audubon Society of New York endeavors to involve golf courses as wildlife sanctuaries. As described by Ronald Dodson later in this chapter, an objective is to emphasize design that reduces adverse effects. Teri Yamada, director of the Royal Canadian Golf Association Green Section, speaks of six areas in which a golf course can be certified in the Audubon Cooperative Sanctuary Program.

- Environmental Planning
- Wildlife and Habitat Management
- Outreach and Education
- Integrated Pest Management
- Water Conservation
- Water Quality Management

Finally, golf architect William R. Love has listed the central environmental questions:[5]

1. Will the course eliminate open or green space?
2. Will it alter wetlands or other sensitive areas?
3. Will it affect significant historical or archaelogical areas?
4. What will the impact be on ecological systems?
5. What will the effect be on the existing character of the site?
6. Is there potential for water pollution and erosion during construction?
7. Will irrigation requirements lead to excessive reduction of water supply?
8. Will long-term application of chemicals cause water pollution from surface runoff or infiltration?

Design in Relation to Wetlands   Use of wetlands themselves for golf is seldom permitted, although mitigation may allow for play across them. Fine holes of the bite-off (heroic) style have resulted when clearing trees is permitted, with or without stump removal.

On the other hand, designing for play across wetlands can produce an overabundance of compulsory carries. These may not be unduly long and may pose no problems to the accomplished golfer. The short hitter faced with repeated carries can handle a few successfully but may become discouraged or tired if they are required often. One answer has been target golf. This involves hitting the ball from one defined landing area to the next (Figures 2.32, 2.33).

In practice, if the course is intended for all types of golfers, as most courses are, carries need to be as short as 60 yards for women and 130 yards for men. It is also mandatory that a course design take into account downhill and uphill shots, together with prevailing winds (our 60 and 130 yard guidelines do not). The designer should also give consideration to shorter carries near the end of the rounds for older or less robust golfers.

Whenever possible, the best policy in course design appears to be avoiding wetlands entirely. Yet the mitigation outlined earlier has proved effective. Another approach,

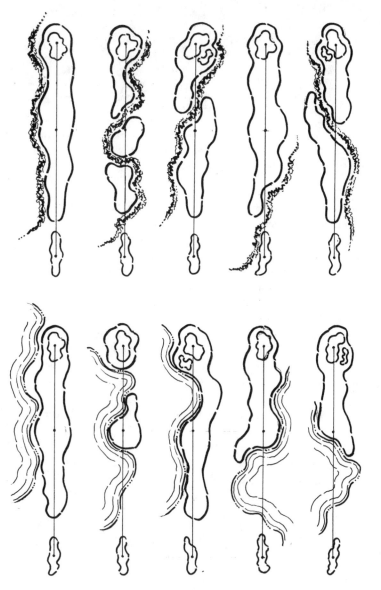

FIGURE 2.32 Here are many variations on target golf in which the water feature (lake or creek) establishes the target area and provides the punishment if the target is missed.

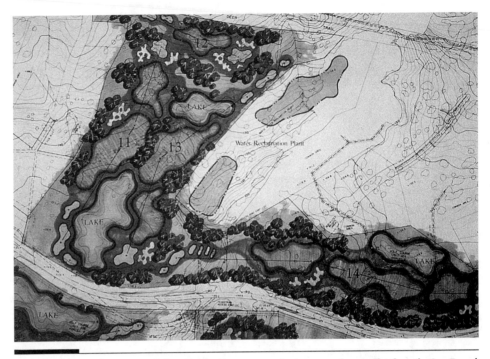

FIGURE 2.33   This is part of the plan for the new second nine recently completed at the Sea Ranch on the California coast. Modern-day target golf and judicious use of native grasses as roughs were reinvented here in the late 1960s for the first nine, located along the coastal bluffs.

involving the creation of new wetlands to compensate for those that are drained or filled, is sometimes permitted but always costly.

Design in Relation to the Americans with Disabilities Act (ADA)   Passage of the ADA in 1990 resulted in accessibility guidelines for golf, neither final nor enforceable but probably imminent at the publication of this book. According to the *USGA Golf Journal* (January-February 1995), golf architects and others are endeavoring to make it possible for disabled persons to reach a teeing area on each hole with an access path no steeper than 5%, to ensure access to fairways from existing car paths at 75-yard intervals if feasible, and to provide access points to each green if safe and environmentally sound.

The USGA and the GCSAA (Golf Course Superintendents Association of America) are jointly involved in research concerning the impact of all assistive devices. Parking near the bag drop, course rest rooms that comply with ADA guidelines, and access to weather shelters are also important considerations for the clubhouse architect.

Integrating Golf with Other Facilities   Many contemporary golf courses are integrated with residential, office, or commercial developments or recreational facilities other than golf. Integration is a trend destined to continue because the presence of a permanent open space—namely, the golf course—enhances surrounding real estate values and the quality of life.

Several considerations to be observed in planning an integrated golf development are outlined in Chapter 3, and a recognized expert on the subject, Kenneth DeMay, prepared Chapter 6 on this subject, while golf architect, William Amick discusses golf courses on otherwise derelict land in Chapter 11.

Golf course communities and resorts provide local employment opportunities. We have observed, too, that a fine layout on its own attracts industry and professionals, including those in medicine, to establish practices in remote communities.

Types of Golf Courses

Course categories are designated by ownership, length, vegetation, design, and landform. None is truly distinct nor definitive. This section provides an outline of the categories.

By Ownership

1. Private clubs, which include nonprofit clubs where members hold equity and profit-motive clubs where members hold no equity. Either of the above can be:
   a. Strictly private: members only
   b. Semi-private: memberships are sold
   c. with daily-fee play permitted
2. Daily-fee courses, which can be publicly owned by municipalities, counties, states, or other jurisdictions, or owned by individuals or syndicates.
3. Resort courses owned by a resort or a hotel.
4. Residential courses, integrated with offices. Developers, home owners, condominium associations, retirement communities, or others may own such facilities.
5. Courses owned by the armed forces or their service organizations.
6. Private estate courses. Varying from a single hole to a full 18-hole course, but often including 3 holes. Courses of this type are for the benefit of the owner, clients, and friends.
7. Industrial and corporate courses owned by companies for their employees and customers.

By Length

1. Full-Length
2. Executive, or Precision
3. Par 3s and approach courses
4. Pitch and Putts
5. Chip and Putts
6. Putting Courses
7. Cayman Golf Courses

By Site or Vegetation   This is the most ambiguous category of all but still can be used to advantage.

1. Links: sandy, grassy, open, and undulating areas similar to the land in Scotland where golf developed
2. Oceanside: situated on headlands well above sea level, as contrasted with links almost at sea level
3. Heathland and moorland (land where members of the heath family of plants predominate)
4. Forest, with holes set in the forest
5. Park or parkland, with holes running through sparsely treed areas
6. Downs: courses on rolling, almost treeless, terrain similar to the English downs
7. Mountain

8. Prairie
9. Desert
10. Jungle

By Design

1. *Core,* where the layout stands as a unit by itself with or without integration with other facilities.
    a. Each nine is a separate unit (Figures 2.34 and 2.35).
    b. The two nines are intermingled (Figures 2.36, 2.37).

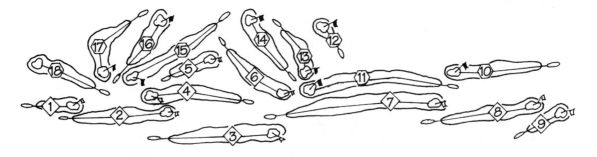

FIGURE 2.34   *This version of the 18-hole loop, core layout is based on Royal Lytham and Saint Annes in England. The nines are kept separate from each other. Often the golf course architect suggests that an 18-hole loop offers better golf for a given site, program, and budget. But commercial interests and golfer desires usually opt for returning nines.*

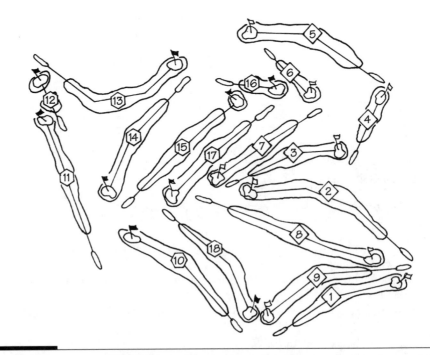

FIGURE 2.35   *Augusta National in Georgia is more a conventional core or lump layout with separate and returning nines. The holes are compacted into an oval shape rather than being stretched out. This style of routing exposes fewer holes to adjacent and, likely, non-golfing features or facilities.*

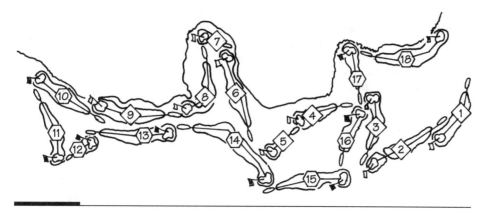

FIGURE 2.36   *This familiar layout at Pebble Beach in California is also an 18-hole loop, but the two nines are intermingled between holes 3 and 4 and 16 and 17.*

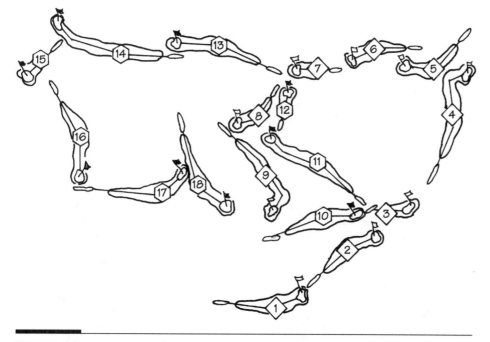

FIGURE 2.37   *By contrast with Augusta National, Eagle Pines in Florida is a combined core shoe-string layout with several holes laid out end-to-end and the nines intermingled at holes 7 and 8 and 12 and 13.*

2. *Integrated* with dwelling and office buildings (Figures 2.38 and 2.40).
   a. Single fairways returning; the two nines are arranged in a figure eight (Figure 2.39).
   b. Double fairways with returning nines (Figures 2.41, 2.42).
   c. Muirhead and Rando also describe continuous double fairways and continuous single fairways, types with only the 18th returning to the clubhouse (see again Figure 2.42).[6]
3. *Hub-and-spoke,* with every third hole returning to the clubhouse (Figure 2.43).

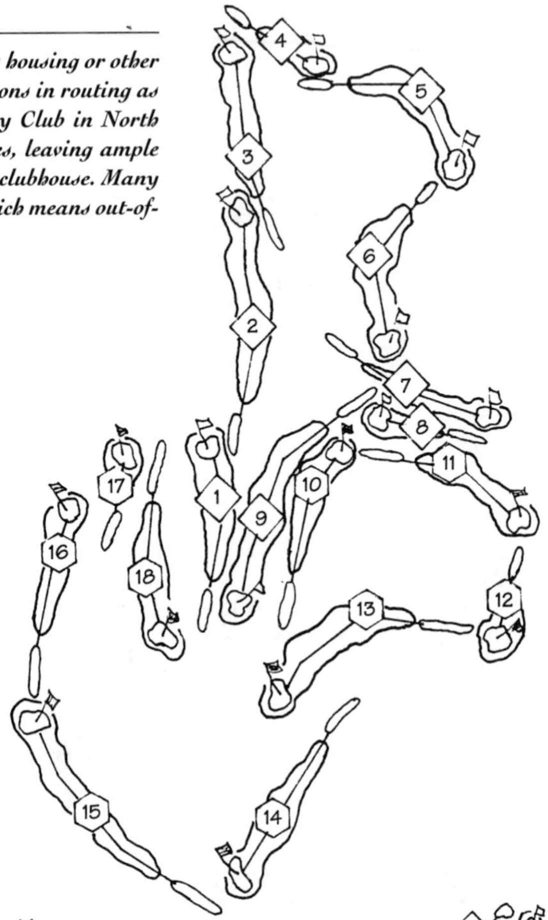

FIGURE 2.38   *When the golf course design incorporates housing or other related features within its layout, we see the same variations in routing as when the golf course stands alone. Forest Oaks Country Club in North Carolina uses a shoestring routing for many of the holes, leaving ample interior areas for development. Each nine returns to the clubhouse. Many holes are open to development on both sides of the hole, which means out-of-bounds as well.*

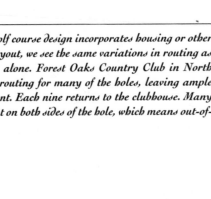

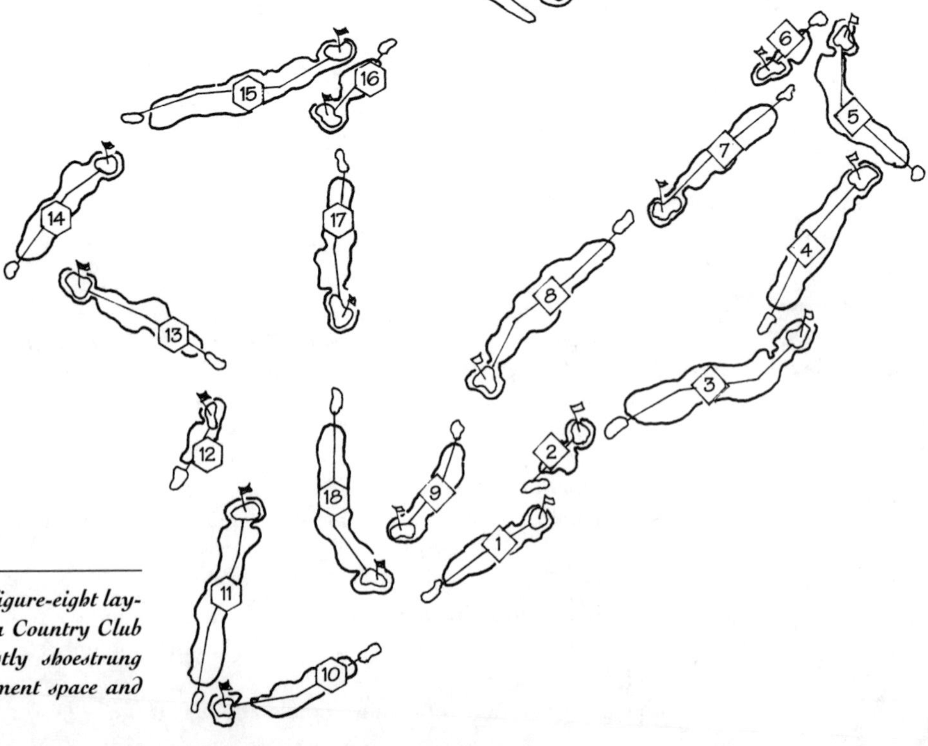

FIGURE 2.39   *This figure-eight layout at Rancho Murieta Country Club in California is mostly shoestrung out, affording development space and returning nines.*

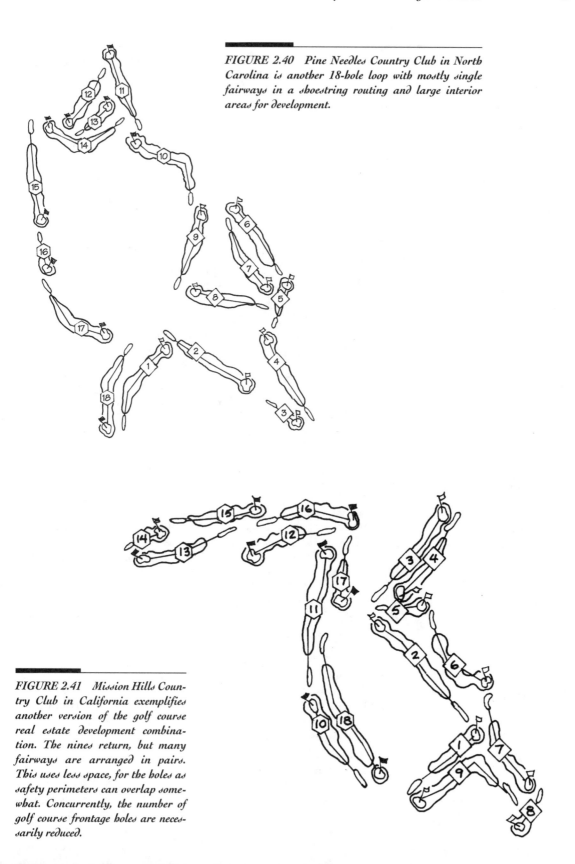

FIGURE 2.40 *Pine Needles Country Club in North Carolina is another 18-hole loop with mostly single fairways in a shoestring routing and large interior areas for development.*

FIGURE 2.41 *Mission Hills Country Club in California exemplifies another version of the golf course real estate development combination. The nines return, but many fairways are arranged in pairs. This uses less space, for the holes as safety perimeters can overlap somewhat. Concurrently, the number of golf course frontage holes are necessarily reduced.*

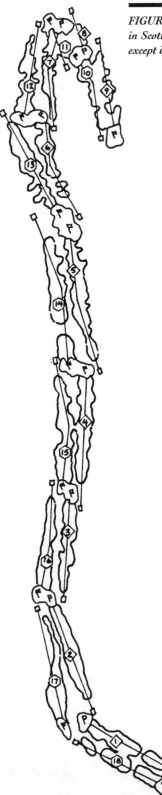

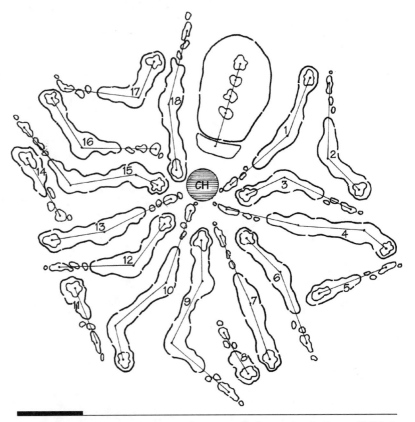

FIGURE 2.42   *The world's oldest and most famous golf course, the Old Course at St. Andrews in Scotland, exemplifies the continuous double fairway, 18-hole loop. A feature seldom seen except in older courses is the crossing fairways of 7 and 11.*

FIGURE 2.43   *A unique routing we have created as an example. Every third hole returns to the clubhouse, which is good for the course as a commercial enterprise. Sale of the "3Bs" (balls, Band-Aids, and beer), as contrasted with the "3 Ps," can raise profits.*

By Landform   Robert Price, Scottish geologist, presents landforms on which the layout is located as still another course classification.[7]

1. Undulating
2. Hillside
3. Drumlins (hills resulting from glaciation)
4. Eskers, kames (an esker is a long gravel ridge; a kame is a ridge of mixed materials)
5. Terrace, sandur, river terrace
6. Raised beach/platform
7. Dunes/sand plan (links)
8. Derelict land (We have added this category to Price's list. British architect J. Hamilton Stutt has used the term *derelict land* to include landfills, gravel and sand pits, slag heaps, and coal sites. See Chapter 11.)

Designing with the Land, Not Over It

by Ronald G. Dodson
PRESIDENT OF AUDUBON INTERNATIONAL,
CHAIRMAN OF THE BOARD,
AUDUBON SOCIETY OF NEW YORK STATE, INC.

Golf and its effect on the environment is a hotly debated topic in many parts of the country. Proponents of golf claim the design, construction, and management of golf courses have no negative environmental impact. Others say golf course development should be considered one of the worst forms of land use ever invented. Somewhere between these two divergent points of view we will no doubt find the facts relevant to this debate.

If development is to take place, a critical first step is selection of the site itself. There must be a commitment to selecting a site that will maximize creative project design while providing necessary buffer areas between the development and sensitive environmental areas.

In most cases it is the developer who chooses the land. It is, however, the architect who can and should assess and report to the developer what changes can realistically and comfortably take place on the site. Modern-day technology and heavy construction equipment have made it possible to move, shove, cut, scrape, pile, fill, and shape nearly any site to fit the most unrealistic dream a developer may have. The fact that this approach is being exercised in many areas of the country has caused the passage of stringent laws and regulations, giving rise to environmental impact statements, public hearings, and extensive court cases.

This expensive government regulatory process, coupled with the use of expensive construction equipment, has driven the cost of development to astronomical levels. Clearly, this approach is unsustainable economically and, most certainly, environmentally.

We must move toward a more sustainable design-style by designing less intrusive, less expensive, and more manageable developments. The golf course architect or designer plays an essential role in decisions regarding both economics and the environment.

Ideally, the design of the course flows with the land. The ultimate goal should be a golf course that, on the first day it is opened, looks as if it has been there forever. One way to achieve this effect is for the designer to take into consideration how wildlife inhabiting the property might use it.

Like humans, all wildlife need the basic elements to survive: space, food, shelter, and water. Considering those elements in designing a golf course not only will help wildlife management efforts but also will ensure greater harmony between the golf course and the land. In addition, randomly and biologically integrating those elements throughout the golf course and allowing the site biology to dictate the design of the course will ultimately maximize the environmental and economic value of the site after development.

Once a commitment to designing eco-centrically is made, fidelity to selecting appropriate vegetation is critical. Besides public concern about the loss of wildlife habitat to golf course development, concern over the unnecessary use of water and chemical products is pervasive. The use of these substances is frequently driven by the types of vegetation selected for use on a development and the environments in which they are raised.

Wildlife Management

All wildlife species require four basic elements to survive: food to eat, water to drink, cover for protection, and the necessary space to carry on the basic activities of life. Understanding these elements and their interrelationship provides a more effective way to assess, design, and manage wildlife on any property.

In planning to attract or sustain wildlife, food availability is often the first consideration (Figure 2.44). Food resources can be manipulated by adopting a landscape plan that includes plants of high food value for a variety of wildlife species.

The availability of water is often the most important factor in sustaining and attracting wildlife (Figure 2.45). Birds, for instance, use water not only for drinking but also to keep their feathers clean in order to retain body heat. Managing water resources should be a primary commitment in sustaining and enhancing the value of property for wildlife.

"Cover" is a general term applied to the aspect of an animal's habitat that provides protection, enabling the animal to carry out life functions such as breeding, nesting, sleeping, resting, feeding, and travel (Figure 2.46). Anticipating the need for cover is related to planning food sources, because animals often will not come to food if no protected place exists for them to eat it.

Wildlife seeking food or water use hedgerows and taller grasses as safe travel corridors. An optimal landscape design includes a variety of flowers, grasses, shrubs, and

FIGURE 2.44 *Wildlife food sources range from set-out feed to a variety of naturally occurring foods from native or introduced vegetation. Leaving old or even dead growth provides habitats as well as a food source. (Courtesy Audubon International)*

FIGURE 2.45 *The lake shown here, next to a fairway at Big Meadow Golf Course in central Oregon, is part of a massive pond, lake, waterway system for the Black Butte Resort. A vast array of wildlife shares the resort with golfers and other recreationists.*

FIGURE 2.46 Truly a spectacular site for wildlife and golf life, Furry Creek Golf Course lies on a mountain slope next to Howe Sound in British Columbia. Black bear on down to the tiniest animal, and dozens of different land and water fowl, called this area home before and after the golf course was developed. Every kind of vegetation, from grasses through the many shrubs and trees, exists here for cover and as food sources.

FIGURE 2.47 This aerial shot of several holes at the Sea Ranch Golf Course in California demonstrates that even with future development adding a few more homes to this picture, the majority of the space is left vegetated. This affords ample room for wildlife to live and prosper. Deer and other animals along with land and water fowl happily share this space with the golfers.

trees to accommodate diverse wildlife, from ground-dwelling species to those who prefer living in treetops. Dead trees, or snags, provide important shelter and nesting sites for many insect-eating mammals and birds. When snags pose no safety hazard, consider leaving them in place. Forest understory also provides cover for safe travel and nesting.

Adequate space is the foundation of the balance of nature (Figure 2.47). An animal will not tolerate an overabundance of its own kind within its living space. This area may be a few square feet for a mouse or a few thousand acres for a grizzly bear.

Within the spatial restrictions for a species, all other basic requirements—food, water, and cover—must be met, or the species will not inhabit the area. Each species has different requirements. At any given time, there is a fixed limit to the kind and number of animals that may live in a habitat. This is called the "carrying capacity."

The physical makeup of space and location—the habitat—determines the numbers and types of wildlife present. A complete habitat is an area that fills the four basic needs of any particular species. Some habitats are obvious. A running stream is habitat for fish; a woodlot is habitat for songbirds. But habitat requirements can be very specific. For example, in a stream "fish habitat" can be further divided into "bass habitat" and "trout habitat." Habitat has the single greatest influence on wildlife.

Interspersion

It is not enough simply to provide food, water, and cover for wildlife. It is critical that those elements are interspersed throughout the space so that wildlife can get all necessary elements for survival without traveling too far. Certain species require "pure" habitat, but the greatest diversity of wildlife species is at the "edge," where one vegetation type meets another (Figure 2.48). For instance, the border between a marsh and a meadow, the border between a woodlot and a field, or the areas between a golf fairway and a pond provide "edge effect." The edge supports more wildlife than pure woods, pure meadow, or pure marsh.

In managing for wildlife, the first step is to determine what habitat is present on the property. The second step is to survey the property for wildlife species presently using the property. Finally, an assessment of present interspersion is essential.

Interspersion analysis requires a property survey to identify where habitats are located. It also requires that missing elements important to a particular species within habitat areas are identified. Interspersion analysis can also identify what is needed to discourage unwanted wildlife. Understanding habitat preferences helps to increase beneficial wildlife and aids in the understanding and control of problem species as well.

FIGURE 2.48   A pond fronting a green at Port Ludlow in Washington demonstrates types of edge habitat where water meets marsh meets grassy meadow. You can see as well where meadow meets brush meets forest.

Vegetation Selection

Vegetation selection affects wildlife management, the economic maintenance of the completed course, and environmental issues of pesticide use and water conservation. Golf course planners should consider four main points in addressing issues of vegetation selection.

Natural Landscaping   To the extent possible, existing vegetation on the property should be identified. Retaining and enhancing areas of vegetation that are already part of the natural habitat of the property makes both environmental and economic good sense. Such areas will continue sustaining wildlife already inhabiting the property, as well as contribute to lower maintenance costs by allowing self-sustaining vegetation in out-of-play areas.

Native Plant Selection   Plant selections are often made for aesthetic reasons which then become poor economic decisions. Rather than selecting plants that have substantial water or chemical requirements for maintenance and survival, choosing plants that are native to a particular area will contribute to wildlife enhancement and lower maintenance costs as well.

Turfgrass Selection   The key traits desired in turfgrass species used on golf courses include rapid recuperative ability, adaptability to required cutting heights, tolerance to soil compaction, and resistance to wear. The turfgrass selected for use should be of a type that is spreading or creeping as it grows, so that it can tolerate close mowing and achieve rapid healing.

From an overall environmental perspective, species and cultivars of turfgrass should have good tolerance to environmental stresses such as heat, cold, drought, and shade and be less susceptible to major disease and insect problems. Species selection should be based on these traits and governed by the ecological region in which the turfgrass will grow. Improper turfgrass results in the need to overwater, overfertilize, and apply extensive amounts of plant protectorants, thus proving economically and environmentally unsustainable.

Biofilters   Biofilters, also known as transition zones, must be established between areas of high golf course maintenance and sensitive environments. Such a zone may be developed between fairways and adjacent water features or on a steep out-of-play bank between the teeing surface and an important wildlife area. These transition zones also provide cover for wildlife.

Summary

Properly sited, designed, and managed golf courses can be environmentally beneficial to any community. The architect, the owner, and the developer can choose to commit themselves to a creative project design that takes into consideration the surrounding human and wildlife community (Figure 2.49). These professionals have the power to create a sustainable golf course, habitable for wildlife, that is economically sensible, aesthetically unique, and accepted by the community. Sustainability ultimately is a matter of present commitment and priorities in light of future consequences, both for the environment and for the golf course industry.

FIGURE 2.49   This golf community is obviously committed to creating a project that takes wildlife, as well as human, use and enjoyment into serious consideration. All will prosper while sharing a mutually compatible environment.(Courtesy Audubon International)

Notes

1. Robert Trent Jones, foreword to *The Golf Course,* by G. S. Cornish and R. E. Whitten (New York: W. H. Smith, 1981), 6.
2. Robert Trent Jones Jr., *Golf by Design* (New York: Little Brown, 1993), 3.
3. George C. Thomas, *Golf Architecture in America* (Los Angeles: Times Mirror Press, 1927), 37.
4. James C. Balogh and William C. Walker, eds., Preface to *Golf Course Management and Construction: Environmental Issues* (Chelsea, Mich.: Lewis Publishers, 1993).
5. William R. Love, *An Environmental Approach to Golf Course Management* (Chicago: The American Society of Golf Course Architects, 1992), 6.
6. Desmond Muirhead and L. Guy Rando, *Golf Course Development and Real Estate,* (Washington, D.C.: Urban Land Institute, 1994), 45.
7. Robert Price, *Scotland's Golf Courses.* (Aberdeen, Scotland: Aberdeen University Press, 1989), 74–76.

Selecting the Site, Routing the Course, and the Role of the Computer

Hills on a golf course are a detriment. Mountain climbing is a sport in itself and has no place on a golf course. Trees in the courses are also a serious defect, and even when in close proximity prove a detriment.

Adapted from *Scotland's Gift GOLF,* 1928, by Charles Blair Macdonald (1856–1939)

Chapter 2 outlined the three basic considerations of course design, playability, practicality, and pulchritude, as analogous to the sides of an equilateral triangle with the interspace as the environment. The environment includes nature, society, and the economy. The triangle and its interspace is therefore the background for the entire course design process, which starts with site selection.

Selecting the Site

Until well into the 1960s the architect played the key role in selecting the site for a proposed course from several under consideration by the owner. As golf became increasingly integrated with other features and the cost of real estate rose, it became more likely that the architect would be asked to report on the suitability of a single site already favored by the owner, pointing out the problems involved and the rationale for or against developing a golf course on it.

With the knowledge of contemporary construction and agronomic practices, the might of modern earth-moving equipment, advanced irrigation and drainage systems, and the availability of mechanical rockpickers together with advanced equipment for preparing seed beds and seeding, it has become possible to reclaim very rough parcels of land that would have been impossible to convert to golf a few decades ago. In addition, more adequate construction budgets are playing a major role in converting forbidding terrain and soil into playing fields for golf.

Still it remains imperative for the owner to obtain an opinion from a golf course architect before becoming deeply involved in any site. The ideal site has the following characteristics:

1. If the course is to be private, a country club atmosphere in the neighborhood is desirable; whereas if a daily fee is to be charged, a location close to populated areas is preferable. Yet contemporary golfers will travel long distances on a regular basis to play an outstanding course. The saying "If you build a better mousetrap the world will beat a path to your door" has repeatedly proved to be applicable to golf.

Witness the fabulous resort courses created in recent years that attract golfers to the United States from other continents.

2. Gently rolling terrain free from sharp drop-offs and steep "cardiac" slopes. While the introduction of golf cars makes such slopes more tolerable for travel, steep grades can lead to an overabundance of objectionable sidehill, uphill, and downhill lies, together with blind shots.

3. Relative freedom from wetlands. Even streams and natural ponds, once desirable in site selection, may contribute to lengthy permit delays in this era of environmental awareness. In some cases, they may rule out the site if permits to play over or across them cannot be obtained.

4. A minimum of 150 acres of usable land for a regulation 18 holes, practice fairway, clubhouse, and other facilities. (Yet numerous outstanding golf courses thrive on less acreage.) However, 150 acres may not be enough if any holes are bounded by homesites or the like. A typical golf course with development on many holes could require as much as 200 acres or more.

5. The shape of the property can also restrict its usefulness (Figure 3.1). However, an Irregular configuration of the tract can lead to a uniquely interesting route plan.

6. With the longest dimensions running north and south (Figure 3.2), this orientation reduces the possibility of facing the rising or setting sun.

7. An adequate source of irrigation water, perhaps wells, city water or agricultural water and sometimes streams and ponds when permits to draw from them are obtainable.

8. The presence nearby of three-phase electricity unless another source of power is available.

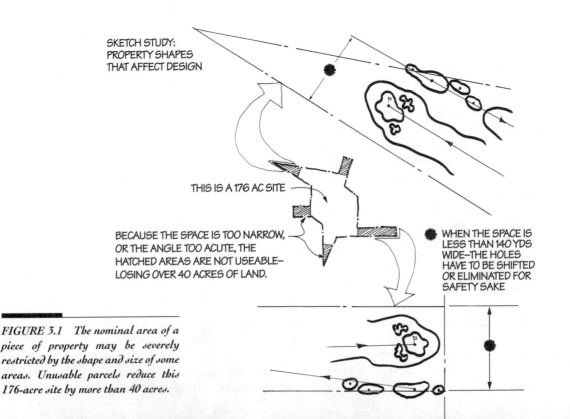

SKETCH STUDY:
PROPERTY SHAPES
THAT AFFECT DESIGN

THIS IS A 176 AC SITE

BECAUSE THE SPACE IS TOO NARROW, OR THE ANGLE TOO ACUTE, THE HATCHED AREAS ARE NOT USEABLE— LOSING OVER 40 ACRES OF LAND.

WHEN THE SPACE IS LESS THAN 140 YDS WIDE–THE HOLES HAVE TO BE SHIFTED OR ELIMINATED FOR SAFETY SAKE

FIGURE 3.1   The nominal area of a piece of property may be severely restricted by the shape and size of some areas. Unusable parcels reduce this 176-acre site by more than 40 acres.

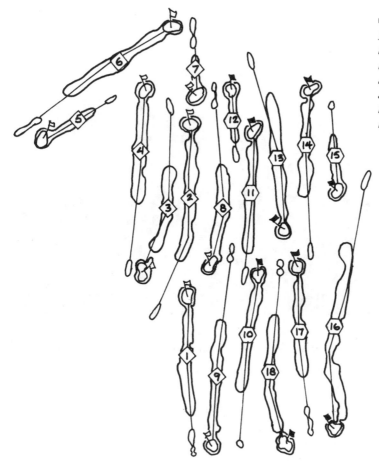

FIGURE 3.2 At Firestone Country Club South, all but two golf holes align either northerly or southerly. Routing somewhat alleviates the potential for monotony, since golfers play only three consecutive holes with same alignment twice during a round.

9. Well-drained soil. Sandy or sandy loam topsoil underlain by porous subsoil with an absence of stones, boulders, ledge rock, and hardpan is ideal. Many—probably the majority—of the world's greatest golf courses are situated on sandy, stone-free soils. Still, as indicated earlier, less desirable soils can now be modified for golf.

10. Tree cover is not mandatory, even on inland courses. Indeed, it is sometimes better to transplant trees of quality from nurseries and other sources. Still, healthy existing trees are a plus, and a hole cleared from a forest has built-in magnificence. If existing trees on some sites are marginal in quality, it may be better to clear the entire area except for specimen trees and those left for animal habitat.

11. No public roads dissecting or crossing the golf course; however, owner, architect, and players are frequently forced to tolerate them.

Notwithstanding these ideal features, contemporary architects and contractors are reclaiming extremely difficult and far from ideal sites and converting them into magnificent layouts. It is probably true that almost any site can be converted to golf if funds are available, the work is permitted, and the cost not excessive.

Peat and muck lands, which may appear attractive at first glance, particularly when under cultivation, are difficult to handle because peat settles unevenly when drained and heaves excessively in spring (Figure 3.3). Furthermore, most are classified as wetlands today, not permitting the modifications needed to accommodate golf. Some peats have been stabilized successfully by placing several feet of fill over them, with per-

FIGURE 3.3 *This site is a fine source of peat but not ideally suited for golf course development.*

haps a geotextile strip inserted between fill and peat to minimize any possibility of future settling. In other instances seed beds have been prepared and planted directly on the peat. Often the result has been excessive unevenness and continuous disruption of irrigation systems, unless flexible pipe has been used.

We recommend the services of a soil engineer when areas of peat are considered for golf. The engineer will require tests to ascertain depth of fill needed to stabilize the peat or to affirm that the peat will remain stable without the fill, which may be the situation when the deposit is shallow. "Breaking the back" is shoptalk for fill being applied until the peat is compressed to a point where no more settling is possible.

For decades, those involved in laying out golf courses used the land itself as their drawing boards with few, if any, plans on paper. The designer spent weeks or months or more on-site, obtaining site data visually. There were no topographical plans. The layout might be recorded on paper, or it could be merely staked on-site. The designer or someone versed in his or her philosophy then supervised development, probably sculpting the land by eye. Some early designs were casual, with Scottish professionals referring to their work as "18 stakes on a Sunday afternoon."

The background of many of these early designers was that of "greenkeeper and professional." Until the heathland era, the acreage used for golf in the British Isles was open, making it possible for designers and those assisting them to hit balls to aid in the decision process (Figure 3.4). (The value of hitting balls and observing others doing so remains paramount even in this computer age. Obviously, forested land, unlike the links, poses a problem in that hitting balls has to be postponed until clearing is well under way.)

With availability of topographical plans, or "topos," by the end of the nineteenth century, more designers took to the drawing board. This trend eventually became universal because owners, contractors, and others had to comprehend the designers' intentions before construction started.

FIGURE 3.4   *The rough grading stage is a good time to hit some balls to test the potential of a golf hole. This budding par 3 at Paradise Valley in Fairfield, California, is under scrutiny by the designers and consultants. Even if the participants' golfing abilities do not match that of future golfers, it's lots of fun anyway.*

Yet, until the present era of increased environmental awareness and permit requirements, designers still produced superb golf courses by eye, using the terrain as their drawing boards. They often placed their layouts on paper once they had planned them on the ground, however, in order to make others aware of their aims and objectives. Sometimes this paper plan was on a scaled, two-dimensional aerial photograph.

Even with today's sophisticated topos and computer technology, there is no substitute for on-the-ground study before, during, and after creation of the route plan. A layout prepared on paper without on-the-ground study can overlook distant, impressive, and important vistas; wind effects; and gentle but subtle contours that do not appear on contour plans.

In practice, golf course design lends itself to thinking on the ground as contrasted to thinking on paper. If the need were not mandatory for others to see the plan, many an architect would still prefer to produce the course by studying the site and staking the resulting concept on the ground with no intermediate paper plans.

Project Data Required for Preparing the Route Plan

Following through on the ground study, a route plan on paper is indeed mandatory today. Ideally, to prepare it the designer will have access to the site data listed in Appendix A at the end of this chapter. In practice the designer may find that some of this information is not available. Still, the more complete and accurate the site data, the greater the opportunity for the designer to achieve a layout of the highest quality consistent with the client's budget and intentions. Site data are part of the inventory that the architect needs and uses to achieve the concept.

The intrinsic function of the base map, a scaled topographical map sometimes referred to as the background plan, is to show the location of existing features on or near the site. *Caution:* The designer should be aware that developers and others may not understand topographical maps.

Appendix B for this chapter outlines the contents of "The Route Plan and the Narrative Report." Once the data in Appendix A are on hand and the designer has studied them, he or she decides whether to produce all studies listed in Appendix B. Surely Allan Robertson, Tom Morris, and many who followed them never produced such studies, but those pioneers analyzed their sites by eye and by hitting balls across them.

Several preliminary plans may be prepared and submitted prior to preparation of the final route plan. First, however, the clubhouse area is determined.

Clubhouse Area

Although its exact site will probably be decided by the clubhouse architect, the course designer often sets aside 4 acres or more for clubhouse, parking, golf car storage, practice green, pool, caddy accommodations and other facilities (Figure 3.5). This acreage does not include starting tees and finishing greens or the practice tee.

Including the pro shop, the clubhouse is the hub of the course layout. Sometimes the course designer is well into a site study before determining the clubhouse area. In fact, the designer may already have selected sites for several holes, though most prefer to select the clubhouse area as an early step, if not the earliest.

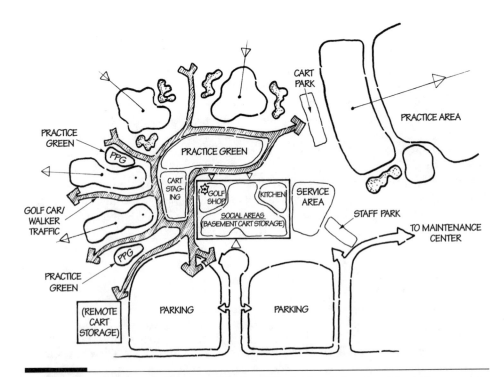

FIGURE 3.5   *This diagram shows one effective way of orienting the interior of the clubhouse to exterior features of the golf course.*

Among the characteristics sought in selecting the clubhouse area are

1. Proximity at least to the two starting tees and two finishing greens plus the practice tee, as well as visibility from the pro shop or starter's building. To accomplish this, it is ideal to be able to radiate holes at 360 degrees from the clubhouse, although 180 degrees makes it possible to accommodate this arrangement from a safety standpoint. Smaller radii, such as 90 degrees, require these features to be at considerable distance from the clubhouse (Figures 3.6 and 3.7).

FIGURE 3.6   With approximately 210 degrees of view arc to work with at Seven Oaks Golf Club, add location the control point (pro shop) can fairly easily "see" all outgoing tees, incoming greens, and the practice range. Only one outgoing tee is partially hidden.

FIGURE 3.7   Even with a 270-degree view arc at Big Meadow Golf Course, the practice tee is partially hidden because of an orientation shift when the clubhouse was constructed.

2. Sufficient area to place the golf car storage building nearby, unless it is to be underground. For underground storage, local building codes must be checked. Some codes preclude car storage under a building where food is served.

3. Sufficient area to place a parking lot of adequate size nearby. For an 18-hole daily fee course in urban or suburban areas, parking for 150 to 200 cars is commonly provided, more if the clubhouse is open for social events and less if the course has restricted play. We find a foursome frequently arrives in four cars, particularly in urban and suburban areas where distances from residences to the course are short.

4. Vistas into the distance and across the course. A view of the finishing hole and practice tee is also important. It has been said that watching golfers settle matches on the finishing green is the most interesting of all clubhouse views. To achieve views, elevation is a must. Still, steep walks from finishing greens to the pro shop are seldom popular.

5. Access to the clubhouse from adjoining roads. Members at private clubs tend to seek the privacy of a clubhouse sited well back from main roads. At daily fee layouts, there is an advantage to placing the clubhouse adjacent to the highway, with the parking lot between the road and the clubhouse (Figure 3.8) or off to one or both sides. This arrangement retains the view of the clubhouse from the highway.

6. Soils sufficiently stable to support the structures.

FIGURE 3.8   The location of the clubhouse at Paradise Valley Golf Club in California, close to a main road, helps hold down entry road costs. Offsetting the parking to the side offers an attractive view of the clubhouse upon entering.

Preparing the Route Plan

Following are the 16 characteristics and features embodied in the route plan in addition to the clubhouse site.

1. Core Layouts   For core layouts where the golf course is perhaps the only feature on-site or the course occupies one contiguous part of it, designers frequently adopt clockwise routing to ensure that out-of-bounds on the maximum number of holes is on the hook side for right-handed golfers, that is, the side that the fewest balls reach. Yet an outside nine with clockwise routing and an inside nine with counterclockwise routing can be desirable because the two nines proceeding in opposite directions (clockwise or anticlockwise) provide varying wind effects.

Architects Rees Jones and Desmond Muirhead, together with landscape architect Guy Rando, have listed configurations other than core layouts for 18 holes with real estate. These are figure eights with clubhouse in the center and single or double fairways, continuous single fairways, and continuous double fairways.

In his later years, old Tom Morris felt it desirable to have the golfer face the wind in four different directions in the first half-dozen holes. This is important on the links and attainable on core layouts but is seldom possible in integrated developments where corridors are determined as much or more by the value of surrounding real estate than by golf.

2. Routing   Careful thought is given to the arrangement of holes. Easy starting holes are included, with no par 3 before the third. This reduces crowding on the first and second tees, and two easy starting holes can be morale builders.

Holes can get progressively more difficult, but not necessarily so. The architect may feel that relaxing "breather" holes in between more difficult ones are desirable.

A few architects prefer easy finishing holes. Nevertheless, most feel that it is mandatory to provide finishing holes on which matches can be decided. Length of tees can offer a happy medium, with long tees provided for those out to excel and seeking challenges and forward tees providing easier finishing holes for the less accomplished and those out to relax.

Two par 3s and two par 5s of varying length and orientation in relation to the prevailing wind can be included on each nine, with length considered in relation to wind and uphill or downhill shots.

3. Orientation   As few east-west and west-east holes as possible, to avoid the rising and setting sun. Starting holes oriented to face the rising sun and finishing holes oriented to the setting sun are particularly objectionable.

4. Variety   No consecutive par 3s or par 5s unless the terrain so dictates. Yet the renowned Alister Mackenzie ignored this guideline in creating one of the world's great layouts, Cypress Point on California's Monterey Peninsula. The Town and Country Club in St. Paul, Minnesota, has three par 5s in a row, a feature that has proved interesting rather than objectionable to members and visitors alike.

5. Continuity   Distances from greens to tees in the range of 200 to 300 feet. Long walks compromise otherwise great layouts. Even for those riding in cars, the sense of continuity and absorption, so important to a golfer, can be lost.

6. Practice Facilities   Addition of a practice area with a northern orientation wherever possible, and orientation to the rising or setting sun avoided. Other practice facilities to be included are the practice pitching and chipping green, the putting green or greens, a practice bunker, and sometimes a practice hole or holes and even a putting course.

7. *Spacing*   A minimum distance of 200 to 250 feet between center lines of adjoining holes.

8. *Overviews*   An overview provided for the starter of tees 1 and 10, greens 9 and 18, and the practice tee. Some designers strive for such an overview from the pro shop in addition to that provided the starter.

9. *Visibility*   A minimum of blind shots. In fact, some architects strive for absolute visibility.

10. *Balanced Length*   The course should accommodate the use of every club. Table 3.1, prepared by golf architect William G. Robinson, indicates one way to achieve this, and Table 3.2 provides an analysis of La Purisima Golf Course near Santa Barbara, California, by golf architect Robert Muir Graves. Such analyses are valuable in checking the balance and other attributes of a course during planning.

11. *Skill Level*   A course should accommodate all types of golfers unless the owner's objective is a course solely for one group.

A course for all can be accomplished if the designer considers all playing levels, for example, by providing three or more sets of tee markers. The contemporary layout truly is several courses in one, with long yardages (6,600 to 7,000), regular (6,000 to 6,400), short (5,000 to 5,800), and perhaps even a shorter course (about 4,800). The strategic design concept can also be important in producing a layout for all golfers. A well-conceived strategy keeps the game interesting for the experienced but does not discourage the less skilled.

12. *Short Course Option*   A forward set of tees providing a short course of about 4,800 yards is becoming popular. This feature arose from golf architect Alice Dye's extensive efforts to create a two-tee system for women. A set of short tee markers is now included on many new layouts and has been added on existing ones. In a poster produced by Dye Designs, Denver, Colorado, architect Dye quotes figures showing the average course length for women nationwide as 5,800 yards, with low handicap women hitting the ball 85% as far as men but those with an average handicap only 75%. Therefore, she concludes that the longer length for women should be 5,400 to 5,800 yards with shorter forward tees measuring 4,600 to 5,400 yards. With watered fairways, Dye maintains, the most pleasurable total length is probably about 4,800 yards.

Dye also points out that these short tees can be used in the junior program and are popular with senior men. (We have observed that if the forward tees — and the red tee — are designated by color only and not as women's tees, they are also used by senior men.) In addition, Dye's short tees play a role in the return of family golf to North America. Parents and children enjoy an occasional round together, sometimes with all playing from the short tees.

13. *Safety*   Contemporary golfers are probably no wilder than their parents. Yet there are many more of them, and American society has become more litigious. The closest attention to safety in regard to players, abutters, and passersby is mandatory.

There is no such thing as absolute safety bordering a golf course. Worse yet, developers may urge designers to disregard safety when millions of dollars in real estate are required for buffers.

Some of these problems may be solved legally by disclaimer codicils in sales agreements to the effect that the real estate has been purchased with normal hazards of golf in

Table 3.1
Estimated Length of Shot—
Balanced Yardage Calling for Use of All Clubs

	Estimated Length of Shot				
Club	Long Hitter	Short Hitter	Club	Long Hitter	Short Hitter
1 Wood	240 yd	210 yd	5 Iron	170 yd	140 yd
2 "	220	200	6 "	160	130
3 "	210	190	7 "	150	120
4 "	200	180	8 "	140	110
2 Iron	190	170	9 "	125	100
3 "	185	160	Wedge	30–120	30–90
4 "	180	150	It is assumed sand wedge and putter would be used.		

Hole	Long Yardage	Club Used	Short Yardage	Club Used
1	380	1W, 8	360	1W, 4
2	400	1W, 6	380	1W, 2
3	540	1W, 3W, W	520	1W, 3W, 5
4	360	1W, 9	340	1W, 6
5	190	2	160	3
6	430	1W, 2	400	1W, 2W
7	500	1W, 2W, W	480	1W, 4W, W
8	150	7	140	5
9	410	1W, 5	390	1W, 4W
	3,360		3,170	
10	370	1W, 8	350	1W, 5
11	520	1W, 3W, W	500	1W, 3W, 9
12	405	1W, 5	370	1W, 3
13	215	4 W	190	3 W
14	340	1W, W	320	1W, 7
15	410	1W, 5	380	1W, 2
16	560	1W, 3W, 9	510	1W, 3W, 8
17	175	4	140	5
18	420	1W, 3	390	1W, 4W
	3,415		3,150	
	3,360		3,170	
	6,775		6,320	

Table 3.2 La Purisma: A Detailed Analysis of a Golf Course

PROJECT: LA PURISMA —   DATE

	HOLE LENGTH			PAR	# APPROACH LENGTH			APPROACH DIRECTION	ELEVATION CHANGE		
	BLUE	WHITE	RED		BLUE	WHITE	RED		1ST SHOT	2ND SHOT	APP. SHOT
1	542	529	447	5	92	159	47	L→R	→	→	↗
2	432	403	337	4	202	33	67	ST	↘		→
3	158	130	98	3	158	130	98	L→R			→
4	340	321	274	4	110	131	4	ST	↘		↗
5	433	400	344	4	203	30	74	R→L	↗		↗
6	566	527	457	5	116	157	57	L→R	→	→	↗
7	427	400	353	4	197	30	83	R→L	→		→
8	437	405	353	4	207	35	83	ST	↘		↘
9	227	201	165	3	227	11	26	ST			↗
OUT	3,562	3,316	2,828	36	AVER: 168	AVER: 80	AVER: 60	ST: 4 L→R R→L: 3 2			
10	465	438	365	4	15	68	95	ST	→		→
11	389	371	329	4	159	181	59	L→R	↘		→
12	609	587	558	5	159	37	28	R→L	→	→	↗
13	169	149	123	3	169	149	123	ST			↘
14	366	366	304	4	194	176	34	ST	↗		→
15	532	503	458	5	82	133	58	L→R	↘	↗	↘
16	436	395	340	4	206	25	70	L→R	↘		↘
17	167	145	118	3	167	145	118	ST			↘
18	410	387	340	4	180	17	70	ST	→		→
IN	3,543	3,341	2,935	36	AVER: 148	AVER: 103	AVER: 73	ST: 5 L→R R→L: 3 1	→ LEVEL	↗ UP	↘ DOWN
TOTAL	7,105	6,657	5,763	72	AVER: 158	AVER: 92	AVER: 66	ST: 9 L→R R→L: 6 3			

(M) LENGTHS (Hole Nos.)	VARIATION	Dogleg L	Dogleg R	Straight
Par 3's 130 145 149 201	15 4 52	—	—	3, 9, 13, 17
Par 4's 321 366 371 387 395 400 400 403 405 438	45 5 16 8 5 0 3 2 .33	2, 4, 7, 8, 16	10, 11, 14	5, 18
Par 5's 503 527 529 587	24 2 58	land 1, 6, 15		6, 12, 15

AVERAGE FIRST and SECOND SHOT LENGTH
B: 230-220
W: 190-180
R: 140-130

PREVAILING WIND

NORTH

mind. Inevitably, however, the developer and, probably, the designer need legal advice before disclaimers are introduced.

Until recently safety problems could be reduced if the community was "adult only." However, such communities in the United States are now considered discriminatory and therefore are not permitted.

Setbacks do not provide absolute safety, although they may reduce danger (Figure 3.9). Whether on the slice or hook side, abutting out-of-bounds real estate, developed or not, each setback requires individual attention. The orientation of buildings near a golf course helps to a limited degree but can compromise the desirability of home sites (Figure 3.10).

Awareness of the location of roadways and players' crossings is also important. Crossings at roadways should be at right angles (Figure 3.11). One-way roads for motorists can sometimes be provided to avoid potential windshield damage.

In sum, there is no substitute for adequate setbacks. Yet even these do not guarantee safety.

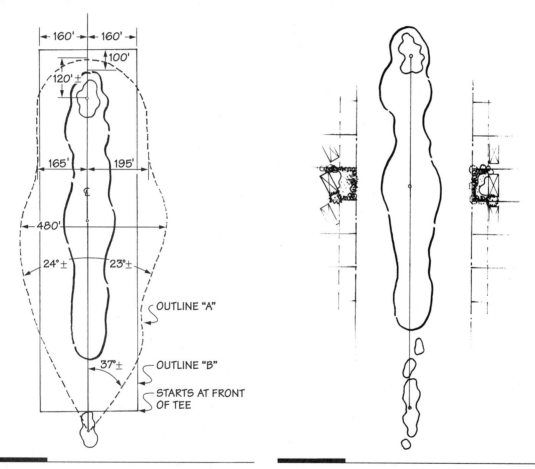

FIGURE 3.9 *Given the infinite distances and directions golfers can hit the ball, it is understandable that the outlines shown, eminating from two separate design offices, are not the same and are not guaranteed to contain all wayward shots. The outlines are a starting point, showing only where* most *golf balls will fall. Each golf hole is different from any other, and the same hole differs day by day due to the combination of wind, hazards, topography, out-of-bounds, vegetation, and turf conditions. The curvilinear shape (outline A) starts at the point where the shot is hit, while the rectangular shape (outline B) is related to tee and green size.*

FIGURE 3.10 *The right side of the golf hole is developed conventionally with the home parallel to the rear lot line. All outdoor living areas are exposed to golf shots. On the left side the homes are angled to protect a portion of the outdoor space.*

To repeat, there is no magic line or space that makes a golf hole "safe". On the contrary, there is a multitude of existing golf holes in spaces smaller than shown here that are quite acceptable to player and neighbor alike.

14. Other Features   Also to be shown on the route plan are golf car paths, shelters, the equipment building, and turf and tree nurseries.

Siting Golf Car Paths   Because so many players use golf cars, all-weather paths are required. At some courses they are provided only in heavy traffic areas. At others they traverse the entire route. Care is needed in siting paths on paper and on the ground. In fact, a golf course can be compromised by placing a path without regard to play, maintenance, or eye appeal. We have observed situations where "the tail wags the dog" and interesting features are compromised to accommodate paths.

In practice, many architects may not undertake the planning of paths. However, in our litigious society it is important that paths be planned carefully. Liability can arise from many circumstances, including, but not limited to:

1. A pathway sloping too steeply from one side or sloping steeply uphill or downhill for a considerable distance.
2. Sharp curves, particularly on steep hills.
3. Inadequate protective railings. Rails themselves, however, can also contribute to accidents.
4. Pathways where drivers encounter shots from another hole.
5. Improper surfacing. Some surfaces are very slippery.

No car path system is ideal. Yet in devising a well-thought-out system, the designer will consider these guidelines:

1. Because most golfers slice, paths should be on the right side of fairways. Exceptions include holes that slope down severely from right to left or dogleg right to left (Figure 3.12).
2. Routing 90 feet from center of pathway to center of fairway is a valuable guideline but by no means rigid. Paths must be brought in closer at tees and greens.
3. A wavy or undulating pathway routing is preferable to a straight line from the perspective of eye appeal. However, if undulations are severe, drivers tend to cut corners (Figure 3.13).
4. The fewer pathways crossing a hole the better. However, with the path crossing just in front of the tee, golfers can leave the path at various points or as directed by signage (Figure 3.14).

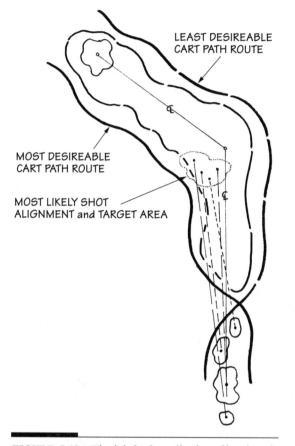

FIGURE 3.12   The left dogleg tells the golfer that the shortest distance to the hole is along the left side, so most shots will head in that direction. The golf car path on the right is so far away from play that many will ignore it as useless or too much trouble.

FIGURE 3.13   A straight car path would likely be as abhorred by nature as any other straight line. However, making the curves too abrupt creates another problem: it seems many golfers are too lazy, careless, or inattentive to stay on the path.

FIGURE 3.14   Here is an example of the path crossing in front of the tee. This is an effective way of controlling turf wear where cars are allowed to leave the path.

5. Parking areas are required at tees greens, and practice areas (Figures 3.15, 3.16). Passing areas may be required along the circuit if on-coming traffic is expected (Figure 3.17).

6. Generally, but with some exceptions, pathways should serve one hole only. Use of one pathway for two adjoining holes can create a dangerous situation: it tends to force golfers to face balls hit from another hole (Figure 3.18).

7. Paths not hidden by trees can often be camouflaged with low mounds (Figure 3.19).

8. If car paths are not continuous over the entire layout, deep holes develop at ends of segments. To prevent this situation, the access and egress ends are swerved so that drivers tend to enter or leave the path at different points (see again Figure 3.14).

9. In compliance with the Americans with Disabilities Act, (ADA) paths must permit egress at 75-yard intervals.

FIGURE 3.15   This parking area is large enough to stage golf cars for a full tournament.

FIGURE 3.16   This car parking area serves a practice range and also allows access through between portions of the golf course. Good parking here encourages golfer use of practice facilities.

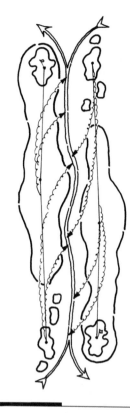

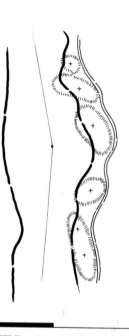

FIGURE 3.17 These pull-out areas are an effective way to park cars, also leaving an access way open for passing. The curbs prevent the cars from being driven up on the tee surface.

FIGURE 3.18 The efficiency of two-directional car paths may be more trouble than it's worth. If the holes are too close together, shots can create a dangerous situation on both holes. If the holes are sufficiently far apart, the path may be too far from both holes for effective use.

FIGURE 3.19 Low-perimeter mounds work well in hiding a car path. Low mounds used in the middle of a fairway can effectively hide a path that must cross the hole. Designing car paths during preparation of the grading plan is the most effective way of integrating the paths into the golf course.

Siting Shelters Shelters, probably designed by the clubhouse architect to harmonize with the clubhouse and other buildings, are sometimes sited on the route plan by the course architect. Varying from elaborate halfway houses that serve refreshments and provide rest rooms to simple rain shelters, they are placed in the vicinity of as many greens and tees as possible (Figures 3.20 and 3.21). In siting, preference is given to those areas of the course located farthest from the clubhouse or at the midpoint of each nine (Figures 3.22 and 3.23), although shelters may be required in areas less remote from the main building as well.

It is important to site shelters, particularly those providing refreshments, well out of range of golf balls. Obvious as this criterion should be, it can be overlooked.

Lightning protection is required, as is access for disabled persons; to this end, overhanging eaves can increase shelter space. Adequate golf car parking is also needed for all who seek shelter in sudden downpours.

Shelters can enhance a layout, with beautiful landscaping including perennial and annual beds, flowering shrubs, and other garden features.

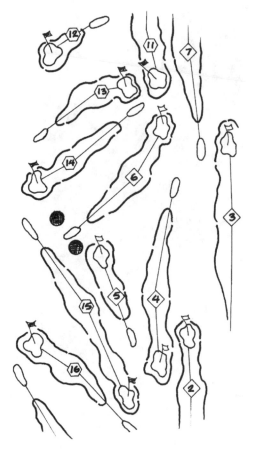

FIGURE 3.20 Based on Figure 2.34, Royal Lytham and Saint Anne's, two excellent locations for a midcourse facility are shown here. The shelters intercept both nines just past midpoint in the round. Another option is to place the facility between holes 9 and 10 at the farthest point from the clubhouse.

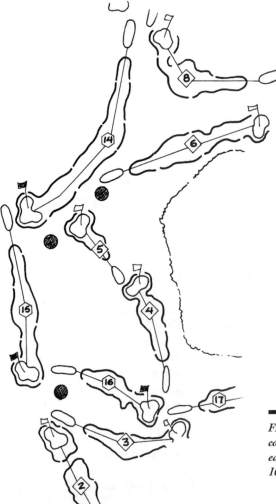

FIGURE 3.21 Based on Figure 2.36, Pebble Beach, the midcourse facility locations shown here are around the middle of each side. The farthest point from the clubhouse is between holes 10 and 11.

FIGURE 3.22 Ranging from a rustic lean-to to a structure rivaling the clubhouse in architectural opulence, mid-course facilities can offer everything from shelter to relief to a steak sandwich. Excepting the rest room feature, many such facilities are being replaced by the drink and sandwich cart.

Siting the Equipment Building The most important building, after the clubhouse and pro shop, is the one that houses maintenance equipment and repair facilities. A reasonably central and secure area, not too conspicuous or close to the clubhouse, is required. In all seasons, there must be access to the building and utilities must be operational. The location of an equipment building in a corner of the property can result in unproductive time for the crew, as they must travel to reach work sites after check-in, and in an integrated development the value of the lot adjoining it may be compromised or, in extreme cases, made unsellable. Some feel that locating the equipment building close to the pro shop improves the relationship between professional and superintendent.

A maintenance area of one or two acres to include the equipment building (Figures 3.23A, B, C, D) a separate chemical storage building, fuel storage, an equipment washing area, employee parking, and sometimes sod and tree nurseries, is shown on the route plan, but seldom in detail.

A

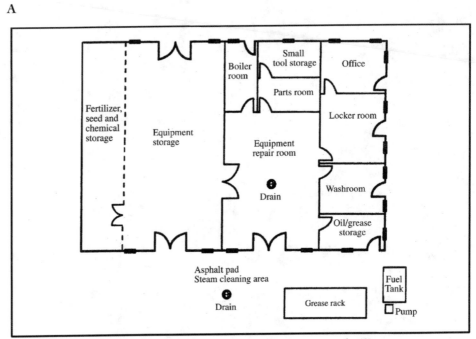

Sample floor plan of golf course maintenance facility.

B

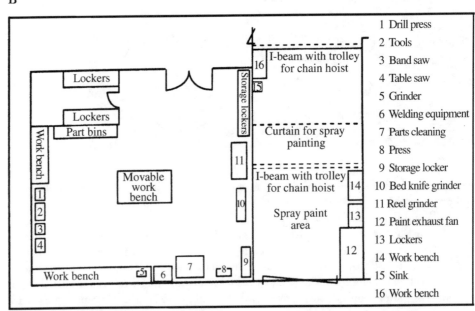

Sample floor plan of shop area of golf course maintenance facility.

FIGURE 3.23 *The GCSAA provides a* Guide to Planning and Design *as well as a multitude of other educational products. These diagrams, furnished by the Golf Course Superintendents Association of America, demonstrate ideas for floor plans.*

C

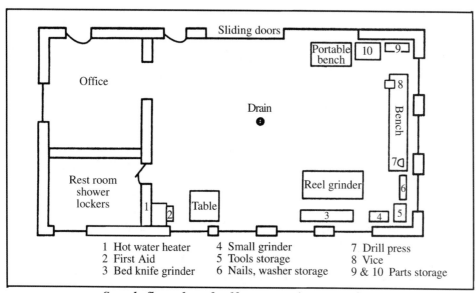

1 Hot water heater   4 Small grinder   7 Drill press
2 First Aid   5 Tools storage   8 Vice
3 Bed knife grinder 6 Nails, washer storage   9 & 10 Parts storage

Sample floor plan of golf course maintenance facility.

D

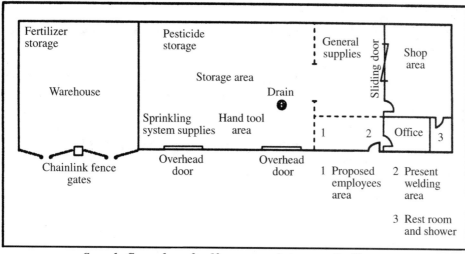

1 Proposed employees area   2 Present welding area

3 Rest room and shower

Sample floor plan of golf course maintenance facility.

FIGURE 3.23   (cont'd)

Turf and Tree Nurseries Turf nurseries to provide sod for repairing greens, tees—and sometimes fairways—were at one time invariably established on new golf courses. Today many commercial sod farms supply quality sod at lower cost than a superintendent can grow it. Therefore, a sod nursery may be unnecessary.

Yet it is still prudent in planning to leave an acre or more, accessible to irrigation, for this purpose. The superintendent may in the future prefer to grow sod on-site. For example, when an existing course is being rebuilt or a new green is being installed, special sod may be needed if players demand identical surfaces to those they are accustomed to. Such sod can be propagated by using aeration plugs from existing greens, planted into a prepared mix on the space set aside for the nursery. Many superintendents prefer the turf nursery close to the equipment building so that crew members can work on it in between other jobs.

On-site tree nurseries with access to irrigation are still common, mostly on new courses where extensive tree planting will be needed. Setting aside an acre or more provides an area where small trees or seedlings are introduced and then transplanted to the course a few years later. Seedling trees may be also planted between fairways, but golfers often trample them.

15. *Future Alterations*   Designers have long realized that holes may require lengthening in the future. Therefore, tees are often sited so they can be extended back if additional length is ever needed, as it often is.

16. *Future Development*   Although the owner may state emphatically that no real estate will be integrated with the golf course, we have observed that as generations and circumstances change—most particularly, as land values increase—this attitude changes. Therefore, designers must give thought to setting aside land for this purpose, and for access to it, to avoid major alteration in the layout if the owner's attitude, or that of any successor, changes.

These 16 items are parts of the graphic layout known as the route plan. While sometimes referred to as the "preliminary plan," we believe that this latter term should be limited to the various plan or plans prepared to complete the true route plan.

The architect will perhaps advise the owner that the plan is diagrammatic and subject to revision and will continue to revise it until all involved are convinced that it is the best possible routing. No doubt several revisions will still be needed. Indeed, each of us has on occasion revised a plan more than 20 times.

Throughout the process, the architect respects the three sides of the design triangle—the game of golf, aesthetics, and future maintainability—together with the environment. At the time of submission of the route plan to the owner, the architect probably submits a complete written report covering some or all of the subjects listed in Appendix B.

The route plan is the framework for the golf course. It serves to show owners and others the intent of the architect and is also needed for

- Preparing preliminary cost estimates
- Publicity
- Financing
- Permitting (authorities sometimes, but not invariably, request more detailed plans)

Appendix C to this chapter outlines the design services required to complete the course following completion of the route plan.

The Role of the Computer in Designing Golf Courses and Holes

Lawrence Sheehan, in *A Passion for Golf*, describes the office of golf architect Michael Hurdzan as "a workplace where the past meets the future in golf course architecture. Drafting tables where golf holes are designed using the latest computer technology share space with a collection of golf antiquities." Sheehan adds that the Hurdzan collection includes "3,000 books on course design and maintenance, some 6,000 wood-shafted clubs and thousands of golf balls."[1]

Hurdzan himself includes an informative case history concerning the role of the computer in the design of Westwood Plateau Golf Course near Vancouver, British Columbia, in his book, *Golf Course Architecture.* In the same chapter, he describes the pioneering work of Edward Connor, an engineer, contractor, and designer who with a laser theodolite, computer, and modeling program records for posterity the exact contours of existing greens, bunkers, and other features.[2]

In this age of computing and rapidly advancing technology, part of a golf architect's training involves computer applications. In practice, every design office uses computers to a greater or lesser extent, whether it owns the system or farms out the work.

Early personal computer use for word processing and basic accounting has progressed to specialized accounting, administration, and business planning applications. In addition, and of particular interest to designers, is CADD (Computer-Aided Design and Drafting).

For golf course architects the computer, and particularly CADD, is a comprehensive and highly refined design tool. Section drawings and perspective views can be provided to show what the grading plans will look like when executed on the ground. This also allows a multitude of opportunities to play "what if" without spending many hours in redrafting plans.

Most CADD systems now have three-dimensional capabilities, allowing the designer to "get inside" the design and look at it from many angles. This is helpful in planning and for presentations and displays to clients, governing bodies, and regulatory agencies.

Indeed, designers can draft a plan for an individual hole or for an entire course by computer, with calculations made for clearing, earth moving, irrigation, drainage, and seed and commodity requirements.

More specifically, there are many CADD functions not necessarily used directly by the course architect but closely related to and necessary for the design of a contemporary golf course. The designer must be familiar with these processes and their products, because they are an essential part of and backup to the preliminary design and important in development and preparation of construction documents.

CADD software was originally used primarily for drafting the designer's plans in two-dimensional forms: plan, profile, and cross-sectional views. This was an aid to the designer, but the more technical mundane tasks—earthwork, drainage, and irrigation quantities among them—were still calculated by hand. This time-consuming process could occasionally compromise the more creative and exciting part of the design process.

The input processes of the first software programs were cumbersome and not always programmed to meet design situations of a particular site. Designers had to take care not to compromise the integrity and aesthetics of the design to suit the input needs of the computer program. However, as computers evolved to faster and more powerful machines, software was developed to facilitate incorporating many time-consuming tasks into the course design process.

CADD software has become more user friendly and versatile. Although these attributes may seem to go hand in hand, the more versatile the options are made, the more complex the design input becomes. To ease the complexities and allow the designer to focus more on design and less on how to input data for the computer, interfaces were developed. For example, one irrigation software program prompts for information and location of the water source, the type of sprinkler and nozzles desired (chosen from a library), and the area to be integrated by outlining the area on a screen. The next options are

- Placing each sprinkler in location and drawing pipes in between
- Placing each sprinkler in location and letting the computer do the pipe layout
- Placing some of each and letting the computer do the rest.
- Letting the computer do everything.

The designer may find it easier to place a few head locations and connect pipes and then let the computer do the rest based on that lead. It is then easy to modify everything the computer creates and play the "what-if" game. With each "what-if" the computer sizes pipe diameter for the amount of flow, the total length of each diameter used, counting the number of sprinklers, elbows, valves, risers, and other fittings required, all within seconds. Coupled with a current price list, a designer could have several irrigation designs with cost estimates in minutes.

Following are particular steps that CADD facilitates in designing a golf course.

Preparation of the Base Map

Nearly all base maps with topography and existing features are developed photogrammetrically from aerial photography. Topographic and other information is first downloaded from a data collector to a computer, where a drawing is prepared at the desired scale.

Site Analysis

Using gridded terrain models, the designer generates and/or analyzes slope maps, showing direction of slope. He or she can then specify and show elevations, analyze visibility, show shadow patterns of trees and surrounding buildings, and create multiple overlay composite maps showing these and other characteristics.

Course Planning

The architect can simultaneously design two- and three-dimensionally and create preliminary routing plans with par 3, 4, and 5 holes, showing their existing and proposed contours and their contour intervals. If spot elevations are needed, the designer can interpolate. Once the route plan is prepared, the designer can draw in roads, car paths, parking lots, buildings and basic tree planting.

Surface modeling is used to create a triangulated irregular network (TIN) in which contours on a rectangular grid can be converted to 3-D graphic representations. The designer can also analyze and design earthworks using slope projections, feature projections, construction nodes for cut and fill depth, and identification of contours. For design of roadways and car paths, slope analysis, drainage flow analysis, volume calculations analysis of terrain data and determination of alignments and profiles may be used.

Landscape Design

Again, the architect can simultaneously design two- and three-dimensionally. A comprehensive plant material plan database is available from software suppliers, covering every climate zone and a multitude of other categories.[3] A growth simulator graphically shows plant growth for any number of years. Plant material tables include symbols for plant species, name, size, and quantity needed to assist the architect in creating the planting plan.[4]

Irrigation Design

In this phase the designer can lay out heads, valves, and piping, performing calculations and perfecting the design using any major manufacturer's equipment. Then he or she sets parameters including sprinkler style or actual model numbers, data files to access, available pressures, and volume of water, as well as wind speed and its direction. Next, the designer generates distribution analyses, summarizes the flow in gallons or liters per minute, determines pressure losses per zone and precipitation rates together with operating time. Piping can be sized for manual or automatic operation, and total length of each size of pipe determined along with other equipment and fittings that are required. See Chapter 10.

Hydraulics and Hydrology

Watershed modeling includes hydraulic analysis for drainage basins, determination of runoff, flood control measures, including detention basins with outlet structures, and hydrographs or water surface profiling. These profiles can be computed through channels and stream networks together with related hydraulic analyses for designing a floodway, bridge, or culvert.

The Future of the Computer in Golf Course Architecture

Despite the immense capabilities and potential of the computer, it is likely that many golf course architects will not create their plans entirely on computer in the near future. Golf architecture is an art form practiced by imaginative and innovative people. As an art form, it seems destined always to require pencil and paper, together with day after day, on the ground studying terrain subtleties, vistas, horizon, and wind effects in order to fully investigate and refine the variety of existing options to be found on the site.

Could the art form be sterilized by neglecting pencil and paper and the ground study? Some building architects fear computer-aided design compromises drawing skills and removes the designer from the basics. Likewise, experienced golf course designers wonder whether the computer will compromise the manner in which a golf course is adapted to the land.

Nevertheless, as recently as a decade ago most designers would have said that the miraculous options available today were impossible. Moreover, the outlook of design professionals is one of vision and, therefore, open-mindedness. Surely this is the appropriate attitude for golf course architects in regard to a new technology that is rapidly advancing and changing the economy of the world and our way of life and, in doing so, creating the need for more golf courses.

This would be an appropriate time for you to review and do Exercise 1 found on page 381, Appendix B.

Notes

1. Lawrence Sheehan, *A Passion for Golf* (New York: Clarkson Potter, 1994), 134.
2. Michael Hurdzan, *Golf Course Architecture: Design, Construction and Restoration* (Chelsea, Mich.: Sleeping Bear Press, 1996), 256f.

3. Software varies considerably where one may have 1000 different landscape materials and plants. Another may concentrate on dozens of trees representing commonly used varieties. The tree forms, including trunk, branch, and leaf structure, can be varied in color and texture in accordance with seasonal changes. Height and width of plants can be specified, along with complexity of the form.

4. One mode allows the designer to generate plants in a very simplified form to note their position. This uses less time, memory, and disk resource. The fully detailed plant can be inserted when the planting plan is finalized.

Site Data Required by the Architect

I. Site Data
   A. Base map (reproducible at 100-scale drawing on photo mylar) of project site and surrounding area, including the following. For CADD purposes, also include DWG files on diskette (Autocad):
      1. Legal boundaries of property, rights of way, easements
      2. Topographical survey (maximum 2 ft contour interval)
      3. Coordinate system for future location of golf course features
      4. Location and general description of existing features, such as buildings, roads, fences, utility lines, together with treed and open areas
      5. Location and general description of any other features within or near the project site affecting golf course development
   B. Aerial photographs of the project site. Scaled verticals are best, yet oblique shots can be useful.
   C. Climatological data, including:
      1. Average monthly rainfall
      2. Average monthly wind direction and velocity (day and night)
      3. Average monthly temperature, humidity, and evaporation rate
   D. Soil analysis (chemical and physical) of topsoil for turf and subsoil for trees. U.S. Department of Agriculture (USDA) soil surveys include information for large general areas on soil maps obtainable from office of the National Resources Conservation Service (NRCS) of the USDA.
   E. Available utilities (location and capacity), including:
      1. Water, potable and for irrigation
      2. Electricity (three-phase)
      3. Storm drainage (water entering and leaving the site)
      4. Sewage disposal
   F. Environmental impact assessment covering issues such as water use, endangered flora and fauna, archaeological sites, wetlands, water quality, health-related or other issues potentially affected by golf course development and future maintenance operations.
II. General Information
   A. Existing or proposed master development plan for the entire project, including the golf course site and adjacent developments, whether or not they are to be integrated with the course.
   B. Proposed participation of owner or representative during construction phase, including:
      1. Labor available
      2. Equipment and tools available
      3. Supervisory personnel available
      4. Contract administrative personnel available
   C. Proposed time schedule for planning and construction phases.
   D. Proposed budget covering planning and construction costs.

The Route Plan and Narrative Report

I. Project Analysis
   A. Schematic master development plan for project site and adjacent areas in narrative and/or graphic form.
   B. Written program covering proposed general characteristics of the golf course and relationship of the course to existing or proposed total land use.

II. Site Analysis Review
   A. Property outline and topography
   B. Major vegetation
   C. Available utilities
   D. Soil characteristics (chemical and physical)
   E. Climate and weather factors
   F. Pertinent planning or design factors limiting or controlling golf course development, including environmental issues. An Environmental Impact Statement prepared by a qualified person may be required at this point unless provided previously to the architect with site data. (See Appendix A, section I.F.)

III. Master Golf Course Development Plan
   A. The graphic layout showing course routing, location, and general characteristics of the golf course and related facilities. Intrinsically, this is the master plan when accompanied by written reports outlined in section IV.
   B. Colored rendering of this plan suitable for public display.

IV. Design Analysis
   A. Description of course and related facilities and their impact on the environment, society, and the economy. (This is not the Environmental Impact Statement.)
   B. Description of each hole in regard to its playability, eye appeal, and maintainability.
   C. General discussion of major construction processes, including:
      1. Erosion and sediment control
      2. Clearing
      3. Rough grading
      4. Drainage
      5. Irrigation water source and pumping station
      6. Irrigation system
      7. Golf course components
      8. Tree planting
      9. Turf establishment
      10. Other environmental issues
   D. Cost estimates for construction of golf course.
   E. Proposed golf course construction schedule and phasing with other related elements to be constructed.

Golf Course Design Services Required Following Completion of the Route Plan and Narrative

I. Components of Golf Course Development
    A. Final design of golf course. This can be an update based on the master golf course development plan (the route plan and narrative). Further site investigation, new project data, or changes in surrounding real estate may require this updating.
    B. The grading plan: this shows existing and proposed contours.
    C. Plans and specifications covering
        1. Protection of the environment
        2. Staking
        3. Clearing
        4. Grading (rough and smooth)
        5. Drainage
        6. Irrigation and pumping system
        7. Fine grading and preparation of seed beds
        8. Turf and tree planting
        9. Related golf course features such as golf car paths, bridges, and shelters
    D. Detailed drawings and specifications covering the construction of
        1. Greens
        2. Tees
        3. Bunkers
        4. Fairway and roughs
        5. Water features
        6. Other major golf course elements
    E. Refined construction cost estimates.
    F. Final construction schedule and phasing plan.
II. Services Provided Immediately Prior to and During Construction Phase
    A. Preparation of contract documents
    B. Assistance in selection of contractors, suppliers, and golf course superintendent
    C. Continual planning and updating as required during golf course construction
    D. Observation of construction
III. Supplement to Golf Course Architectural Services
    A. Aid in implementation of operations and maintenance programs, including "grow in."
    B. Continuing consultation and assistance as an agent and/or advisor. In this regard, numerous design problems and other difficulties may arise in the early weeks following opening, particularly when the course superintendent was not present during construction. The architect and his or her staff can often solve these without resorting to major reconstruction.

Design of a Golf Hole

Every hole should have a different character.

From *Golf Architecture*, 1920, by Alister Mackenzie (1870–1934)

"God created golf holes, it is the duty of the architect to discover them." Attributed to Donald Ross, this influential quotation indicates that many an imagined golf hole can become reality by following existing contours and moving little earth. Yet the might of contemporary earth-moving equipment enables the creation of a golf course on a site with few natural golfing characteristics. For example, construction of Shadow Creek near Las Vegas by Tom Fazio involved moving millions of cubic yards of earth to remake a desert landscape into 18 holes. On the other hand, Sand Hills Golf Course at Mullens, Nebraska, by Coore and Crenshaw, required modifications only of existing contours with no major earth-moving efforts.

General Principles

Whether natural or a designer's creation, each hole is a composition with the green as its focal point. This chapter reviews parameters to be considered in planning that composition. Because it is a work of art, these are guidelines only: they are not fixed rules or regulations. An artist has license. Indeed, the final form emerges from the designer's judgment and vision. Influential architect Tom Fazio has said, there are really no rules in golf course design.

Development of the Composition

Landscape architect Kenneth K. Helphand says, "One can dissect the form of any design, a building, a garden, or a golf hole, for example, and examine component parts."[1] However, the various parts of a golf hole—green, tee, bunker, which all have Scottish origins—can be natural, man-made, or man-modified.

There are strategic, penal, and heroic holes; there are the classics, as described in Chapter 2; and there are holes barely manifesting any of these characteristics. Likewise, in golf, as in any game, there are players with exceptional skill, those with little skill, and players of all calibers in between. In general, the architect tries to accommodate all. Yet in achieving this objective, the integrity of individual holes for the accomplished golfer must not be compromised. Furthermore, medium and high handicap golfers still want the layouts they play to be courses of integrity even though they may be playing forward tees. A duty of the architect is to encourage the golfer to improve his or her game. Risk-reward holes contribute to this by providing the player another way to play a hole as his or her game improves.

Par

A first consideration is *par*, the closest of any parameter to being a rule, in that it is defined in the Rules of Golf. The ruling bodies put forward yardages, as shown in the table on this page, with each hole measured horizontally from the middle of the appropriate tee to the center of the green. Unless the hole is straight from tee to green, it is measured first to the bend (pivot or turning point) and from there to the center of the green. That measurement, according to the rules, should follow the line of play designated by the architect, generally down the geographic centerline of the hole.

Par	Men	Women
3	up to 250	up to 210
4	251 to 470	211 to 400
5	471 and over	401 to 575
6		576 and over

Measured length is the criterion for par. Exceptional conditions, however, including severe problems such as steep uphill or downhill shots and strong prevailing winds, may permit modification of even this parameter. Nevertheless, length is the most important factor in regard to the difficulty of a hole.

Design for Women

Contemporary course design calls for layouts more friendly to women. Jeff Brauer, past president of the American Society of Golf Course Architects (ASGCA) in 1995, emphasizes that in addition to length the playability of a hole from tee to green must be thought out by the architect. The architect may then provide a portion of each green accessible for a run-up, more chipping areas, and, if a bunker is deep, one shallow face for a sideways escape. Brauer forecasts that golf courses of the future will be played by more mixed foursomes — a trend we have observed.

Trees and Golf

The links are devoid of trees. Yet as golf spread from Scotland to England and Ireland and then around the world, trees became an important element of the game, and today they exert a profound influence on play, maintainability, and eye appeal of a hole. Trees situated anywhere on a golf course are beautiful, yet haphazard planting or lack of thought during clearing operations compromises many a great hole.

There are seven common oversights in clearing or tree planting operations that contribute to serious problems as the trees mature:

1. Inadequate widths provided from tree line to tree line
2. Failure to consider the mature tree and silhouette (Figures 4.1a and 4.1b).
3. Trees left or planted too close to putting surfaces and tees
4. Inadequate thought given to air circulation
5. Trees that block distant vistas or breathtaking vistas from hole to hole (Figure 4.2)
6. Gallery space reduced by an overabundance of trees (Figures 4.3 and 4.4)
7. Trees between a bunker and the target that create double penalties (Figure 4.5)

BEFORE

AFTER

FIGURE 4.1a   In the "before" stage, there is sufficient density for a proper green background but still plenty of sunlight and air circulation space.

FIGURE 4.1b   In the "after," more mature, stage, failure to anticipate the ultimate size and density of the background creates too much shade and too little air circulation for healthy turf growth.

FIGURE 4.2   A spectacular view of the city of Bend, Oregon, backed by the mountains at River's Edge Golf Club, may disappear without judicious pruning and thinning of the trees below the green.

FIGURE 4.3   The treed border on this par 4 at La Purisima in Lompoc, California, is heavy enough to define the hole and dictate golf play but open enough that spectators have a clear view of the action. (Courtesy David Bauer)

FIGURE 4.4 Clearing work on this par 3 at Port Ludlow in Washington is sufficient to allow sunshine and air circulation but does not permit easy access or space for spectators.

FIGURE 4.5 This fairway bunker/tree complex demonstrates the double penalty. However, a strong case can be made that whether you're in sand or turf, you will lose a shot either way if you're close behind the tree.

Whether they are planted or left standing during clearing operations, trees should be sited with several objectives in mind, including safety, depth perception or shot definition, aesthetics, shade—mostly at tees—shade effects, wind breaks, and boundary planting (Figures 4.6, 4.7, 4.8).

Yet in achieving these objectives, unfavorable microclimates, characterized by absence of air circulation, dense to moderate shade, and direct root competition with the greensward, result from close proximity of trees and shrubs to turfgrass. In turn, these adverse microclimates contribute to low-quality turf.

Trees poorly situated in relation to play compromise a hole and, in extreme cases, make it a "freak" hole as they mature. Specimen trees carefully left near the line of play can substitute admirably for a bunker or other hazard. Although they may be considered unfair or even "freaky" early on, as time passes, they become an integral part of the hole

FIGURE 4.6 *This row of cypress trees was originally planted as a windbreak for ranching activities. They were left in place since they make such a fine background for this green at the Sea Ranch in California.*

FIGURE 4.7 *The effects of shade can be very dramatic but, late in the day, may obscure the details of a golf hole, making shot evaluation difficult.*

FIGURE 4.8 Here a golf hole is bounded on one side by a linear roadside planting and on the other by an orchard. The two plantings are both necessarily linear in character hence great for definition but do not add much to the beauty of the hole.

and are revered by the regular players. Others are responsible for worn traffic areas on the turf, make maneuvering of maintenance equipment difficult, or preclude opening a shaded hole for play following frost on otherwise ideal mornings in early autumn. Still others contribute to prolonged ice buildup, which can have devastating effects.

Although trees contribute to the magnificence of our inland courses as contrasted with links layouts where few trees are present, it is significant that numerous established courses today are involved in tree removal rather than planting programs. Truly, many a golf course has become an outstanding arboretum at the expense of playing values and turf quality.

Single specimen trees can be pleasing features of holes (see Figure 4.12), but owner, architect, and superintendent should be aware that they can disappear because of disease, high winds, lightning, and other factors. Experience shows they cannot be relied on as permanent features, although arboricultural expertise and sometimes the addition of lightning rods can prolong their lives.

Clearing widths specified for construction vary. Any space less than 200 feet at greens or 180 feet across the fairway and rough, leads to problems. Architect Douglas Carrick recommends 200 to 240 feet from tree line to tree line. At tees, an absolute minimum of 100 feet is mandatory for turfgrass health, with more generous widths desirable whenever possible, and no tree at a green should be closer than 60 feet to the edge of the putting surface[2] (Figure 4.9).

Except on boundaries and for protection of other features, straight-line planting is generally to be avoided in favor of drifts and clumps (Figure 4.10). Similarly, and more often than not, an undulating clearing line produces a more beautiful and interesting golf hole than a straight line, in regard to both play and aesthetics (Figure 4.11), and a few magnificent specimen trees on the edges of clear-cut areas further enhance eye appeal (Figure

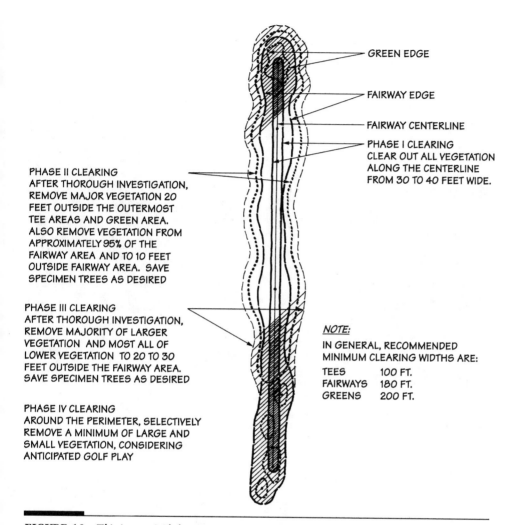

GREEN EDGE

FAIRWAY EDGE

FAIRWAY CENTERLINE

PHASE I CLEARING
CLEAR OUT ALL VEGETATION
ALONG THE CENTERLINE
FROM 30 TO 40 FEET WIDE.

PHASE II CLEARING
AFTER THOROUGH INVESTIGATION,
REMOVE MAJOR VEGETATION 20
FEET OUTSIDE THE OUTERMOST
TEE AREAS AND GREEN AREA.
ALSO REMOVE VEGETATION FROM
APPROXIMATELY 95% OF THE
FAIRWAY AREA AND TO 10 FEET
OUTSIDE FAIRWAY AREA. SAVE
SPECIMEN TREES AS DESIRED

PHASE III CLEARING
AFTER THOROUGH INVESTIGATION,
REMOVE MAJORITY OF LARGER
VEGETATION AND MOST ALL OF
LOWER VEGETATION TO 20 TO 30
FEET OUTSIDE THE FAIRWAY AREA.
SAVE SPECIMEN TREES AS DESIRED

PHASE IV CLEARING
AROUND THE PERIMETER, SELECTIVELY
REMOVE A MINIMUM OF LARGE AND
SMALL VEGETATION, CONSIDERING
ANTICIPATED GOLF PLAY

NOTE:

IN GENERAL, RECOMMENDED
MINIMUM CLEARING WIDTHS ARE:
TEES   100 FT.
FAIRWAYS   180 FT.
GREENS   200 FT.

FIGURE 4.9   *This is a typical clearing program starting with a narrow centerline space and widening out in increments so that no more trees are removed than absolutely necessary.*

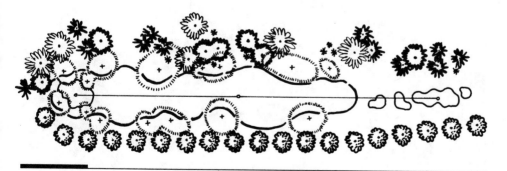

FIGURE 4.10   *All efforts to create a naturally shaped and graded golf hole are diminished along the left side by the rigid, linear planting. On the right, the drifts and clumps of trees blend comfortably with the golf hole.*

4.12). Yet architect and superintendent must beware of even these few specimen trees. They can cause problems unless their positioning in relation to prevailing winds, sunlight, and the greensward has been thought through. Planners must also realize that as years go on it may not be possible to remove such trees, because of player resistance. Sometimes they are planted as family memorials, making their removal even more difficult.

FIGURE 4.11   This hole at Canterwood Golf Club in Gig Harbor, Washington, demonstrates how an undulating clearing line and variations in the treatment of lower-growing plants create a naturally attractive setting for golf.

FIGURE 4.12   The huge old ponderosa pine was retained in a very strategic position at the right-front of the green. It dictates the tee shot as well as the approach shot on this short dogleg left par 4 at River's Edge in Bend, Oregon.

Doglegs

If not overdone, doglegs add interest to a round. In planning a dogleg, consider the following:

1. The inside angle of a dogleg should never be less than 90 degrees (Figure 4.13). In fact, 90 to 100 degrees is often too sharp. When the angle is less than 90 degrees, golfers sooner or later learn to cut the corner—there have been instances of greens on par 4s and even par 5s reached on the drive. This can occur when trees between the tee and the green disappear as a result of disease, windstorms, a change in the water table during construction, or other factors.
2. Double doglegs on par 5s also add interest. They must be planned so the golfer is not penalized by a long drive resulting in him or her having to use a wedge or short iron to get around the second corner (Figure 4.14). Golfers abhor these "wasted" shots.
3. As a rule (with many exceptions), the architect should not take the driver out of the golfer's hand for the tee shot. Several architects long ago experimented unsuccessfully by forcing the golfer to use a short iron off the tee with a longer iron or wood to the green (Figure 4.15). This situation still occurs most often on doglegs, but sometimes elsewhere. For example, a pond that cannot be carried from the tee could require a short iron off the tee (Figure 4.16).

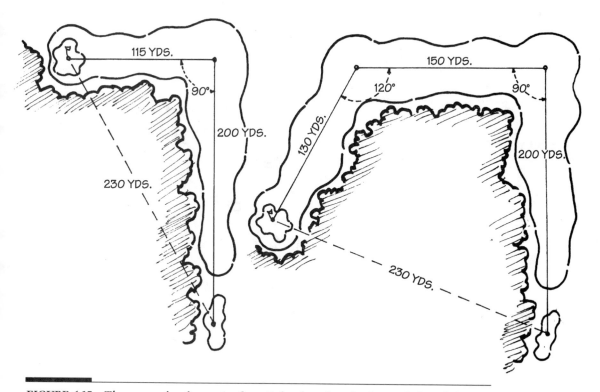

FIGURE 4.13   These examples of a par 4 and par 5 show how short the shot can be directly from tee to green. Without heavy tree cover (and sometimes even with tree cover), some golfers will decide they can hit the shot. Then there is a very dangerous situation, in which no one on the green is expecting incoming shots.

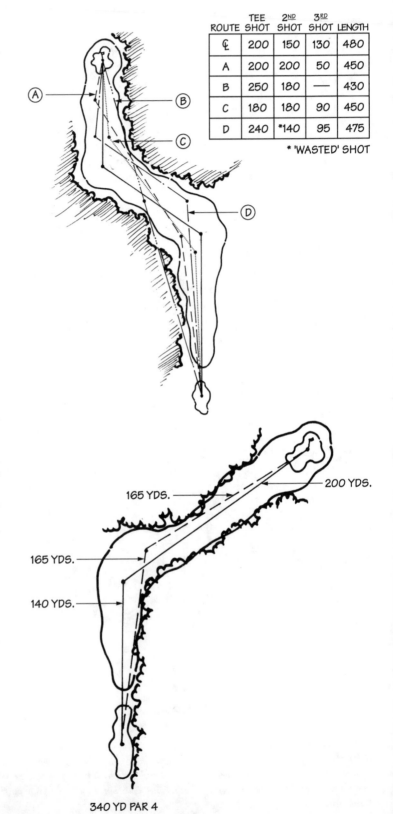

FIGURE 4.14   This par 5 is a three-shot hole by definition, albeit a short one. The all-too-common idea is that if you can't hit a wood or long iron on the second shot, it is wasted. It's not wasted but simply determined by where the golfers hit their tee shots.

ROUTE	TEE SHOT	2ND SHOT	3RD SHOT	LENGTH
₵	200	150	130	480
A	200	200	50	450
B	250	180	—	430
C	180	180	90	450
D	240	*140	95	475

* 'WASTED' SHOT

FIGURE 4.15   The tree size and density next to the tee may well obligate a short shot to the corner and a long approach shot, changing the usual sequence. This may rankle some golfers who either don't realize or don't accept that there is no rule in golf that prescribes a wood shot off each par 4 or 5 tee.

165 YDS.

200 YDS.

165 YDS.

140 YDS.

340 YD PAR 4

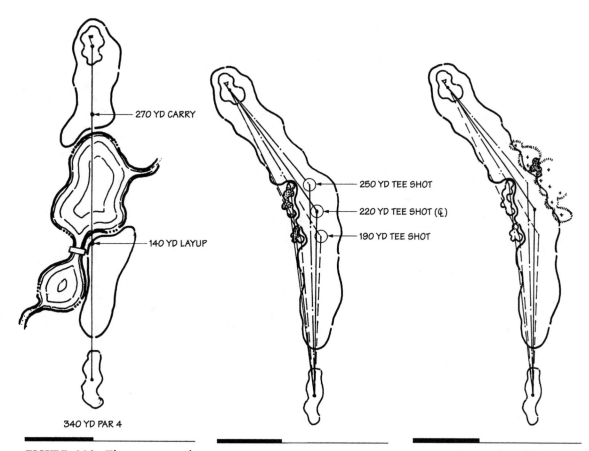

270 YD CARRY

140 YD LAYUP

340 YD PAR 4

250 YD TEE SHOT

220 YD TEE SHOT (₵)

190 YD TEE SHOT

FIGURE 4.16   The same non-rule applies here as in Figure 4.15. The very strong golfer can try to carry the lake. The rest of us must lay up as close as possible to the lake edge and then either use our most dependable club to carry the water or take our 200-yard club to the green.

FIGURE 4.17   Three variable-length tee shots . are well placed for the approach shot(s) to the green. By daring to cut too close to the bunker, or missing left, the same-length tee shot ends up in trouble.

FIGURE 4.18   The golf hole shown in Figure 4.17 is illustrated here with some golfer aids added. The bunker offers a distinct target to aim for, and the mounding will keep an almost properly hit shot from going too far off the fairway.

4. The architect should ensure that the player on a dogleg par 4 hole can go for the green following a well-placed tee shot (Figure 4.17).
5. Definition can be added to a dogleg with bunkers, mounds, or both on the far side of the turn (Figure 4.18). These also can reduce the number of balls running through the fairway into the woods or other rough.

Target Golf

Target golf requires playing from one landing area to another over rough and hazards. It involves risk, reward, and strategy and was a common practice until after World War I, when it went out of vogue (see Figures 2.20 and 2.21). With increasing environmental awareness, particularly in regard to wetlands issues, target golf has been revived with the intention of playing over existing wetlands. Target golf can be of interest on a few holes but is sometimes overdone, particularly if the carry is constantly penal, involving right-angled carries rather than diagonal shots (Figure 4.19).

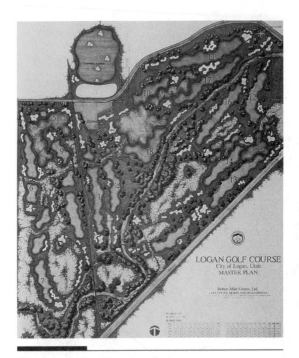

FIGURE 4.19 The municipal golf course in Logan, Utah, was developed on a heavily treed and low-lying site with a river traversing and creating numerous wetlands. Fairways were kept as wide as was prudent but golfers are still faced with several carries over the wetlands, creating "target" golf on some holes.

FIGURE 4.20 The small track-layer is often the machine of choice, but many other shapers prefer the rubber-tired "brush" for their artistic endeavors. (Courtesy Phil Arnold)

Sculpting the Earth

Features created by sculpting or modifying existing terrain can be impressive. For this operation, the artist's "brushes" are the equipment operators, with the shaper as the key person. The shaper refines and finalizes features as planned by the architect, although they may have been roughed out by the other operators. More than any other "brush," the shaper produces the spectacular and dramatic routes from tees to greens that add so much to the playing fields of the game (Figure 4.20).

Parts of a Golf Hole

The architectural axiom "Form follows function" dictates size, shape, and height of greens, tees, bunkers, and other features. Yet the game, as interpreted by the architect, determines what these functions are. In designing parts of a hole, the architect's knowledge of turfgrass science as well as maintenance equipment and use are called upon constantly.

Size of the Putting Surface

Until after World War II the average putting surface was less than 4,000 square feet. These greens are now known as "postage stamps," after the classic 8th at Troon in Scotland. Donald Ross was an exponent of these small greens; many of his were in the range of 2,500 to 3,500 square feet. Yet by the 1950s immense putting surfaces had become common, some of them 10,000 square feet or larger. Putting, the stroke already requiring the most attention, required still more. Experience showed that these huge surfaces contributed to slow play because of the unusually long putts they called for.

Maintenance costs also rose. Consequently, the trend has been toward putting surfaces smaller than monsters but larger than postage stamps. The contemporary size is often in the range of 4,000 to 6,000 square feet, with five or six major cupping areas (Figure 4.21). In line with the axiom "Form follows function," the longer the approach the larger the putting surface should be, but that is a decision for the architect.

FIGURE 4.21   This green at Furry Creek in British Columbia measures around 5,800 square feet—about average in this day and age. At least 40% of the area is available for cup placement, which is more than ample.

Grades of Putting Surface

Moderate rolls and depressions can be accommodated on those greens requiring a short approach. The watchwords in regard to their severity are *gentle* and *mowable*. Surface drainage in at least two directions on the green is mandatory, yet drainage in more than two directions is preferable. With golfers demanding ever faster greens, these grades are seldom steep. When they are, golfers constantly putt off the green. Common grades today, except on rolls and terrace slopes, are 2 to 3% down from back to front with 1 to 2% from one side to the other or, on crowned putting surfaces, in both directions. On these crowned surfaces the grade should be only 1 to 1.5%.

Configuration of Putting Surface

Greens present innumerable shapes, including, but not limited to, crescents, ells, teardrops, kidneys, squares, and free forms (Figure 4.22). Oval and egg shapes are abundant on many established layouts. Yet these may not be what the architect originally intended (Figure 4.23). More often than not their mundane configurations arose from decades of mowing, with no correction to compensate for the putting surface closing in at each mowing, most particularly at turns. This tendency toward oval shapes on older courses was also aggravated by years of mowing with triplex mowers.

Many architects provide "unique" cupping areas in the corners of their greens to bring a bunker or other hazard into play. Unfortunately, decades of mowing may have eliminated these areas as well (Figure 4.24).

BASIC GREEN SHAPES

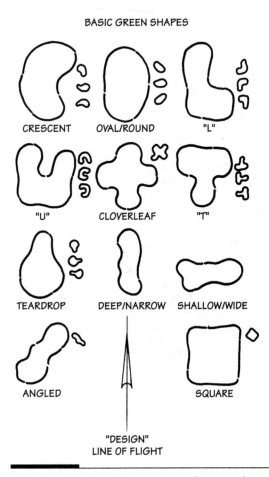

CRESCENT   OVAL/ROUND   "L"

"U"   CLOVERLEAF   "T"

TEARDROP   DEEP/NARROW   SHALLOW/WIDE

ANGLED   SQUARE

"DESIGN"
LINE OF FLIGHT

FIGURE 4.22 Use of certain green shapes, such as a crescent, L, U, cloverleaf, or T, may create areas where, by virtue of these shapes, pin placement, and green contour, the golfer may not find a direct putting line to the cup from portions of the green. This can be exacerbated or eased by the height of cut in the collar area surrounding the green. When the collar is cut low enough, the golfer may be able to putt directly to the cup.

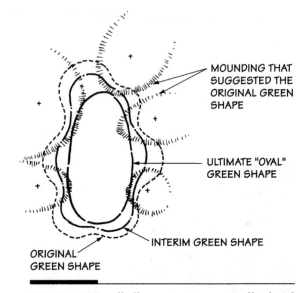

MOUNDING THAT SUGGESTED THE ORIGINAL GREEN SHAPE

ULTIMATE "OVAL" GREEN SHAPE

INTERIM GREEN SHAPE

ORIGINAL GREEN SHAPE

FIGURE 4.23 All efforts to create a naturally shaped green, backed by mounding in all the right places, have been counteracted by a green mower's determination to make his or her work easier.

UNIQUE CUPPING AREAS

FIGURE 4.24 Here again, certain green shapes may create areas where, because of shape, pin placement, and green contour, golfers may not find a direct putting line to the cup. This may be exacerbated or eased by the height of cut in the collar area. When the collar is cut low enough, the golfer may be able to putt directly to the cup.

Elevation of Green in Relation to Fairway Level

Early greens were often located in hollows protected from the strong winds of the links land. Later, some were located on natural plateaus. "Hollow" and "plateau" greens are still created. Yet many contemporary greens are massive, sculptured, and picturesque, most raised above fairway level and with a break between fairway and putting surface (Figure 4.25). The break provides a more interesting approach. It may also assist air to circulate across the turf, ice to melt earlier in the spring, the green to drain faster in periods of heavy precipitation; it also prevents surface water on surrounding areas from running across the putting surface. Yet subsurface water may still require interception by an underground drainage system (Figure 4.26).

FIGURE 4.25 *This green at the Sonoma Golf Club in California was recently restored as closely as possible to its original, early 1920s character. Raising the green, and particularly the bunker cluster, achieves all the attributes noted in the text and also effectively precludes a run-up shot.*

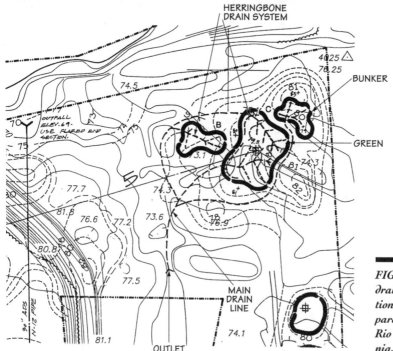

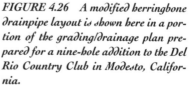

FIGURE 4.26 *A modified herringbone drainpipe layout is shown here in a portion of the grading/drainage plan prepared for a nine-hole addition to the Del Rio Country Club in Modesto, California.*

Since the introduction of fairway irrigation the "bump-and-run" shot is rarely called for and, in fact, verges on the impossible on lush, irrigated turf. Yet if the architect calls for bump-and-run, the green is often fairly level or depressed in relation to the fairway (Figure 4.27).

The depth of the green must be considered. With exceptions, depth too depends on "Form follows function", meaning the longer the approach the deeper the green (Figure 4.28).

FIGURE 4.27   Although not actually depressed, this green at Widgi Creek in Bend, Oregon, is close to the grade of the green entry and open enough to encourage bump-and-run shots.

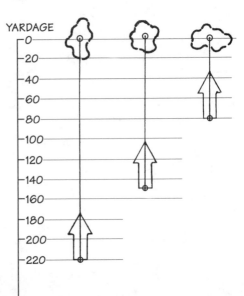

FIGURE 4.28   This diagram shows a general relationship between shot length and green shape, a rule of thumb often broken.

Mundane but Important Considerations
Concerning Greens

A. W. Tillinghast, among others, pointed out that the green is the face of the hole and the destination of the golfer. It is, therefore, the focus of the composition. General considerations in regard to planning a green have been outlined, yet there are several other important considerations:

1. Is there room for turning the green mower off the green rather than on the putting surface?
2. Is surface drainage free of narrow channels that will remain saturated long after a storm has passed (and in northern areas hold ice late into spring)?
3. Are green mounds and banks off the green mowable?
4. Are walk-offs to the next tee or to the golf car parking area planned so that they will not create worn traffic patterns (Figure 4.29)?
5. Standing on the approach, can one see the ball roll on the putting surface?
6. Are grades and rolls configured so that the green can be mowed in all directions?

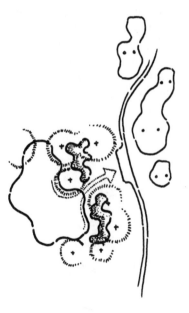

FIGURE 4.29   The relationship between the green/ bunker/mound complex and the car parking area was not well thought out in this example.

Entrance to the Green and Collars,
Fringe or Chipping Swales

Width of entrance to the green is an important factor, "Form follows function" again determining its width and shape as well as the superintendent's mowing pattern. Yet some architects specify these widths (Figure 4.30). In doing so, they try to prevent the creation of traffic areas that will wear.

When planning collars, the architect realizes they are subject to additional wear from mowers turning off the green, golf carts pulled across them, bags dropped on them, and spectators crowding in. Architects generally provide 2- to 5-foot collars (or aprons) around the greens, maintained at a slightly higher cut than putting surfaces but still puttable. Approaches to the green may also be mowed at this lower height.

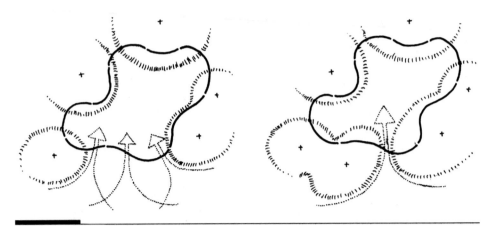

FIGURE 4.30 *The example of green mounding on the left has kept traffic in mind. The example on the right, with the same green shape and background, allows the mounds to crowd the front so that there is only one way to enter.*

In conjunction with collars, many architects provide "fringe" or "chipping" swales. These are commonly situated in depressed areas surrounding greens, but are sometimes placed on uphill and downhill slopes and level areas. They are mowed to collar height, thus forcing the accomplished golfer to make a club selection whereas the less talented tends to putt. Experience has shown these swales to be interesting and popular features. Nevertheless, for variety, some depressions in the surrounds must be maintained at rough or fairway height (Figure 4.31).

FRINGE OR CHIPPING SWALE

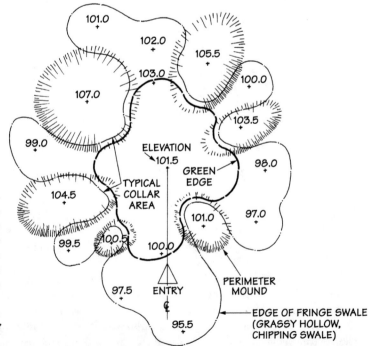

FIGURE 4.31 *This diagram shows a number of ways that a fringe or chipping swale can be created by extending collar height turf out between mounds or into low areas. This adds a new dimension to the game around the green. Although not as well defined, virtually every green at St. Andrews has low-cut grass adjacent, allowing putts from a considerable distance off the green.*

Placement of Greenside Bunkers

Figure 4.32 indicates the siting of greenside bunkers in three different eras. Until World War II, greenside bunkers were located on the very edge of the collar and sometimes even on the edge of the putting surface. This was ideal from the standpoint of play and eye appeal. Unfortunately, huge quantities of sand reached the putting surface, where it damaged the bed knives of mowers and perhaps the grass itself.

Following World War II, when maintenance budgets were low, greenside bunkers were placed 40 feet or more from putting surfaces. This allowed the superintendent to mow between bunker and green with tractor-drawn mowing units. It also eliminated the possibility of sand reaching the putting surface. However, it was found that the only players reaching these far-flung hazards were high handicappers with troubles enough. Furthermore, the exceptionally long recoveries required to reach the putting surface from the sand proved too much for many. Moreover, tractor-drawn mowers contributed to compaction.

A compromise was reached, with sand some 10 to 12 feet from the putting surface. At this distance sand still reaches the green, but not in huge quantities. The placement of greenside bunkers, as practiced in three different eras, is an example of the endless compromise required in course design.

Inadequate thought given to bunker placement in relation to golf car parking and the next tee inevitably results in worn traffic areas in the future, as was shown in Figure 4.29.

UNTIL WORLD WAR II   FOLLOWING WORLD WAR II   COMPROMISE

FIGURE 4.32   The green shape and bunker shapes shown here represent the three eras noted in the text.

Placement of Fairway Bunkers

Figure 4.33 provides an indication for siting fairway bunkers, yet the architect may site them in many other positions, sometimes to guide players rather than penalize them. Wind effects and terrain (uphill or downhill) also affect their placement.

Greenside and Fairway Mounds

In accordance with links principles, architects use mounds around greens to aid in depth perception, to create a target, and to keep balls within a reasonable distance of the flag. The sharper the mound, the more it enhances depth perception. Still, with few exceptions, all mounds should be mowable (Figure 4.34).

Fairway mounds are provided to enhance depth perception and to prevent balls from rolling too far from the fairway. Yet they must be shaped so that the ball can be advanced. Otherwise, they may provide a penalty far greater than the architect intended (Figure 4.35). Several design firms line fairways completely with mounds to produce an

FIGURE 4.33   In the diagram on the left, the bunkers are situated in relationship to the ideal landing area and subsequent approach shot required. The diagram on the right is based primarily on distance from a certain tee, the white tee in this case.

1. Play is from the white (men's regular) tee.
2. The hole site is relatively flat.
3. The ball lie is good, the stance and proposed landing areas are all relatively easy to deal with.
4. There is no appreciable wind.

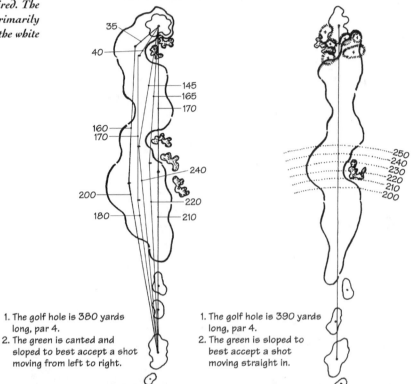

1. The golf hole is 380 yards long, par 4.
2. The green is canted and sloped to best accept a shot moving from left to right.

1. The golf hole is 390 yards long, par 4.
2. The green is sloped to best accept a shot moving straight in.

FIGURE 4.34   The mounds in back of this green at the Lightning-W Ranch Golf Club in Nevada not only set up the approach shot with enclosure and depth perception tools but also effectively reflect the character of the hillsides behind them.

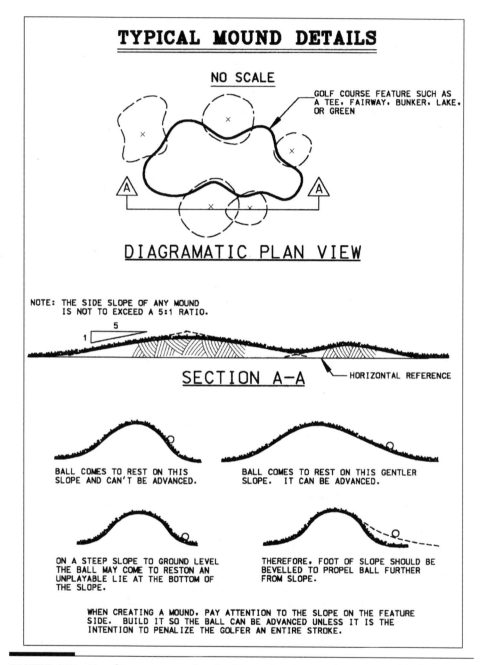

TYPICAL MOUND DETAILS

NO SCALE

GOLF COURSE FEATURE SUCH AS A TEE, FAIRWAY, BUNKER, LAKE, OR GREEN

DIAGRAMATIC PLAN VIEW

NOTE: THE SIDE SLOPE OF ANY MOUND IS NOT TO EXCEED A 5:1 RATIO.

SECTION A-A

HORIZONTAL REFERENCE

BALL COMES TO REST ON THIS SLOPE AND CAN'T BE ADVANCED.

BALL COMES TO REST ON THIS GENTLER SLOPE. IT CAN BE ADVANCED.

ON A STEEP SLOPE TO GROUND LEVEL THE BALL MAY COME TO REST ON AN UNPLAYABLE LIE AT THE BOTTOM OF THE SLOPE.

THEREFORE, FOOT OF SLOPE SHOULD BE BEVELLED TO PROPEL BALL FURTHER FROM SLOPE.

WHEN CREATING A MOUND, PAY ATTENTION TO THE SLOPE ON THE FEATURE SIDE. BUILD IT SO THE BALL CAN BE ADVANCED UNLESS IT IS THE INTENTION TO PENALIZE THE GOLFER AN ENTIRE STROKE.

FIGURE 4.35 *Mounding can purposely or inadvertently create an almost impossible shot, perhaps requiring the golfer to hit sideways or into yet another awkward situation.*

impressive appearance. This can speed play, because mounds tend to keep balls on the fairway. Golf car paths must be routed to provide visibility of the fairway, since mounds that reduce visibility from a path contribute to slow play.

Shaping and positioning of mounds requires close attention by the designer. For example, a round mound directs a ball in all directions, whereas a berm type mound directs it in only one or two (Figure 4.36).

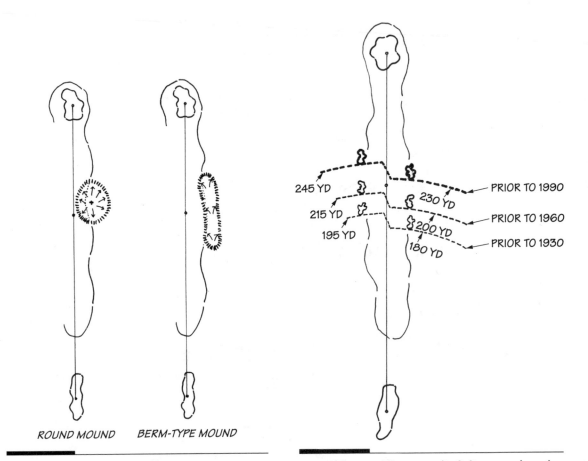

ROUND MOUND   BERM-TYPE MOUND

FIGURE 4.36 *Natural or artificial mounding is one way of returning the traditional element of luck to the game. The ridge simply offers fewer possibilities than the rounded mound.*

FIGURE 4.37 *This generalized diagram shows how bunkers have necessarily been pushed ever farther from the tee as the golfer's reach has lengthened over time.*

Checklist for Greenside and Fairway Bunkers

In planning a greenside or fairway bunker, whether it is level, raised, or a pot, there are a number of considerations:

1. Position in regard to play. Golfers continue to hit balls farther. Consequently, fairway bunkers are placed farther from tees (Figure 4.37).
2. Generally, but not always, the axis of a fairway bunker converges on the axis of the fairway (Figure 4.38). In practice, this means the farther a player hits the ball, the more accurate he or she must be—although we find this axiom controversial with some touring professionals.
3. Partial or entire visibility. In fairness to golfers, we prefer bunkers to be visible in their entirety. If this is not possible, a flash of sand visible to the golfer contributes to fairness.
4. Adequate depth. Generally, but with exceptions, the closer to the green it is, the deeper the bunker should be and the steeper its face (Figure 4.39).

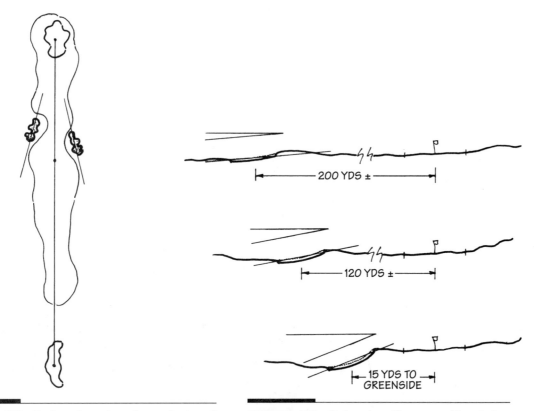

FIGURE 4.38 *Rather than place the emphasis and risk-reward premium on length or strength, this type of bunker alignment demands accuracy as well. The farther you choose to hit the ball, the more accurate you must be.*

FIGURE 4.39 *Unless the golf course architect is bent on penal design or severe punishment regardless of proximity to the green (or goal), it makes sense to allow the golfer farthest from the target to be able to advance the ball farthest.*

5. Seldom should the contemporary architect penalize a player an entire stroke on reaching a fairway bunker. Rather, the design should allow the player to advance the ball.
6. Seldom if ever should a greenside bunker be such that a player can putt from it (Figure 4.40).
7. The bunker should be protected from surface water by a swale, a berm, or both (Figure 4.41).
8. As much of the sand area as possible should be rakeable with a mechanical bunker rake (Figure 4.42).
9. A player should be able to enter or leave a bunker without scrambling up or down a steep face. A sincere effort should also be made to accommodate disabled persons.

Bunkers enable the architect to provide an accent to his composition. Therefore, they are planned with an immense variety of shapes, the utmost in eye appeal, and with no rigid rules for their placement. Yet contemporary designers seldom use steep sand faces for this visibility as they did until recently. More often, the slopes are grass (sod faced), thus obviating the shoveling of sand following heavy downpours, as is often needed on sand-faced bunkers (Figures 4.43 and 4.44). Faces change because sand

FIGURE 4.40   Not all designers or golf course operators agree, but in fact it is seldom that golfers can putt from a bunker. Rather, they are obligated to learn yet another shot in order to get the ball into the hole.

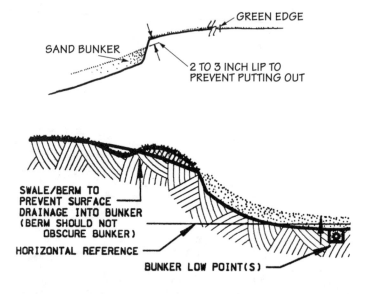

FIGURE 4.41   This design/construction concept is practically mandatory on steeply sloping sites or where bunker interior slopes are easily scoured by water draining into their basins.

FIGURE 4.42   Labor costs often dictate that maximum golf course maintenance be accomplished by faster mechanical means. There can be a downside: the same machinery can create one maintenance problem while solving another.

FIGURE 4.43   Besides being difficult to play from, such a steep bunker face requires many man-hours of raking and shoveling to keep the sand in place.

FIGURE 4.44 Here the steep sand faces have been replaced with grassy slopes over sod banks. They do not show up as well to the oncoming golfer but are much easier to maintain.

splashes onto the sod. This kills the grass. The tendency is then to convert these areas to sand. Over a period of decades, one of the authors has observed sod faces converted to sand, then back to sod, and back again to sand. Presently they are being converted to sand.

The Old Course at St. Andrews, which was once penal, became strategic as fairways were widened to accommodate increasingly heavy play in the nineteenth century. These widened fairways allowed golfers to play around intimidating bunkers rather than over them, although the safer routes were longer. Nevertheless, until the 1920s the predominant placement of bunkers in North America was penal, with cross bunkers calling for compulsory carries. Today placement is strategic, with bunkers placed laterally.

An objective for decades was to bring these hazards into play for golfers of all calibers, assuming that each group would use the tee provided for its own caliber. At that time, the emphasis was on providing similar landing areas for all.

Today many architects are placing fairway bunkers so that the higher handicappers do not reach them from their tees. In addition, it has become increasingly apparent that a player of this caliber requires a second landing area on all par 4s longer than some 360 yards unless the second shot is downhill or subject to a strong prevailing tail wind (Figures 4.45 and 4.46).

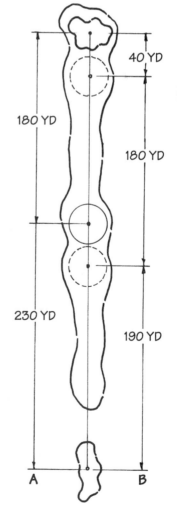

FIGURE 4.45 Whereas the stronger golfer reaches out ever farther with the tee shots, weaker or less accomplished players often cannot reach a green in the standard number of shots. The second- or even third-more comfortable landing area helps these players to enjoy the game and keeps the pace moving as well.

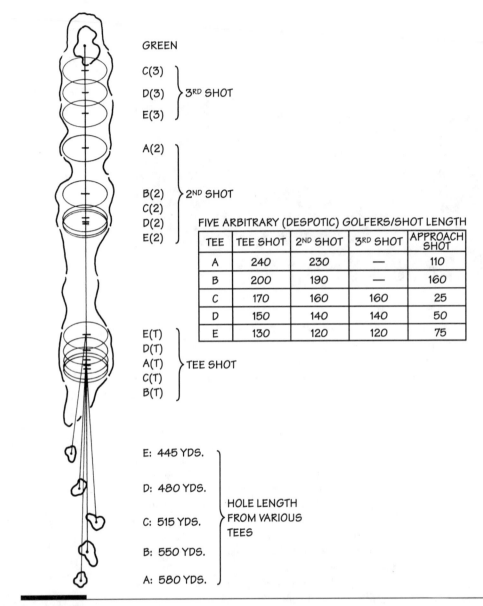

GREEN

C(3)
D(3) } 3RD SHOT
E(3)

A(2)

B(2)
C(2) } 2ND SHOT
D(2)
E(2)

FIVE ARBITRARY (DESPOTIC) GOLFERS/SHOT LENGTH

TEE	TEE SHOT	2ND SHOT	3RD SHOT	APPROACH SHOT
A	240	230	—	110
B	200	190	—	160
C	170	160	160	25
D	150	140	140	50
E	130	120	120	75

E(T)
D(T)
A(T) } TEE SHOT
C(T)
B(T)

E: 445 YDS.

D: 480 YDS.

C: 515 YDS. } HOLE LENGTH FROM VARIOUS TEES

B: 550 YDS.

A: 580 YDS.

FIGURE 4.46

1. General Notes

   a. *We often read or hear about a particular golf hole, its features and characteristics, and how they will affect a golfer's shot. You must ask the question: Affect whose golf shot; which golfer are we talking about?*

   b. *Remember that only a select few golfers actually hit the ball exactly where they want to, and they can't do it every time.*

   c. *Note that in this example, nominally a par 5 or 3 shot hole, only two of the five golfer types can get on in three shots.*

   d. *In this example, after the tee shot or second shot, where could you put a hazard for one category of golfer that would never affect another category of golfer?*

   e. *There are hundreds of scenarios that can be set up like this hole and with differing arbitrary shot lengths, hole conditions, and playing conditions. But the results are always the same; it is difficult, if not impossible, to predict what will happen with any assurance, particularly when you design for one caliber of golfer and neglect the rest. (cont'd)*

FIGURE 4.47   (Cont'd

    f. We cannot dictate, quantify, or otherwise account for luck any more than we can accurately anticipate the multitude of other variables, including the wild shots we are capable of hitting.

    g. The best designer is the one who does the best and most thorough job of handling these variables consistent with his or her client's program and budget for golf course development.

2. Assumptions

    a. All golfers, regardless of ability and strength, are trying to keep the ball in the center or desired target area with maximum reliable shot length.

    b. There are no weather or site conditions that would dictate a special shot.

    c. The shot lengths per golfer category are arbitrary, but result from decades of observation and consultation with golf pros, operators, and golfers.

    d. Golfer shot lengths chosen for this study will easily range from the low handicapper to the beginner.

    e. The tees are spread laterally for greater clarity of proposed shot line and, in this case, to demonstrate clustering of the tee shots.

    f. The elliptical shot landing areas all center on the perfect shot, with deviations inside the ellipse of 15 yards in length and 25 yards in direction.

Waste Bunkers

Waste bunkers are large areas of unraked sand in the roughs, where players are allowed to ground their clubs. Waste bunkers have not always proved functional. For one thing, they compromise the immaculate grooming of many contemporary courses. And while some architects once thought they would assist in reducing chemical percolation to lower levels of the soil, they soon realized that grassed depressions are far more effective in this regard.

Tees

Long rectangular tees to accommodate several sets of markers are functional. Yet these "airstrips" become monotonous when presented 18 times (Figures 4.47 and 4.48). Old-time square tee boxes divided by strips of rough grass (Figure 4.49) can be more interesting, and free-form shapes created during construction, or by contour mowing of "airstrips" during later maintenance, are also more attractive (Figure 4.50).

FIGURE 4.47   Such long, linear tees are not often seen in Ireland. This one is an exception.

FIGURE 4.48 The Sinners Golf Club in Florida featured a very long, narrow tee. In this case the tee serves two holes.

FIGURE 4.49 These two rectangular tees contrast with the natural shapes of distant parts of the golf hole. When more mature, the rough grass between tees may soften the contrast.

FIGURE 4.50 The plan and perspective views demonstrate how a tee built along geometric lines can be remodeled with the mower into a more curvilinear or natural shape as long as the resultant tee space is large enough for the amount of play.

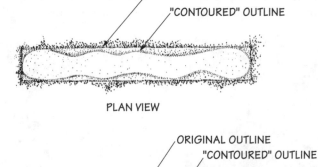

"CONTOURED" OUTLINE

PLAN VIEW

ORIGINAL OUTLINE
"CONTOURED" OUTLINE

PERSPECTIVE VIEW

Alternate or separate tees have enjoyed popularity because of the variety they afford, but not invariably so (Figure 4.51). In fact, golfers who play at a country club or at a daily fee layout on a regular basis prefer to play round after round from one tee, despite the variety afforded by playing a certain tee one day and a different one the next. Yet at resort courses the experience has been almost opposite, with guests preferring variety. Nevertheless, one long tee, regardless of shape, allows more flexibility in placing markers.

The height of the tee is determined by the height needed for visibility of the landing area. It is ideal for the player to see his or her shot roll on the fairway (Figure 4.52).

The Green Section provided a guideline for the size of tees on par 3s and the first hole: 200 square feet for each 1,000 rounds of golf played annually, with 150 square feet on the par 4s and 5s. The tee space provided for an estimated 40,000 rounds annually would then be 8,000 and 6,000 square feet, respectively. In this regard, it is significant that architects and owners often underestimate the number of rounds in their projections, and practice swinging on the first tee may be overlooked.

FIGURE 4.51   At Big Canyon Golf Club in Southern California, the multiple tees shaped and stepped into the sloping site offer much variety for the golfer who cares to take advantage of it.

FIGURE 4.52   A tee need only be high enough, in relation to the area to be viewed, to allow the golfer to see and evaluate the problem at hand. Excessive tee height, although appearing natural on the tee, may look awkward and out of place as seen from behind or beside.

The Green Section has indicated that the square footage in these guidelines can be reduced if the quality of tee construction is high and shade is not a major factor. Under these more favorable conditions, the guidelines are 150 and 100 square feet, respectively.

Generally, more than three-quarters of the wear occurs on the men's regular tees. Therefore, three-quarters or more of that total tee space must be allocated to them (Figure 4.53).

Tee surfaces can be crowned, sloped side to side, down to the front if the landing area is below the tee, flat (but very rarely), or sloped down, front to back, at 1% (Figure 4.54). The latter is the most common and preferred grade. Because a tee surface is relatively flat, the 1% grade is adequate for surface drainage, unlike a putting green with an undulating surface.

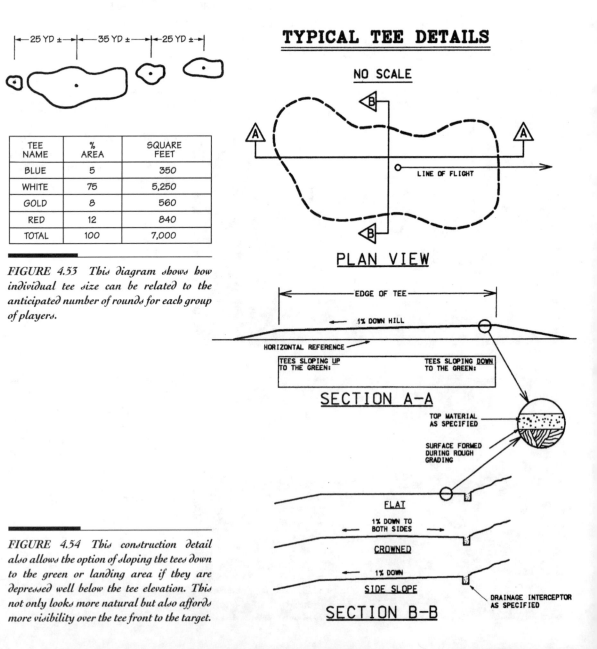

TEE NAME	% AREA	SQUARE FEET
BLUE	5	350
WHITE	75	5,250
GOLD	8	560
RED	12	840
TOTAL	100	7,000

FIGURE 4.53   This diagram shows how individual tee size can be related to the anticipated number of rounds for each group of players.

TYPICAL TEE DETAILS

NO SCALE

PLAN VIEW

LINE OF FLIGHT

EDGE OF TEE

1% DOWN HILL

HORIZONTAL REFERENCE

TEES SLOPING UP TO THE GREEN: TEES SLOPING DOWN TO THE GREEN:

SECTION A-A

TOP MATERIAL AS SPECIFIED

SURFACE FORMED DURING ROUGH GRADING

FLAT

1% DOWN TO BOTH SIDES

CROWNED

1% DOWN

SIDE SLOPE

DRAINAGE INTERCEPTOR AS SPECIFIED

SECTION B-B

FIGURE 4.54   This construction detail also allows the option of sloping the tees down to the green or landing area if they are depressed well below the tee elevation. This not only looks more natural but also affords more visibility over the tee front to the target.

Grading of Fairways and Grassed Roughs

Roughs on most courses include

1. An intermediate strip, frequently but not always, the width of a riding mower (6 to 8 feet) adjoining the fairway and mowed ¼ to ½ inches above fairway height.
2. Grassed roughs, also known as primary roughs, the area beyond the intermediate strip mowed an inch or two higher than fairway height. Specimen trees and even outcropping of rock ledge may be present in this type of rough.
3. Treed or remote roughs. These roughs vary; some include underbrush and others are planted with grasses and mowed (Figure 4.55). The latter are known as "English parks." On treeless links the vegetation is often composed of links plants such as gorse (Figure 4.56).

Until recently, the grading of fairways and roughs was limited to modifying landing areas and ensuring surface drainage and visibility. With the advent of higher construction budgets and ever-mightier earth movers, some architects began to sculpt the fairways to create contours similar to those found on the links or other interesting landforms. The results have been impressive and dramatic. Recently, however, there has been a return to minimalism, with cuts and fills executed for functional purposes only.

FIGURE 4.55   Much of the rough at Black Butte's Big Meadow Golf Course in Oregon has both grass and brushy rough interspersed with large trees.

FIGURE 4.56   The renowned links of Scotland are treeless, but the equally famous gorse, heather, and tall grasses provide all the challenge—and beauty—from vegetation that most any golfer requires.

FIGURE 4.57 *Here in Scotland, the naturally occurring bumps and hollows are left as is or only mildly subdued to create challenging lies and golf problems to solve. Again, the element of luck is allowed its rightful place in the game.*

Undulating, as contrasted with flat, surfaces produce the most interesting lies and more exciting golf (Figure 4.57). Therefore, architects need to give great thought before flattening existing contours.

Architect Douglas Carrick emphasizes smooth, flowing, and generous fairway contours. He also recommends that there be no fairway or rough area with less than 2 to 3% surface drainage.[3] We find that the Carrick specifications for surface grades should be amended to steeper grades on saline and alkaline soils to accelerate the runoff of salts.

"Oakmont" Ditches

The renowned Oakmont Country Club near Pittsburgh, Pennsylvania, features several depressions or ditches located in strategic areas and played as hazards, with the player not permitted to ground the club. Other clubs have copied this feature, with mixed results. Oakmont ditches are apparently too frustrating for those golfers out to relax.

Contour Mowing

Contour mowing refers to mowing an undulating line usually between fairway and rough (Figure 4.58). Because of the striking eye appeal and playing interest that result, the adoption of contour mowing has been almost universal since 1980. Introduction of lightweight mowing encouraged this trend, because the smaller mowers necessitated less fairway acreage. Many a course using gang units mowed 40 to 50 acres of fairway; with lightweight mowers, the range is 20 to 30 acres.

Yet ruling bodies may frown on contour mowing for major tournaments, because the very long roughs provided for these events call for wider fairways than those for daily play, where roughs are mowed no higher than 1½ to 2 inches to speed play and provide more pleasurable golf for the majority. Many medium and high handicappers find it difficult to advance the ball from very tight fairway lies. Therefore, play may be faster on courses with less fairway acreage and roughs mowed fairly close, from which less accomplished golfers can advance balls.

This method of improving a golf course is very effective for tees and greens as well as fairways and at the same time is inexpensive. This is not a new concept but one well worth any good golf club's consideration. The word *contour* is really misapplied here,

FIGURE 4.58 At Port Ludlow in Washington, the shapes of the perimeter mounds dictate the contoured shape of the mower's pattern. Previous consideration of space requirements for the various anticipated golf shots dictated the shape, size, and placement of the mounds.

excepting where contour (or hump and hollow) is used to dictate the shape of the turf edge.

It amounts to changing from common, ordinary straight-edge mowing of turf areas to a more naturalistic, usually curvilinear, shape. At the same time, this practice, whether or not coupled with forced carries, can actually reduce turf maintenance requirements by 10–30 percent or more, as noted on page 114.

- *Tees:* Here we are often limited in size, so, in maintaining the required usable tee area, we may have to conform to a more rectangular or other geometric shape, whether we wish to or not. Where space allows, the difference in the tee cutting height and fairway height creates an edge that can fit our contour format, even though the tee is essentially level.
- *Fairways:* Where width allows, we can manipulate the edge of the fairways inward and outward for the natural appearance that we want. At the same time, we try to blend the shape to existing contours or other natural features of the site, such as tree masses. Above all, we must consider the playability of the hole in terms of each calibre of golfer.
- *Greens:* As in tees, we cannot restrict the green area to where there is insufficient number of pin placements or area to hit to. Where possible, we can greatly enhance the picture that the green area affords by avoiding the usual circular or oval shapes in favor of natural forms that relate carefully to other existing features, such as humps, hollows, bunkers, or trees.

A side issue could be that reducing fairway area and increasing first (or second) cut rough could also reduce irrigation water requirements.

Other Hazards

Water   As stated earlier, water can be the most exciting and memorable hazard on a golf hole. Water hazards may come into play in the same way as bunkers, although they generally call for more compulsory carries because ponds are larger than bunkers (Figure 4.59).

FIGURE 4.59 *This diagram shows many ways that water in the form of a lake or creek can be used as a hazard and design feature in a golf hole, fitting the several major styles of design.*

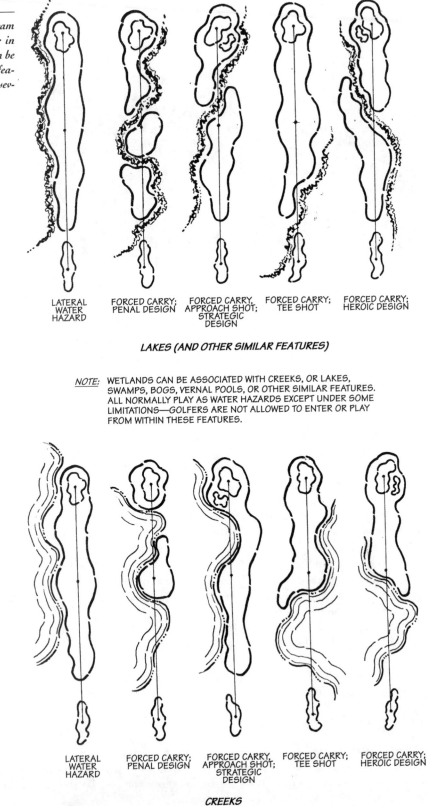

LATERAL
WATER
HAZARD

FORCED CARRY;
PENAL DESIGN

FORCED CARRY;
APPROACH SHOT;
STRATEGIC
DESIGN

FORCED CARRY;
TEE SHOT

FORCED CARRY;
HEROIC DESIGN

LAKES (AND OTHER SIMILAR FEATURES)

NOTE: WETLANDS CAN BE ASSOCIATED WITH CREEKS, OR LAKES,
SWAMPS, BOGS, VERNAL POOLS, OR OTHER SIMILAR FEATURES.
ALL NORMALLY PLAY AS WATER HAZARDS EXCEPT UNDER SOME
LIMITATIONS—GOLFERS ARE NOT ALLOWED TO ENTER OR PLAY
FROM WITHIN THESE FEATURES.

LATERAL
WATER
HAZARD

FORCED CARRY;
PENAL DESIGN

FORCED CARRY;
APPROACH SHOT;
STRATEGIC
DESIGN

FORCED CARRY;
TEE SHOT

FORCED CARRY;
HEROIC DESIGN

CREEKS

Excavation of a pond provides fill for other purposes, and the pond may then function as a reservoir. Permit requirements today can be difficult, however, and in periods of severe drought owners in some jurisdictions may not be allowed to use their own water.

Bulkheads and Railroad Ties   Bulkheads for ponds and other areas, common in North America before World War I, were reintroduced by Pete and Alice Dye in the 1960s following their extended visit to the links of Scotland. Railroad ties, with their rugged appearance and durability (if treated) are appropriate for bulkheads, although some say they are "contrived," an objectionable concept in design. We can point out they are in the links tradition and that they make it possible to utilize corners and edges of property not otherwise usable. Moreover, their vertical or near vertical faces can call for a precise shot over water to a cup placed near the water's edge, in contrast to a shot to a green with a long grass slope from water to the putting surface.

The use of railroad tie bulkheads in bunkers is another Dye reintroduction, but it is not always as well accepted in North America as the use of pond bulkheads. Yet these features add to variety in recovery shots.

Similarly, sod revetting of bunker walls (Figures 4.60 and 4.61) — that is, pieces of sod piled one on top of the other — has been introduced off and on in North America. However, these sod walls have not always fared well, particularly in areas with high summer temperatures.

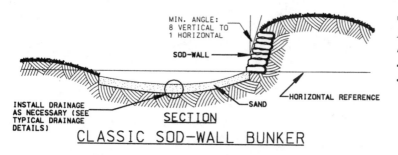

FIGURE 4.60   *Sod walls have been used, probably for a century or so, to solve the problem of eroding and sloughing off of steep banks.*

FIGURE 4.61   *While solving a maintenance problem, the sod wall created a golf problem for one of a pair of Aussies enjoying St. Andrews. The tables were fairly turned at a subsequent hole.*

Retaining Walls   Among the several types, three common constructions are

1. Wood (Figures 4.62a and 4.62b).
2. Natural rock or stone (Figure 4.63).
3. Gabion baskets filled with stone (Figure 4.64).

FIGURE 4.62a   Whether sawn timber, as shown here, railroad ties, or rough-split logs and poles, wood often is selected as the means to solve a grade-change problem or to create more playing space.

FIGURE 4.62b   Here ties or split logs are laid back at an angle to further strengthen the wall.

FIGURE 4.63 *Native rock, artfully placed for stability without mortar, creates an effective, attractive, natural appearance on this lake at the Lightning W Ranch Golf Club in Nevada.*

FIGURE 4.64 *The gabion used to stabilize a creek bank at the Sonoma Golf Club in Northern California, while not as natural appearing as native rock, does a practical and economical job where native rock is not available. Turf and creekside planting will soon soften the sharp edges already obscured from the green area. (Photo courtesy of Robert Holmes)*

Stone walls are laid with or without mortar. In the interests of good taste, it is recommended that only one type of retaining wall be used on a course. However, we have seen instances where the use of all three, even on a single hole, has produced dramatic results.

Spectator Mounds   Spectator mounds, particularly around finishing greens and related to televising of golf, have become features of stadium and other tournament courses. This is still another outcome of the Pete Dye influence, which in turn was influenced by former PGA Tour commissioner Deane Beman. Both architects and spectators take advantage of existing mounds. Holes at La Purisima near Santa Barbara, for example, are set in valleys with surrounding hills ideal for spectators (see Figures 2.22 and 2.23).

Shot Value

A golf hole is planned as a composition in relation to the overall layout and its sequence in the round. Yet dissecting a golf hole, as Kenneth Helphand puts it, does not necessarily explain why it is an exciting and interesting hole. Golf architecture remains an art form with its end result an artistic composition: artistic as to playability, maintainability, and aesthetics. Playability, in turn, also embraces what an ancient Scottish golfer is reputed to have said: "Gawf ye ken neids a heid" ("Golf, you know, needs a head").

This statement leads to the consideration of "shot value," a concept of paramount importance but frequently misunderstood. In fact, individual architects and professional golfers use and describe the term differently. We offer the following brief discussion and conclusion to outline our concept of shot value.

Shot: "Stroke and resulting movement or journey of the ball" (Peter Davis, *Historic Dictionary of Golfing Terms*).

Value: "Worth in usefulness or importance to the possessor. Utility or merit. Principle, standard or quality considered worthwhile or desirable" (*American Heritage Dictionary*).

Although important, the concept of shot value is vague and has been described differently by various golf course architects. Here are three interpretations:

"The reflection of what the hole demands of the golfer and the relative reward or punishment it metes out for good and bad shots" (Kenneth Killian and Richard Nugent).

"The architect should seek to get the most out of the ground while letting play take care of itself. Each hole must be designed to balance risk and reward" (Thomas Doak).

"The value of a required golf shot as related to its difficulty or allowable margin of error" (Michael Hurdzan).

For us, shot value refers to the worth or usefulness of a particular shot made on a particular hole at a particular instant. If all elements are right, the shot has a great value because the golfer accomplishes the desired result (Figure 4.65).

When we discuss a particular hole and its value to the enjoyment and challenge of the game, we really speak of the "shot requirements" of the hole: What does the hole require you to do to get the ball from its present location to the desired landing area or stopping point? Shot requirements of a hole are therefore affected by

1. Distance from where the ball lies to the desired stopping point
2. The lie of the ball (flat, sloped, buried, solid, fluffy)
3. The golfer's stance (flat, sloped, hard, soft, slippery, stable)
4. Wind direction and speed (at the ball, en route, and at the desired stopping point)
5. The desired stopping point (flat, sloped, hard, soft, close-cut, average, or deep grass)
6. Hazards or other problem areas either in the desired line of play or near enough to be of concern if the shot is missed
7. Shot requirements of the next following shot if the present shot is successfully made or if it is missed

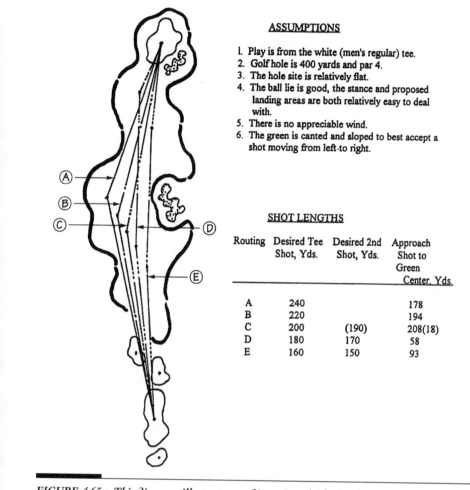

ASSUMPTIONS

1. Play is from the white (men's regular) tee.
2. Golf hole is 400 yards and par 4.
3. The hole site is relatively flat.
4. The ball lie is good, the stance and proposed landing areas are both relatively easy to deal with.
5. There is no appreciable wind.
6. The green is canted and sloped to best accept a shot moving from left-to right.

SHOT LENGTHS

Routing	Desired Tee Shot, Yds.	Desired 2nd Shot, Yds.	Approach Shot to Green Center, Yds.
A	240		178
B	220		194
C	200	(190)	208(18)
D	180	170	58
E	160	150	93

FIGURE 4.65   This diagram illustrates our discussion of "shot requirements" versus "shot value."

Refer again to Figure 4.65, where shot requirements are illustrated for various lengths. The "value" of being able to hit it long but particularly to place your shot where you want it is obvious.

Symbolism in Golf Course Design*

by Desmond Muirhead,
GOLF COURSE ARCHITECT

A symbol is a visible sign of something invisible, often an object suggesting an abstract concept: a cross for faith, a sword for valor, a dove for peace. Symbols can have multiple meanings: the color green may evoke nature or jealousy, the lion courage or wisdom. Symbols invested with myth, mystery, and religion are evident even in Paleolithic cave

---

* There are those in any profession who strive to extend the horizons of their art form. Golf architect Desmond Muirhead, whose forte is symbolism, is the designer of three successful symbolistic layouts in the United States and several abroad.

paintings. The ability to derive abstract understandings from symbols is one of the distinguishing features of humankind.

Carl Jung (1875–1961), a psychologist of enormous intelligence and mental capacity, is well known for his research into symbols. Jung believed that we all possess a personal as well as a collective unconscious. The many forms in the collective unconscious he called "archetypes." We all inherit this set of internal blueprints, the combined historical unconscious of the human race.

Jung was amazed to find that archetypes from antiquity reappeared both in his patients' dreams and in the images induced from their thoughts and drawings while they were in analysis. He believed that symbolic archetypes had unlimited energy and could provide powerful messages to individual thoughts and memory. Jung found that under psychoanalysis archetypes could be called up from the subconscious and their forms expressed by different symbols.

Among the many archetypes Jung identified, he particularly emphasized the significance of the *mandala,* which in Sanskrit means "magic circle," a design that signifies the complete integration of opposites to create a whole. A mandala usually consists of a circle with a described center plus a form involving fours, such as a square, a cross, or the cardinal points. Often, considerable decoration is involved.

Many designs, paintings, buildings, and town plans consciously or unconsciously employ the mandala. The layouts of ancient Babylon and Kathmandu, Angkor Wat, and Mexico City, as well as Viking camps and modern-day Brasilia, all pay homage to the mandala. Mandalas are found everywhere—in Gothic rose windows, Leonardo DiVinci's paintings, Russian ikons, and Navajo sand paintings. All over the world people have found comfort in the psychic wholeness projected by the mandala with its reconciled contrasts of color, shape, and form.

From a background in architecture, planning, and urban design, I was familiar with archetypes as they apply to cities. The mandala and the cosmic tree developed into the Christian cross with outstretched arms, exemplified in the design of St. Sophia in Istanbul and the great Gothic cathedrals such as Chartres. A cathedral city based on the mandala unified humankind and the cosmos and reconciled all opposites.

In the early 1960s I faced the task of integrating a golf course with its surrounding community. While designing Boca Raton West, Florida (later called Boca West) and Mission Hills in Palm Springs, California, I discovered it was the golf course that determined the form of the community, not the other way around. I found that these developments, to which we gave the name "golf course communities," balanced building forms and green space very effectively.

The symbolism of the golf course community was on a large scale. This was a simple group of English or Mediterranean villages where everybody shared a large, informal English garden—the golf course. In addition, the building area and green space were sharply divided, which was itself a nurturing feature. This sharp definition between buildings and green space nurtured symbolism.

Buildings in these communities were designed in a series of clusters or groupings, symbolizing security and togetherness. From there it was a short step to employing symbolism on the golf course.

The principles of strategic design of golf courses, which are independent of symbolic influence, have grown from St. Andrews, Muirfield, Carnoustie, and other Scottish golf courses. Yet archetypal symbols add layers of memory and meaning to these traditional golf course landscapes as well as to more contemporary ones.

Since ancient times the landscape environment has been identified with symbolic archetypes such as Mother Earth, Eden, Paradise, and the Promised Land. The circular walls of Chinese gardens enclosed symbolic mountains, forests, and lakes, with huge palaces scattered throughout the grounds. On the Mediterranean island of Crete are palaces within gardens or similar enclosures. In one of these gardens, I came upon twin mountain peaks that symbolized the breasts of Mother Earth. Symbolically, the designs of these gardens were close to what I eventually drew upon 25 years ago when I started using overt symbols in golf course design.

The development of symbols on golf courses goes far back into unrecorded history. The Old Course at St. Andrews was in play during the Middle Ages, at least five hundred years ago, but little is known about its development before A.D. 1700. The Old Course is filled with symbols, most of them religious, deriving from the Calvinist tradition of the town. Even today the Old Course is closed on Sundays, the day when people of St. Andrews use the course for picnics and walk the fairways with their dogs. Symbols such as Hell Bunker, Lion's Mouth, the Valley of Sin, and Hole O'Cross abound on the Old Course. Other more secular symbols—such as the Maiden at Sandwich, the Sahara at Prestwick, and the Postage Stamp at Troon—are common on many other links courses of the British Isles.

In America during the 1920s and 1930s, a few golf courses—usually single holes— were built with symbolic implication. At the same time, baroque abstract symbols, in the form of bunkers, were developed. However, without the wind and weather that had formed the originals on the links of Scotland, these bunkers often looked contrived. Bunkers like these are still used today, and their architects hopefully label their courses "natural."

Outside Jungian psychology, I was influenced by the forms of artists such as Joan Miró, whose emphasis was abstract form, philosophers such as Soren Kierkegaard for whom choice was a prime issue, and linguistic theorists such as Noam Chomsky, whose emphasis is deep structure.

The mandala influenced communities that our firm was designing in the 1960s, such as Desert Island in Rancho Mirage, California, and later in the 1990s our new town of Lippo Karawaci (Lippo Village) in Jakarta, Indonesia. The combined influences of Jung, Chomsky, Kierkegaard, and Miró gave rise to the design of a flood of new golf holes, some spontaneously generated from my collective unconscious. I was searching for passion and meaning in these new symbolic forms.

The first durable symbol occurred at Aberdeen, a course then under construction at Boynton Beach, Florida, where I noticed a fairway shape sandwiched between two lakes we had just built. It was in the natural form of a mermaid. I added the hair, the scales, the tail, and the breasts, using grass mounds and white sand (Figure 4.66). The composition looked terrific from the air, but from the ground it appeared somewhat like a conventional hole—in essence, almost links-like. Yet even on the ground one could sense something new and different about this hole. Stone Harbor in New Jersey followed. This course design was based on classical mythology. The 7th at Stone Harbor, Clashing Rocks, came straight out of my subconscious where it had probably been lingering stubbornly for some time (Figures 4.67 and 4.68).

Although both these golf holes can be explained by Jung's symbolic theories, Clashing Rocks has a wider range of meanings than the Mermaid. First of all, it is a mandala, the primary Jung archetype. As a mandala with the cup as the center, the hole represents the integration of opposites which, through its symmetry, makes a powerful statement of psychic wholeness. As a mandala, it calls on both history and tradition, the cosmic pattern and the collective unconscious.

Moreover, Clashing Rocks depicts in Jungian terms both *anima*, the feminine part of the male personality, as embodied in the rounded forms and curved lines, and the *ani-*

FIGURE 4.66 This is the symbolic mermaid that evolved during construction of a golf hole at the Aberdeen Golf Club in Florida. (Courtesy Desmond Muirhead)

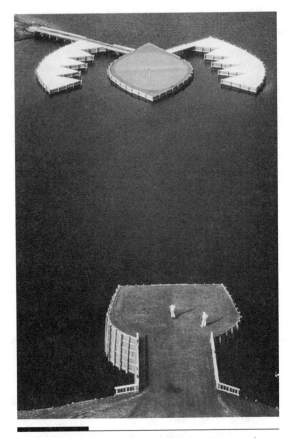

FIGURE 4.67 At a hole called Clashing Rocks at Stone Harbor in New Jersey, the familiar golf hole features of tee, green, and bunker along with water are combined in a particularly unusual form. (Courtesy Desmond Muirhead)

FIGURE 4.68 A close-up view of the green bunker/water complex at Clashing Rocks. (Courtesy Desmond Muirhead)

mus, the masculine part of the female personality, represented by the straight and jagged lines in the design. Both these themes are complexly interwoven in Clashing Rocks, yet the hole displays an unconscious spontaneity from its primordial origins in my subconscious and mythology. It takes little imagination to see others of Jung's archetypes lurking happily in the bilateral symmetry of Clashing Rocks, such as the trickster and the shadow, writhing with the stress and tension of opposites. I could sense many other unconscious influences—a symbolic use of mood from Muench, a use of direct line and flatness from Picasso, a sense of depth and structure from Chomsky—as well as the shades of meaning derivative of Jung.

Since then, I have designed many symbolic golf holes and entire courses that include symbolic concepts probably discovered as the work proceeded (Figure 4.69). A golf hole is a sum total of its designer's site experience, fields of study, creativity, and intuition (which is to say, his or her stored mental experience). I wanted a golf hole with a sense of place—a place with a spirit. I decided that I had to discover the spirit, trap it, energize it, and reveal it in a recognizable form.

Well-wrought symbols must be expressed as art, not kitsch. They need content and meaning as well as form, essence as well as existence. I wanted my golf holes and courses to have—like Jung's symbols—greater power than the personal experience from which they came.

One thing is certain. If memorability is an important aspect of golf course architecture, these symbols are impossible to forget. Symbols have been in golf course architecture for a long time. They are not going to go away. Admittedly, today's symbols are different, but as Winston Churchill reputedly said: "an art without a tradition is like a flock of sheep without a shepherd, but an art without innovation is a corpse."

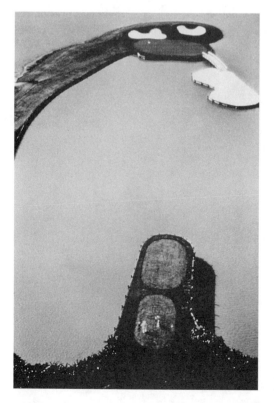

FIGURE 4.69 Is there a dedicated golfer who has not encountered one hole that defeated him/her during every round and haunted him/her in his dreams? The 8th hole at Florida's Aberdeen Golf Club may personify this experience. (Courtesy Desmond Muirhead)

Review

At this point we recommend the reader complete Exercise 2, and following that, complete Exercise 3.

Notes

1. Kenneth Helphand, "Learning from Linksland," *Landscape Journal* (spring 1995): 77.
2. *Greenmaster* (February 1995). (Official publication of the Canadian Golf Course Superintendents Association.)
3. *Greenmaster* (February 1995).

Planning Major Changes

Despite the best conceived designs of any architect, nearly every course sooner or later requires updating. . . . The task of updating an architect's work may fall upon a generation of subsequent designers.

From *The Golf Course,* 1981, by Geoffrey S. Cornish and Ronald E. Whitten

With the exception of a handful of hallowed layouts, the playing fields of golf are altered from time to time. Although these alterations generally contribute to excellence, some are obviously ill-advised. Because a golf course is a living thing, it cannot remain static. Therefore, many courses opened for play a quarter of a century or more ago are now undergoing or planning changes.

Time physically erodes and changes the course and, to a degree, the game. Time also alters shot values and shot requirements, as do changes in playing equipment. Moreover, refined greenswards and the longer carries of contemporary golfers compromise objectives and the interesting problems posed by particular courses. Yet as architect Marzolf pointed out in Chapter 1, these changes are profound, but not absolute.

Changes required to update a layout vary in extent and may involve any of the following:

1. Complete rebuilding of the course with little or no reference to the existing layout. In effect, a new course is created.
2. Restoration of the course to what it once was—particularly if it was the creation of a widely recognized architect.
3. Renovation or reconstruction of the existing layout. This involves rebuilding and/or modifying all or some features, with the original and basic layout retained.
4. Combinations of the preceding approaches.

In general, the objective of updating an existing layout is to enhance the basic considerations of golf design—the integrity, beauty, and maintainability of the layout—along with the beneficial environmental impact of its open space.

Higher green fees can be the objective for updating daily-fee layouts, whereas resort courses improve their layouts to attract more guests, at higher rates, to their hotels. One incentive for change at private clubs has been the scheduling of a major event on their courses with sponsors of the event requesting alterations.

On occasion, updating is made necessary by land taking or an owner's decision to sell real estate (Figures 5.1 and 5.2). Sometimes it is prompted by the knowledge that a neighboring and competing course is already involved in such a program. Still another reason is that one or more new courses with excellent facilities have opened in the vicinity. Most often, however, if funds are available, golf courses are changed to satisfy the everlasting yearning of golfers for excellence and playing interest, reflecting the universal trend toward increasingly magnificent and impressive layouts.

FIGURE 5.1 *The city of Livermore needed to expand an airport runway into the existing 18-hole golf course.*

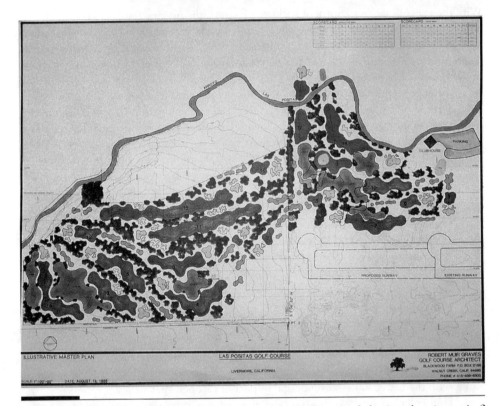

FIGURE 5.2 *With the use of adjacent land and careful planning, nine holes (not shown) remained untouched and in play while the new nine, along with a nine-hole executive course, was developed.*

Minimizing Interference for Players

Whatever the change in a golf course, thoughtful planning is needed.

Rerouting and rebuilding all 18 holes is sometimes called for to achieve better balance, more length, and maximum advantage of natural features, such as wind and vistas, and to reduce out-of-bounds on the slice side. Rerouting is also called for when the existing layout does not sustain high golfing standards.

Complete reconstruction often causes major disturbance to play. Yet there are instances in which interference was minimal at layouts that were completely reversed, even while new greens, tees, and other features were being built (Figures 5.3 and 5.4).

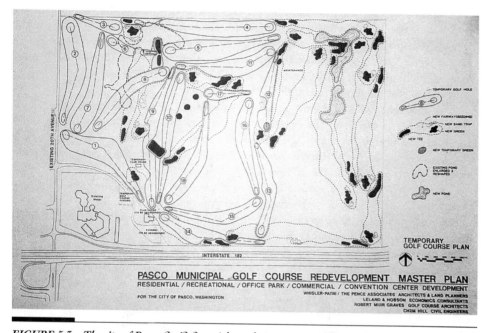

FIGURE 5.3 *The city of Pasco decided to pick up their existing 18-hole golf course, move it 650 feet easterly, but keep it open for play the entire time. With comprehensive planning and dedicated participants, it worked out fine. The dark spots are new tees and greens.*

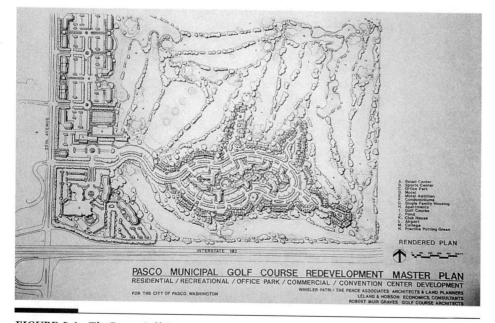

FIGURE 5.4 *The Pasco Golf Course is in play while development of residences and the business park progress.*

Sometimes the clubhouse and other structures, including parking, car storage, maintenance center, and entrance road, are relocated. These alterations may require further changes, such as moving the finishing greens and starting tees. Such restructuring can be disruptive to play, as can land takings by eminent domain.

With today's growing demand for practice fairways, clubs and other courses are finding that room must somehow be found for these facilities. Extensive rerouting is probably required, which players will tolerate if they are convinced that a fine practice fairway facility will emerge. On the other hand, they will be disappointed if after changes involving several holes and lengthy disturbances, the new practice fairway is inadequate—particularly as to length and width.

Increasingly, state-of-the-art irrigation and drainage are being added at established courses. In the hands of experienced installers this work does not have to be excessively disruptive, especially if it is limited to one hole at a time and no trenches are left open over weekends and other periods of heavy play. Sometimes, too, installation can be achieved entirely during off-seasons.

Some changes are less extensive. For example, tees located in dense shade, those that are too small, too low for visibility, or sited poorly in relation to bunkers and landing areas will probably have to be rebuilt, as will those that have settled extensively or become very bumpy. Disturbance to players can be minimal if the tee is relocated or if one portion is rebuilt at a time.

Fairways may need extensive cuts and fills to create visibility and landing areas that are free of severe sidehill, uphill, and downhill lies (Figure 5.5). Thoughtful planning, combined with the might of modern earth-moving equipment, can reduce disruption to play. Fairways with bumpy surfaces may call for resurfacing and reseeding with more suitable grasses. One technique employed, after reducing fairway acreage to 25 acres or less, is to burn off the existing turf with glyphosate, remove the dead sod using a commercial sod cutter, cultivate, fine grade, then prepare and reseed the fairway. On the other hand, if a fairway does not require resurfacing, it can be converted to more desirable grass by overseeding existing or burnt-off turf and adjusting cultural practices to favor the introduced grass.

FIGURE 5.5 For years the Waverley Country Club golfers played a long downhill par three to a partially hidden green that sloped away from the shot. This resulted from changing a hole with a northerly direction to one with a westerly direction and not changing the green design. This section drawing (with an exaggerated vertical scale) shows how lowering the area in front of the green and regrading the green while adding some rear mounds created a more attractive and fair golf hole.

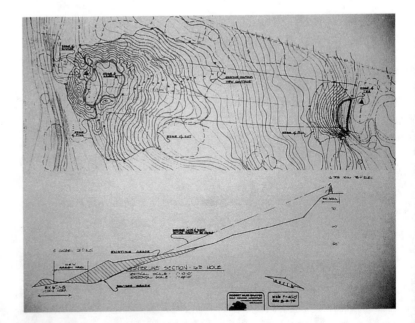

Extensive bunker work is often called for, which can involve rebuilding existing bunkers, building new ones, and eliminating others (Figure 5.6 and 5.7). Neglected bunkers do well as those that are hidden, too shallow, or unprotected from surface runoff may have to be rebuilt completely, with drainage and new sand added.

Rebuilding greens and surrounds can also disrupt play. Nevertheless, if they lack playing interest and eye appeal and are low-quality construction, they probably should be rebuilt. Yet we have observed greens rebuilt at great expense and with major disturbance to players, only to deteriorate within a few seasons to the quality of those they replaced. In such cases the problems were not due to construction. Two common causes were dense shade and destructive traffic patterns.

Redesign Objectives

Experience indicates the following to be common contemporary objectives in redesigning a course, unless a new layout and style are called for. Reaching the objectives may involve rerouting and adjustment of holes.

1.   Adding a balanced short course, perhaps only about 4,800 yards in total length, by creating forward tees.
2.   Adding more adequate practice areas.
3.   Adding ponds for strategy, eye appeal, and use as reservoirs.
4.   Adding or removing trees. In recent years tree removal, as opposed to tree planting, has become increasingly important.
5.   Redetermining the relationship between length of holes in the circuit and their shot values.
6.   Enhancing safety.
7.   Renovating bunkers to provide drainage, new sand, and protective berms. This includes the elimination of some and the addition of others, perhaps with some pot bunkers added as well.
8.   Adding fringe swales.
9.   Adding mounds on sides of fairways or in roughs to aid depth perception and to prevent balls from rolling into wooded areas (Figure 5.6).

FIGURE 5.6   This bunker at Orinda Country Club, which had a rather drab appearance, ended up out of play due to a changing green mowing pattern. See also Figure 5.7.

10. Rebuilding or coring of greens ("coring" refers to removing 16 to 18 inches of existing material and replacing it with tile and USGA-specified layers).
11. Restoring putting surfaces to former shapes and sizes.
12. Converting fairways to bent grass in cool, humid regions, or to superior Bermuda grasses in warmer areas. This conversion is often accompanied by a reduction in fairway acreage, achieved by contouring the fairway down to 25 acres or less.
13. Improving green surrounds by adding mounds and other features.
14. Some owners strive for surplus real estate to develop into homes or commercial buildings. To accomplish this, holes are relocated. Sometimes, but not invariably, this has been accomplished, with success depending on the cyclical market for real estate and the time it takes to bring the new holes into play, often a minimum of two years.

Restoration Objectives

Precisely, *restoration* in this context means restoring a course to what it once was. In practice, however, the term is arbitrary. For example, carrying a bunker sited 170 to 190 yards off a tee may be no challenge to a contemporary golfer, even though a half century or more ago that same bunker may have decided many an important match. Siting the bunker farther down the fairway may restore the challenge. Yet purists say doing that is not true restoration.

Tree stands pose another problem in restoration. It is likely that since the time a course was opened, its trees have grown and others have been planted. Therefore, the hole cannot be played the same way it once could unless many trees are eliminated.

Golf architect Michael Hurdzan points out that a restoration program probably becomes an improvement program rather than absolute restoration, in light of the limitations on removing entire stands of trees.[1] Moreover, maintenance practices and equipment have changed, which in turn leads to different playing conditions.

We have made similar observations: for instance, that when an architect is asked to prepare a restoration program, he or she must point out that, intrinsically, a true restoration is limited to returning to the original architect's style, restoring historical features and, wherever possible, shot values and strategy. Nevertheless, there are examples of successful restoration of individual holes to exactly what they once were.

Plans and Planning

Many private clubs and others require a long-range plan on file as a blueprint for the future of their layout and to obviate unwarranted changes (Figures 5.8–5.10). Background plans similar to those for planning a new course are therefore called for, although some architects work entirely with a scaled aerial photograph.

Among golf architects there are two schools of thought concerning the preparation of a master plan. The methods described in the following paragraphs are used in developing plans for member-owned clubs and are adaptable to other ownerships.

Method A

The first method is for the architect to prepare and submit one or several plans, not necessarily working closely with the owners group in preparing them. A committee selects one

FIGURE 5.7   This "after" picture, from a different angle, shows the bunker's new character as it also moved closer to the action at the green edge.

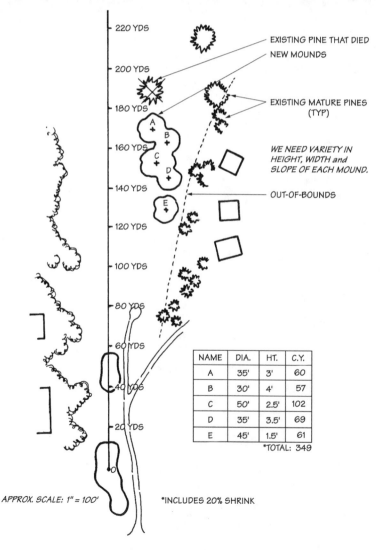

FIGURE 5.8   A diagram based on a vertical, scaled aerial photo was all that was needed to fix a problem at Black Butte Ranch, where a large tree, critical to the strategy of the golf hole, had died. The new mounding helps dictate play, while the dead tree that was left in place, less its top, becomes a habitat tree for locals.

NAME	DIA.	HT.	C.Y.
A	35'	3'	60
B	30'	4'	57
C	50'	2.5'	102
D	35'	3.5'	69
E	45'	1.5'	61

*TOTAL: 349

APPROX. SCALE: 1" = 100'   *INCLUDES 20% SHRINK

FIGURE 5.9   Rogue Valley Golf and Country Club needed to expand its practice facility and generally upgrade the golf course. Here we see the complete 27-hole facility master plan.

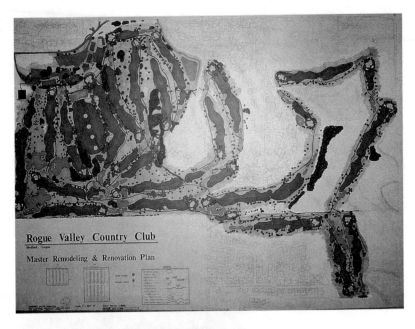

FIGURE 5.10   This blowup of the western area shows more detail, such as green and bunker perimeter mounding and reshaping. New lakes that will become part of the golfing experience and will also furnish fill soil for course re-modeling work are indicated.

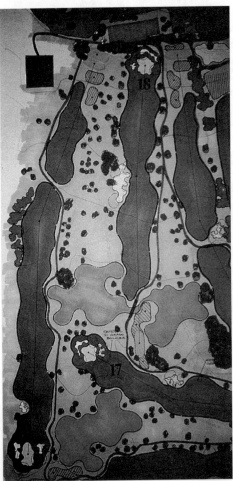

plan. According to this school of thought, it is the duty of the architect to prepare the plan because he or she is the one most qualified and experienced to do so. The club (or other owner) wants the architect's signature on its layout and may resent ideas arising "in-house."

Method B

Using the second method, the architect generates the plan by working closely with a select committee including members of different playing abilities, the club professional, and the superintendent. These are people who know the layout intimately through regular play. This method calls for the architect to embrace the concepts of the select committee and includes the following steps:

- The architect meets with the select committee and is advised of problems that have been encountered, as well as the traditions, aims, and objectives of the club. The architect then prepares a plan.
- At a second meeting, the plan is discussed. The architect then revises it in light of this discussion.
- At a third meeting, the new plan is discussed.
- This procedure is repeated until the select committee and the architect are convinced that the best possible plan has been achieved. (We have found that a minimum of three to four meetings is required.)

This second method of planning is the route taken by many clubs. Embracing the thoughts of those who know the layout intimately, practitioners of this school can ensure that the finest characteristics of the existing layout, those the membership cherishes most, will be retained. Yet the architect still introduces new ideas.

During preparation of a master plan, rumors may arise. It is therefore important to keep the membership informed by newsletter or notice board. Some committees canvas the membership for ideas to be given to the architect. Excellent suggestions have been put forward, and club members gratified that they have been given the courtesy of being permitted to express their views. However, it is mandatory that members' views be submitted to the chairman in writing. When verbal submissions are permitted, we have observed a member submitting an idea one day and the opposite the next.

Once the committee thinks the best possible plan has been achieved by the committee and the architect (or submitted by the architect if the first method has been adopted), it may be voted on by the entire membership. If approved, it is entered in the club's bylaws so that no major changes are allowed for a period of years, except in accordance with the plan. A resolution commonly used states: "Resolved, that no major changes will be allowed on the course for a period of — — — years except those included on the plan dated — — — unless the Board of Governors directs otherwise." This resolution does not state that everything in the plan must be executed. It states that nothing is to be done except in accordance with the plan. This obviates a problem in those states where an existing board is not permitted by law to encumber a future one financially. Yet it satisfies the need of a member-owned club to have a blueprint for the future of its course on record.

If the resolution is to be voted on at the annual meeting, an informational meeting is held a week or so in advance for questions and discussion, preferably with the architect present. This avoids discussion concerning the plan at the annual meeting where other important items of business are put forward.

A plan entered in the bylaws prevents what the Green Section of the United States Golf Association (USGA) has called "the musical chairs type of planning," whereby a chairperson adds a feature one year and his or her successor eliminates it the next, all at excessive expense and player inconvenience.

A plan entered into a club's bylaws (or the equivalent) becomes the blueprint for the future layout. If not in the bylaws, experience shows that the plan may be disregarded by future chairpersons.

There are a number of other considerations concerning the execution of long-range plans:

1. In order to ensure continued progress in execution of the plan, a club may assure that someone remains in office or create a special committee to monitor its continued progress in future years.
2. The special committee conducts regular reviews of the plan to update and modify its concepts and to consult with the architect. Such changes must be authorized by the Board of Governors in order to maintain the integrity of the long-range plan.
3. Scheduling of execution is flexible in order to accommodate:
   a. Continuing play and maintenance during reconstruction
   b. Availability of funds and vagaries of the weather
4. The special chairperson must realize that players will tire of constant reconstruction unless it ensures minimum player interference. Experience points to 5 years as the limit, although some groups have taken 10 to 20 years, perhaps including years when no work was executed.
5. When extensive changes are to be made, some member-owned and other clubs choose to close for an extended period, probably a year to 18 months, and to execute all work within that period. There have been instances of a club renting a nearby facility for its exclusive use for a year or two. This option is possible when a new course in the vicinity is ready for opening but has accepted few members. Such an arrangement eases pressure for reopening too soon, an ever-present danger.

   Some clubs close one nine. Yet that is seldom acceptable unless the layout includes 27 holes or more. If the course is not to be closed, with work proceeding piecemeal over a period of years in accordance with the long-range plan, the problems may be eased by establishing an extra temporary hole on each nine and producing well-sited temporary greens, maintained at the highest possible standard with regular mowing, watering, fertilizing, rolling, and heavy top dressing often with sand.
6. Plans furnished by the architect may include
   a. Plans during the preliminary process (if method B has been adopted). Some clubs have reduced one or more of these plans in size to use as placemats in the grill or dining room so as to stimulate interest in the program.
   b. A final plan and/or individual plans of each hole showing proposed changes.
   c. A colored print for clubhouse display.
   d. A written report listing what is to be done on each hole, a cost estimate at current-year prices (no one can tell what path inflation will take), and the architect's recommended priorities, emphasizing those are flexible.
7. Once the master plan has been approved by the membership, detailed plans and specifications will be needed to execute work on the ground. Some clubs obtain these in one packet, others when items of work are about to proceed.

Notes

1. Michael J. Hurdzan, *Golf Course Architecture* (Chelsea, Mich.: Sleeping Bear Press, 1996), 366.

Planning the Adjacent Real Estate

by Kenneth DeMay, FAIA
SASAKI ASSOCIATES, INC.

In recent years more than 50% of all newly developed golf courses have been integral parts of resort-orientated real estate projects or residential communities.

Adapted from *Golf Courses and Country Clubs*, 1992, by Arthur E. Gimmy, MAI,
and Martin E. Benson, MAI, of the Appraisal Institute

Golf courses are frequently combined with residential development in order to realize the natural benefits that each component can gain from the combination. For example, the presence of an adjacent golf course increases the value of residential uses. Similarly, profits from residential sales can make golf course construction financible. Thus, a value premium is created wherein the value of the combined golf and residential uses is greater than the sum of these uses as separate elements (Figure 6.1).

FIGURE 6.1   A veil of trees softens the residential edge. (Architect: Dann Norris Batting, Chester, NH. Developer: The Green Company Inc., Newton Center, MA. Golf Course Designer: Cornish Silva and Mungeam, Uxbridge, MA. Photographer: Cymie Payne, Berkeley, CA)

The following list highlights the benefits of golf/residential communities.

- The creation of a community theme that makes the community a special place in which to live.
- With its varied shades of green, a golf course constitutes a lastingly memorable landscape feature.
- Golf provides adjacent residents with everyday visual enjoyment of a well-maintained greensward with long vistas and low-density activity.
- A golf course aids in the sculpting of a life-style that includes a convenient and omnipresent visual and recreational amenity.
- A golf course permanently provides open space.
- Golf offers convenient opportunities for recreational activity that eases the stress of contemporary life.
- The combination of golf and residential uses discourages automobiles in favor of walking.
- The environmental impact is less than that produced by a site filled with impervious roads and buildings.
- An economy of scale is achieved; utility mains for the residential development can also serve the golf component.
- Golf can create wildlife areas that are accessible to the residents and/or to the public.
- Golf creates a "visual backyard" whose size and expanse generates the real estate premium.

In designing such a community, the first challenge is to begin with a site that can accommodate a golf course and the necessary residential improvements. To evaluate a site for this purpose, the designer must develop

- A good understanding of golf
- A good understanding of the residential marketplace
- A thorough understanding of the particular site and its idiosyncrasies
- An ability to balance all of the site's features within a harmonious composition

There are basically two kinds of courses. First, there are those that pay their own way and can exist financially without adjacent real estate development. These "playing" courses are frequently located on high ground in order to capture views of the horizon and other dramatic vistas. Second, there are courses that exist only because of adjacent residential development. These "real estate" courses are usually located on lower land, allowing residential development, situated at higher elevations, to overlook their grounds.

Regarding residential design, this chapter addresses only low-rise housing, for three reasons. First, the American population nationally prefers low-rise housing by approximately 10 to 1 over mid- and high-rise housing. Second, low-rise housing is much less of an entrepreneurial risk because any number of such homes can be built at one time. Thus, low-rise housing is "tunable," or adjustable to temporary market realities. Third, low-rise housing has a greater influence on golf design, because it is spread over a larger area and is better integrated with golf than mid- or high-rise housing, which is usually built on a single site.

This chapter assumes that the reader has a working knowledge of the principles of golf course design as presented so far in the previous chapters of this book. In fact, all the rules of course design apply to golf within a residential context. Of course, many more criteria and challenges are added when adjacent homes are introduced into the composition. For example, the distances between greens and the next tees will probably have to be increased because the residential component frequently is in the pathway.

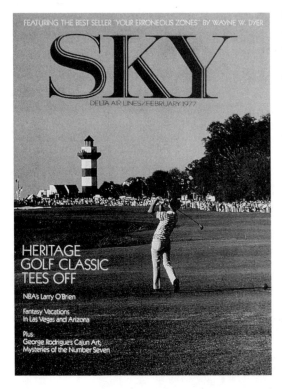

FIGURE 6.2   *Local landmarks can be incorporated into the golf routing plan. (Client: Sea Pines Corporation. Master Planners: Sasaki Associates, Inc., Watertown, MA. Golf Clubhouse and Villa: Thomas E. Stanley & Associates, Savannah, GA. Golf course design: Pete Dye, Jack Nicklaus)*

Existing features such as landform, views, and existing vegetation areas can all add great character if they are preserved. Thus, each project presents a new set of opportunities and challenges. Because each community is unique and highly responsive to its particular environment, there are relatively few hard-and-fast rules to follow (Figure 6.2).

In general, golf and residential components must be carefully coordinated in order to maximize the benefits of the combination while enhancing the integrity of each. In any case, it is always wise to move as little earth as possible and to be extremely cautious about cutting down healthy trees.

The purpose of this chapter is to enable designers to understand the major issues, to appreciate various points of view, to apply them to actual site considerations, and to combine them into a coordinated golf and residential community of exemplary design.

The Design Process

A question frequently asked is, "Who starts sketching first, the golf architect or the land planner?" The answer depends on whether golf or housing is the primary consideration. If golf is the primary consideration, the golf course architect should take the first step so as to articulate the important issues of the golf sequence and the reasons behind the design of each particular hole, its solar orientation, and so on. If the residential component is the primary consideration, the land planner should begin by sketching alternative golf solutions, the housing concepts that seem most appropriate, and all other opportunities such as topography, detention basins, irrigation ponds, clubhouse/entrance locations, and so forth. In either event, these professionals must work together in a cooperative manner, with continuing feedback and appropriate adjustments.

To begin the design process, the designer must grasp the essential opportunities and constraints of the physical site, the law, and the market. All are important, but the most critical opportunities and constraints are the following:

- About 300 acres minimum net usable land area (NULA): To accommodate a typical 18-hole regulation golf course, the site must minimally contain between 160 and 180 acres of net usable land area (not wetland, not steep slopes, not restricted land, etc.). Most golf/residential developments have an additional minimum of about 100 acres dedicated to residential uses.
- With some exceptions, a 5 to 10% land slope is the usual maximum for uphill and side slopes of golf holes.
- Most subdivision regulations have a 10% maximum slope for residential roads.
- There is no maximum for downhill par 3s, but by environmental regulation, slopes steeper than 20% are increasingly required to be preserved in an undisturbed condition.
- Subdivision regulations can specify the allowable length of cul de sacs.
- Environmental regulations may or may not allow for replacement wetlands or for the clearing of trees within a wetland.
- The buying market may be interested in any of a number of housing types: attached, detached on small lots of less than one acre or on large lots of more than one acre, high- or mid-rise buildings, congregate, resort, conference hotel, or a mixture of types.
- Other amenities, such as tennis, a spa, a marina, or a town center, may be proposed.

Site Planning Procedures

This section outlines standard office procedures for on-site planning of large land designs. Its step-by-step organization has two purposes. The first is to make certain that tasks are performed in a sequence that ensures the minimization (or elimination) of wasted time. Fundamental constraints and opportunities are identified and addressed before details come into play. The second purpose is to make certain that every necessary step is individually scrutinized, not overlooked. In this sense, the following outline is very much like the checklist a pilot reads before take-off (Figure 6.3).

FIGURE 6.3 Again, a veil of trees softens the residential edge. (Architect: Dann Norris Batting, Chester, NH. Developer: The Green Company Inc., Newton Center, MA. Golf Course Designer: Cornish Silva and Mungeam, Uxbridge, MA. Photographer: Lyn Weisman Mayewski, Epping, NH)

I. Introductory Phase
   A. Get control of land (purchase or option to buy)
   B. Obtain aerial survey
   C. Establish political feasibility
II. Initial Physical Analysis
   A. Perform on-site physical analysis
      1. Wetlands
      2. Flood plain
      3. Groundwater conservancy overlay district
      4. Restricted areas
      5. Building setbacks
      6. Parking setbacks
      7. Steep slopes
      8. Rock outcroppings
      9. Sub-soil (from federal maps)
      10. Drainage pattern, including watershed definition
      11. Detention requirements
      12. Sewage disposal
      13. Water supply
      14. Hazardous waste
      15. Historical artifacts
      16. Grave sites
      17. Vegetation
      18. Endangered animals
      19. Sun orientation
      20. Views from the site
      21. Easements, rights of way
      22. Limits resulting from flight paths
      23. Landscape features
      24. Existing buildings
      25. Utility lines
   B. Perform off-site physical analysis
      1. Access points
      2. Water supply
      3. Sewage disposal
      4. Views into site
      5. Surrounding land uses
      6. Acquisition potential of adjacent lands
   C. Conduct special studies
      1. Traffic
      2. Notice of intent
      3. Federal Emergency Management Agency (FEMA) regarding flood-plain
      4. Historical
      5. Underground ledge topography
      6. Hazardous waste
   D. Determine site premium costs
      1. Utility connections
      2. Leveling steep slopes
      3. Ledge moving

            4. Unusual plan configurations
            5. Roadway inefficiencies
            6. Buffering from unsightly environs
      E. Identify NULA (net useable land area)

III. Initial Legal/Zoning Analysis
      A. Current zone (matter of right)
      B. Alternative zones available in zoning area
      C. Adjacent zones to avoid spot zoning
      D. New zoning
            1. Consultant goes for a zone change
            2. Get zone accepted
            3. Get land into new zone
            4. Get site plan approval
      E. Regulatory permitting process
            1. Agencies with jurisdiction
            2. Appropriate sequence
            3. Time limits for each
            4. Submission requirements
            5. Scale requirements
      F. Subdivision regulation
            1. Cul-de-sac length
            2. Roadway slope
            3. Roadway radii

IV. Initial Market Analysis
      A. What do authorities want?
            1. Units
                 a. Lots ready for development
                 b. Lots with detached units
                 c. Clustered units
                 d. Attached units
                 e. Other
            2. Streets
                 a. Curb types
                 b. Lighting types
                 c. Street trees
                 d. Alignment variety
            3. Tree preservation
            4. Design controls
            5. Amenities
                 a. Golf
                 b. Recreation
                 c. Retail
                 d. Conference center
                 e. School sites
                 f. Equestrian
                 g. Other
            6. Image(s)
                 a. One or more images?
                 b. Privacy
                 c. Security

       d. Environment
    7. Phasing
       a. Utility runs
       b. Road length
       c. Clean access to completed phases
       d. Construction access separate
  B. What do authorities want to avoid?
    1. Bare earth atmosphere
    2. Uniformity
  C. Financial realities
    1. Market definition
       a. Sale range of units
       b. Lease range of units
       c. Site improvement costs
       d. Other
    2. Pro forma by phase
    3. Cash requirements by phase
    4. Return on investment
    5. Downside risks
    6. Market elasticity
V. Site-Plan Alternatives
  A. Land use patterns
  B. Maximized views and privacy
  C. Density
    1. Unit density
    2. Linear density for views
  D. Overall circulation
    1. Right of way to meet public standards
    2. Minimum pavement width for low traffic
    3. Opportunities for long vistas
  E. Visual variety within unity
  F. Resolve conflicts between lost opportunities and high expenditures
  G. Market elasticity
  H. Parking
  I. Open space designing
    1. Hierarchy of open space(s)
    2. Opportunities for long vistas
VI. Select and Refine Preferred Alternative
  A. Adhere to all regulatory requirements or articulate appeals
  B. Phasing issues
    1. Infrastructure costs by phase
    2. Market appeal
       a. Best foot forward
       b. Save best for last
       c. Some of both
       d. Start with next to best
    3. Maximize flexibility in later phases. If possible, each phase should look complete because it is difficult to ensure that later phases will be carried out as originally envisioned.
  C. Signage and entrance(s)

VII. Present to Political Powers as a Courtesy
VIII. Rework If Needed
IX. Obtain Citizen Support or Neutrality
    A. Universally critical issues
        1. Traffic impact
        2. Viewshed impact
        3. Construction
            a. Noise impact
            b. Dust impact
            c. Runoff impact
        4. Loss of natural open space
X. Negotiate/Redesign as Needed
XI. Obtain Official Regulatory Approvals
    A. As in a political campaign, seek the alliance of a larger number of citizens to speak in favor of the proposal than objectors can assemble to speak against it.
XII. Litigation by Objectors
    A. Usually only the nuisance of expense and time incurred by owner and planner
XIII. Appeal by Objectors
    A. Usually only the nuisance of expense and time
XIV. Approvals Upheld
XV. Land Values
    A. Raw land with no approvals
    B. Raw land with approvals
    C. Approved land with all roads and utilities
    D. Sale of multiple lots/areas to individual developers
    E. Sale of individual lots/condos to buyers
    F. Fully developed site
XVI. Marketing and/or Fund-Raising
XVII. Site Civil Engineering
XVIII. Full Architect/Engineering (A/E) Services
XIX. Ground Breaking
(Figure 6.4)   XX. Ribbon Cutting

FIGURE 6.4 Expansive glass windows allow panoramic views of golf. (Architect—Garden House: Richard Bertman, CBT/Childs Bertman Tseckares, Boston, MA. Master Planners: Ricardo Dumont and Sasaki Associates, Inc., Watertown, MA. Builder: The Green Company, Inc., Newton Center, MA. Developer: Willowbend Development Corp., Mashpee, MA. Golf Course Designer: Michael Hurdzan. Photographer: Frank Foster, West Harwich, MA)

Extent of Integration—
Golf and Residential Components

The most basic challenge for the planner is to accommodate golfers' wish for bucolic isolation while providing a direct view of the course to as many homes as possible. It must be understood that these two worthy goals are in conflict (Figure 6.4).

Single Fairways   To maximize residential frontage on a golf course, one would design a golf corridor with single fairways only. Housing would be lined up on both sides for the entire length. However, such a highly interlocking plan, if carried through the entire course, may not lead to the most enjoyable golfing experience (Figure 6.5).

Double Fairways   Doubling up some fairways provides the opportunity to locate mounds, tree clumps, and ponds in between the fairways, adding to the interest of the course. Inasmuch as most players slice, the right hand (slice) side of the fairways should be aligned along the center of the golf corridor in the interest of safety (Figure 6.6).

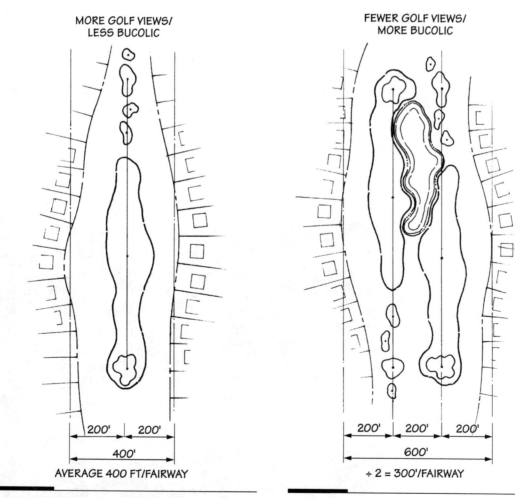

MORE GOLF VIEWS/
LESS BUCOLIC

FEWER GOLF VIEWS/
MORE BUCOLIC

200'	200'
400'	

AVERAGE 400 FT/FAIRWAY

200'	200'	200'
600'		

÷ 2 = 300'/FAIRWAY

FIGURE 6.5   Like playing down a "canyon" of homesites.

FIGURE 6.6   This is more enjoyable golf and takes less space than two separate holes.

FEWEST GOLF VIEWS/
MOST BUCOLIC

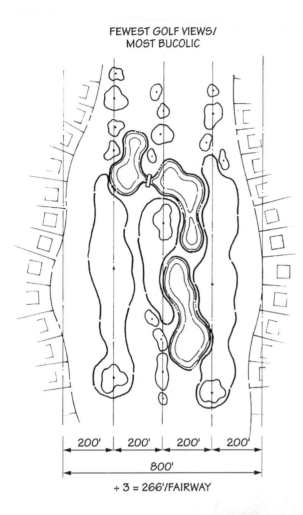

|← 200' →|← 200' →|← 200' →|← 200' →|

|←——————— 800' ———————→|

÷ 3 = 266'/FAIRWAY

FIGURE 6.7   *Again, a relatively better golfing experience but at the cost of golf perimeter residential lots.*

Triple Fairways   Multiple fairways conserve land and provide a more bucolic golf experience. However, they cannot give as many homes a direct view of the golf course (Figure 6.7).

A Veil of Trees   One obviously good way to create a bucolic setting for golf is to include a screen of new or existing trees between a fairway and the abutting lots. Lower tree branches can be selectively pruned to allow views of the course from the homes while the remaining treetops form a strong green edge as viewed from the fairway. An advantage of this technique is its effectiveness in softening long, continuous building facades such as those produced by attached town homes, as shown in the photograph of Kings Way (Cornish Silva and Mungeam Golf Course Architects, The Green Company, Developer) (Figure 6.8).

Trees Between Lots   If residential development is composed of detached homes on lots of about 80 feet or wider, another screening technique can be considered. As shown in Figure 6.9 preserving or planting trees and shrubs densely between these lots increases neighbor-to-neighbor privacy and relieves the golfer of seeing homes as a long architectural row.

FIGURE 6.8   *Golf greens are a favorite focus for views at Kings Way in Yarmouthport, MA. (Developer: The Green Company, Inc., Newton Center, MA. Master Planners: Ricardo Dumont and Sasaki Associates, Inc., Watertown, MA. Architect: Dann Norris Batting, Chester, NH. Golf Course Designer: Cornish Silva and Mungeam, Uxbridge, MA. Photographers: Cymie Payne, Berkeley, CA; Lyn Weisman Mayewski, Epping, NH)*

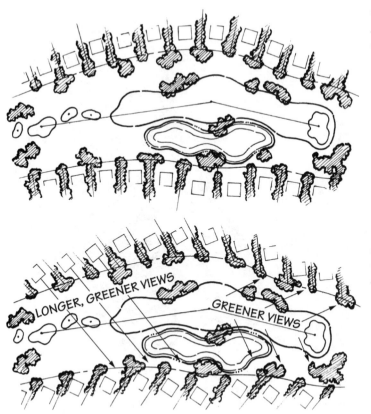

FIGURE 6.9   Tree screens shown between a conventional lot layout.

FIGURE 6.10   Tree screens between angled lots do double duty in creating a greener view for golfer and home owner.

Trees Between Angled Lots   As a refinement of the previous concept, trees can be placed to advantage on angled lots. Golfers look ahead toward the green, not back toward the tees. Therefore, angling lot lines, as shown in Figure 6.10, allows golfers to look at trees rather than houses. This arrangement also means longer angled views from the homes toward the fairway. Moreover, angles screen the views of homes across the fairway, making these views greener.

The Residential Enclave

A golf course and an adjacent residential development should not be considered as two independent components. If they are allowed to interact, a great deal of variety is possible (Figure 6.11).

Interstices between fairways can be used to great advantage. For instance, such an area can contain a grove of trees and/or a pond for either detention or irrigation (Figure 6.12) or serve as a large "estate" site for a high-end home with a private driveway (Figure 6.13).

The most effective way to make golf a pastoral experience is to truly surround a significant number of holes with nature. As shown in the site plan for Purchase Estates and the Country Club of Purchase (Jack Nicklaus, golf course architect), holes 4, 5, and 6, and holes 12, 13, 14, and 15, as well as the 18th hole, are located away from residential areas (Figure 6.14). They impart a profound sense of being surrounded by a natural environment rather than a built environment of homes.

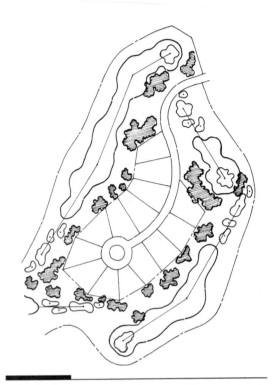

FIGURE 6.11   Given enough space, golfers can enjoy the golf course and home owners can enjoy their homes.

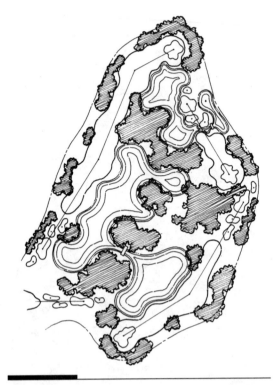

FIGURE 6.12   The inner space is used to develop a parklike area for possible multiple use rather than for homesites.

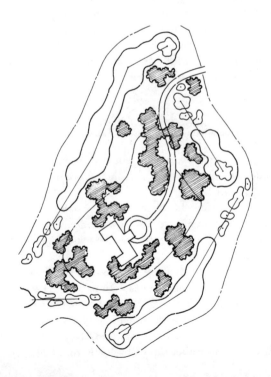

FIGURE 6.13   A third possible use for the inner space is the "estate" lot.

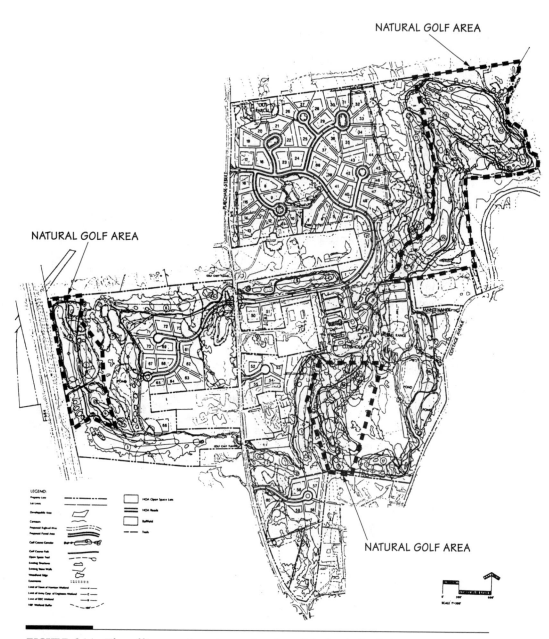

FIGURE 6.14   The golfing experience is greatly enhanced by developing holes in a natural environment.

Of course, this solution dramatically decreases the number of homes that have views of the course. It is appropriate only when there is a clear understanding that the greater appeal of the golf experience is worth the decreased visibility from the adjacent residences. The crucial determination can be reached only through realizing what constitutes the developmental driver: housing or golf.

Thus, for Purchase Estates, although the residential lots were designed with great care in regard to variety and livability, the basic decision was to have the golf experience dominate the overall intentions.

Designing the Site Perimeter

Because of the large acreage needed by a golf/residential development, the site perimeter is always of sufficient length to warrant careful planning. The following paragraphs offer a number of guidelines.

Buffer   Where the land abutting the perimeter is not yet developed, but has that potential, preserve a treed buffer of about 100 feet. Whether the perimeter use is golf or residential, this buffer can provide protection from any unsightly neighboring development should one ever be constructed (Figure 6.15).

Single-Loaded Road   A perimeter residential road that is single loaded (houses on one side only) is basically an inefficient use of an expensive roadway, considering the necessary clearing, grading, paving, utilities, lighting, and so on (Figure 6.16).

Double-Loaded Road   Siting homes on both sides of a perimeter road is a more efficient use, but it includes many homes without any view of the golf course. However, depending on the particular market conditions, there are frequently home buyers who, because of the lower price, would appreciate the opportunity of living in a golf/residential community even without such a view from their homesites (Figure 6.17).

Variety   A residential perimeter road can be partly singleloaded and partly double loaded. This arrangement relieves visual monotony, particularly in longer roads. It can also provide some very interesting views of the golf course from the road (Figure 6.18).

Topographically Low Site Perimeter   If the site perimeter is at a lower elevation than the internal road that serves the adjacent homes, golf should be on the perimeter in order to allow views of the course from homes on the higher elevation (Figure 6.19).

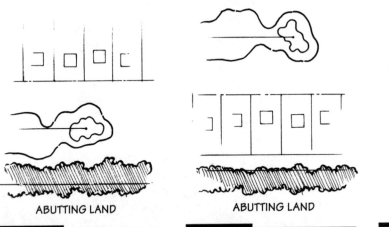

ABUTTING LAND

ABUTTING LAND

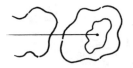
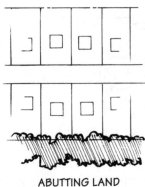

ABUTTING LAND

FIGURE 6.15   The golf hole and homesites are protected from future development.

FIGURE 6.16   Single-loaded roads are to be avoided if possible.

FIGURE 6.17   The lack of a golf view can be successfully offset by the lower price.

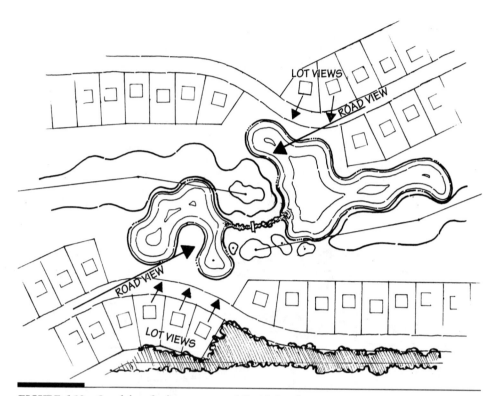

FIGURE 6.18   *Careful road alignment, coupled with lot placement, creates excellent golfing views for both users.*

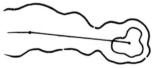

ABUTTING LAND

FIGURE 6.19   *The buffer becomes part of the view as well as a background for golfing views.*

Perimeter with Superior View   In the case of a perimeter location with a permanent superior view of off-site open space, the designer has two options. One is to place a double-loaded road on the perimeter (Figure 6.20). The other is to have perimeter golf with an internal double-loaded road. With this arrangement, the internal homes have a golf view and the external homes have an extra benefit: the permanent superior view (Figure 6.21).

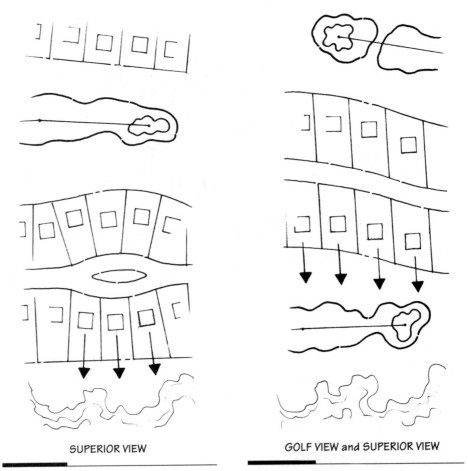

SUPERIOR VIEW   GOLF VIEW and SUPERIOR VIEW

FIGURE 6.20   Here the lack of a golfing view is replaced by the permanent superior view.   *FIGURE 6.21   Two views can add appreciably to the value of these perimeter lots.*

Two Perimeter Options   In designing a site perimeter, a very interesting question immediately arises. Should the most expensive housing product (a large home on a large site) or the least expensive (a narrow town house connected to others) be located on this kind of supervaluable site?

In some super locations (such as Pebble Beach) a few very expensive homes overlook both the golf course and the Pacific Ocean. Thus, their value is greatly enhanced, but that is meaningful only if there is a ready market for these exceedingly costly homes.

In other super locations (such as Harbour Town at Sea Pines Plantations, South Carolina) many attached town houses overlook both the 18th fairway and the Intercoastal Waterway (Figure 6.22).

FIGURE 6.22   At Harbour Town, SC, the homes on the right enjoy both a golf view and a water/ horizon vista, as shown in Figure 6.21. (Client: Sea Pines Corporation. Master Planners: Sasaki Associates, Inc., Watertown, MA. Golf Clubhouse and Villa: Thomas E. Stanley & Associates, Savannah, GA. Golf course designers: Pete Dye, Jack Nicklaus)

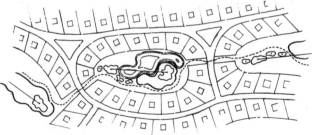

FIGURE 6.23   This represents maximum use of the golf edge as a homesite amenity. However, unless very carefully developed, it can diminish enjoyment of golf.

Of course, each will significantly increase in real estate value because of the double amenity. But which increase is better from an overall developmental point of view? The answer usually comes from market considerations.

There are many concepts that a site planner can employ when joining golf and residential components. Wrapping the fairways with lots represents the maximum of interlocking. Except for the golf car paths, the full perimeter of the fairway is lined with homes, and the homes wrapping the tees and greens enjoy the longest views up and down the fairways (Figure 6.23).

A neighboring green (a traditional green, not a golf green) can serve as a focus in a key location. If some smaller lots are appropriate, they may be located near the neighborhood green to provide emphasis to its design. A planner may also consider the use of a hammerhead, which is an acceptable alternate to a turnaround or cul-de-sac in some jurisdictions (Figure 6.24).

Undulating the residential edge can add considerable variety on either side of the collecter road. Creating a cul-de-sac, a close, or a loop road can provide a real sense of identity as opposed to merely lining up lots on either side of a road. The undulations can also add interest to the golfer's perspective. For example, the solar orientation of fairways can be significantly varied (Figure 6.25).

Also illustrated in Figure 6.25 is the concept of overlapping a green and the next tee, which can sometimes be key to accommodating the necessary hole lengths in a limited length of site.

FIGURE 6.24   The neighborhood green is a modern adaptation of a centuries-old concept. The hammerhead is a relatively new idea for the end of a street.

HAMMERHEAD   NEIGHBORHOOD GREEN SPACE

FIGURE 6.25   Here is an interesting lot arrangement, coupled with a varied residential edge for the golf holes. Note overlapping holes providing additional length to the golf course.

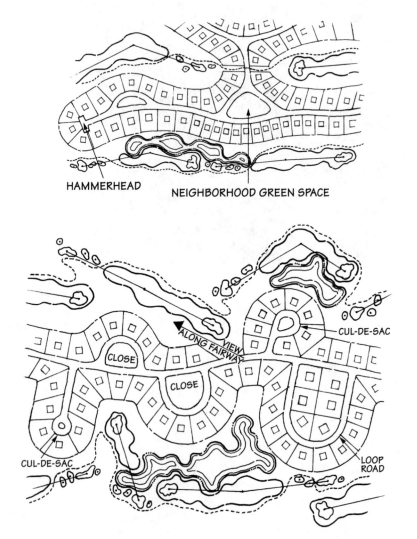

CUL-DE-SAC

VIEW ALONG FAIRWAY

CLOSE

CLOSE

CUL-DE-SAC

LOOP ROAD

View Easements

The views enjoyed by owners of low-rise homes that abut golf fairways also add substantially to the value of their real estate. To protect this investment, view easements are frequently established, requiring the golf course owner/manager to get the home owners' permission before (for example) planting a dense evergreen hedge that would block their view of the course. Such a view easement could also extend to some part of the home owners' association (HOA) lot (or even an abutter's lot), which could be planted in such a manner as to block a valuable view.

Executive Courses

Executive courses are designed to include homes with all the benefits of a golf course but without the land consumption of a full 18-hole regulation course. If there is not enough land to accommodate a regulation course, an executive course is a logical alternative. At Kings Way on Cape Cod, the developers bought land that already had a design for a 9-hole course (which can be seen in the southwestern corner of the site shown in Figure 6.26). To augment this facility, Cornish and Silva, Golf Course Architects, added nine more executive-length holes in a single-fairway configuration. This back nine contrasts very comfortably with the more open front nine. Since an 18-hole regulation course is always preferred, a market study should be undertaken to verify the local market acceptability of an executive course.

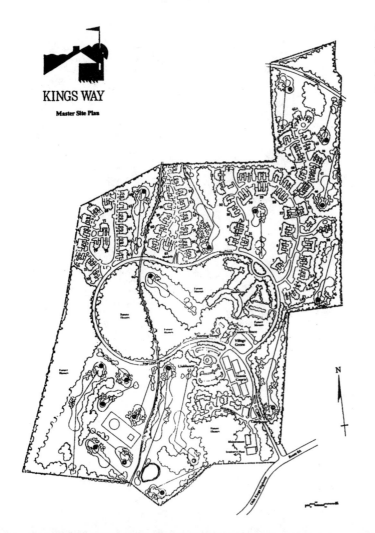

FIGURE 6.26 Note the golf holes surrounding the federal airport beacon in the southwest corner. (Developer: The Green Company, Inc., Newton Center, MA)

Long-term flexibility must be considered. For example, after half the homes were sold at Kings Way, the existing federal installation (contained within the rectangular fence) amid the existing nine holes was abandoned by the federal government and the site became available to the developer. A quick analysis by the planner revealed that by changing two par 3 holes, many more homes with golf views could be substituted. All factors were evaluated. Because residential use was the driver, the decision of the developer and the planner was to increase the number of "view homes" with necessary alterations in the golf course. Because flexibility had been provided in the original plans, this was accomplished with reasonable costs and no disruption to play (Figure 6.27).

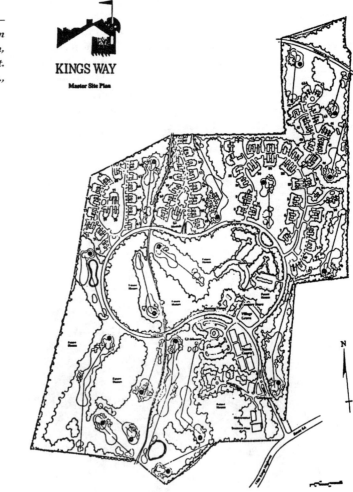

FIGURE 6.27   Note golf hole configuration after removal of the federal airport beacon, leaving the space for future development. (Developer: The Green Company, Inc., Newton Center, MA)

KINGS WAY
Master Site Plan

Other Considerations

Number of Lots on a Site

The designer should always bear in mind the total number of lots that are likely to be located in any golf/residential community (Figure 6.28). The site plan for Purchase Estates shows 73 house lots for sale (see Figure 6.14). In addition to house lots, the site planner should always anticipate the possibility of three more lots:

FIGURE 6.28 At Samoset Village, several homes can share an entrance courtyard. (Client: Samoset Resort Investors, Inc. Architect: Sasaki Associates, Inc. Master Planners: Sasaki Associates, Inc. General Contractor: Laukka Construction, Rockport, ME. Photographer: Brian Vanden Brink)

1. A "golf lot" usually contains
   a. The golf course itself
   b. Any practice facilities
   c. The clubhouse
   d. The maintenance area
   e. The entrance road from a public right-of-way to the clubhouse parking area
2. A home owners' association (HOA) lot containing
   a. Open space(s) for the use of all home owners
   b. Amenities such as community tennis, jogging or walking trails, pool, picnic facilities—that is, all HOA spaces for active and passive recreation
   c. Circulation roads leading from a public road to all residential lots
   d. Incidental planted areas, such as turnarounds at cul-de-sac ends
3. A "public lot" containing any facilities to be used by the general public. In the case of Purchase Estates, this consists of an active recreation field at the extreme southern end of the overall site, where it is easily accessible to all town citizens and yet isolated enough not to be a visual or audible nuisance.

Road Crossings

Although crossing any road when playing golf (either walking or with a golf car) is undesirable *in abstractum*, the necessary interlocking of golf and residential components usually makes such crossings inevitable. As the site plan in Figure 6.29 shows, the Purchase Estates site is bisected by a busy state roadway. To avoid conflict, two underground tunnels were built connecting hole 2 to hole 3 and 8 to 9. An alternative sometimes seen in other golf courses with similar situations is a golf car path crossing on grade with the protection of a hand-activated red light.

At Purchase, the only other road crossing, from hole 9 to hole 10, is over a quiet internal private road where road striping is adequate. Sometimes white road striping is combined with either speed bumps or a cobblestone rumble strip.

Kings Way has eight crossings, but they are all over quiet internal private roads where striping is adequate.

Phasing

Low-rise residential components are usually built over a number of years in order to minimize financial risks as well as to allow fine-tuning in response to changing market preferences. A phasing concept must be developed that allows minor adjustments and minimizes the nuisances of a lengthy construction period. The conventional wisdom is to design a phasing system wherein there will be

1. A clean and finished (nonconstruction) access road to the completed homes in each phase
2. A separate construction access road that isolates the construction nuisances of later phases away from the completed areas
3. An absence or a minimum of future infrastructure costs superimposed onto earlier phases

At Purchase Estates, Phase One includes the 11 lots on the two cul-de-sacs and the main entrance, as shown in Figure 6.29. Phase Two includes the next 11 lots north of the clubhouse. Clean access is via a northerly road extension from the clubhouse area.

FIGURE 6.29   *The circled numbers indicate each phase of development in sequence. See also Figure 6.14 for a clearer plan view.*

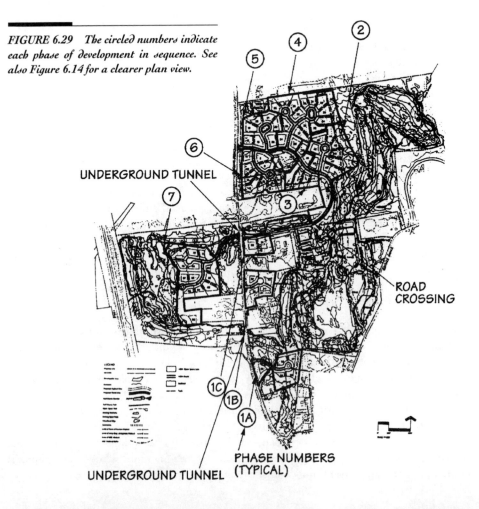

Construction access is via the extended roadway northwesterly to Purchase Street. Phase Three consists of 7 lots. Phase Four contains the 15 lots that are served by the Y-shaped cul-de-sac. Phase Five has 6 lots, and Phase Six's 10 lots complete all the construction in the northern sector of the site. Phase Seven includes the 13 lots that are located on the west side of Purchase Street. In summary, this phasing concept conforms to the three criteria listed earlier.

Residential Site Planning

In the United States there is strong preference for dwelling units (DUs) that have individual exterior front doors rather than share an entry corridor with other DUs. Thus, this section focuses on homes that enjoy "their own front doors." Detached homes are of primary importance because national statistics indicate an overwhelming preference for this housing type. Yet, the primary goal of siting any residence in a golf community is to orient major viewing windows toward the golf fairways. This generates the need to understand the functional organization of internal spaces, the direction of the golf view, the issue of lot width, and the building width that is allowed by zoning. The section is organized in this sequence.

Functional Organization of Internal Spaces

Active Cluster   Generally, there is a close relationship between living, dining, and kitchen areas. In larger houses, there is frequently also a family room nearby. In homes with children, it is highly desirable to have a place where they can play; realistically, that area should be somewhere near the kitchen, which is usually a center of daily activity. Close connections between the garage and the kitchen simplify the carrying of food bundles. For convenience, the proximity of these active areas to the front door is also useful.

Quiet Cluster   Bedrooms and bathrooms usually form a quiet cluster somewhat removed from the active cluster.

Unique Characteristics of Golf-Oriented Housing

Although market preferences vary, and although most rooms benefit from golf views, a survey of priorities reveals that most home buyers in golf communities think that the view is most important from the family/living room and the master bedroom. Furthermore, since many buyers see such a house as a retirement venue, there is a strong preference for single-floor living and, thus, for the location of the master suite on the ground floor. A responsive designer therefore envisions a floor plan that places the family/living room and the master bedroom on the ground floor on whatever side faces the fairway. The detached building in Figure 6.30 is roughly 60 feet wide. On the ground floor are the living room, dining room, master bedroom suite, and two-car garage. Three additional bedrooms are on the second floor. The concept is popular with a large number of home buyers, especially "empty nesters" whose children may be away much of the time (Figure 6.31).

Rearage   Most homes have the golf view at the rear of the building where the living/dining/kitchen area and the master bedroom have an unobstructed view of the

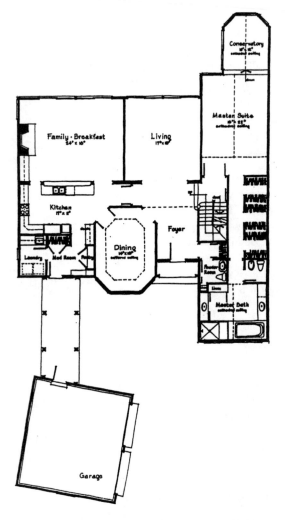

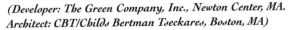

FIGURE 6.30   Ground floor plan.

(Developer: The Green Company, Inc., Newton Center, MA. Architect: CBT/Childs Bertman Tseckares, Boston, MA)

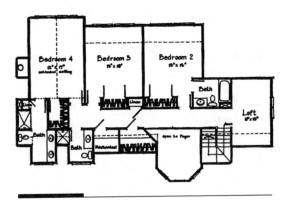

FIGURE 6.31   Second floor plan.

course. This is extremely important to the real estate value of the house. It should not be obstructed by a rear yard garage; the garage should be in front or in the basement (Figure 6.32). The concept of rearage was developed by The Green Company.

Another rearage consideration is grading. Green fairways are most spectacular when seen from above. Thus, the level of the primary viewing rooms must be at least a few feet higher than the fairway for maximum visual impact.

Yet another issue is privacy from neighborhood homes. This can be accomplished either by projecting an architectural element (note the conservatory on the first-floor plan (in Figure 6.30) by a privacy fence, or, better yet, by a heavy planting screen such as was mentioned earlier in this chapter.

Frontage   In golf/residential communities, most homes are approached by cars on what may be called the front of the building (Figure 6.33). Here the two customary cars are usually parked and, in higher-end situations, garaged. This frontage gives the first impression of the home and must therefore be sensitively designed. The important benefit of locating the garage on the ground level is that, combined with a ground-floor living room/dining room/kitchen plus a ground-floor master bedroom, it allows "one-floor living" for the owners of the house (see Figure 6.32).

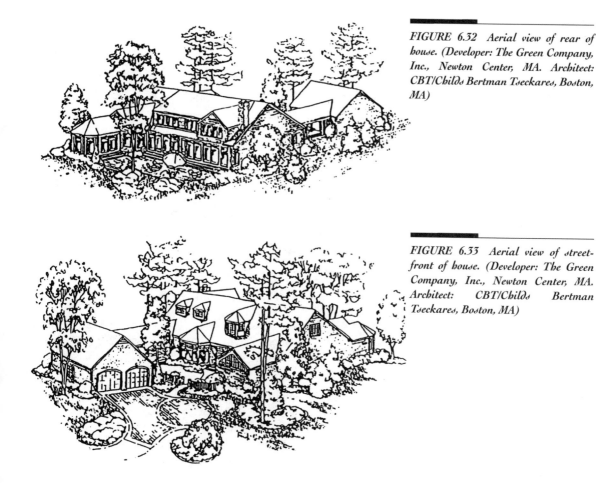

FIGURE 6.32 Aerial view of rear of house. (Developer: The Green Company, Inc., Newton Center, MA. Architect: CBT/Childs Bertman Tseckares, Boston, MA)

FIGURE 6.33 Aerial view of street-front of house. (Developer: The Green Company, Inc., Newton Center, MA. Architect: CBT/Childs Bertman Tseckares, Boston, MA)

The first architectural challenge is to make a 22-foot by 22-foot garage aesthetically inviting. A first step is to turn the garage doors away from the street, as shown in Figure 6.33. A second step is to use articulated door panels, arched soffits, a strip window above the doors, or another pleasing design feature. A third step is to install decorative pavement on the driveway, along with fences, gates, lighting fixtures, and, especially, planting. The garage can be used to provide privacy for part of the house. The minus of having to go past the garage is counterbalanced by the increased width of the rear view. An alternative is to locate the garage in the basement via a sloping driveway through the side yard. However, this will require the residents to climb stairs on a daily basis, which will not provide the one-floor living that is preferred in many market areas.

Another completely different frontage issue is illustrated in Figure 6.34. The lots with single asterisks have a golf view from the front of their homes. Raised porches, like those on classic Victorian or Queen Anne houses, are useful in such situations. In these circumstances, rear yard garages are most appropriate. Although the golf view must be seen across the road, the rear yard is completely private, which may be preferred by some families.

Sideage   Local zoning codes establish the side yard dimension between the home and the side property line. In the interest of privacy, on narrow sites it is advisable to install a fence on the side property line and/or plant heavily for 5 or 10 feet from the line. On

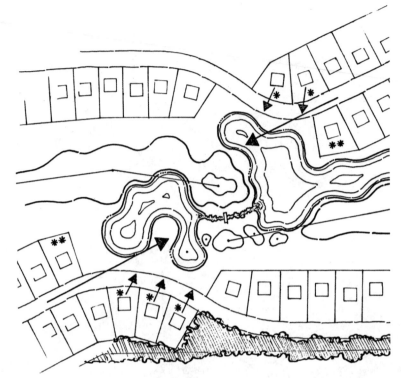

FIGURE 6.34 *The single asterisk indicates a golf view from the front of the home. The double asterisk indicates both a rear golf view and a side view down the fairway length.*

narrow lots, the practicality of having windows on the side of a house largely depends on the presence or absence of side windows in the neighboring home. Occasionally, there may be a major sideage opportunity, as also illustrated in Figure 6.34. The lots with the most spectacular golf views are those with the double asterisks because in addition to having a rear golf view, they each have a side view down the length of the fairway.

Lot Width

Within the realm of low-rise housing—detached, semidetached, attached town homes, and walk-up units—value is positively influenced by the presence of a golf view. Thus, the width of the lots in a golf/residential development is crucial because their cumulative width will determine how many will enjoy preferred golf views. We must, therefore, confront two opposing forces. The wider the lots, the more privacy from neighbors and the more amenities (pools, tennis courts, etc.) that can be accommodated on each lot. The narrower the lots, the more lots that can overlook the fairways.

Detached   Generally speaking, detached house lots tend to be a minimum of 60 to 70 feet. For conceptual simplicity, suppose the narrower lots contain a 30-foot-wide dwelling unit. This assumes a first-floor living/dining/kitchen bay of about 15 feet next to a master bedroom of about 14 feet, with about 1 foot for walls and partitions. On the second floor, two bedrooms of 14 or 15 feet width at the rear and one or two bedrooms at the front could be accommodated (Figure 6.35).

Semidetached   To achieve a lot width of less than 60 feet or so, the site planner should consider semidetached homes (Figure 6.36). In order to enhance a sense of residential individuality, every attempt should be made to separate the two entry doors so that they are not visible from each other.

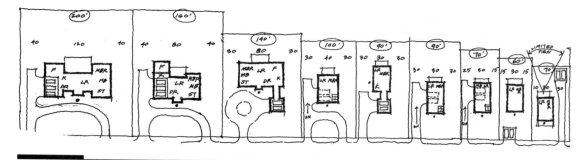

FIGURE 6.35   Detached housing on a narrow lot.

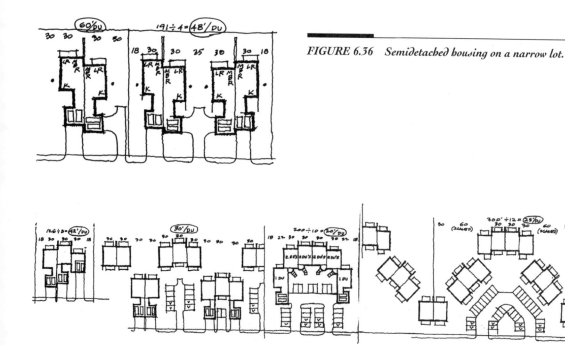

FIGURE 6.36   Semidetached housing on a narrow lot.

FIGURE 6.37   Single-family attached housing.

Single-Family Attached   To achieve a lot width between 40 and 24 feet, a "town house" concept can be appropriate, as shown in Figure 6.37. Parking for two cars for residents, plus ½ car for visitors, per dwelling unit will be very important in the site design process. Gang parking lots as shown may have to be used.

Although each project is unique, all will be high-end developments. If home buyers are looking for detached homes on large lots of 1 acre or more, the designer's efforts will be relatively simple. If they are looking for attached units, siting the driveways and/or parking lot will make the design process more complicated.

Town Houses Over Flats   Each home discussed so far has had its own footprint on its own ground. In order to reduce widths to 20 feet or so, two-story homes stacked above flats will probably be necessary. Parking for two cars for residents, plus ½ car for visitors, per home will be dense enough to dominate the design process.

Summary

Planning the real estate abutting a golf course can be an incredibly rewarding experience, along with making good business sense. In a planned golf/residential community, the combined uses can complement and lend character to each other in a sensitive and enriching manner.

Practice Facilities, Short Courses, and Cayman Golf

The shortest, most direct line to the hole, even if it be the center of the fairway, should be fraught with danger.

From *Concerning Golf,* 1903, by John Laing Low (1869–1929)

In this era of apparently limitless expansion of golf, practice facilities and short courses have become popular for beginners, others wishing to improve their games, and golfers of all calibers out to enjoy themselves. Golf architects are called upon to plan these facilities as features of existing or new courses, as well as those that stand alone. Practice facilities have become increasingly sophisticated and beautiful, with ever higher construction and maintenance standards. (Commercial driving ranges and miniature putting courses are not discussed in this text, although they add to the world of golf. The National Golf Foundation provides information on these facilities.)

Practice Fairways

One of the most important facilities of any golf club is the practice fairway. Practice fairways are valuable assets for private clubs as well as daily-fee layouts, from the standpoints of both player satisfaction and the bottom line. Golfers often feel their presence is mandatory in selecting vacation destinations. Yet a limiting factor to their inclusion can be lack of space.

Sometimes rearrangement of holes to accommodate a practice fairway is possible. Fencing can also be a solution, as well as excavating the fairway many feet in depth and building mounds at ends and sides with the soil if soil conditions are favorable and drainage possible (Figures 7.1 and 7.2).

FIGURE 7.1 The practice range at Woodcreek Oaks Golf Course in Fairfield, California, was completely depressed, with much of the excavated soil used to raise perimeter mounding. This reduced the height of the safety screen and its cost. Note the ground-level night lighting to illuminate the landing area and pole lights for the tee.

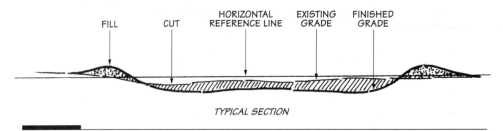

FIGURE 7.2   This section drawing shows relationship between existing and finish grades at Wood-creek Oaks.

Some say that today's golfers are not hitting balls significantly farther than their parents did. Yet a practice fairway 800 feet from front of tee to the end was adequate until recent decades. Now 900 feet is needed, and, possibly, low fencing, to prevent balls from rolling even farther. These lengths are subject to modification when shots are uphill or downhill.

The ideal practice fairway is characterized by

- Proximity to the pro shop and the first tee.
- Visibility of the fairway from the tee.
- 300 yards from front of tee to end, where a fence may still be needed.
- A grass tee with a minimum surface area of 20,000 square feet and width enough to accommodate at least 12 to 15 golfers with 10 to 12 feet allotted for each, plus one or more practice bunkers. Larger teeing areas are better. Several courses have established grass tees an acre or more in size (Figure 7.3).

FIGURE 7.3   This is a typical practice tee at a public golf course, Blue Rock Springs in Vallejo, California. The tee is on an arc, with the center out about 160 yards. This orients each tee area inward toward the center, helping to keep balls inside the range. Notice the special teaching area, lower left.

- A strip of all-weather material. If this is inserted forward on the tee, the superintendent's crew can perform work on the tee when the strip is in use.
- A private area for lessons by the professional.
- A "clinic" tee at the far end of the fairway, but with its front 325 yards from the front of the regular tee, because fencing is not possible with tees at both ends. Depending on circumstances, the clinic tee is often one-half or less the area of the main tee.
- Orientation with a north-south axis is desirable, with north preferable (Figure 7.4). Northwest to northeast is satisfactory, considering whether the use is likely to be in the morning or afternoon.

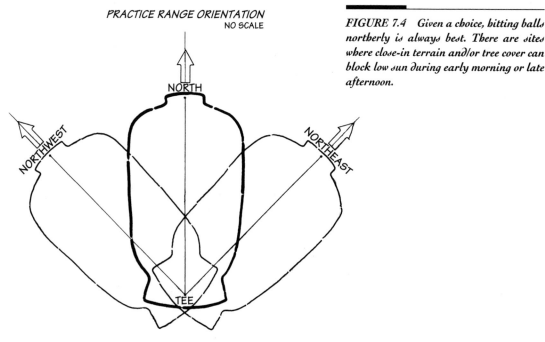

PRACTICE RANGE ORIENTATION
NO SCALE

NORTH

NORTHWEST

NORTHEAST

TEE

FIGURE 7.4 Given a choice, hitting balls northerly is always best. There are sites where close-in terrain and/or tree cover can block low sun during early morning or late afternoon.

- Other orientations are acceptable if the tee is not directed into the rising or setting sun, the very hours when most golfers wish to practice. In establishing where the sun rises and sets in different seasons, planners may inquire at local meteorological stations. Also, consider whether close-in terrain or tree cover will block objectionable early morning or late afternoon sun. For example, at the latitude of Boston, Massachusetts, the sun sets in the northwest at the height of the playing season, even though many say it sets in the west. Orientation to the south can work where latitude and time of year keeps the sun high during most of the midday.
- Target greens with bunkers situated at different distances from the tee. In placing them, it should be observed that players prefer staggered positions. Still, if space is constrained, target greens in line down the center help direct shots toward the center and away from out-of-bounds. Each green has an area of 2,000 to 3,000 square feet. To assist in retrieving balls, the bunker "sand" may be limestone of a type that will harden, allowing the ball retriever to pick balls from it more easily (Figures 7.5 and 7.6).

FIGURE 7.5   The target green sizes and outlines can vary, but having them all bowl shaped and sloped down to the front helps everyone to see where the ball hits and also helps to collect the shots.

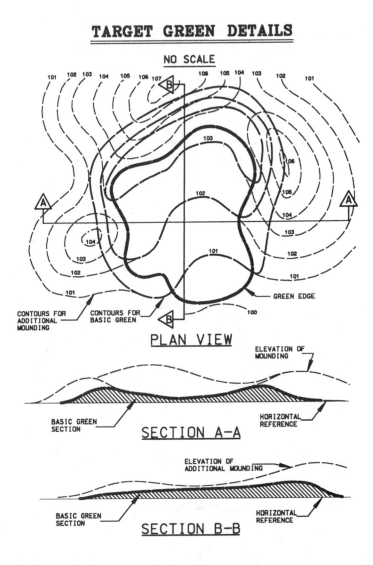

FIGURE 7.6   The target greens don't show very well because of mowing height, but the bunkers help to locate them.

- Irrigation for the tee and, ideally, the fairway.
- A beautifully landscaped tee. Chairs in alcoves set among shrubs in the rear of the tee are popular, and landscaped parking areas with aesthetically pleasing surfaces add to eye appeal.
- A tee of the highest quality.

Aqua Ranges

Where space is limited, some owners using floating balls adapt reservoirs and other expanses of waters for practice fairways. Aqua ranges are functional and appear popular, partly owing to their novelty. However, a "floater" does not fly as far as a regulation ball, and the novelty can wear off (Figures 7.7 and 7.8).

FIGURE 7.7 This water collection basin, part of a hotel complex in Reno, Nevada, was effectively developed for the additional purpose of a golf practice range. Although the ball reacts differently (shorter distance carried), particularly with the longer clubs, this is still an effective way to practice.

FIGURE 7.8 The large lake directly north of the clubhouse was needed as part of the irrigation water storage system. Using floating balls, it doubles nicely as a practice fairway.

Practice Putting Greens

Ideally, the practice putting green is located between the pro shop and the first tee (Figure 7.9). Yet a second green can be favorably received when set elsewhere, even on the front lawn of the clubhouse or in the entry circle. The latter location, however, can lead to accidents if golfers step off the pavement. Siting a second or third practice green near the 10th tee is also popular.

Superintendents prefer the total area in a putting green to be 12,000 square feet or more but have found that two separate greens, each about 6,000 square feet, are more functional for maintenance than a single large one.

The putting surface, including contours and putting qualities, should resemble the 18 greens as closely as possible. Nevertheless, most of the green should be flat so that golfers can work on distance and straightness before practicing putts that break. Construction of the highest quality is required.

FIGURE 7.9 Located ideally between the clubhouse and the first tee, this practice green at Widgi Creek Golf Club in Bend, Oregon, has every type of putt, from flat to steep.

Practice Pitching Greens

Pitching and chipping balls to the practice putting green can create a hazard or prevent others from putting. Therefore, a separate green is needed, often at a site some distance from other practice facilities where players may shag their own balls (Figure 7.10). Features of such greens include

- An area of 3,000 square feet or more with contours and texture of turf equal to those of greens on the course. In this era of increased golfing sophistication players expect this close relationship.
- One face bunker, and probably a second requiring the player to play over sand.
- A grass pot and a sand pot even if there are no pot bunkers on the course. Players want to practice from pots before visiting other layouts in the vicinity or before traveling to the British Isles where pot bunkers are commonplace.
- Fairway and rough areas for pitching and chipping, along with a fringe swale.

PRACTICE PITCHING /CHIPPING GREEN
APPROX. SCALE: 1" = 30'

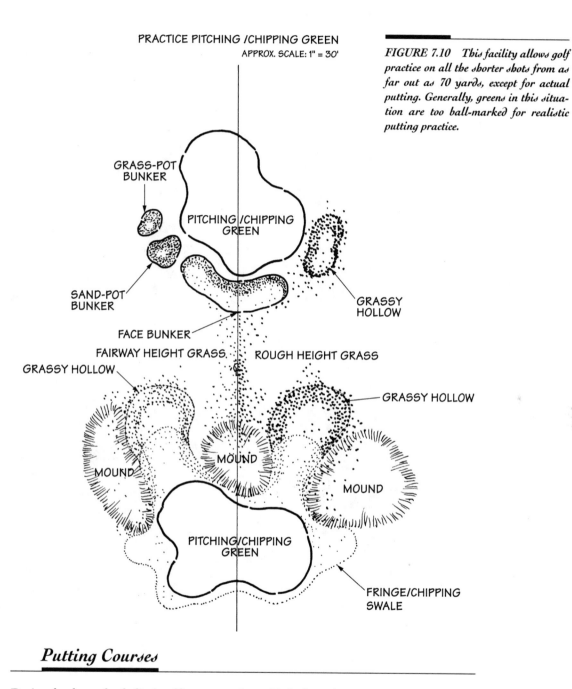

GRASS-POT
BUNKER

PITCHING /CHIPPING
GREEN

SAND-POT
BUNKER

GRASSY
HOLLOW

FACE BUNKER

FAIRWAY HEIGHT GRASS   ROUGH HEIGHT GRASS

GRASSY HOLLOW

GRASSY HOLLOW

MOUND

MOUND

MOUND

PITCHING/CHIPPING
GREEN

FRINGE/CHIPPING
SWALE

FIGURE 7.10   This facility allows golf practice on all the shorter shots from as far out as 70 yards, except for actual putting. Generally, greens in this situation are too ball-marked for realistic putting practice.

Putting Courses

Dating back to the ladies' golfing ground established in the 1800s at St. Andrews, putting courses are popular at clubs, resorts, and other layouts around the globe (Figures 7.11 and 7.12). In fact, several stand on their own as daily-fee layouts. Often flood-lit for night play, they require ½ to 2 acres of land.

Putting courses are not always laid out as one very large putting surface, as is the ladies' course at St. Andrews. Rather, they can be 9 or 18 ribbons of putting surface, each 20 to 90 feet in length, set between grass roughs, collection areas, sand, water, ledge rock, trees, and out-of-bounds. Doglegs can be included, with the "fairway" contoured to permit a putt to the hole, and shot values can be incorporated.

FIGURE 7.11 *This putting course at Angel Park in Las Vegas, Nevada, is part of a complete golf facility including an 18-hole golf course and practice range.*

FIGURE 7.12 *Langdon Farms, near Wilsonville, Oregon, features this putting course, along with an 18-hole standard golf course and practice range. (Photo by J. D. Mowlds, P.G.A.)*

The possibility of emulating their own full-length layout in miniature when planning a putting course has been discussed by several clubs, and architect Scott Miller actually imitated the routing and numbers of the Old Course at St. Andrews for a senior center in Mission Viejo, California.

Children's Courses

Children's courses with three or more holes have been introduced at clubs and daily-fee layouts with varying degrees of success. Problems have arisen, in that sooner or later the space is needed for another program, or parents playing with their children demand maintenance standards that are too high and too expensive. Hole yardages provided for children under 12 years are 100 yards or less (Figure 7.13).

FIGURE 7.13 Children's golf courses, such as this diagram depicts, provide shots from 60 to 130 yards with many angles to deal with over and around guarding bunkers.

Warm-up Courses

Some clubs and daily-fee courses provide two or three holes for players to warm up before embarking on the 18-hole round (Figure 7.14). These facilities are assets when maintained at the standard of the regular layout.

FIGURE 7.14 An expanded version of the children's golf course, this layout provides shots ranging from 95 to 385 yards with just about every in-between length covered.

Par 3 and Approach Courses

Par 3 and approach courses of 9 or 18 holes have been popular to a greater or lesser degree at established clubs and daily-fee layouts for many years. (Approach courses are par 3 layouts with no tees, thus allowing players to select shots.) Sometimes par 3 layouts operate on their own as for-profit ventures. Blue Rock at South Yarmouth on Cape Cod, opening as a daily-fee course in the early 1960s, attracts players from far and wide. Established on some 40 acres with a separate practice fairway, it calls for the use of all clubs. Greens average about 5,000 square feet, with water and sand hazards approximating those on regulation layouts. Blue Rock's score card is as follows:

Hole	Yards	Hole	Yards
1	103	10	147
2	113	11	111
3	113	12	200
4	130	13	150
5	248	14	181
6	145	15	177
7	170	16	141
8	153	17	120
9	160	18	170
Out	1,335	In	1,397
		Out	1,335
		Total	2,732

Pitch-and-Putts and Chip-and-Putts

On limited acreage, with greens averaging 500 to 2,000 square feet, pitch-and-putt and chip-and-putt courses have been added at several established clubs (Figure 7.15).

FIGURE 7.15   Hillcrest Country Club located in Los Angeles, California, added an interesting amenity to its facilities by converting a 2-acre parcel near the clubhouse to a 6-hole pitch-and-putt course. Lengths range from 20 to 50 yds. It is maintained to the same exacting specifications as the club's 18-hole golf course.

More often they are daily-fee layouts floodlit for night play and operated with a profit motive.

The pitch-and-putt at Turnberry Hotel in Scotland has long been a model world-wide (Figures 7.16 and 7.17), while Hillman's at Elmwood Park, New Jersey, which ranks among the oldest commercial pitch-and-putts in the United States, has been open since 1954 on seven acres with this card:

Hole	Yards	Hole	Yards
1	50	10	45
2	75	11	50
3	45	12	80
4	60	13	70
5	45	14	40
6	40	15	50
7	60	16	40
8	50	17	60
9	60	18	45
Out	485	In	480
		Out	485
		Total	965

FIGURE 7.16   Here is a portion of the popular pitch-and-putt course at the Turnberry Hotel in Scotland. It allows a variety of iron shots and is a favorite with golfers of all age groups and skill levels.

FIGURE 7.17   The Turnberry Hotel short course features bunkers and mounding similar to those encountered on the big course. It's a great place to practice your short game or to warm up for Turnberry's two full-length courses.

Executive (or Precision) Courses

With total length somewhere between a par 3 and a regulation course, executive (or precision) layouts appeal to many golfers (Figure 7.18). An 18-holer can require 80 acres plus an area for a practice fairway. Numbers of par 3s, 4s, and 5s in the circuit vary, but with par 3s exceeding the total number of 4s and 5s. Greens and tees are the same size as on regular layouts. The card for Kingsway at Yarmouth Port on Cape Cod, Massachusetts, is the following:

Hole	Yards	Par	Hole	Yards	Par
1	346	4	10	215	3
2	198	3	11	193	3
3	155	3	12	297	4
4	375	4	13	167	3
5	124	3	14	167	3
6	189	3	15	138	3
7	157	3	16	181	3
8	147	3	17	211	3
9	409	4	18	354	4
Out	2,100	30	In	1,923	29
			Out	2,100	30
			Total	4,023	59

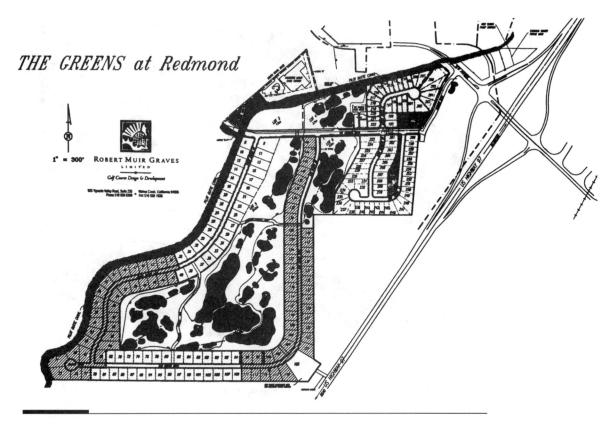

FIGURE 7.18   *This executive golf course is essentially a core layout with two par 4s and the rest a variety of different length par 3s ranging from 78 yards to 210 yards.*

Learning Centers

Learning centers are comprehensive practice facilities slanted toward teaching. The majority function strictly as learning centers or schools, although some are also open to the public on a green-fee basis.

These facilities first came into being in the 1960s. An early objective was to attract people to major ski resorts in summer months when room occupancy was low.

The Stratton Golf School at Stratton Mountain, Vermont, was a pioneer in 1969 (Figure 7.19). First conceived as an instruction facility for youths, it soon evolved into a school for all age groups.

Originally, Stratton's elaborate practice facility featured ponds, with youthful attendees retrieving balls when swimming in the evening. As it evolved to include all age groups, the ponds were eliminated because of problems encountered in recovering balls.

An increasing number of golf schools have emerged in recent decades. Some are commuting schools with little or no connection to hotels or motels. A number of courses use their existing practice facilities for schools, but many construct specially designed areas similar to the Stratton's (Figure 7.20).

Architect Michael Hurdzan describes a learning center of his design near Cincinnati in the November 1995 issue of *Golf Course News*. It includes a 9-hole executive layout, a circular driving range divided into three sections including a 49-tee area, a 25-tee

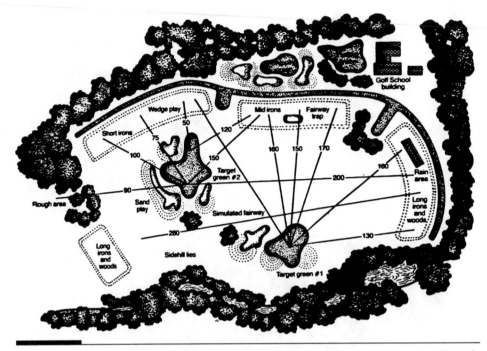

FIGURE 7.19 *The Stratton Golf School, on 22 acres at Stratton Mountain, Vermont, allows the golfer to hit shots from any number of different locations. This practice area offers two large target greens, wide fairway areas, bunkers, and an expansive putting green for chipping and pitching.*

instruction area, and a 1½-acre bent grass green with mounds, bunkers, chipping areas, and depressions.

Foy and Beljan describe World Wood Golf Club, Brooksville, Florida, as offering the ultimate. It includes a 22-acre practice park with eight separate teeing areas, a 2-acre putting green, three practice holes, an iron range, and a 9-hole short course.

Rustic Golf

Short courses and learning centers have become "sandlots" for golfers. Yet until after World War II, rudimentary layouts established on pastures, open areas in parks, other large lawns, abandoned golf courses, and real estate available for a season or more were sandlots for many.

Rough hewn as they were, these rustic layouts provided many a person his or her first experience of the Royal and Ancient game. Unfortunately, today's litigious society poses the constant fear of liability, and owners of open spaces are less likely to permit this use of their vacant property. Still, the role of rustic golf in North America is in many ways similar to the role of the links and their free play in the early centuries of the game.

Rustic golf lingers in many forms. One sees cowboys in the West playing from tee mats over sagebrush and prairie grasses to areas cleared for greens and sometimes oiled. It seems dedicated golfers worldwide who have no formal courses manage to find rustic areas for rudimentary layouts.

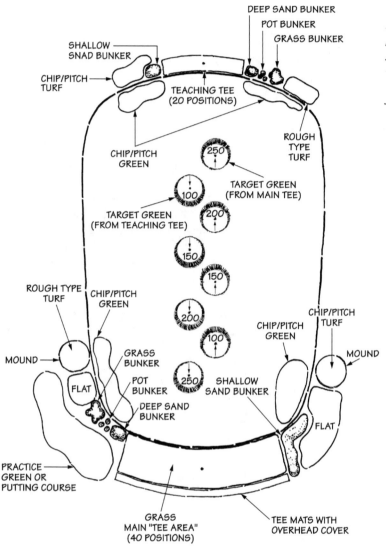

FIGURE 7.20 *Here is a complete practice area where the dedicated golfer can work on every type of golf shot, either from the normal usage tee or the teaching-end tee. A unique feature includes the mounds in the rough and chip/pitch turf areas where golfers can work on uphill, downhill and side-hill lies.*

Golf on Fewer Acres—Cayman Golf

by William Amick
Golf Course Architect,
Daytona Beach, Florida

In the 1930s, Indianapolis-based golf course architect William H. Diddel originated the concept of reducing the size of courses by using a ball less lively than the standard ball. In the early 1980s, Jack Nicklaus persuaded the MacGregor Golf Company to manufacture a ball for a small course that his design company was developing on Grand Cayman Island in the Carribean. An improved version of that ball is now manufactured and sold by the Cayman Golf Company of Albany, Georgia. The company's president, Troy Puckett, holds the patent. At first the game was termed "modified golf." Now, the ball is named "the Cayman," and the game is called Cayman golf.

Advantages to Cayman Golf

- The Cayman ball is easier to get airborne; therefore it motivates beginners and, in turn, golf teachers like it.
- The ball is lightweight, making it less dangerous to passersby and property.
- Cayman golf provides exciting golf with a competitive game on courses a fraction the size and cost of regular courses. They are also shorter to walk and, accordingly, quicker to play.
- A reduced set of clubs may be possible.

Such advantages make Cayman golf enjoyable, at lower fees, for occasional and less serious men golfers, many women, senior men, young people, disabled persons, and beginners.

Eagle Landing, near Charleston, South Carolina, provides an example of how such courses can be laid out (Figures 7.21, 7.22, 7.23). Designed by the writer of this section, Eagle Landing was the first 18-hole Cayman course in the United States. Several other courses have since been constructed in Japan, England, and the United States. The card for Eagle Landing is as follows, with the yardage equivalent for the standard ball:

Hole	Par	Back Tee Yardages	Approximate Equivalent Yards with Standard Ball
1	4	245	408
2	5	343	571
3	3	98	163
4	4	222	370
5	4	278	463
6	4	263	438
7	4	260	433
8	5	290	483
9	3	125	208
Out	36	2,124	3,537
10	4	210	350
11	3	112	187
12	4	218	363
13	3	138	230
14	5	350	583
15	4	250	416
16	4	272	453
17	5	305	508
18	4	252	420
In	36	2,107	3,510
Out	36	2,124	3,537
Total	72	4,231	7,047

FIGURES 7.21, 7.22, 7.23   Here are three views of the popular Eagle Landing Golf Course in Charleston, South Carolina. The first Cayman golf course in the United States, Eagle Landing measures 4,231 yards from the back tee. (Photos by William Amick)

Construction
and Grow-In

Constructing the Golf Course

> *Bunkers should be used sparingly by the architect. Except on one-shot holes they should never be placed within 200 yards of the tee. Ridges and depressions are the best way of controlling the entrance to the green. The best hazard on a course is a fairway bunker 200 to 235 yards from the tee, placed 5 to 10 yards off the accomplished player's most favorable line to the green.*
>
> From *Concerning Golf,* 1903, by John Laing Low (1869–1929)

This chapter outlines construction procedures in one of several logical sequences. Generally, the constructor is responsible for determining sequence, means, methods, and techniques for executing the work described in the contract documents prepared by the architect. However, the architect may specify that certain percentages be completed by certain dates. The architect may also specify that environmental measures and sediment control be completed according to plan by specified dates. The architect should also review the contractor's critical path, or sequencing of his work, but should agree to flexibility to accommodate weather and other factors.

Erosion and Sediment Control

Golf courses yield innumerable environmental benefits. Yet there are negative aspects. Overall objectives embraced in course design are to enhance beneficial and reduce negative environmental impacts.

The construction period is one in which environmental degradation, sometimes immense, can occur. For weeks or months the land is devoid of vegetation and subject to excessive wind, water, ice, and gravity erosion. Techniques for partial control of erosion and sediment during this critical "unvegetated" period and the weeks following, when turfgrass covering is sparse and root growth is shallow, include the following:

1. Using rapidly germinating cover crops prior to seeding when the ground would otherwise be bare. Two species commonly used are the cereal winter rye, in seasons subject to freezing, and buckwheat in frost-free periods. Each provides a cover crop for otherwise bare ground. In addition, these crops can be sown immediately prior to or over the permanent grass seed to provide early cover and thus fortify the seedling grass against erosion. (Both disappear with regular mowing.)
2. Including rapidly germinating grasses such as ryegrass in the seed mixture, if this will not compromise the future greensward as it would a bent grass green or fairway.
3. Hydroseeding, along with use of mulches, natural or synthetic, applied dry or hydraulically.
4. Using erosion control blankets of various types, with or without seed contained in them.

5. Sodding areas where runoff is rapid or concentrated, such as steep banks and channels.
6. Limiting traffic close to stream banks and installing as few temporary crossings as possible.
7. Installing water bars or berms to deflect water on slopes and in channels before it gains sufficient volume and momentum to cause scouring (Figure 8.1).
8. Using straw bales, silt fences, sediment ponds, and basins to catch sediment once it has started to move (Figures 8.2 and 8.3).
9. Incorporating biological and engineering principles. John McCulla, landscape architect, states that management practice may integrate biology and engineering principles to achieve erosion control.[1] Examples include the use of live cuttings on stream banks, vegetated gabions, and cellular confinement systems involving three-dimensional mats with cells planted to grass or other species.
10. Preserving existing trees and other vegetation, including weeds when possible and desirable.
11. Controlling dust by providing parking lots for the construction crew and visitors, limiting traffic in all possible ways, planting stockpiles with cover crops or covering them with erosion control blankets, using water trucks, refraining from cultivating and smoothing seedbeds until immediately prior to seeding and perhaps letting weeds flourish until then. Use of toxic chemicals for dust control is seldom possible on golf courses. Yet research may provide products in the near future that can be used.

FIGURE 8.1   Beginning at the top, this shaper is creating a swale/berm that will intercept surface water before it reaches the golf course. (Photo by Phil Arnold)

FIGURE 8.2   *At Woodcreek Oaks in Roseville, California, straw bales, silt fences, and other means were used to control erosion during construction.*

FIGURE 8.3   *Silt fencing was also used to keep out vandals and curious passersby while the important work of studying, identifying, and protecting the wetlands was under way.*

   D. N. Austin and T. Driver emphasize that keeping soil in place is far more effective than trapping it once it has been suspended in water or air.[2]
   Specifications for erosion and sediment control are included with the contract documents. They are generally prepared by the architect, working with an engineer or environmental consultant who is skilled and experienced in their preparation and in meeting with the authorities who will review them.

Staking and Clearing

These important links in the critical path or chain leading to a great golf course involve:

1. Staking and clearing a center line on each hole. Staking is executed by a surveyor, who follows the architect's plan to place stakes at 100- to 200-foot intervals and at pivot points (Figure 8.4; see also Figure 4.9).
2. The architect checking this center line, making adjustments when needed.
3. Clearing up to 75% of the width of the hole. Final clearing widths are often 100 feet minimum at tees, 200 feet at greens, and 180 to 250 feet on the rest of the hole.
4. Flagging the final clearing limits in accordance with the plan. This flagging is often executed by the architect, who recognizes the importance of an undulating tree line (Figure 8.5).
5. Clearing to these limits, with the architect designating specimen trees that are to remain. The architect may also call for removal of trees that will in the future

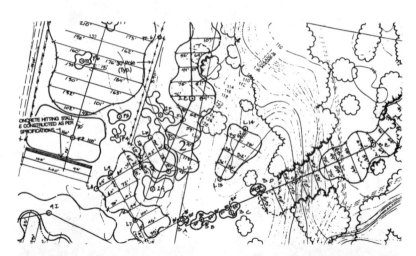

FIGURE 8.4   This portion of a staking plan demonstrates how off-set dimensions, spaced at appropriate intervals, can be used to lay out or field check the size and shape of a tee, fairway, lake, or other large feature. Greens and bunkers are typically shown at a larger scale on separate drawings.

FIGURE 8.5   Using the surveyed center-line stake, with a PVC pipe extension for visibility, the golf course architect is often faced with the unpleasant task of deciding which trees must be moved or removed during clearing operations.

shade greens, tees, or other areas, causing ice problems and curtailing air circulation.

6. Clearing pathways from greens to tees, as well as maintenance paths from hole to hole.

Clearing

Tree removal involves clearcutting and removing trees and their stumps on playing areas, along with selective clearing of woods adjoining these areas (Figure 8.6).

Clearcutting is required on all playing areas, including greens, surrounds, tees, fairways, grassed roughs, and paths (see Figure 4.9). There are two methods for clearcutting:

1. Bulldozing trees and stumps directly into piles and burning them, a procedure no longer permitted in many jurisdictions.
2. Felling trees and disposing of them by one of the following means:
   a. Burning, if permitted.
   b. Deep burying on each hole, if permitted and if soil conditions are such that the wood will not rot and cause settling in the future. Thorough compaction of debris is mandatory, with no voids left, followed by covering it with 4 or more feet of fill plus topsoil. A permit for burying is probably required. Many such dumps require drainage in the form of tile, otherwise the area above or near the dump may take on boglike characteristics. Rotting wood may also produce an oily substance that oozes from the pit and damages turf.
   c. Carting all trees to conveniently located central dumps on- or off-site.
   d. Chipping. Chips are disposed of through sales or used elsewhere for development.
   e. Selling timber for lumber or firewood. Branches are then buried or chipped.

FIGURE 8.6   Clearing in heavy forests requires massive amounts of machinery work and hand labor. Often the timber removed in clearing has some market value that helps offset construction costs.

Selective Clearing

Selective clearing is executed in areas 40 feet or more from the edges of the clearcut, sometimes from hole to hole and on some courses wall-to-wall on the entire tract. Areas out of play are not selectively cleared, in order to provide cover for wildlife. Four objectives of selective clearing are to permit air circulation and light across the greensward, to speed play by helping golfers find balls, to reduce unplayable lies, and to allow remaining trees to develop impressively.

Selective clearing includes the following steps:

1. Removing windfalls, logs, and underbrush, along with dead or dying trees and stumps, fences, and all other debris.
2. Pruning lower branches—dead, dying, and living—to a height of 6 to 8 feet, taking great care to remove sharp branches that can cause eye injuries and other harm.
3. Removing sufficient trees to permit mowing if the area is to be grassed.
4. Removing surface stones to prevent golf club damage, whether or not the area is to be grassed.
5. On occasion, grassing these areas to produce a beautiful "English park" effect. From the standpoints of play, maintenance, and eye appeal this grassing is desirable, but not necessarily so for wildlife. Here the architect's judgment is called upon to create both cover for wildlife and pleasurable golf.
6. Conserving pine needle roughs. Pine needle ground covers can be attractive and playable in forest areas.

Grubbing of Clearcut Areas

Once trees are cleared, all remaining stumps and surface stones must be removed. This operation, termed "grubbing," involves the following:

1. Stumps are removed with root rakes attached to bulldozers and are then disposed of. Backhoes and power shovels can also be used. The area must then be further grubbed to remove lateral roots and other debris. Large chippers are sometimes available to chip stumps.
2. If the grubbing operation involves removing medium- to large-sized stones and boulders, the grubbing by bulldozer with attached root rake is completed at least once the length of the hole and then at right angles. The specified depth of grubbing varies from 8 to 12 inches, although depths below 8 inches may not be attainable.
3. Selectively cleared areas are grubbed on occasion, although extensive damage to roots of remaining trees can occur if painstaking care is not taken. Stumps in these areas are sometimes removed chemically or by grinding.

Other Tree Work

When preparing specifications for clearing, both clearcutting and selective, the architect may include branch pruning at 6 to 8 feet above ground. Sometimes the architect specifies arboricultural or tree surgery, particularly on specimen trees in proximity to playing areas, and root pruning of trees bordering the greensward. More often than not, arboricultural work and root pruning are done later, after the course is opened for play and under direction of the superintendent.

Lightning rods installed on specimen trees may also be specified or recommended.

Earth Moving

In contrast with minimalist layouts where existing contours are merely modified, creating a sculpted golf course requires moving immense quantities of earth—sometimes more than a million cubic yards for 18 holes. For any course, however, whether sculpted or minimalist, some amount of earth is moved. This reshaping of natural terrain is one measure of an architect's talent (Figure 8.7).

FIGURE 8.7   The mass earth moving is completed, and now the smaller "cat" must smooth out the work and ensure uniform soil quality throughout the golf course.

Stripping and stockpiling the topsoil is mandatory to conserve this valuable resource. When doing so, the constructor ensures that the area stripped is large enough that the stockpile does not have to be moved a second time to complete the earthwork needed to bring the feature to the subgrade stage. Contractors remove and stockpile topsoil from the first area to be worked, grade the area, and then topsoil it with material from the second area, proceeding progressively. This reduces the number of times topsoil is removed.

Heavy Earth Moving

Heavy earth moving involves bringing greens, tees, ponds, bunkers, and other features to subgrade. It is also required to

- Create landing areas that allow golfers reasonably even, if not absolutely flat, stances as contrasted with sidehill, uphill, or downhill lies
- Ensure visibility
- Ensure surface drainage
- Create water bars to deflect water that would otherwise erode the soil, forming channels and steep banks (see Figure 8.1).

Ledge Rock

Earth moving may involve removal and disposal of ledge rock. Ledge is encountered as solid rock outcroppings or boulders on the surface or below ground. Boulder size to qualify as ledge is specified by the architect. Ledge is also encountered as trench rock during trench excavation.

Because quantities of ledge and trench rock are difficult to estimate, a price per cubic yard for removal and disposal is usually called for on the bid or proposal form. Different prices apply for rock requiring drilling and dynamiting, boulders that can be removed by heavy equipment, and "soft" ledge that can be ripped and then removed.

Shaping

The final shaping of features following heavy earth moving is critical to the creation of a course of distinction. Talented shapers are available to create the features envisioned by the architect. Or the architect may supervise this operation personally because of its intrinsic importance to playability, aesthetics, and his or her own reputation. When earth moving, it is essential to avoid overuse of a haul road that causes severe compaction, which can compromise turf quality far into the future.

Pond Construction

Ponds are created on golf courses to provide playing interest and beauty, to act as reservoirs, and to provide fill and topsoil for other purposes. Varying from a few thousand square feet, or even less, to more than several acres, some ponds are truly lakes.

Obviously, planning a pond requires a source of water. Depending on circumstances, the sources can be adjoining streams, wells, runoff, or a year-round high water table.

There are two types of golf course ponds. One is a dug pond, a hole excavated below ground level. The other is created by an embankment or dam. There are also combinations (Figure 8.8). Generally, a minimum 6-foot depth of water is called for in wet regions, while 15 or more feet may be required in arid regions and in cold areas to allow fish to survive under ice. Greater depths are better to inhibit weed growth and to keep water fresh and cool.

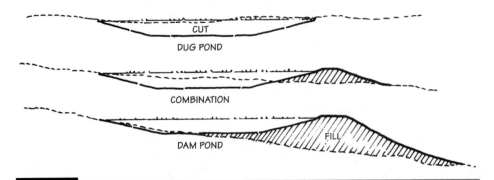

FIGURE 8.8   The three generalized methods of lake construction are shown here. The combined method is the most prevalent, whereas the dam method is used least. Blending a dam into a natural landscape is not an easy task.

If banks above water level are to be grassed and mowed, as contrasted with bulk-heading, a slope not to exceed 1 foot vertical for each 3 feet horizontal is desirable, although somewhat steeper slopes may be mowable. Banks below water level should be as steep as physically possible and as local and other ordinances permit. Generally, a 1 to 3 slope is maximum for installation of a plastic membrane with soil cover. A steep bank below the water line reduces weed growth and can be achieved in stable soils such as clays, but not in sand or gravel (Figure 8.9). Unfortunately, steep banks can be hazardous. Critics claim that they can contribute to drowning accidents. From the standpoint of safety, a 5 to 1 (or 1 to 5) slope is desirable.

TYPICAL LAKE CROSS SECTIONS

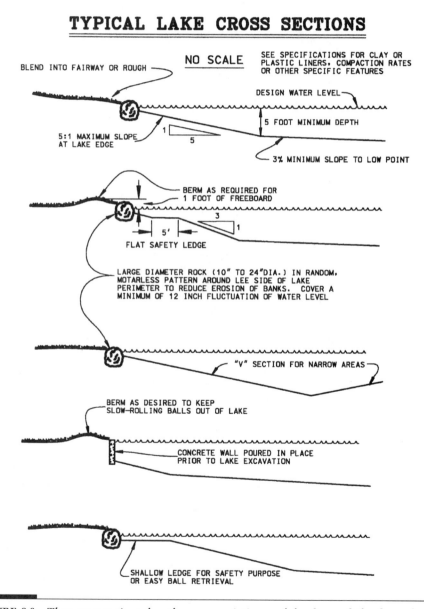

FIGURE 8.9 *These cross sections show the many variations on lake edges and the edge embankment. Each has advantages and disadvantages. Safety, ball retrieval, aquatic weed growth, and other maintenance considerations must be addressed.*

Freeboard, the distance from water level as determined by the overflow to the top of the surrounding bank, is regulated in some jurisdictions. Adequate freeboard is desirable because too high a water level in a pond will affect drainage on surrounding playing areas, although a pond with water level flush with the fairway produces a soothing appearance.

If a stream is the source of water, it should seldom enter the pond directly, because it can cause sedimentation. Exceptions to this rule can be made if the pond is intended as a silt basin or if the pond is merely the widening of a water course. A method to prevent sedimentation in a golf pond is to create a bypass whereby water from the stream is fed into the pond through a pipe leading from a barrel placed upstream (Figures 8.10, 8.11).

FIGURE 8.10   Here the barrel is remote from the stream source but still can function to collect sediment.

FIGURE 8.11   With the barrel as the inlet, water goes directly to the lake. To remove sediment, there must be an outlet on the bottom to a termination point. Otherwise the barrel sediment would have to be pumped out.

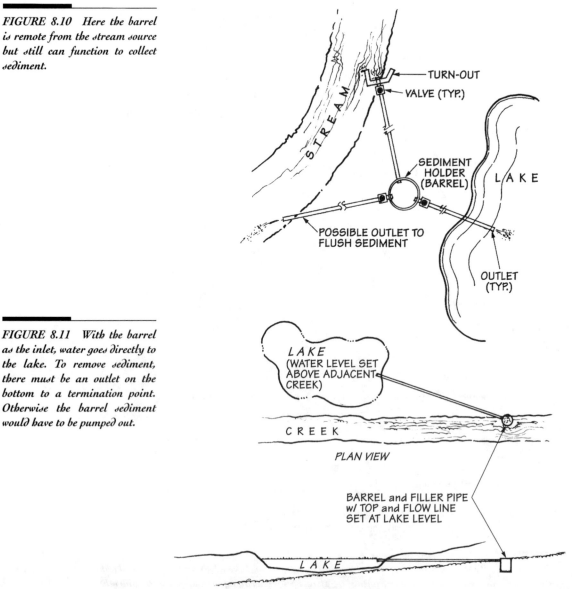

Bulkheading pond banks with wood (often railroad ties), stone, or concrete to stabilize embankments by preventing wave action, rodent intrusion, and other forms of
erosion can create a striking effect. This also enables the architect to require shots over
water across nearly vertical bulkheads to the green, as contrasted with shots over water
and a long grass bank sloping down to it (Figures 8.12 and 8.13).

*FIGURE 8.12   At Seven Oaks Golf Club in Bakersfield, California, a concrete bulkhead or wall
was poured first and then the lake was excavated. When filled with water, the concrete is well hidden.*

*FIGURE 8.13   The most natural juncture between water and grass is the grassy slope. However, it
provides little protection against the wind and wave action that can cause scouring and sloughing off
of the banks.*

An outlet from the pond is also needed. A device that meets this requirement and yet allows the pond to be drained is a trickle tube (Figure 8.14). The tube is fabricated to permit lowering or raising the pond level or draining the pond entirely in order to remove silt and other sediments and to retrieve balls. If complete drainage of the pond is not called for, it can be drained by a horizontal pipe set at the desired water level (Figure 8.15).

Golf course architects should be aware of a telescoping valve (T-valve) used primarily for engineering projects such as water treatment plants. For very small or shallow ponds a T-valve would not be cost effective as compared with the more prevalent overflow pipe and valve system. However, in large and deep lakes where more constant water level control is important, the T-valve with its telescoping inlet could be the answer.

In a golf course drainage study, Theodore L. Bohlander Jr., civil and sanitary engineer, states:

> It is the application of the adjustable height overflow pipe with the capability to empty a reservoir that seems most appropriate to [this] line of work. Recreational lakes and ponds require periodic maintenance along the shoreline including trimming of grasses, removal of brush and weeds, and the removal of nuisance aquatic growth lying submerged just off shore. It is a nice feature to quickly adjust water levels so that these tasks can be accomplished. For those conditions requiring the structure to be empty (removing accumu-

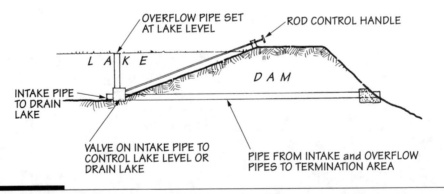

FIGURE 8.14   *This trickle tube is simply a vertical overflow pipe to a junction where a valve can be installed to let water out as desired.*

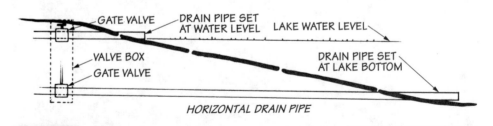

FIGURE 8.15   *This simple drain is inexpensive but with the pipe installed at water level does not offer much in the way of level control. Closing the valve will allow the level to rise, but there is no way to change the lower levels except by filling and water usage or seepage. Installing the pipe at the lake bottom simply allows the lake to be drained for maintenance work.*

lated sedimentation [and] deep water aquatic growth) or perimeter bank repair of the pond (lake), the valve can be placed in its fully retracted position.[3]

In addition to the controlled outlet, an emergency spillway is needed for flood periods. The spillway must be reinforced by strong turf or, in some cases, by concrete or wood.

Pervious soils may require sealing, achieved through the use of clay soils purchased or derived on-site. Bentonite is the preferred clay type. Sealing is also achieved through use of synthetic liners. Several types are on the market. All are flexible membranes. Critical to their effectiveness are the selection of the appropriate thickness, gluing the sheets together, and anchoring the perimeters (Figure 8.16).

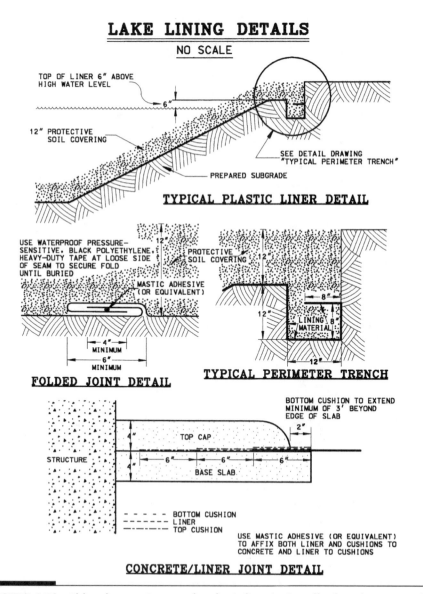

FIGURE 8.16 *Although expensive, use of a plastic liner is virtually the only way to achieve a 100% seal.*

There are laws, rules, and regulations governing installation of ponds and lakes, and special permits are often required. It is therefore recommended that the planner engage the services of a registered engineer or proceed only after close consultation with the National Resources Conservation Service of the U.S. Department of Agriculture.

Still, the architect is the person who plans the configuration of the pond because it creates beauty, strategy, and interest. Indeed, pond configuration may be the dominant feature of a hole.

Irrigation and Drainage Installation

Drainage and irrigation systems are discussed in detail in Chapters 9 and 10, respectively. System installation follows completion of shaping but precedes the returning of topsoil. This sequence reduces later settling over pipelines and the possibility of stone and debris generated by trench excavation becoming mixed with the topsoil.

Topsoiling

Topsoiling involves returning stripped topsoil and, if needed, adding additional topsoil to fairways and roughs, along with preparing or purchasing special root zone mixes for greens and tees.

Once topsoil (or a root zone mix) is in place, the area is ready for preparation of seed beds and seeding.

Golf Course Structures

Required structures on golf courses include shelters, paths, stream crossings, steps or stairs, and an equipment building. Shelters and the equipment building require state-of-the-art lightning protection. (An alarm system for players and others on the course, if installed, is generally housed in the clubhouse.)

Paths

Golf cars and all-weather paths make it possible to play golf late into life. They also accelerate play and make the game more attractive for many, especially on hilly courses. Their use nationwide has increased profitability and numbers of people playing golf.

The surfacing of car paths is commonly asphalt, concrete, stone preparations, or stone dust. In recent years colored (often red) brick paving stone, although costly, has become popular because of its handsome appearance.

Stone dust tends to scour in early spring or other periods of heavy runoff if situated on steep slopes. This material and other stone preparations also present dust problems in dry periods if irrigation water does not reach them. Yet both are functional if constantly replenished. Later, when necessary, they can be topped with asphalt or concrete if they are originally laid carefully with adequate drainage.

Organic materials have been tried, including barks and other components of several tree species—tanbark, wood chips, licorice roots, and nut hulls. Unfortunately, they decompose rapidly on a permanent car surface and must be replenished constantly. Still, they are useful for temporary surfaces and can provide attractive finishes for pedestrian walkways through wooded areas. Seashells have also been used. Although striking in appearance, they too deteriorate.

Curbs on pathways are needed at greens and tees to prevent golfers from driving golf cars onto tee slopes and green surrounds. Curbing a path and shaping it to carry water during periods of heavy runoff has been tried as a form of drainage. A problem arises, however, in that these "aquapaths" ice over on cold nights in spring and autumn and remain slippery late into the morning. Even on summer days, following rainstorms, they may remain slippery for several hours. Accordingly, the use of paths as water channels is seldom recommended.

Some recommend the use of curbs for the entire length of a path to keep cars on it,[4] with a standard width of 5 to 8 feet with one architect installing 12- to 14-feet wide double-lane paths. We have observed that 6 to 8 feet is a common range for path widths. One of several methods for constructing hard-topped car paths is described in Figure 8.17.

FIGURE 8.17   *Slip form concrete is about to be poured here. The car path has been graded to leave the concrete surface flush with the adjacent soil. The machine will pour on top of the grade if desired, as no extra form is needed. (Photo courtesy of Gary Paumen)*

Materials are available for strengthening turf at both ends of a path to prevent the development of holes. These include plastic and other materials fabricated so that grass grows through them. New and promising materials for this purpose continue to reach the market. Chemicals once available to stabilize existing soil along the entire route are seldom used today. Swerving the path also reduces such wear (see Figure 3.14).

Golf car and pedestrian pathways through woods can be attractively landscaped and become features that impress players.

Stream Crossings

Culverts, preferably with a headwall at each end, suffice for many crossings. Yet environmentalists may not approve culverting of streams. In practice, a permit will be needed. A problem also arises concerning size, in that the pipe must be of sufficiently large diameter to carry the entire flow during periods of exceptional runoff, unless some form of overflow is provided for such periods.

Bridges may therefore prove to be most satisfactory, although more expensive. Yet they can add charm to a golf hole. Among the various types that can be used are stone bridges (Figures 8.18 and 8.19), reminiscent of the ancient bridge on the Old Course, and the red brick bridges that attracted wide attention at the Senior Open at Cherry Hills Country Club near Denver Co. in 1993. Boardwalks over wetlands appear to be acceptable environmentally and are attractive as well (Figures 8.20 and 8.21).

FIGURE 8.18 This is certainly the most photographed bridge in the golf world, over Swilcan Burn at St. Andrews. Coauthor Cornish advises all who would practice golf course architecture to visit St. Andrews, crossing this bridge in their search for the roots of our profession.

FIGURE 8.19 A mini-version of the bridge at St. Andrews, the bridge at Port Ludlow, Washington, suggests an attractive end treatment for the asphalt cart path road undercrossing.

FIGURE 8.20 A boardwalk is the most acceptable means for crossing wetlands.

FIGURE 8.21 These bridge abutments at the Sea Ranch Golf Course in Northern California will support a prefabricated wood bridge but could also be used for other platforms, such as old railroad flatcars.

Covered bridges appropriately landscaped and reminiscent of the Colonial past are features on courses in New England and in the Atlantic provinces of Canada (Figure 8.22). They also serve as shelters. Creative architect Pete Dye once adapted a railroad car for a covered crossing (Figure 8.23).

A wide variety of striking prefabricated wooden bridges, some arched, are available. One type is portable and requires no abutments. It can be stored in winter and may be preferred by environmentalists. Another is the "breakaway" across streams that are dry most of the year but are subject to gully washes in flood periods. One end of the bridge is anchored while the other gives way in high water, to be reset as the water subsides.

FIGURE 8.22 Covered bridges have a long history in the United States, spreading from coast to coast. This covered bridge for a car/maintenance path is located at the Crooked Stick Golf Club in Carmel, Indiana. (Photo courtesy of Alice Dye)

FIGURE 8.23 Also located at Crooked Stick Golf Club is a further adaptation of the covered bridge. This one employs an old railroad car for cover and features a classic advertising slogan. (Photo courtesy of Alice Dye)

Correct siting of a bridge is important, particularly if it is one that is difficult and costly to move. Generally, the desirable location is on one side of the hole where it and the ramp leading to and from it are out of play but sited near the area where most balls land. Bridges must also be placed in conjunction with the routing of car paths. If crossings are needed, with one on each side of the hole, one may be provided for golf cars with the other accommodating pedestrians only.

Maintenance equipment must also cross streams. Golf car bridges can provide these crossings, but special bridges may be needed. To keep them at a minimum, maintenance routes must be considered in planning (Figures 8.24 and 8.25).

FIGURE 8.24   *As the only access, this boardwalk must be strong enough for golf cars and most maintenance vehicles as well as for golfers on foot.*

FIGURE 8.25   *More bridge than is normally associated with a golf course, this concrete structure at the Santa Clara City Golf Course in California spans four lanes of traffic, a railroad, a light rail system, and pedestrian traffic.*

Protection of Stream Banks

Unless water flow is intermittent or of low velocity, seeding of banks may not be successful even with mulch. More often, bank protection calls for sodding. Erosion control blankets may succeed in keeping seed in place, and in some cases a bank can be planted to willows and other trees.

Other protective measures include the use of wood, concrete or stone bulkheads, riprap (stones thrown together on pond and stream banks to reduce erosion), gabions (sometimes vegetated), log cribwalls interplanted with other species, and three-dimensional honeycomb metal or plastic mats topsoiled and seeded. Selection depends on the volume and velocity of water flow. Architects are giving increasing attention to bioengineering, a combination of vegetation and engineered structures.

Steps

Access by steps to raised areas on a course, particularly tees, is required unless the slopes of ramps and banks are gentle. At the point where the top step meets the teeing surface, a wear area soon develops that eventually becomes a hole. To prevent this, steps are flared (Figures 8.26 and 8.27), with the first step narrow, and the top one wide.

Grassy or other types of ramps may also be needed by disabled persons in order to reach the tees, and in some instances railings are required by all golfers.

FIGURE 8.26 *Flaring the top of the steps to each side allows golfers to head to the center or either end of the tee without wearing a path.*

FIGURE 8.27 *These beautiful, wood-round steps can't dissuade some golfers, mostly hand cart pullers, from wearing out a path alongside.*

The Equipment Building, Storage, and Covered Top-Dressing Areas

To house equipment together with office and work areas, an enclosed minimum space of 6,000 square feet is required for an 18-hole course (see Figure 3.23 A–D); larger areas are better.

Sited by the architect, the equipment building is most often planned by the building architect. Yet its design will be enhanced if the course superintendent also plays a role in siting and planning it. Refer to Figure 3.23 for detail on various components of this building. Several prefabricated equipment buildings available for this purpose have proved functional, with the manufacturer providing the benefit of his experience. Many states require a separate chemical building constructed to rigid specifications.

Other areas are needed, including a separate area for top-dressing preparation, a parking area for crew and visitors, a special area for fuel storage, and an area for washing maintenance equipment to obviate chemicals entering streams and the underground water table. As discussed in Chapter 3, a 1- to 2-acre arrangement for siting the various facilities is required at the equipment building, in addition to space for the sod and tree nursery.

The Role of the Golf Course Superintendent During Construction

Many dividends, tangible and intangible, arise from having the future golf course superintendent on-site during construction and as early as possible. Indeed, if that person has had construction experience, he or she may be qualified to direct the operation as construction superintendent. More often, however, the future superintendent acts in an advisory capacity or may be on-site merely as an observer. Even this involvement is immensely valuable. For example, watching the installation of irrigation and drainage will be as helpful in future years, or even more beneficial, than a sophisticated computer-aided "as-built," although the latter is still needed.

The maintenance superintendent's contributions during construction include, but are not limited to

1. Consulting on specifications for preparing seedbeds and the selection of grasses
2. Consulting on irrigation and drainage systems, as well as golf course features such as tees and greens
3. Consulting on planning the maintenance buildings and access to them
4. Listing maintenance equipment requirements and course furnishings and acquiring them
5. Assisting in or directing the grow-in
6. Assisting in or directing the sampling and analyzing of soils and water before and during construction, including physical and chemical soil tests and water quality
7. Preparing future maintenance budgets
8. Assembling the future maintenance crew
9. Assisting with permit requirements and advising on materials that are environmentally friendly

In practice, the architect looks to the superintendent to monitor every aspect of design and construction that affects future maintainability.

Notes

1.   John McCulla, *Landscape Architect and Specifier News* (February 1996). *BMPs of Erosion Control*.
2.   D. N. Austin and T. Driver, *Erosion Control* (January/February 1995).
3.   From a letter report of one of the author's own projects.
4.   *Golf Course Management* (October 1995).

Drainage

Nothing induces more to the charm of the game than perfecting putting greens. Some should be large, but the majority would be of moderate size, some flat, some hillocky, one or two at an angle, but the great majority should have natural undulations, some more and others less undulating. It is absolutely essential that the turf be very fine so the ball will run perfectly true.

Adapted from *Scotland's Gift GOLF* 1928, by Charles Blair Macdonald (1856–1939)

Emphasizing the importance of drainage, British golf architect Fred W. Hawtree stated at a University of Massachusetts turfgrass conference in 1975 "Drainage, drainage, and more drainage is the key to better turf in Britain." Visiting many climatic zones, we find his statement to be true worldwide. Indeed, some architects refer to it as "The Hawtree Law." Planning a drainage system is difficult, and the system once installed requires constant additions, upgrade, and repair.

The dominant objectives of drainage are to remove excess water so that the turf may flourish, to enhance comfort for golfers walking, driving, and hitting balls, and to ensure that they and the maintenance crew encounter a minimum of puddles and mud as they play or work. Well-drained playing areas are also less prone to rutting by equipment and golf cars, and in arid regions drainage provides a means to remove and flush salts from alkaline and saline soils. Even in cool, humid regions the ability to flush a green or other feature is eminently worthwhile.

A unique concern in golf course drainage is to remove excess water rapidly, more rapidly than on many agricultural lands, because golfers expect to play and the superintendent must resume maintenance operations as soon as a rainstorm is over and as early as possible following snowmelt in spring.

Golf courses require surface, subsurface, and air drainage.

1. Surface drainage is achieved by
   a. Grading the land so that it sheds water
   b. Installing open ditches, swales, and channels
   c. Creating water bars and furrows
2. Subsurface drainage is achieved by installing
   a. Tile drains and pipe
   b. Mole drains
   c. Vertical drains
   d. Slit trenches
   e. French drains
   f. Curtain or interceptor drains (which can be in the form of surface or subsurface drainage)

3. Air drainage is achieved by selecting sunlit sites exposed to wind and by removing trees, low branches, hillocks, and other features that obstruct air flow.

An entire system of subsurface drainage includes collecting drains leading to a main drain, which in turn lead to an outlet (Figure 9.1). The effectiveness of subsurface drainage depends on, and may be limited by, the type of outlet used. Possible outlets are the rough (if it slopes away or is porous with a deep water table), existing main and lateral drains and swales, ditches, ponds, and streams. Regulations may govern these exits. In practice, their selection has become increasingly complex because outlets into ponds and streams are often not allowed.

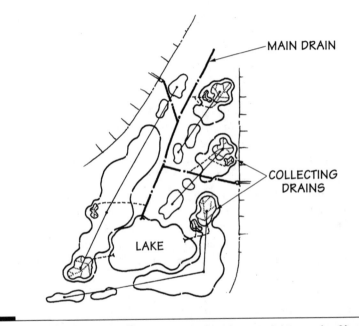

FIGURE 9.1   *In this simulation of a four-hole complex, the main drain can handle residential as well as off-road drainage water. Collecting drains under greens and bunkers can also terminate in the same main drain. It all ends up in the lake or some other appropriate area.*

The outlet can also be a sump, pit, or catch basin to which the water is led (Figure 9.2). If the soil is porous, the water then drains from the sump. If not, it is pumped from the sump or the sump itself is drained by a pipe or tile.

Sumps on golf courses are sometimes left open, but because of danger to passersby they are more often filled with stones or gravel with sides and top lined with straw or synthetic materials to filter out silt that would otherwise enter the gravel. The filter material may then be covered with topsoil (Figure 9.3). Sometimes a grated manhole is provided (Figure 9.4).

On occasion, a lake, creek, or drain swale can be used as a drainage termination. If appropriate, drain water can be discharged in an area that is out of play (Figure 9.5).

Those planning drainage from a surrounding housing development, even when golf and housing are integrated, must not look on the golf course as a giant sump. In practice, when homes or other structures are integrated with or surround a course, a master drainage plan is required to coordinate drainage from the course and the development.

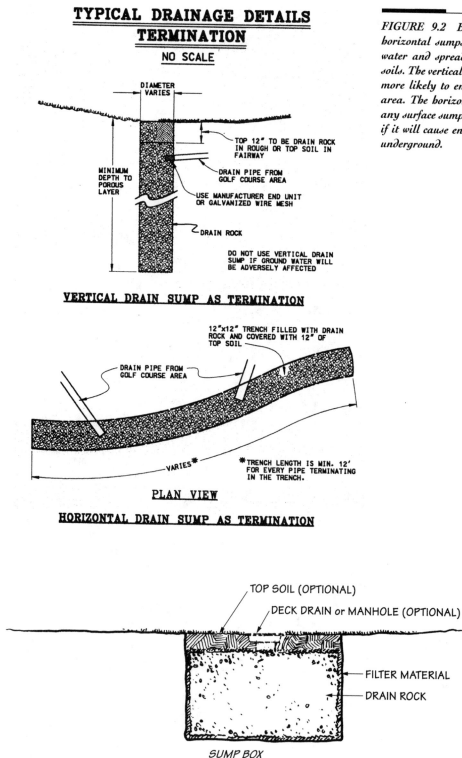

TYPICAL DRAINAGE DETAILS
TERMINATION
NO SCALE

DIAMETER VARIES

TOP 12" TO BE DRAIN ROCK IN ROUGH OR TOP SOIL IN FAIRWAY

DRAIN PIPE FROM GOLF COURSE AREA

USE MANUFACTURER END UNIT OR GALVANIZED WIRE MESH

MINIMUM DEPTH TO POROUS LAYER

DRAIN ROCK

DO NOT USE VERTICAL DRAIN SUMP IF GROUND WATER WILL BE ADVERSELY AFFECTED

VERTICAL DRAIN SUMP AS TERMINATION

12"x12" TRENCH FILLED WITH DRAIN ROCK AND COVERED WITH 12" OF TOP SOIL

DRAIN PIPE FROM GOLF COURSE AREA

VARIES *

* TRENCH LENGTH IS MIN. 12' FOR EVERY PIPE TERMINATING IN THE TRENCH.

PLAN VIEW

HORIZONTAL DRAIN SUMP AS TERMINATION

TOP SOIL (OPTIONAL)

DECK DRAIN or MANHOLE (OPTIONAL)

FILTER MATERIAL

DRAIN ROCK

SUMP BOX

FIGURE 9.2 Both the vertical and horizontal sumps can collect drainage water and spread it out into adjacent soils. The vertical works best, as you are more likely to encounter a porous soil area. The horizontal acts the same as any surface sump. Neither is acceptable if it will cause environmental problems underground.

FIGURE 9.3 A sump is simply a large container to collect drainage water from other concentrated sources. Its bottom and side surface areas allow dispersal in several directions.

TYPICAL DRAINAGE DETAILS: COLLECTION

NO SCALE

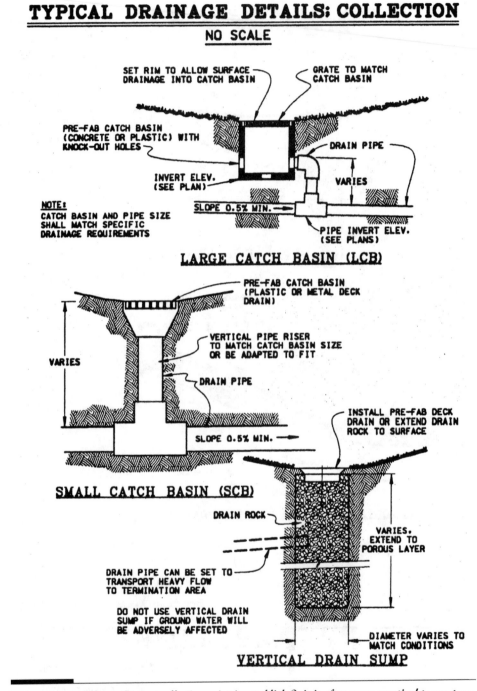

SET RIM TO ALLOW SURFACE
DRAINAGE INTO CATCH BASIN

GRATE TO MATCH
CATCH BASIN

PRE-FAB CATCH BASIN
(CONCRETE OR PLASTIC) WITH
KNOCK-OUT HOLES

DRAIN PIPE

INVERT ELEV.
(SEE PLAN)

VARIES

NOTE:
CATCH BASIN AND PIPE SIZE
SHALL MATCH SPECIFIC
DRAINAGE REQUIREMENTS

SLOPE 0.5% MIN.

PIPE INVERT ELEV.
(SEE PLANS)

LARGE CATCH BASIN (LCB)

PRE-FAB CATCH BASIN
(PLASTIC OR METAL DECK
DRAIN)

VERTICAL PIPE RISER
TO MATCH CATCH BASIN SIZE
OR BE ADAPTED TO FIT

VARIES

DRAIN PIPE

SLOPE 0.5% MIN.

INSTALL PRE-FAB DECK
DRAIN OR EXTEND DRAIN
ROCK TO SURFACE

SMALL CATCH BASIN (SCB)

DRAIN ROCK

VARIES.
EXTEND TO
POROUS LAYER

DRAIN PIPE CAN BE SET TO
TRANSPORT HEAVY FLOW
TO TERMINATION AREA

DO NOT USE VERTICAL DRAIN
SUMP IF GROUND WATER WILL
BE ADVERSELY AFFECTED

DIAMETER VARIES TO
MATCH CONDITIONS

VERTICAL DRAIN SUMP

FIGURE 9.4   *When a distinct collection point is established, it is often more practical to create an open route down to the transport pipe.*

TYPICAL DRAINAGE DETAILS
TERMINATION
NO SCALE

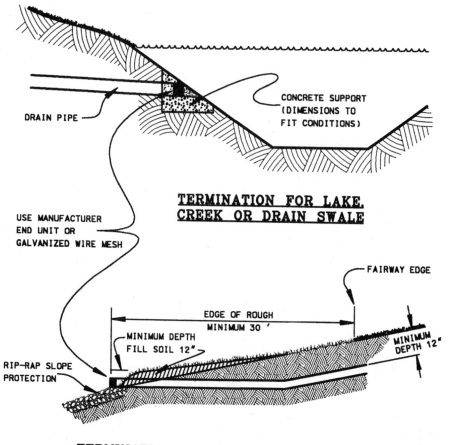

TERMINATION FOR LAKE, CREEK OR DRAIN SWALE

TERMINATION IN OUT OF PLAY AREA

FIGURE 9.5 Another termination for drainage water can be a nearby water feature or an area located out of play where saturated soil will not be a problem.

Surface Drainage

Surface drainage is the most critical and effective type of drainage for greenswards and can be achieved in a number of ways.

Grading the Land

In grading the land, the objective is to accelerate runoff by gravity over the surface of the ground without piping. In practice, surface drainage of every turfgrass area on a golf course is critically important, even on very porous soils. Infiltration on porous soils is reduced when the soil is frozen or has become heavily compacted by years of play and maintenance. All large and small pockets that would hold water must therefore be removed.

Allowing surface water to flow across greens and tees from surrounding areas in any season of the year damages the turf. These features must therefore be raised above surrounding levels or protected by open interceptor drains or swales.

A 2 to 3% pitch appears to be minimum grade for surface drainage of close-clipped turf. Lesser pitches do not carry water off fast enough for golf courses, although gentler grades, no less than 1%, are sometimes used in creating runoff in a second direction on greens and tees. Where soils are alkaline or saline, grades steeper than 2 to 3% assist in carrying away salts.

Installing Open Ditches and Swales

A second means of surface drainage is an open ditch (Figure 9.6), with almost vertical sides if the existing soil is stable, as are some heavy soils. On less stable soils, such ditches require sloping sides with grade of slope determined by the stability of the soil.

A varient of an open ditch is a swale, which is a depression as wide as 30 feet or more and mowable, with a depth varying from a few inches to several feet. A minimum pitch of not less than 2% is required (Figure 9.7).

Open ditches on or near playing areas, unless they are mowable swales, annoy golfers and are expensive to maintain. Therefore, they are generally located in roughs well away from playing areas. Sometimes, however, ditches are installed across fairways as a temporary measure and piped later after it is established that they will be effective. In the history of golf architecture many such ditches have evolved over the years into accepted hazards and have not been piped because they enhanced interest and became a tradition of the layout. Yet ditches with intermittent waterflow contribute to maintenance problems.

FIGURE 9.6   An old vertical walled ditch, likely first installed to handle drainage water from a nearby area, has become an integral part of a Scottish golf hole.

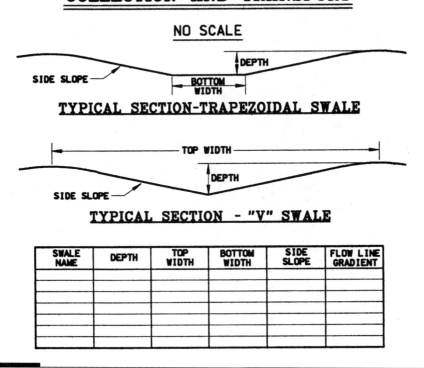

TYPICAL DRAINAGE SWALE DETAILS
COLLECTION AND TRANSPORT

NO SCALE

SIDE SLOPE

DEPTH

BOTTOM WIDTH

TYPICAL SECTION-TRAPEZOIDAL SWALE

TOP WIDTH

DEPTH

SIDE SLOPE

TYPICAL SECTION - "V" SWALE

SWALE NAME	DEPTH	TOP WIDTH	BOTTOM WIDTH	SIDE SLOPE	FLOW LINE GRADIENT

FIGURE 9.7 *Swales are a popular means of transporting drainage water. They can also add topographic interest to a golf hole and will generate fill soil.*

Swales on playing areas are less obnoxious than ditches because they are mowable when dry. On most soil types, however, their floors remain wet long after surface water flow has ceased. In this case, tile must be installed under the swale (Figures 9.8 and 9.9). This tiling is of increased importance when the gradient of the swale is minimal or if the swale meanders.

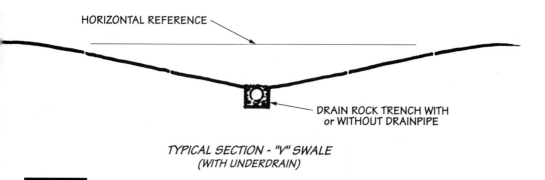

HORIZONTAL REFERENCE

DRAIN ROCK TRENCH WITH
or WITHOUT DRAINPIPE

TYPICAL SECTION - "V" SWALE
(WITH UNDERDRAIN)

FIGURE 9.8 *A swale bottom may stay wet from irrigation as well as from rainfall. Then a centerline or flow-line drain is necessary to speed drying.*

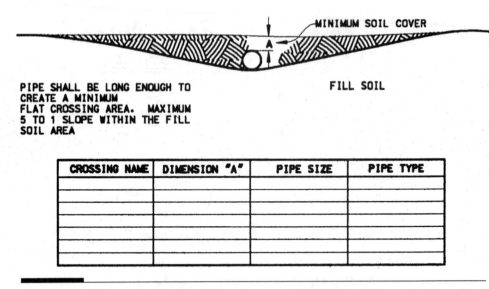

PIPE SHALL BE LONG ENOUGH TO
CREATE A MINIMUM
FLAT CROSSING AREA.   MAXIMUM
5 TO 1 SLOPE WITHIN THE FILL
SOIL AREA

CROSSING NAME	DIMENSION "A"	PIPE SIZE	PIPE TYPE

FIGURE 9.9 *If a swale stays wet and must be traversed by foot or vehicle traffic, the architect should plan to install a crossing consisting of a drain pipe along the flow line and sufficient fill to allow access.*

Furrowing

A furrow is a narrow swale with minimum meandering, often but not always with a berm on its lower side (Figure 9.10). Furrows are sometimes placed across steeply sloping fairways, where they are referred to as water bars.

The objective of water bars is to divert water to the sides before it gains sufficient volume to start scouring. They are valuable during seeding operations and grow-in but can exert a beneficial impact for years to come if constructed so they are mowable.

FIGURE 9.10 *The berm on the lower side of a water bar effectively increases the capacity and uses excavated soil from the swale.*

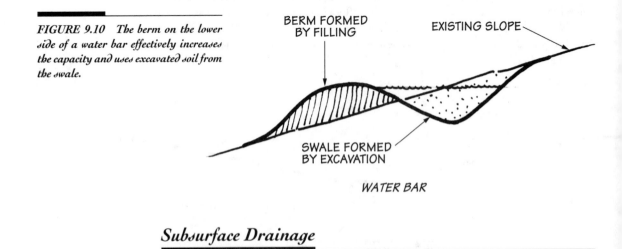

Subsurface Drainage

Tile drainage installed according to recognized methods is the most common form of subsurface drainage on golf courses. Patterns for tile drainage include herringbone, grid, and random systems (Figures 9.11, 9.12, 9.13).

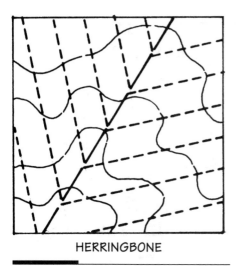

HERRINGBONE

FIGURE 9.11 The herringbone is best suited to fairly uniform slopes if they are not flat.

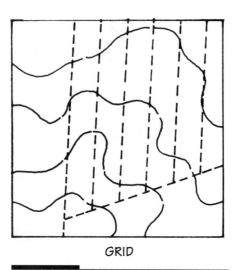

GRID

FIGURE 9.12 The grid pattern is best suited to flat or uniform slopes.

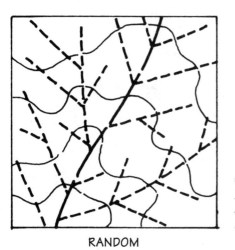

RANDOM

FIGURE 9.13 The random pattern is ideally suited to variations in the surface slope and can be made to fit any situation effectively.

    If excess water is to be collected along the route of the drain, the tile must be porous wall, jointed, or with openings so that water can enter. All are often surounded by gravel. However, if water is to be conducted from a spring or other source to an outlet with no water to be collected along the route, the tile or pipe can be solid with no surrounding gravel (Figure 9.14).

    When gravel is used, the size most often specified is ¼ to ⅜ inch (pea stone), although some engineers prefer larger sizes, particularly where a sloping drain line may be scoured out by run-off. On fairways and roughs the gravel can be brought to the very surface with no topsoil placed over it. This arrangement speeds removal of excess water and contributes to rapid drainage; however, it can prove objectionable for play and maintenance for months following installation (see slit drain on Figure 9.14). Yet grass will eventually cover it if the material is not more than ⅜ inch in diameter. When the gravel is of a larger diameter, coarse sand or finer gravel may be used to top it to a 2- or 3-inch depth to assist the grass in forming a turf. In fact, in a few years dense thatch may

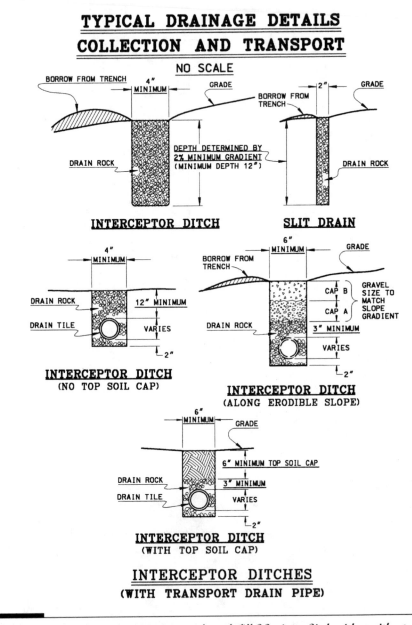

FIGURE 9.14 *There are many variations on the rock-filled drainage ditch, with or without a drain pipe. If the pipe is nonperforated, gravel generally is not needed.*

have formed over the stone, which requires removal with a sod cutter. If not removed, the thatch compromises drainage.

Outlets and inlets for tile and pipe on a golf course are often protected by headwalls of stone or manufactured metal aprons to minimize scouring (Figure 9.15). Open ends may also need protection to prevent rodents from entering the tile, where they can be trapped and block the pipe. A means to flush the system is also desirable, particularly for tile systems on greens. This is achieved by installing a riser at the top end of the pipe to which a hose can be inserted when flushing is needed (Figure 9.16).

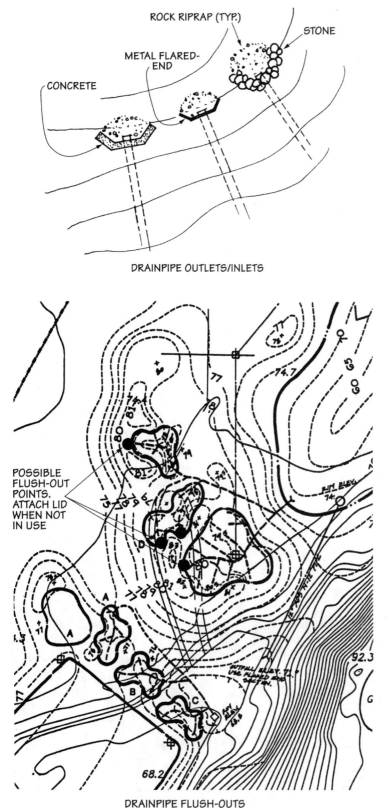

ROCK RIPRAP (TYP.)

STONE

METAL FLARED-
END

CONCRETE

DRAINPIPE OUTLETS/INLETS

FIGURE 9.15   Here are three common means to treat a drain pipe outlet or inlet. If used as an inlet, the riprap may not be required.

FIGURE 9.16   Each separate main drainpipe is a potential location for a flush point. The lid can be solid or a deck drain for air circulation.

POSSIBLE
FLUSH-OUT
POINTS.
ATTACH LID
WHEN NOT
IN USE

DRAINPIPE FLUSH-OUTS

Tile is usually laid in trenches on an inch or more of the specified gravel and then surrounded and covered by the same gravel (Figure 9.17).

Trench width varies, depending on the size of the pipe, the depth of the trench, and, sometimes, the soil type. A 6-inch wide trench may be adequate on many soils when tile with a diameter of 4 inches or less is to be installed.

Pipes and culverts used for golf course drainage may be of plastic, concrete, clay, metal, or the old-type clay tiles. Depending on type of drainage needed, tile may be solid, perforated, or porous. It can be flexible or rigid, but flexible tile is preferred on soils containing boulders and ledge.

On greens, tile is laid in trenches with a pitch similar to or steeper than the general grade of the green, often 2 to 3%. It is not always mandatory that subdrainage of greens and other turfgrass flow in the same direction as the surface drainage. On fairways and roughs the 2 to 3% pitch of tile drainage is desirable but sometimes not obtainable. The minimum functioning pitch on such areas is 1%, but drainage will then be slow (Figure 9.18).

FIGURE 9.17   Regardless of the type of green- or turf-growing medium, it is often prudent to install a drain rock blanket or envelope with a drainpipe system.

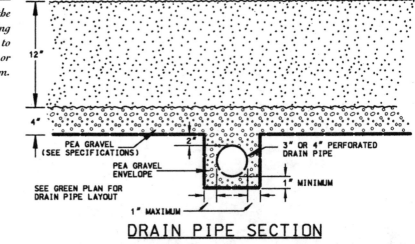

FIGURE 9.18   This is a typical drainpipe installation before the drain rock blanket is added. (Photo by Phil Arnold)

Protecting tile and the surrounding gravel has long been achieved by enveloping these materials with straw, hay, or tar paper. Now several effective envelope materials, mostly unwoven geotextiles manufactured for this purpose, are available. The entire system of tile and surrounding gravel is installed in a manner that permits wrapping on three or four sides with the geotextile (Figure 9.19). Drainage pipe already wrapped with a geotextile is also available.

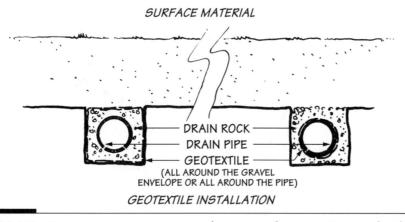

FIGURE 9.19   Here are two ways to use a geotextile to protect a drainpipe. Care must be taken that the geotextile does not ultimately prevent drainage water from reaching the drainpipe.

Golf architects collaborating with engineers develop ingenious systems of drainage. For example, Pete Dye installed a system at the Old Marsh Golf Club in Florida whereby excess water is collected and returned to the irrigation reservoir, from where it is pumped back to the course. Golf architect William G. Robinson created a combined golf course and water treatment plant on Meadow Lake in Prineville, Oregon, involving the creation of ponds into which some 600,000 gallons of treated wastewater are pumped daily to become an odorless irrigation source. An extensive pipe system prevents the water from reaching a nearby river or entering the water table. Murray Parkway Golf Course in Utah, by coauthor R. M. Graves, filters runoff from a freeway before it enters a river.

Mole Drains

Mole drains are unlined channels, generally round, installed 2 or 3 feet below ground level. They are created by pulling a steel ball or lug, the "mole," through the subsoil to an outlet. A device similar to that employed in installing wire, television cable, and irrigation pipe is used to pull the mole. The resulting underground channel, although unprotected, is effective for two or three years on heavy soils. The operation of pulling the mole through the soil also creates a slit above the channel so that water can reach the mole drain. In turn, this produces beneficial cracking of the soil adjoining the slit (Figure 9.20).

Mole drainage on a contemporary golf course can be hampered by the miles of wiring installed for automatic irrigation. And, if in place before the wire and irrigation pipe, the mole drains can themselves be disturbed when these are installed.

Several types of subsoilers developed for agriculture, and one specifically for turfgrass, have also been used with success to lead water away by creating a network of temporary channels in the subsoil under a green or a tee.

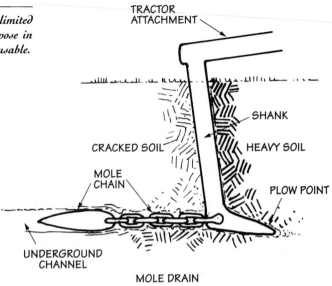

FIGURE 9.20 *Although it affects a rather limited area, the mole drain does serve a useful purpose in heavy soils. Very rocky soils make this tool unusable.*

TRACTOR ATTACHMENT

SHANK

CRACKED SOIL

HEAVY SOIL

MOLE CHAIN

PLOW POINT

UNDERGROUND CHANNEL

MOLE DRAIN

Vertical Drains

Vertical drains are functional on playing areas where the topsoil is separated, by a layer of impervious soil, from the porous sand or gravel beneath it (see Figure 9.2). In bunkers a vertical drain is sometimes a well filled with stone similar to that specified for the gravel blanket of USGA greens.

Vertical drainage of entire fairways and other playing areas is functional if the material beneath the impervious subsoil is truly porous. Wells or trenches leading downward to the porous layer are excavated and filled with a specified type of gravel (Figure 9.21). At one time it was a practice to shatter impervious layers by dynamiting. Although the result was effective for a few years, dynamiting had to be repeated from time to time. Because of the presence of contemporary irrigation systems, however, dynamiting is no longer practical and, in fact, is not permitted in many districts. Vertical drains are forbidden on some soils because of their potential for contaminating groundwater.

Curtain or Intercepting Drains

Curtain (or intercepting) drains can be shallow swales or deeper ditches with or without tile or pipe (see Figure 9.14). On golf courses, they are generally situated on slopes above playing areas. The objectives are to intercept surface water flowing down a slope, to collect underground water, and to lower the water table on the area below. Curtain drains or intercepting drains are also installed on boundaries to collect surface and subsurface water and lead it away before it reaches the course (see Figure 9.14).

Perhaps the notorious "Oakmont ditches" were installed originally as intercepting drains. Becoming widely known and feared by golfers, they were imitated by other clubs, at times purely to act as hazards.

Slit Trenches

Slit trenches are constructed by excavating a drainage trench and filling it with gravel but with no tile (see Figure 9.14). They can be effective for a few months, but become

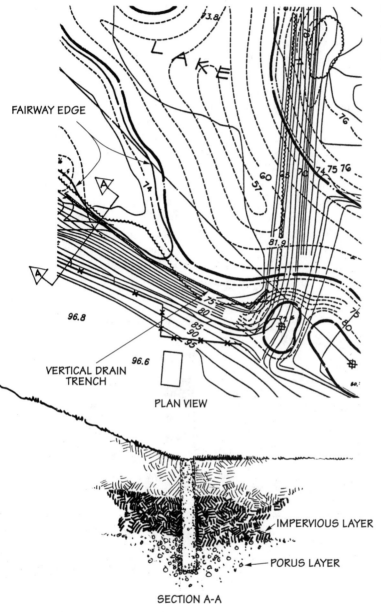

FIGURE 9.21 *This drawing shows how a vertical drain trench could be used to protect the edge of a fairway at the base of a slope.*

FAIRWAY EDGE

VERTICAL DRAIN TRENCH

PLAN VIEW

IMPERVIOUS LAYER

PORUS LAYER

SECTION A-A

ineffective within a year or two as the gravel clogs with sediment. Envelopes of hay, straw, tar paper, or manufactured products surrounding the gravel lengthen their effective lifespan. Still, at best, slit trenches are temporary measures. In the majority of cases, tile drains are more cost-effective because they last for decades if carefully installed.

French Drains

The term "French drain" has been applied to several types of drainage systems, including slit trenches and even tile drains. Golf architects use the term specifically in relation to underground drainage channels created by placing stones to conduct water (Figure 9.22). Effective in agriculture for centuries, French drains appear to have limited life on golf courses even when enveloped with natural or synthetic materials. This short life-span is probably due to constant equipment traffic over playing areas.

"French drain" has also been used to describe ditches excavated during construction and filled with fieldstone from the site. This is a useful technique for disposing of rock. Yet its drainage value is short-lived. In New England, for example, stone walls built for centuries on farms are bulldozed into trenches with the hope that they will enhance drainage. Initially they do, but they are effective for only a few years.

Golf course drainage in humid areas is ongoing. It is both a construction and a maintenance procedure. During construction, drainage is installed on all areas that obviously require it. Yet as years pass, additional drainage is an inevitable requirement on most soil types. Moreover, the life of golf course pipe is limited despite the best efforts of all concerned. In mountainous country and other rough terrain, new springs erupt and channels unexpectedly fill with water. In granular soils, they can shift, plugging old conduits and creating new ones. Months or years after construction, tile collapses and outlets clog even though the original drainage plan was prepared with the utmost care and installation was of the highest quality. Many golf course soils, despite their turf coverings, are not completely stable in the first years following construction. This instability adds to the ongoing need for additional drainage and repair.

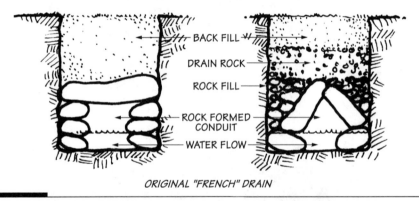

ORIGINAL "FRENCH" DRAIN

FIGURE 9.22   *Many types of drain systems are referred to as "French" drains. But this is the original version, going back many years, when its normal use was to develop farm fields.*

Air Drainage

In golf course development, as in agriculture and horticulture, one must think of air drainage. Lack of air circulation, as well as shade, contributes immeasurably to ice accumulation in winter or spring, to air stagnation in hot, humid summers, to frost remaining on putting surfaces after play has commenced on autumn days, and to constantly wet and fungus-prone turf surfaces.

Conversely, the evaporation of moisture resulting from air drainage is of major significance in removing excess water from playing areas and in keeping turf surfaces dry. This free water evaporation must never be overlooked in clearing operations or in maintenance. Unfortunately, the onset of inadequate air drainage on an existing layout as a result of tree growth can be gradual and is easily overlooked. Ensuing problems may be attributed to other factors, but limited sunlight and stagnant air are the basic causes of difficulties encountered in providing the turf a golfer wants.

Inadequate air drainage is mostly caused by trees and, to a lesser extent, by structures and natural features, including surrounding hills and cliffs. Features located in depressions may suffer from poor air circulation (Figure 9.23). Probably little can be done about the structures and natural features except to relocate a green or a tee or to remove an offending hill, although the use of huge fans to increase air circulation is becoming more common.

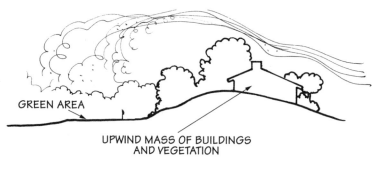

GREEN AREA

UPWIND MASS OF BUILDINGS
AND VEGETATION

INADEQUATE AIR DRAINAGE

FIGURE 9.23 The combination of the rear slope with a building and sizable, thick vegetation deflects the prevailing wind up and over the green.

A newly developed patented device, "subair," for pumping air into a green and withdrawing it and excess water, could also develop into a useful device to achieve quality turf in the unfavorable microclimates on many golf courses.

Tree planting has been overdone on many North American layouts. One reason this has occurred is that the golf or landscape architect did not consider the mature heights and silhouettes of trees he or she sited. In addition, at the time of clearing it may have been overlooked that remaining trees grow more luxuriantly when others around them have been removed. Fertilizing and irrigating of the greensward also stimulate tree growth because some of the fertilizer and water inadvertently reaches the trees.

To enhance air circulation, tree stands that are to remain can be thinned during selective clearing operations. Air channels created from hole to hole by removing trees are also beneficial (Figure 9.24). Underbrush remaining in surrounding roughs, even when remote from playing areas, reduces air circulation, as do low branches. The

FIGURE 9.24 Proper tree removal and thinning of lower branches and brush allows adequate airflow throughout this green and adjacent golf holes at Canterwood Country Club in Gig Harbor, Washington.

removal of brush for many feet back from clear-cut areas benefits the greensward. Yet this measure is sometimes inconsistent with the objective of providing cover for wildlife. On many a course a compromise can be reached, with underbrush left in areas where few balls land.

The lesson is that when planting new trees before or after a course opening, planners must give thought to their impact on the greensward as they mature. In this regard, architects often specify that no tree be left during clearing and no tree planted closer than 60 feet to a putting surface.

Many greens are rebuilt at great expense and player inconvenience in cases where removing trees and underbrush could have corrected the problem. If densely shaded, even a well-rebuilt green will revert to its former unsatisfactory state.

Conclusion

Surface, Subsurface, and air drainage are intrinsic to the beauty, maintainability, and playability of the playing fields of golf.

Golf Course Irrigation

by James McC. Barrett
GOLF COURSE IRRIGATION ENGINEER AND CONSULTANT
MONTCLAIR, NEW JERSEY

The architect must allow the ground to dictate play. The good architect sees that there is a special interest for the accomplished golfer in each stroke, just as the billiard player always has in mind the next stroke or strokes.

From *Concerning Golf*, 1903, by John Laing Low (1869–1929)

For five hundred years, golf has been played on grass. Although there have been attempts to use other materials, it is clear that golfers prefer natural turf. As long as grass remains the playing surface of choice, irrigation water will remain the most important single factor in the establishment and maintenance of golf courses.

Water obviously provides for the direct moisture requirements of a plant. It makes up for losses resulting from evapotranspiration (ET). The ET rate is determined by a combination of climatic conditions such as solar radiation, wind, temperature, and humidity. Water is the vehicle that transports needed nutrients and chemicals to the plant roots and acts as a cooling agent. Water is also used to flush or leach unwanted materials out of the root zone.

As the popularity of golf has grown over the last few decades and players have demanded better and better playing conditions, irrigation component manufacturers, system designers, and superintendents who operate the systems have responded with systems and procedures that are cost-effective, reliable, efficient, and environmentally responsible.

Irrigation systems must apply water where it is needed, when it is needed. They are tools that, when properly designed and operated, allow the superintendent to respond accurately and precisely to the moisture requirements of every part of the course.

Plant Irrigation Requirements

In addition to the obvious differences related to site location and climate, moisture requirements can vary tremendously within a given course. They are affected by a wide range of conditions including soils, topography, turfgrass type and height of cut, drainage, player and vehicle traffic, compaction, and exposure to sun, shade, and wind. In a given area, any one (or combination) of these conditions can make the plant moisture requirements significantly different from those of the turf only several feet away.

A common example occurs on an east-west fairway that has a high, thick tree line on the south side. The north side of the fairway is in the sun all day. The south side, however, is shaded for the part of the day that includes the hottest sun. The two sides have substantially different irrigation requirements.

If the fairway is covered by a single-row system, the superintendent cannot apply the additional water needed by the north side without overwatering the shady side. The same problem exists in a two-row system if two (or more) heads are paired across the fairway on one controller station. The operator must irrigate the entire width for whatever run time he or she assigns the station. If the operator sets the run time based on the needs of the shady side, the sunny-side turf will be thin and weak and the ground hard. If run time is set according to the requirement of the sunny side, the shady side will be too wet. In addition to creating undesirable playing conditions, this situation wastes water and pump power and could lead to turfgrass diseases and other maintenance problems.

The optimum irrigation system allows discrete control of each area, regardless of size, that has unique requirements. Thus, in the preceding example, a well-designed system would have at least two-row coverage. Either individual head control or, in the case of a block valve system, control zones including heads on only one side of the fairway would allow the superintendent to set different runs on each side.

Moisture requirements also change significantly during the irrigation season according to weather patterns and the growth cycle of the turfgrass plant. The irrigation system must be flexible enough to allow easy adjustments, on a daily basis, to accommodate these changes.

Water Supply: Quantity and Quality

Overall irrigation requirements depend primarily on location and climate, acreage to be watered, and type of turfgrass to be established. Daily use can range from less than 100,000 gallons in cool, humid regions to several million in hot, dry areas. Annual usage varies from less than 10,000,000 gallons per year in the Northeast to more than 150,000,000 gallons for hot desert courses.

The best sources of irrigation water include existing lakes, ponds, canals, and rivers or streams that flow throughout the drier summer months. Assuming environmental and other regulatory authorities will grant the necessary diversion permits (including limits on withdrawal rates), these sources can generally provide sufficient water of acceptable quality for turfgrass purposes. Use of these sources frequently precludes the need for construction of a storage pond and avoids the added cost of recharge pumping.

Drilled wells, tapping aquifers, are another source, and they usually provide high-grade water. Permits are required even to drill test wells, and withdrawal from production wells will be limited in terms of daily and annual rates by state and regulatory agencies. Some systems pump directly from one or more wells into the irrigation system, but there are inefficiencies associated with this procedure. It is usually preferable and more cost-efficient to pump from a well into a storage pond, from which a separate pump station discharges water into the irrigation system.

Storage Ponds

Storage pond capacity depends on site-specific conditions such as climate, irrigation requirements, and source reliability. However, achieving maximum practical depth is desirable regardless of location. A deeper pond has fewer problems with algae and aquatic weeds, and its irrigation water stays colder. Increased depth also lessens evaporation losses by minimizing surface area. In many new construction projects, the irrigation storage pond is often a source of fill material needed for feature construction, so the cost of excavation is not applied solely to the irrigation system.

Municipal Source

Municipal potable water systems are used as a source at many courses, usually where there are no alternatives. The cost of the water is high, and booster pumps are needed because very few municipal systems operate at the pressure required for golf course sprinkler heads. Expensive backflow prevention devices are usually required to comply with health code regulations concerning cross-connection.

Another problem with municipal systems is the possibility of the supply being shut off (when it is most needed) during periods of severe drought. Local, regional, and state authorities have been known to restrict or cut off water to golf courses for reasons that are politically popular, rather than for reasons based on practical evaluation of potential losses and damages.

Wastewater

Wastewater, or sewage effluent, is another source of irrigation water. At least 200 courses in the United States now use wastewater, and the number is growing. Typically, it is cheaper than potable water, especially if pumping and other related costs are excluded. However, the cost may increase as municipalities begin to view effluent as a sellable product rather than a disposal problem.

Wastewater treated to only the secondary level has been used successfully. However, tertiary (or beyond) treatment is preferable from an agronomic perspective, in terms of compliance with local codes, and in regard to health hazards perceived by an often poorly informed public.

Regardless of the level of treatment, a thorough investigation of wastewater content relative to the specific soils found on the project must be undertaken by qualified personnel before the decision is made to use the effluent. Key factors to be determined include biochemical oxygen demand (BOD), total suspended solids (TSS), total dissolved solids (TDS), fecal coliform levels, and levels of certain trace elements. These and other criteria must also be tested on a regular basis while an effluent irrigation system is in operation. Additional costs may be incurred if factors in the effluent need adjustment. For example, additional soil amendments and/or additional water for leaching may be required to offset high salt levels. Pond management costs may rise because of increased nutrient content. Some courses have reported increased fertilizer, pesticide, and herbicide costs owing to effluent use.

Many regulations restrict the use of effluent, and they must be carefully researched before making the decision to use wastewater. In most states, buffer zones are required between effluent spray zones and buildings or property lines. Wetlands, endangered species zones, and freshwater ponds or streams typically have buffers, as do outdoor drinking fountains and potable water well fields. As a result, many courses with effluent systems must install a parallel freshwater system throughout much, if not all, of the course to cover the areas where effluent is not permitted. This is also done to accommodate sensitive ornamentals and, in many cases, to water putting surfaces.

Another concern is the requirement for storage. If the course is obligated to take a fixed amount of effluent on a daily, weekly, or monthly basis, there must be capacity to store a certain amount when rain reduces or removes the need for irrigation. Certainly, any agreement with an effluent supplier must cover the issue of what is done with the wastewater beyond the irrigation season.

In spite of the many cautions and problems, effluent irrigation systems are becoming increasingly common, and not only in areas where regulations or other conditions leave no other option.

Water Analysis

It is important to note that, regardless of the proposed source, water quality and the availability of adequate quantities must be thoroughly investigated and proven satisfactory very early in the planning process for a golf course construction project. Many test laboratories are equipped to analyze irrigation water quality and are familiar with golf course requirements. Analyses typically report pH, hardness, electrical conductivity, sodium absorption rate, levels of bicarbonate, carbonate, total soluble salts, sodium, chloride, and various nutrients. In some cases, injection of additives may be required to mitigate high levels of key properties.

Drinking Water

A final but extremely important supply issue concerns the use of the irrigation system to supply drinking water to fountains, bathrooms, and halfway houses (guest shelters). Regardless of the water source, the direct connection of irrigation piping to potable water outlets is a cross-connection. This is a clear violation of the National Standard Plumbing Code and all local health codes. It presents a potentially serious health hazard and possible liability for the owner or operator of the course. All potable water feeding drinking fountains, bathrooms, halfway houses, and other such facilities must be supplied via piping separate from the irrigation system.

Pump Stations

Most of today's golf course pump stations are skid-mounted preengineered units that include multiple pumps, all required valves, and manifold piping. They typically have solid-state programmable logic controllers that sequence pumps on and off in response to irrigation system pressure and flow senses at the pump station. Also included are automatic safety circuits that retire the pumps when they sense a fault condition that could damage components of the pump station or the irrigation system. Such faults include phase failure on the incoming power, which could burn out a motor; low inlet water level, which could cause a pump to seize up; and high discharge pressure, which could burst pipes or fittings in the irrigation system. In addition, an accurate flow meter, with totalizer, should be included. It is needed for control purposes and provides important information to the superintendent for water management purposes and required usage reports to regulatory agencies.

Unless the pump station is fed by a flooded suction or is a booster station, vertical turbine pumps are preferred over horizontal centrifugal units. Vertical turbines have the bowls actually submerged, eliminating concern over maintaining prime, which is so often a problem with horizontal pumps in a lift suction situation. Vertical turbines are generally more efficient at typical golf course pump locations. Low-speed (1,800 vs. 3,600 rpm) pumps and motors are also preferred because they last longer, although they cost more.

Variable frequency drives (VFD), which have recently become popular, automatically vary the speed of a pump in response to system demand, thereby avoiding the waste of horsepower associated with a constant-speed pump not operating at the most efficient point on its curve. VFD units can reduce electric bills, especially where power is expensive and systems are operated year-round. Another benefit of VFDs is that they provide "soft" starts, meaning a motor is gradually ramped up to full speed instead of being started across the line. In the latter case, there is a very high current inrush, and severe pressure shocks potentially damaging to irrigation components are generated. VFD units are expensive, and a cost/benefit analysis should be done before including them in a pump station.

A typical turbine station is installed on a concrete slab with the pumps extending down into a concrete wetwell. An inlet flume, of concrete or PVC pipe, runs from the bottom of the wetwell out to the pond. The flume is set 1 to 2 feet off the pond bottom to avoid silt. A screening device (a simple box screen or an automatic self-cleaning unit) prevents large items such as sticks and fish from entering the flume.

Filtration

The need for filtration equipment depends on water quality. Automatic self-cleaning mechanical screen filter units are available and effective for most problems, including the presence of zebra mussels and freshwater clams. However, they cannot handle organic material. Sand-media filters are more effective for algae, but they require a lot more space than screen units.

Algae growth and related problems are better handled in the storage pond. Introduction of oxygen into the water through diffusers located on the bottom, combined with submerged circulation pumps to prevent stagnant water, will minimize algae and aquatic weed growth.

The Pumphouse

A simple building of block or stud construction is erected over the station. The building must have a roof hatch (often a prefabricated skylight) to allow removal of the pumps, adequate light for maintenance and repair, a louvered intake, and a thermostat-controlled exhaust fan to provide adequate air movement to keep motors cool. Heat and insulation are seldom absolute necessities, but they are often included in pump buildings in northern areas.

Power

Proper power must be supplied at the pump station, and this can be a significant expense. Usually 480-volt, 3-phase, 60-hertz power is preferred, although it is not available in all locations. The size of the service depends on the capacity and horsepower of the pump station, but 400 amp is usually the smallest acceptable.

Some utility companies provide underground cables, which the owner then installs from the nearest power lines. Some power companies also have rebate programs that pay a customer to replace existing units with more efficient ones. Rate structures vary from one utility to the next, but most include demand charge and time-of-use (peak and off-peak hour) clauses, which can be important in irrigation and pump station design. Most power companies also have specific restrictions concerning motor starting and control devices. All of these power considerations must be investigated early in the design procedure.

Pump Capacity

Pump station capacity (and therefore that of the irrigation system mainline piping) used to be determined by comparing the amount of water needed for a complete cycle with the time available between the end of play in the evening and the start of maintenance procedures the next morning. A simple calculation provided the flow rate needed. Today, with higher levels of maintenance, increased costs, and tighter environmental regulations, other factors determine pump station capacity: the need to syringe (lightly spray) all the greens, or even all the fairways quickly during the afternoon stress period; the need to quickly water in a fertilizer or other expensive material before its effectiveness is lost, or before heavy rain washes it off the course; the desire to water in a certain chemical before play begins; the need to keep large areas constantly moist during planting and early grow-in; or the need to complete various cycles quickly to take advantage of off-peak power rates.

Fertigation

Fertigation (the application of liquid nutrients and trace elements through irrigation systems) has been used on U.S. courses for more than 30 years. Started in Florida, this technique is now used on most courses in that state and, in spite of resistance among some end users, is spreading throughout the country. Although uniformity of application is important to fertigation, there have been surprisingly good results with even single-row quick coupler systems.

One of the greatest values of fertigation is realized during grow-in of a new course. Some courses even claim to have recouped the initial cost of the fertigation components during this period alone. After grow-in, one of the main benefits of fertigation is the ability to economically and accurately apply small amounts of nitrogen (N), for example, on a regular basis. This keeps a relatively constant level of N in the soil and produces a more constant color in the turf and a slow, steady growth rate. It avoids the undesirable fluctuations in color and growth that result from infrequent and heavier applications.

Another key benefit of fertigation is the level of control afforded the superintendent. The small amount of N put down in a typical fertigation application will be used by the grass in a few days, whereas N put down in a conventional granular application is used over a period of four to six weeks or more. The rate of release of N from controlled-release materials is affected by moisture and temperature, among other things. Because each fertigation application will be taken up in a short period, the turf manager can choose a period when he or she is certain that conditions will remain advantageous. The manager cannot do this given a four- to six-week uptake period.

Blended liquid products are comparable in price to equivalent dry materials. Although there are labor and equipment savings in the application of liquid products, there are also added initial costs. Storage tanks must be installed in or adjacent to the pump station. Secondary containment and a series of safety devices must be included. If the tanks, injection pumps, and controls are to be installed in the pump station building, an additional 1,200 to 1,500 square feet will be required.

Materials

Virtually all systems installed today use PVC pipe (Figure 10.1). Mainline pipe, usually 4 inches and larger, typically has gasket joints. These joints allow for movement due to expansion and contraction and are more tolerant of installation errors than solvent weld joints. Smaller pipe can also be gasketed, although solvent weld joints are required if installation is to be by the vibratory plowing method (Figures 10.2 and 10.3).

FIGURE 10.1   *Solvent welding a fitting to PVC pipe. (Photo by James Barrett)*

FIGURE 10.2   *Installing pipe and wires by vibratory plowing. Plywood sheets prevent ruts in the turf. Note minimal disturbance of turf in the background. This process is used only on smaller pipe sizes. (Photo by James Barrett)*

FIGURE 10.3   *Boom trencher in operation. Note that the sod was lifted prior to trenching. This process is used for larger pipe and in rocky soil. (Photo by James Barrett)*

Typically, SDR (standard dimension ratio) 21 or SDR 26 PVC, with pressure ratings of 200 psi and 160 psi, respectively, is installed. SDR-rated PVC pipe has the same pressure rating in all sizes. Schedule-rated pipe (Schedule 40, Schedule 80) does not. Although Schedule 40 pipe is sometimes used in smaller sizes (2 inches and less) where its pressure rating is above that of SDR 21, it is never used in the larger sizes. Other classes of PVC pipe (SDR 13.5 and AWWA C900, for example) are available for extremely high pressure systems.

Pressure ratings must be used with caution. American Society of Agricultural Engineers (ASAE) Standard S376.1 states that surge pressures in PVC pipelines should not exceed 28% of the pipe's pressure rating. Thus, if surge is not known, working pressure in SDR 21 (200 psi) pipe should not exceed 144 psi, and in SDR 26 (160 psi) pipe, working pressure should not exceed 115 psi. If surge pressures are known, the total of working pressure and surge pressure must not exceed the pressure rating of the pipe.

The designer of the irrigation system must be knowledgeable and experienced in these areas. Velocities should be kept below 5 feet per second, and competent designers size mains so that velocities are much lower than that. Higher velocities can lead to fatigue failure resulting from long-term cyclic surges. They also are a major contributor to water hammer, which is a destructive overpressure situtation resulting from abrupt changes in velocity caused by the sudden opening or closing of a valve or by the sudden start or stop of a pump.

Other types of pipe, such as ductile iron, black steel, and high-density polyethylene, are used in special situations. Asbestos-cement pipe was popular in the 1950s and 1960s, but it is no longer manufactured. Galvanized steel was also used in the past, but it is seldom installed today because it can fail owing to the corrosive action of irrigation water or of the surrounding soil.

Pipe Fittings

Pipe fittings must also be selected with care, especially in terms of anticipated pressures. Although PVC fittings are used in smaller sizes (2½ inches, 2 inches, or smaller), the current trend is to ductile iron fittings with push-on gasket joints in the larger sizes. Saddles are sometimes used in place of service tees and tapped couplings in certain pipe sizes, but they must be specifically made for use with PVC and very carefully installed.

Most swing joints today are prefabricated PVC assemblies with O-ring gasket joints and Acme or buttress threads. Some Schedule 40 galvanized steel swing joints are still used, but they must be coated, especially on the exposed threads with bituminous material.

Mainline isolation valves (3 inch, 4 inch, or larger) are usually ductile iron, resilient seat gate valves with push-on gasket ends. Smaller isolation valves are bronze units. Gate valves have been the norm, but ball valves are becoming common in the small sizes. The latter usually last longer but cost more.

Air release/vacuum relief valves are a necessity with PVC piping, and proper sizing and location are very important. Drain valves are typically installed at low points for maintenance purposes, but they are not intended to completely drain the system when it is winterized. Compressed air is used to blow out the water for this purpose.

Sprinkler Heads

Many different types of sprinkler heads are available, although the majority of heads used on golf courses are the pop-up type that are installed flush with grade and raise their nozzle turrets 1 to 4 inches when they are activated (Figure 10.4). Radii can vary from 40 to nearly 100 feet, with flows from 10 to 80 or more gallons per minute, depending on nozzle selection and available pressure. Some heads are manufactured of cast bronze, brass, or stainless steel, and a few still have cast iron cases. Others are made of high-impact plastics. Some heads have plastic cases with metal internals. Rotation is achieved by cam or lever-type impact drive or by a drive assembly that includes a turbine and a series of reduction gears. Most types of heads are available with adjustable part-circle arcs, and there are also full-circle models. Check valves are available on most models.

FIGURE 10.4   *Sprinkler head on a galvanized steel swing joint. (Photo by James Barrett)*

A basic head is connected alone or in a group to a remote control valve by lateral pipe. The remote control valve is on pressurized pipe, and when it is activated by a signal from a controller, it opens and allows the water into the lateral pipe. Pressure and flow cause the head(s) to pop up and rotate. When the valve is closed by the controller, flow into the lateral pipe stops and the heads retract to the closed position flush with grade. This configuration, known as a block valve system, requires that check valves be installed in most of the heads so they do not drain unwanted water onto the turf after the remote control valve closes.

Remote control valves can be activated either electrically or hydraulically, although the former is by far the most common means. If the system fails, electric valves fail closed and normally open hydraulically valves fail open.

Valve-in-head sprinklers are pop-up units that incorporate the remote control valve into the sprinkler body. This arrangement removes the need for a valve box to house a remote control valve. It also facilitates valve maintenance, because all components can be accessed through the head without any digging. The most common valve-in-head unit is electrically activated, but hydraulically activated models are also available.

Valve-in-head sprinklers make individual head control more practical and economical than the combination of a separate remote control valve and a basic head. In block valve systems, the distinction is not so clear, especially if more than two heads are connected to a valve. Nonetheless, electric valve-in-head sprinklers are frequently grouped through wire splicing so that two or more run on one controller system.

Although valve-in-head sprinklers facilitate maintenance procedures and have design advantages in terms of control, they do add to long-term maintenance considerations by virtue of the number of valves involved.

As nozzle designs have improved, "low-pressure" heads have recently become available from most manufacturers. These require 2 to 30 psi less pressure than previous heads, resulting in lower pump station discharge pressures and, in turn, lower-horsepower motors and smaller electric bills. These heads also perform well in windy conditions, as their spray has larger droplets than that of higher pressure heads.

Control Systems

Control systems have advanced dramatically since the introduction of solid-state components and computers. Electromechanical controllers are still manufactured but are used less and less as continuing developments in the modern units bring prices down. The modern controllers are more reliable and much more precise in terms of timing. Most important, they are infinitely more sophisticated and flexible, including functions such as multiple repeats and timed pauses between repeat cycles to allow water to soak in, simultaneous operation of a group of stations and sequencing of such groups, two-way communication allowing feedback of information from the field, flow management systems that limit velocities in piping and keep system flow at or near the point of highest pump station efficiency, alarms and switches, and cancel, pause, and resume features that react to input from remote devices such as wind, rain, and moisture sensors. Central control systems can automatically calculate station run times from ET data received from a weather station or from manual input. They can also provide reports that detail water usage totals and summarize system operation and faults.

Most of today's systems include a central programmer and a series of satellite controllers located throughout the course. The latter are connected to the remote control valves or valve-in-head sprinklers by direct burial wires or hydraulic tubing. Satellites are connected to the central communication cable or radio, although they can be programmed to operate in a stand-alone mode if the central or the communication system fails. Satellites are also used for local, nonprogrammed operations in various maintenance procedures.

Radio communication from central to satellite is becoming more common and is especially advantageous in irrigation retrofit projects on existing courses. Another recent innovation gaining in popularity is hand-held radio remote operation. By use of a keypad on a portable voice radio transceiver, the superintendent can start individual heads or groups, and even programs, from any location on the course. This system eliminates the need for line-of-site visibility from the satellite to its heads, allowing satellite boxes to be located farther out of play and view. It also could eventually lead to the elimination of all, or most, of the programming capability in satellites, thereby significantly reducing their cost.

On-site weather stations provide accurate local reference ET figures (Figure 10.5). After a crop coefficient is applied (manually or by the central controller) to adjust for the specific turfgrass type, the central can precisely calculate run times so only the amount of water needed to replace losses is applied. Weather stations range from expensive and elaborate computerized assemblies to simple atometers costing very little.

FIGURE 10.5 An on-site weather station calculates the evapotranspiration rate. (Photo by James Barrett)

Lightning Protection

Lightning protection is a concern with any computerized control equipment. Protective systems are available that detect approaching lightning activity and disconnect controller wiring prior to arrival of a storm. Some of these systems are combined with audible alarms to warn golfers off the course.

Design

Early automatic systems were designed primarily by irrigation equipment distributors. In the late 1960s, a number of independent irrigation designers in California began to take over the design function in that area. The concept of the independent irrigation consultant has slowly spread across the country and, in the not too distant future, distributors will essentially be out of the golf irrigation design business. The primary value of independent designers to course builders or operators and to architects is that they do not have a vested interest in one manufacturer. Accordingly, they can choose from all the systems and distributors available and thus select the best one for a given project.

At the start of a project, the irrigation designer needs comprehensive site information, most of which the architect can furnish. In addition to site data (local climatic and soils information), the route plan and grassing plan are essential, as are subsequent changes to either. Topography is needed, with tree lines and indications of limits or buffer zones concerning wetlands, endangered species areas, other factors, and property lines. The pumping location is obviously critical, and the source must be thoroughly investigated with a view toward water quality and quantity, as well as pertinent regulatory issues. The designer must also know where the maintenance buildings will be located and where 120-volt power will be available for the satellite controllers.

General system guidelines must be established through early discussions that include the architect, the irrigation designer, and the owner's representative. Guidelines should include the extent of coverage, supplemental coverage in green complexes, system capacity versus operating time, isolation capacity, desired level of control system sophistication and flexibility, and ancillary items such as weather stations, hand-held radio remotes, and fertigation capability. Obviously, all of these factors must be considered in view of the construction budget.

Coverage

Coverage in fairway and rough areas is defined by width, but not necessarily by only the number of sprinker rows. A given width can be achieved with two rows of 90-foot-radius sprinklers spaced at 90 feet or three rows of 65-foot heads spaced at 65 feet. The differences are distribution uniformity and precision of control. The three-row layout will produce maximum uniformity over more width than the other system. In addition, each large radius head covers 25,500 square feet, whereas the smaller one reaches only 13,300 square feet. Assuming individual head control, the three-row system can discretely control a much smaller area. Combined with careful location of heads (and part-circle sprinklers in some cases), this allows the operator to water the sunny area but not the adjacent shade, the slope or ridge but not the nearby swale, and the approach but not the putting surface.

Obviously, budget considerations are important, but smaller heads at closer spacings with individual head control can provide the most uniform irrigation coverage and, therefore, the most uniform playing conditions. They can also ensure the least waste of water and power in the long run.

Sprinkler selection is based, to a large extent, on uniformity. There are several technical measures of uniformity, and computer software is available that allows modeling of different combinations of head layouts, spacings, nozzles, and pressures. The combinations can then be compared to select the optimum solution for a given project, but experience is needed to make proper evaluations.

Supplemental coverage around greens is now provided in most designs. Because of differences in grass type, soils, height of cut, and topo, the moisture requirements of the putting surface are substantially different from those in the surrounding areas. Some designs use individually controlled part-circle heads throwing away from the collar. Others have groups of small (12-foot to 15-foot radius) spray heads, run by remote control valves, located on the slopes and ridges framing putting surfaces and greenside bunkers. There have even been a few experiments with subsurface drip in slopes and collars, but not enough to properly evaluate the technique.

Hydraulics

The hydraulic part of irrigation design requires knowledge of factors such as static and dynamic pressure, friction loss, velocity, water hammer, pipe and fitting pressure ratings, hydraulic looping, irrigation system operation, pump operating curves, and installation procedures in order to route and size a piping network that will be cost-effective and safe to install and to operate over the life of the system. The electrical part of design requires knowledge in areas such as wire sizing and voltage loss, conductor and insulation types, splicing systems and procedures, grounding and surge protection, and code requirements.

Conclusion

The foregoing discussion is intended only as an introduction to some of the key principles, components, and concerns related to the irrigation of golf courses. All the aforementioned irrigation design/construction concepts are even more difficult to implement when installing a system on an existing golf course. The designer must also consider golfer dissatisfaction, daily play disruption, scheduling conflicts, safety factors, and additional costs (Figures 10.6 and 10.7). This is a complex subject and is becoming increasingly more so. System design and preparation of plans and specifications should be left to a professional, independent consultant. Nonetheless, the golf architect must have a working knowledge of irrigation systems and their planning and installation if a project is to be successful.

FIGURE 10.6 The length of trench on an established course is generally no longer than that which can be piped, backfilled, and resodded in the same day. (Photo by James Barrett)

FIGURE 10.7 Here a rotary broom cleans up backfilled trench prior to sod replacement. (Photo by James Barrett)

Golf Courses
on Derelict Land

All really great golf holes involve a contest of wits and risks. No one should attempt to copy a great hole, because so much may depend on its surroundings as well as some feature miles away in the background which influences and affects the play of the hole. If the terrain is suitable, some of the character of the original hole might be incorporated elsewhere.

From *Concerning Golf,* 1903, by John Laing Low (1869–1929)

It has become increasingly difficult and expensive to acquire land for golf near population centers. Therefore, planners are turning their attention to the use of derelict land, including strip mines, slag heaps, collieries, gravel pits, sand pits, and, especially, sanitary landfills. Successful and uniquely interesting golf courses have been created on all.

Before strip mines and collieries are converted to golf courses, chemical and physical tests are required to establish whether toxic materials are present that may contaminate topsoil or sand placed on them. Tests can assure that the existing material will not compact to a degree that prevents subsurface drainage.

Many towns and cities are considering the development of golf courses on their landfills as desirable recreational features and revenue producers. William Amick, who is probably the golf architect most experienced in handling landfills for golf, contributes the following discussion to this chapter.

Golf Courses on Landfills

by William W. Amick
GOLF COURSE ARCHITECT
DAYTONA BEACH, FLORIDA

Affordable and available land for new golf courses is often scarce in populated areas. Yet there are few active uses for completed landfills. Fortunately, provided that certain critical construction and maintenance requirements are met, many landfills can be—and have been—turned into attractive and popular golf courses.

In 1995 there were more than 60 golf courses in the United States that were partially or entirely built on landfills. A few more are built each year, mainly by municipalities. Three long-established and very successful courses are the Santa Clara Golf and Tennis Club, Santa Clara, California, by Robert Muir Graves (Figure 11.1); the Renaissance Park Golf Course in Charlotte, North Carolina, by Michael Hurdzan; and the Mangrove Bay Municipal Golf Course in St. Petersburg, Florida, by William Amick (Figure 11.2). Their lush tees, fairways, and greens have emerged from sites that were once debris.

FIGURE 11.1   *California's Santa Clara Golf and Tennis Club in the foreground is part of a complex that includes a hotel, tech mart, convention center, and parking garage. With the exception of the lakes, the entire golf course was constructed on landfill.*

FIGURE 11.2   *This is the 14th tee at Mangrove Bay Municipal Golf Course. (Photo by William Amick)*

Nevertheless, because of the instability of old dumps, perhaps completed with no filling, dumping, or capping specifications, and even modern sanitary landfills with rigid fill specifications, a course can quickly become a disaster area if sound building practices are not employed (Figure 11.3). Following are several issues that are typically of critical concern in planning and constructing a golf course over a landfill.

FIGURE 11.3   Here is another successful 18-hole golf course, developed for the city of St. Petersburg, Florida, built on landfill. (Photo by William Amick)

Permits, Requirements, and Monitoring

All requirements included in federal, state, regional, and local permits for operating, closing, and then maintaining a landfill must be studied and followed during placement of material in a landfill, in capping and monitoring it during construction of the golf course, and in future maintenance. These requirements are usually strict, yet liability is minimized by following them carefully. Monitoring groundwater for leachates and the handling of all waters from the site are particularly critical issues.

Settling

With the passage of time, substantial settling occurs in landfills as the refuse decomposes. This settling proceeds for many years and in varying amounts in different parts of the same landfill. Settling is of immense concern to the golf course architect. Tees may settle unevenly, depressions may occur in playing areas, irrigation pipes or wire may be broken by uneven shifting, and drainage lines under greens or elsewhere may fail. (Figure 11.4) Because the rate of settling is impossible to predict for individual landfills and even different parts of the same fill, hard rules cannot be set as to when a landfill is "ready" for golf course construction. Five to eight years after all parts are completed and capped seems to be the minimum period required before actually starting construction of the course. There are cases in which construction has begun sooner or even immediately after capping. Most of these courses have suffered a combination of difficulties disruptive to play and costly to correct.

Gases

Methane and other gases are produced by decomposing solid waste. To avoid the possibility of fires or explosions endangering construction workers, maintenance crew, and golfers, as well as future damage to turfgrass and trees, these gases must be properly handled. Protection is usually achieved with a network of perforated collection pipes and solid removal pipes laid in the refuse. The gases are either vented into the air, burned off, or piped to be used as energy. The Mountaingate Country Club near Los Angeles, by architect Ted Robinson, has collected up to 5 million cubic feet of gases daily, which is piped and used by the University of Southern California for heating, cooling, and other purposes (see Figure 11.4). Design of a gas collection and removal system calls for an engineer, with the resulting system operated exclusively by qualified and accomplished service personnel.

FIGURE 11.4   *Mountain Gate Country Club near Los Angeles, California, has a history of severe settlement and shifting of golf course features. But, as the photo shows, it is a very attractive golf course today.(Photo by D2 Productions, Murphy/Scully))*

Capping

Today in the United States, capping landfills with several feet of soil is a requirement with few, if any, exceptions. Sometimes a heavy plastic membrane cap is also specified. These and other steps must be executed to complete a landfill for a closing permit. Yet much more must be accomplished to build a proper golf course over the cap (Figure 11.5).

Golf course architects' recommendations for the minimum depth of capping soil range from 3 to 8 feet for all playing features of the course. The average recommendation is about 5 feet. If the capping soil is heavy, 6 to 12 inches of sand or sandy topsoil is probably desirable on top of the cap. Greater depths are needed for tee and green complexes. Sometimes geotextile fabrics are placed under the sand. It is mandatory that the golf course architect and developer use the services of a civil engineer who is experienced in landfill development.

The cap of soil, and possibly topsoil, is a major factor in the high cost of landfill-golf course construction as compared with construction on natural sites. Unless soil for capping, the grading of course features, and the topsoil can be derived by stripping and stockpiling before the landfill operation, these materials must be transported from an off-site location. Purchasing the soil, loading, hauling, and distributing it can be very costly. Yet, if only part of the course is on landfill, the natural portion of the site can be a nearby and less costly source of material.

FIGURE 11.5   When landfills are not properly developed and capped, the results are water and air infiltration, decomposition, settling, and leachate formation, seen at the bottom of this photo.

FIGURE 11.6   This brave tree tried to grow with virtually no topsoil cap and nothing but garbage for a root zone. The results are obvious.

Trees for landfill-golf courses require deeper soil than does turfgrass (Figure 11.6). Trees can be planted in "tree mounds" containing 6 to 8 feet of soil. It may be desirable, but sometimes not allowed by permits, to plant trees with long taproots that can penetrate the refuse. Accordingly, species of trees for a landfill-golf course must be specially selected for both suitability and survival.

Designing the Fill to Shape the Golf Course

A limitation to building most golf courses on landfills is that disturbing refuse once it is in place is not permitted, or if it is permitted, can be impossible or impractical. This limits shaping to the use of costly fill brought onto the site. Therefore, the ideal preparation of a landfill as a site for a future golf course requires early involvement of the course architect in cooperation with the consulting engineer in planning placement of the refuse. Such planning is done before the landfill is started and many years prior to construction and completion of the course. If finished contours are planned before dumping starts, the advantages and cost savings can be immeasurable.

Even though limited to fill over only the cap, the landfill's contours can be approximately shaped for each hole and the practice range once refuse is in place. The golf course can thus be more interestingly shaped, and the holes will have more possibilities for golf strategy and interest. Earth moving, and therefore construction costs, can be minimized in this manner. Pond sites may even be possible. All of these objectives are accomplished by the course architect as he or she completes routing and grading plans, taking into account the engineer's estimates for eventual settling. The resulting grading plan then becomes the basis for determining how to place the refuse in the landfill (Figure 11.7).

At its completion, the landfill is capped and allowed to settle the required number of years, as specified by regulations. At the end of that time, with a minimum of earth movement, the site will present outstanding contours for a golf course. This preparation was done for the Toytown Sanitary Landfill in St. Petersburg in anticipation of a golf course being built on it in the future. (see Figure 11.7).

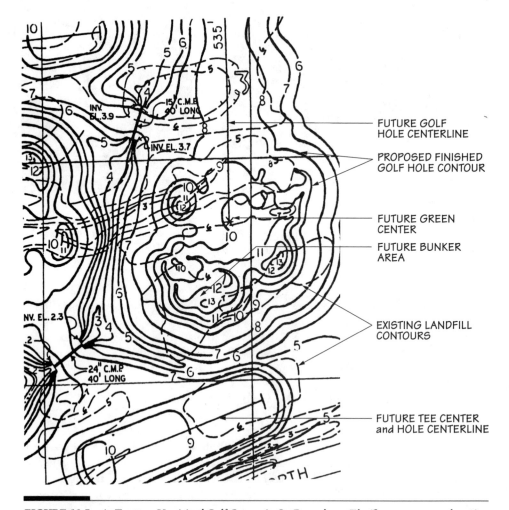

FIGURE 11.7 *At Toytown Municipal Golf Course in St. Petersburg, Florida, you can see the existing landfill contours and the finished contours desired by the golf course architect. Landfill work could then continue to where the golf course shape and contour evolved and the golf course construction could then be completed.*

For the reasons discussed earlier, the cost of construction of a golf course on a landfill can be half-again to twice or more times the cost of a comparable course created on a natural site. Moreover, maintenance costs, primarily during the first few years, are likely to be greater than for other new golf courses.

Judging from a number of excellent examples across the country, it is apparent that the additional problems and extra costs of building on a landfill are justified for a municipality, for an operator when the course is leased to him or her, and for golfers who enjoy the course. Who would argue that a beautiful golf course packed with enthusiastic golfers is not superior to a completed but sterile and derelict landfill, unused and unloved?

Grassing the Golf Course

Whether this or that bunker is well placed has caused more intensely heated arguments (outside the realm of religion) than has ever been my lot to listen to. Rest assured, however, when a controversy is hotly contested over several years as to whether this or that hazard is fair, it is the kind of hazard you want and it has real merit. When there is unanimous opinion that such and such a hazard is perfect, one finds it commonplace. I know of no classic hole that does not have its decriers.

Adapted from *Scotland's Gift* GOLF, 1928, by Charles Blair Macdonald (1856–1939)

Grassing the Course

Golf is played on grass. A vigorous and groomed greensward of permanent grasses is therefore a primary objective in design of the course and the preparation of specifications for its construction. In practice, the quality of the greensward is said to be the first thing that players notice, and many golfers deem it the most important aspect of the layout.

A beautiful greensward becomes a reality on irrigated areas following grow-in when there is

1. An adequate depth of topsoil or root zone mix
2. Surface, subsurface, and air drainage
3. A seedbed with meticulously graded surfaces
4. Nutrients and soil conditioners sufficient to provide productive soil
5. Ideal varieties of grass

Specifications must therefore include comprehensive chemical and physical soil testing of topsoil and subsoil:

1. *Depth of topsoil.* On fairways and adjoining roughs, the minimum is a 4-inch settled depth, and on tees, 6 inches. Greater depths are better. The type and condition of the subsoil also has a bearing on depth of topsoil. On greens, the minimum depth of root zone mix is as specified for the method used. For example, the USGA method requires a uniform 12-inch compacted depth.

2. *Drainage.* This involves grading to create surface runoff, installation of underground drainage where needed, and the removal of trees to create air drainage.

3. *Surfacing, removing rocks and debris.* "Surfacing" is smoothing the surface, not the grading achieved by cutting and filling with heavy equipment. Mechanical rock pickers and rakes are used to create level areas and surface drainage, as are homemade floats of several sorts pulled by tractors. The objective is a smooth surface free of small humps and hollows, one that surface drains and that is mowable at low heights of cut with no "scalping" of the turf.

Yet this surfacing of fairways does not involve elimination of natural undulations. As Alister Mackenzie emphasized,[1] the objective is not a dead flat fairway. Although the architect may specify removal of some, natural undulations add intense interest. These gentle undulations, however, probably do not show on the topographical plan. They are found by walking the site and contribute to the traditional element of luck in golf.

On greens and tees, total rock and debris removal is required. Unless a prepared mix is purchased, screening is necessary because even meticulous mechanical or hand-raking will not remove all stones.

Fairway soils and those of mounds and tee slopes are sometimes screened. More often rocks and debris are removed by mechanical rock pickers and rakes, and this is sometimes accomplished by hand-raking and picking.

4. *Soil conditioners and plant nutrients.* Soil conditioners are added following rough grading. Soil reaction (pH), as determined by testing, can be too acid or alkaline for turfgrass. If soils are too acid, lime is needed; if too alkaline, sulfur or acid-reacting fertilizers may reduce alkalinity. Where soils are alkaline or saline, gypsum is added. It is also used when soil pH is favorable or high but the element calcium is lacking.

When the desired surface has been achieved, fertilizers and soil conditioners are added. Soil analysis may indicate what is needed. Still, the architect draws on his or her own knowledge, or that of consulting agronomists or the superintendent, to determine actual requirements.

Almost always nitrogen, phosphorus, and potassium (N, P, and K) are needed, and, on occasion, minor elements.[2] Environmentalists prefer organic nitrogen sources. Yet some architects have observed that inorganic complete (N,P,K) fertilizers can result in an earlier grass cover than that produced by an organic fertilizer, thus reducing the critical period in which the land is devoid of vegetation.

Except on California greens, organic matter, often peat moss, is part of the prepared mix for greens and tees, as on occasion is a sandy topsoil. A host of other materials, including sawdust and bark dust, are sometimes used. An analysis of each is needed.

The preferred method for mixing sand and other amendments is mixing off-site— that is, off the feature, not necessarily off the golf course. This mixing is effected with a blender or similar equipment (Figures 12.1 and 12.2). A former method, mixing several buckets of sand with several of organic matter and soil according to the specified ratio and then turning the pile repeatedly, does not produce a uniform mix unless the pile is turned many times (Figure 12.3).

FIGURE 12.1 A 966 Cat front-end loader is feeding the peat hopper of a custom soil blending machine. Precision accuracy is key in the development of a root zone medium. (Photo by Greensmix)

On-site mixing involves spreading the organic matter on the surface of the green
or tee and then mixing it into the sand or topsoil with a rotary plow or by thorough disc-
ing. On-site mixing may be satisfactory when a very small amount of organic matter is
to be incorporated. It is not ideal when a larger amount of organic matter is added. In

practice, on-site mixing of organic matter into sand can produce a perched water table in the top few inches of the green and a saturated condition in the upper inches of the root zone.

Other materials sometimes added to the top mix are calcined clays, calcined diatomites, humates, seaweeds, sewerage sludges, perlite, porous ceramics, vermiculite, and zeolite. Seaweeds and their extracts have produced positive results on some soils and appear to be particularly beneficial on sands. These amendments, along with fertilizers, are frequently mixed in on-site, although some architects and superintendents prefer off-site mixing.

Peat and sand mixes may lack beneficial organisms required for healthy turf. A more rapidly decomposing form of organic matter is then needed, or a percentage of sandy topsoil. Rapidly decomposing forms of organic matter include sewage sludge, seaweed, and well-decomposed manures (if the manures are truly weed-free).

Soil Fumigation

Fumigation has long been practiced in turfgrass propagation. The objective is to remove all pests, including weed seeds, insects, and fungi. At one time, soils for greens were sterilized by oven heating. Weeds were also reduced by fallowing the soil, an operation seldom considered today because it can result in severe erosion. Fallowing allows seeds to germinate; cultivating then eliminates them. Today the treatment is most likely chemical fumigation. However, at time of writing the compound long used, methyl bromide, is being phased out. Other materials may soon be on the market to replace it. Moreover, architects, contractors, and superintendents pay less attention to fumigating now that many greens are sand-based.

Grasses for the Golf Course

The important subject selecting grasses for the golf course is discussed in Chapter 13 by the national director of the Green Section of the USGA. Purchasing seed is introduced in Chapter 14.

Wildflowers, ornamental grasses, ground covers (including pachysandra and myrtle), links plants (including gorse, heather, sea lyme and marram grass), together with bulbs (particularly daffodils for early spring color), are appropriate in out-of-play areas. Seedsmen and extension services are sources of information concerning their use.

Mulching Newly Seeded Areas

"Mulching" refers to techniques for protecting seedbeds from erosion and dessication. Generally, mulching accelerates germination and early growth of seedling grasses. A mulch is selected for its ability to conserve moisture and heat and yet not cut off oxygen. It is also mandatory that the mulch permit water to move through it into the soil.[3]

Mulching materials include natural products such as untreated hay and straw, although hay introduces weeds unless it is harvested from salt marshes or other areas free of noxious weeds. Synthetic materials are therefore preferred. One commonly used is a woven polyethylene cover developed originally for winter protection of existing greens. It is long lasting, and, when used in initial construction, is also adaptable to later maintenance practices.

A preferred method for applying hay, straw, and some synthetic mulches is hydromulching, which is hydroseeding with a mulch added to the slurry in the tank of the hydroseeder.

Application rates for synthetic materials are those recommended by the manufacturer, whereas straw and marsh hay are frequently applied at the rate of ½ to 1 standard bale per 1,000 square feet. Synthetic mulch materials are biodegradable, as indeed are natural materials, but the latter may have to be removed in whole or in part as the seedling grass develops and when temperatures rise, even in otherwise dormant periods.

Some mulches, such as natural ones, must be fastened to the soil in areas exposed to wind and subject to scouring in periods of heavy runoff. Glues, tar, or other viscous substances can be used for this purpose. Mulches can also be secured by nets made of biodegradable material that does not require removal before the first mowing.

Mulching is almost always a useful practice after seeding greens and tees and on steep slopes of fairways and roughs. In fact, often entire golf holes are mulched.

Closely related to mulching is the use of erosion control sheets of various types through which the grass grows. Several brands that contain seed are available, although it may be difficult to find one impregnated with the desired variety unless the erosion mat is made to order.

Except for sodding, mulching is probably the most effective means of controlling erosion, although a high percentage of fast germinating species in the seed mixture also helps. Fine-bladed ryegrasses can be used for this purpose, but their content should not be high. In practice we find that in a bluegrass-ryegrass mixture the ryegrass will dominate the resulting stand if it makes up more than 15 to 20% by weight of the mixture. This is due to its rapid germination and the vigor of its seedlings, which crowd out bluegrass. The bluegrass may then take years, if not forever, to assert itself.

Another means to control erosion is to seed cereal rye or any rapidly germinating cereal that disappears with mowing. Cereal rye is sown at the rate of 40 to 80 pounds per acre. The permanent mix is then sown over it. Sometimes following hydroseeding an empty cultipacker-type seeder is pulled over the seeded area to ensure that the cereal rye makes contact with the soil. In frost-free seasons, buckwheat can also be used in this manner.

Constructing Golf Course Features

Construction procedures vary for different features. Appendices A and B at the end of this chapter provide draft specifications for materials used in constructing USGA and California greens.

Greens and Collars

Many, perhaps the majority, of greens built today are constructed to USGA specifications involving a perched water table (Figure 12.4). This is intended to provide the superintendent with the best of both worlds in that it contains a reservoir in dry periods above the gravel blanket and rapid drainage though the green profile in periods of heavy precipitation.

The reservoir is created because water moving downward through a layer composed of fine particles is retained above one composed of coarser particles until sufficient head develops to force the water to move by gravity through the gravel and into the tile.

USGA recommendations allow two methods for putting green construction: one including an intermediate coarse sand layer between the gravel blanket and topmix; and one without this coarse layer, with topmix placed directly on the gravel blanket (Figure 12.5).[4]

FIGURE 12.4   This is the typical USGA green that evolved from Dr. Marvin Ferguson's work in the 1950s. (Courtesy USGA)

USGA GREEN DETAIL
NO SCALE

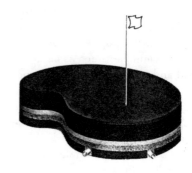

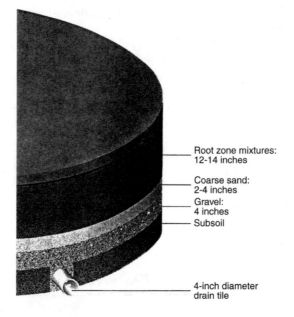

Root zone mixtures:
12-14 inches

Coarse sand:
2-4 inches

Gravel:
4 inches

Subsoil

4-inch diameter
drain tile

FIGURE 12.5   This diagram, prepared by the USGA, shows at left the green cross section with the 2- to 4-inch intermediate coarse sand layer. An alternative cross section on the right deletes the coarse sand layer, leaving the rest of the cross section the same.

Analyses of sand and gravel by approved laboratories are mandatory to determine whether a coarse sand layer is required and to select the correct sand and gravel size. Methods other than those of the USGA include, but are not limited to:

1. Purr-wick (Figure 12.6). Developed by W. H. Daniel of Purdue University, this patented system employs compacted sand over a plastic barrier. The sand, stabilized by the turf, remains moist and playability is constant. This system has proved successful in building greens and even more successful for tees, where grades are flat as contrasted with rolling greens. (Still, rolls can be accommodated on the Purrwick system.)

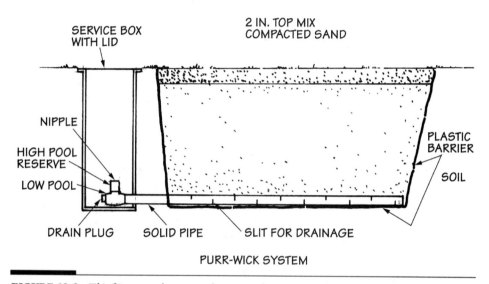

FIGURE 12.6   *This diagram shows one of many such components separated by an internal divider formed by a plastic barrier and reinforced by wood or fiber house sheathing. An internal divider is installed for every 6 inches of elevation change on the green surface.*

2. *California method* (Figure 12.7). This method, developed at the University of California-Davis, involves a 12-inch depth of pure sand situated over a tiled subbase with or without an intermediate gravel layer.
3. *Other patented methods.* Several other systems have been developed. An example is the cell system, which provides trickle irrigation and drainage.

Some architects construct greens with a topmix or a sandy topsoil placed on a tiled subbase without a gravel base, advising their clients accordingly. We have observed that many such greens produced at lower costs have been highly successful and are less likely to allow saturation of soil within a few inches of the surface.[5] Sometimes tile is omitted when the subbase is very porous, although in northern areas ice may disappear more rapidly in springtime on tiled greens.

Architects in northern regions have experimented with draping topmix and gravel over the sides of greens and tees rather than placing them in a cavity (Figure 12.8). Drainage appears to be enhanced. In fact, tile may have to be installed at the foot of the draped material to carry off water in wet periods, especially in early spring. Draping probably compromises the perched water table.

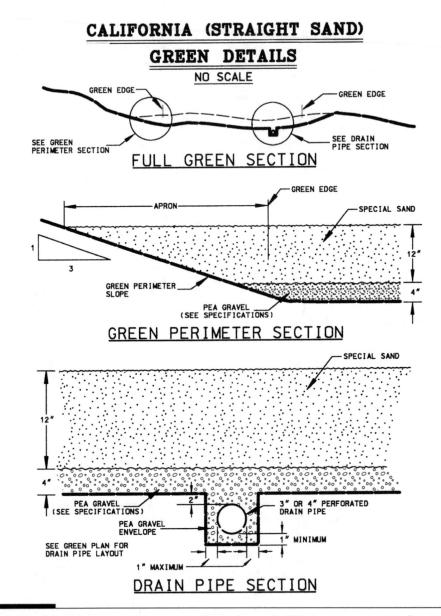

FIGURE 12.7 *This cross section is generally similar to the USGA green except (1) there is no intermediate layer and (2) the growing medium is straight sand versus a mix.*

Once the subgrade of a green (other than those of patented systems) is in place and compacted, the steps involved include the following:

1. Tile* is installed in a herringbone, grid, or random pattern, with spacing between laterals dependent on the texture of the subbase soil. A flusher or cleaner is installed at the top end of the main tile to permit flushing the system with a hose. The Green Section recommends that drainage trenches in the subbase be a minimum of 8 inches deep below the subgrade.

Note: The old term "tile" and the new term "drainpipe" are interchangeable.

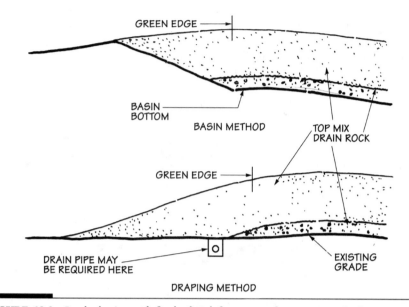

GREEN EDGE

BASIN
BOTTOM

BASIN METHOD

TOP MIX
DRAIN ROCK

GREEN EDGE

DRAIN PIPE MAY
BE REQUIRED HERE

EXISTING
GRADE

DRAPING METHOD

FIGURE 12.8 In the basin method, the finished green grades must match the perimeter. In the draping method, the green material is placed on top of a subgrade and virtually every green would have a side slope up to the green surface.

2. The layers are added, including the gravel blanket, the coarse sand layer (if used), and the root zone mix.
3. Fertilizers and soil conditioners are added. Type and rates are determined by analysis.
4. The surface is fine-graded by raking and floating and then seeded, sodded, or vegetatively planted with stolons or sprigs. Sodding methods include use of turf grown on matching soils, washed sod, and sod grown on plastic sheets.
5. Seeding is followed by the grow-in period, involving frequent fertilizing and special irrigation to keep the surface constantly moist.

Tees

Methods for constructing tees after the subbase is complete include the following:

1. The USGA Green Section method for greens, most often with the coarse sand layer omitted
2. The Purr-wick method
3. Other methods, under the following circumstances:
   a. If the subsoil lacks uniformity, a gravel base is added with 6 or more inches of sandy topsoil or topmix placed over it (Figure 12.9).
   b. If the subsoil is uniform and porous, the sandy topsoil or topmix is placed directly on it.

Once topsoil or topmix is in place and compacted, construction proceeds in steps similar to those for greens, with the side slopes of the tees treated in the same manner as fairways. Sodding of side slopes is commonly specified to prevent erosion. Newly introduced laser graders are now used to produce "billiard table" teeing surfaces as demanded by contemporary golfers.

Because the tee surface is uniformly flat except for a slight surface pitch (Figure 12.10), tile is not always needed, except at the foot of terraced slopes (Figure 12.11) or at the hillside edges of those tees notched into hillsides (Figure 12.12) where tiles are needed as curtain drains.

FIGURE 12.9   The gravel base smooths out the uneven subgrade, allowing tee material to be added evenly for a proper turf growing medium, either in a basin or draped as shown here.

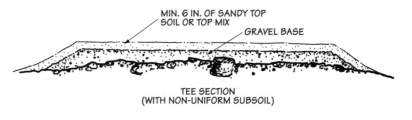

MIN. 6 IN. OF SANDY TOP
SOIL OR TOP MIX
GRAVEL BASE

TEE SECTION
(WITH NON-UNIFORM SUBSOIL)

FIGURE 12.10   Generally, the only time the longitudinal cross section of the tee drops down to the front is when the landing area is well below the tee level. Otherwise, the lateral cross section is up to the golf course architect's discretion.

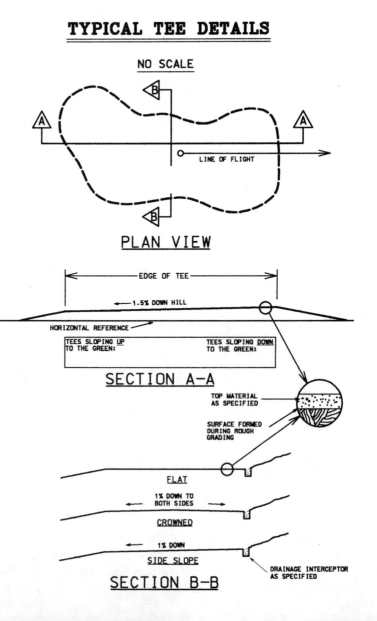

TYPICAL TEE DETAILS

NO SCALE

LINE OF FLIGHT

PLAN VIEW

EDGE OF TEE

1.5% DOWN HILL

HORIZONTAL REFERENCE

| TEES SLOPING UP TO THE GREEN: | TEES SLOPING DOWN TO THE GREEN: |

SECTION A-A

TOP MATERIAL AS SPECIFIED

SURFACE FORMED DURING ROUGH GRADING

FLAT

1% DOWN TO BOTH SIDES

CROWNED

1% DOWN

SIDE SLOPE

DRAINAGE INTERCEPTOR AS SPECIFIED

SECTION B-B

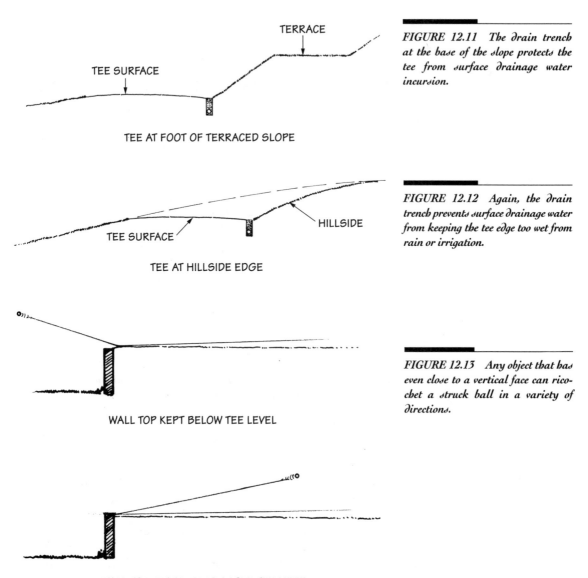

TERRACE

TEE SURFACE

TEE AT FOOT OF TERRACED SLOPE

FIGURE 12.11 *The drain trench at the base of the slope protects the tee from surface drainage water incursion.*

HILLSIDE

TEE SURFACE

TEE AT HILLSIDE EDGE

FIGURE 12.12 *Again, the drain trench prevents surface drainage water from keeping the tee edge too wet from rain or irrigation.*

WALL TOP KEPT BELOW TEE LEVEL

FIGURE 12.13 *Any object that has even close to a vertical face can ricochet a struck ball in a variety of directions.*

WALL TOP PROTRUDING ABOVE TEE LEVEL

If retaining walls are used on sides of tees to conserve real estate by precluding long grass slopes, care is then necessary to ensure that the walls do not protrude above tee level. Otherwise, dangerous ricochets can occur (Figure 12.13).

Fairways

Preparation and fine grading must be painstaking to create a mowable surface free of stones and other debris, humps that scalp when mowed, and hollows that will hold water. Preparation involves these steps:

1. *Subdrainage* of a portion or all of a fairway unless the existing soil and subbase are porous, as they are in sandy regions. If fairway tile is installed to drain the fairway itself, rather than as a conduit to lead water from one area to another, the gravel

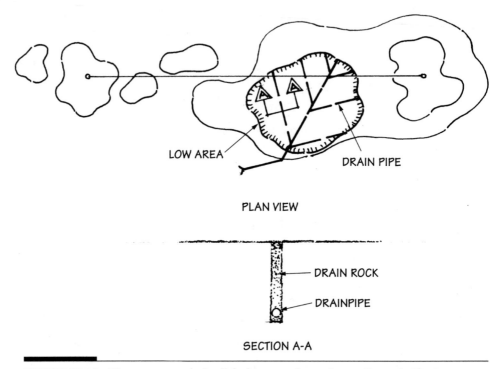

LOW AREA

DRAIN PIPE

PLAN VIEW

DRAIN ROCK

DRAINPIPE

SECTION A-A

FIGURE 12.14   The narrow trench should be kept open for unobstructed travel of drainage water down to the drainpipe. Growing turf can quickly cover and hide the drain rock.

surrounding it is brought to the very surface, because even a shallow depth of top-soil over the gravel compromises the system (Figure 12.14).

2. *Topsoiling* to a minimum 4-inch compacted depth, depending on the subsoil. Sands close to USGA specification can be used in place of topsoil if a sophisticated fair-way irrigation system is installed. Some architects specify a physical test of the subsoil.

3. *Adding fertilizers* and possibly soil amendments, such as lime.

4. *Grassing.* Fairway turf cover is most often established by seed or sprigs. Yet fair-ways are on occasion completely sodded, or sod is specified on steep slopes, in drainage swales, and other areas where erosion can be excessive. Strip sodding is sometimes a good technique in these areas. Water bars are created on steep slopes and in channels to deflect runoff before its volume and velocity are great enough to cause erosion.

Roughs

Grassed roughs extending for some 50 feet or more out from fairways are prepared in the same manner as fairways, but grassed with other species.

Remote and treed roughs are seldom refined carefully but are grassed with a rough mixture. Yet it is desirable that these areas be mowable, and some architects strive for "English park" roughs in treed areas.

Bunkers

A method for the construction of bunkers includes the following steps (Figure 12.15):

TYPICAL BUNKER DETAILS

NO SCALE

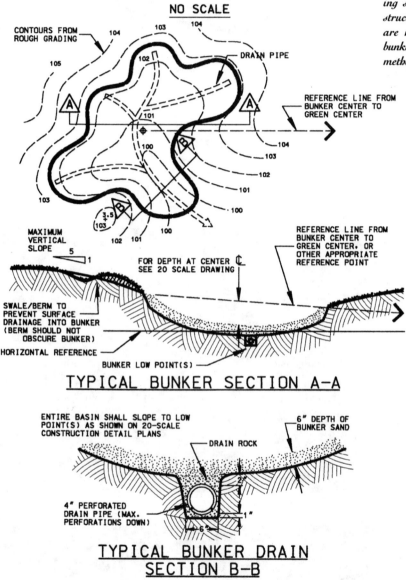

FIGURE 12.15 *This detail draw-ing shows one basic way of con-structing a sand bunker. There are many differing types of sand bunkers, each requiring a different method of construction.*

1. Excavating the bunker to the specified depth (Figure 12.16).
2. Constructing a berm, swale, or both, around the entire bunker to prevent surface water from entering it (see Figure 12.15).
3. Establishing a 1-foot vertical lip around the entire bunker to reduce wind erosion of sand (Figure 12.17). On sandy or unstable soils, this sharp drop-off may require stabilizing with flexible plywood or sandbags filled with heavy soil (Figures 12.18 and 12.19).

   If the 1-foot vertical lip has been installed, sand is added later at the green end of the bunker to provide a 3-inch lip and 12 inches at the tee end to prevent an unplayable lie (Figure 12.20).

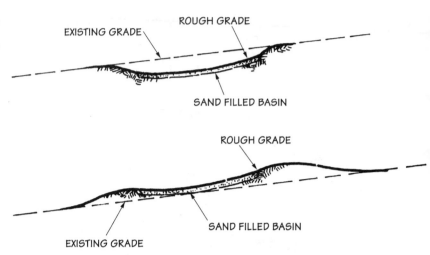

FIGURE 12.16   These diagrams demonstrate two basic methods of bunker construction. In the upper diagram, the bunker is completely excavated from the existing grade. In the lower diagram, the bunker is constructed from fill material. There are a multitude of variations and combinations of these two methods.

FIGURE 12.17   Rather than a vertical lip, shown here, a bunker edge may be sloped instead.

FIGURE 12.18   Thin, pliable plywood or fiberboard can be formed to achieve the curves desired in the bunker outline.

FIGURE 12.19 *Another excellent way to form the capes and bays of a sand bunker involves the use of soil-filled sandbags. The bags later rot away and disappear.*

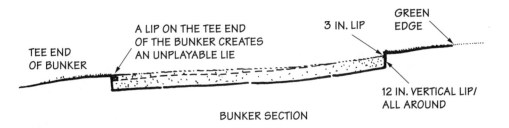

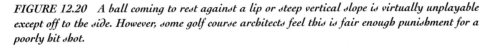

FIGURE 12.20 *A ball coming to rest against a lip or steep vertical slope is virtually unplayable except off to the side. However, some golf course architects feel this is fair enough punishment for a poorly hit shot.*

4. Installing tile. Standard and random patterns are used. If stone is placed around the tile, a barrier of straw, tarpaper, or geotextile is placed between it and sand to prevent stone contaminating sand.
5. Lining. Although the practice is controversial, a few architects prefer to line a bunker with geotextiles or other materials that permit passage of water. This is done on very stony soils to prevent stones from becoming mixed with the sand.
6. Sodding a strip around the edges if irrigation is available during construction.
7. Special perimeter irrigation installation for surrounds is specified by some architects.

Because of the Dye influence and the links tradition, architects may face their bunkers with railroad ties installed in a laid-back position to prevent ricochets that would occur if the walls were vertical (Figure 12.21).

Bunker walls and the mounds surrounding them are generally grassed in the same manner as fairways or roughs, but with no bentgrass in the mixture.

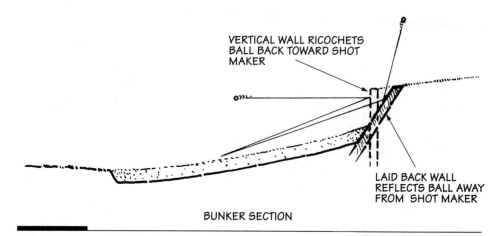

VERTICAL WALL RICOCHETS
BALL BACK TOWARD SHOT
MAKER

LAID BACK WALL
REFLECTS BALL AWAY
FROM SHOT MAKER

BUNKER SECTION

FIGURE 12.21   Constructing a vertical wall here would create a dangerous situation (see also Figure 12.13). Again, some golf course architects feel this is simply another problem for the golfer to solve, usually requiring the use of a shot off to the side in order to ultimately reach the green.

Mounds

Mounds in the rough are grassed in the same manner as the roughs, whereas fairway mounds are treated as fairways. Although they are often seeded, sodding produces an early finished effect that is aesthetically attractive.

Grow-in: Cool Season Grasses

Grow-in involves watering, mowing, fertilizing, and topdressing of the new stand. The program for this critical period is not necessarily specified in detail by the architect, although he or she may outline it in general terms or return periodically to advise. Most often it is left in the hands of the maintenance superintendent. Although there are contractors specializing in grow-in, its execution may not be part of the construction contract.

Major points to observe in creating playable stands of bentgrass are outlined in the following paragraphs. Yet it is emphasized that no rigid directions can be put forward. These vary according to innumerable circumstances, and "fertigation" has revolutionized the fertilizing of new stands.

Blankets During Grow-in

A common practice following seeding, particularly autumn seeding, is to cover the seeded area with blankets similar to those used in northern areas to reduce ice cover. These blankets, of which there are several types, hasten germination and reduce erosion. With managed care their use can be prolonged into the seedling period and over the winter and thus accelerate the maturing of the turf. Yet problems can arise with their use. For example, they may have to be removed in warm periods, even in winter, and their final removal in spring can be critical.

Guideline rates for fertilizing given below are for each 1,000 square feet. It is important to note that the grow-in period can result in extensive damage to new equipment. Owners therefore make arrangements for the rental of used equipment.

Putting Surfaces and Collars

Putting surfaces and collars, whether seeded or sodded, must be kept moist until there is a mature stand and never allowed to undergo water stress. Seed sown during droughts may not be injured, except by erosion when it remains unwatered and ungerminated.

Soon after germination, an application of ½ pound of nitrogen (N) per 1,000 square feet is required, plus phosphorus (P) and potassium (K). The utmost care is required to prevent burning. This application is repeated once every two weeks in the growing period. For example, if a green is seeded or sodded in early September in the Boston area, the first fertilizer application can be in the third week of that month with at least two more applications by freeze-up, followed by a dormant fertilizing, using an organic nitrogen source at the rate of 1 pound of nitrogen plus P and K, each at about half the rate of N but varying.

The following spring, once growth has restarted, possibly by mid or late April, the ½-pound N plus variable P & K applications once every two weeks are resumed and continued throughout the season; some superintendents stress 1 pound of nitrogen for the first application in spring. This program involves some 4 to 10 pounds of N during the first full season, plus P and K, at variable rates. This heavy N range does not appear to reduce root growth, as do more frequent or excessive applications involving more than 10 pounds in a growing season.

If the weather is dry, watering must be resumed. In fact, April is a month even in cool, humid climates when seedling stands can be lost in whole or in part by dessication.

Early and frequent top dressing with sand, plus organic matter or perhaps a sandy topsoil, creates a true putting surface. The top dressing material used for the root zone mix is often recommended for this purpose.

Initial mowing is recommended when the bentgrass is ½ to ¾ inches high, perhaps two to three weeks after seeding, with no more than ¼ inch of the grass blade removed. This is followed by gradually lowering the cut to ⁵⁄₁₆ inch and retaining this height for the entire first growing season. Reducing the height of cut even more enhances ball speed, but at the expense of root growth. Indeed, the combination of close clipping and heavy nitrogen applications may reduce root growth appreciably and adversely affect the quality of the putting surface well into the future.

When players complain about slowness of greens during the first season, as they typically do, superintendents find that periodic rolling reduces complaints. Still, it is best to keep the height of cut at ⁵⁄₁₆ inch or even as high as ¼ inch. Dividends in depth of root growth and density of turf soon become apparent.

Throughout grow-in, superintendents must be vigilant in regard to disease, insect pests, and localized dry spots. The latter can often be corrected with the use of wetting agents, and the former call for use of pesticides—often at rates lower than those used on mature turf.

Both tine and water injection aeration are beneficial on new stands if the surface has become compacted. On sodded stands, most of all those established from washed sod, aeration is needed to encourage root penetration.

Bentgrass Tees and Fairways

Bentgrass tees and fairways require watering practices similar to those for greens and collars, and, generally, ½ to ¾ of the fertilizer amounts used on those areas.

The first mowing is recommended when the grass is ¾ to 1 inch high, with ¼ inch removed on the first cut and a gradual lowering to ½ inch or the desired future height of cut. Lightweight mowers are recommended, because gang units can cause extensive damage to the seedling grass.

Top dressing of tees, as for greens and collars, is recommended to produce or maintain a "billiard table" surface, as demanded by contemporary golfers and considered to be a standard of excellence.

Erosion Repair

Despite painstaking precautions, erosion can occur in the early grow-in period. It appears as three distinct types or combinations of these types.

1. Sheet erosion, when an area is denuded of seed and topsoil to a shallow depth
2. Rivulet erosion, when small rivulets, from ¼ inch to several inches in depth, are produced by runoff
3. Gully erosion, when deep channels are formed by cascading water

Early repair followed by protection of the eroded area is the best practice. Sheet and rivulet erosion require retopsoiling, refertilizing, and reseeding. In most cases, sowing cereal rye at 2 pounds per 1,000 square feet—or some other fast-germinating cover crop—on top of the grass seed, rolling the rye in, and protecting the reseeded area by mulching or blanketing is almost mandatory. Some sow the cereal before sowing the permanent seed.

Sodding is often recommended for repair of gullies, because reseeding will not preclude further washing. When sod is not available, gullies can be reseeded with the desired species plus cereal rye. If carefully protected by mulching or erosion control blankets, the repair job can be a success.

Bermudagrass Putting Green Establishment and Grow-in

by John H. Foy
DIRECTOR, STATE OF FLORIDA
USGA GREEN SECTION

Once the actual putting green construction/renovation process is almost complete, preparing for turf establishment and development of proper surface conditioning begins. A good grow-in is critical for both short- and long-term success. The following suggestions are based on successful grow-ins at many facilities over the past several years.

Preplant Fertilization

Following laboratory testing of the root zone mix components and determination of the physical characteristics of the mix, a chemical soil analysis should be performed. The results should be used for amending the root zone with lime or other needed materials during the actual mixing operation. This is also the ideal time to have the preplant fertilizer thoroughly incorporated into the root zone mix. As a general guideline, incorporating the equivalent of 2.0 pounds of actual nitrogen per 1,000 square feet from an organic slow release source, such as Milorganite, is suggested. In addition, incorporating 2.5 to 3.0 pounds of phosphorus per cubic yard of root zone mix is a good starting point, and, for surface preplant applications, a 5-20-20 material can be broadcast at a rate of 10 pounds per 1,000 square feet and then lightly incorporated.

Surface Preparation and Planting

A firm and smooth soil surface is required for a successful grow-in and long-term top-quality conditioning. This is an aspect of putting green construction often overlooked but critically important. A board float setup can be used for the final smooth grading operation and development of the desired and appropriate surface contours. The depth of the root zone mix should not vary more than plus or minus 1 inch for proper putting green performance. An old golf club shaft or piece of rebar can be used for random probing of the root zone. Then, to firm the root zone mix, a combination of supplemental irrigation and wheel tracking is typically repeated several times. Ideally, only minimal footprinting occurs once the root zone has settled and been firmed prior to planting.

The standard means of planting bermudagrass putting greens is still vegetative sprigging. For normal summertime plantings, increasing the sprigging rate to 25 to 30 bushels is appropriate, but exceeding this range does not increase the rate of turf establishment. As a matter of fact, excessive sprigging rates can actually slow turf establishment because of intraspecies competition. Thus, it is a waste of money.

Turf Establishment and Surface Development

Immediately after sprigging, a thorough irrigation should be conducted to reestablish good soil moisture. Until good root system development has occurred, the upper root zone must be kept moist but not saturated. Frequent and light daytime irrigation applications must be made for the first 3 to 6 weeks and will vary depending on weather conditions. Overwatering is just as detrimental as underwatering. A good strategy to follow with new plantings is to "treat them like a baby—put them to bed dry (on the surface) and wake them up wet."

In 7 to 14 days after planting, new shoot growth should start to appear, and with this the grow-in process begins. To encourage maximum turf growth, the rule of thumb for grow-in fertilization has been to supply 1 pound of actual nitrogen per 1,000 square feet per week. Very good results have been achieved with alternating a readily available nitrogen source, such as ammonium sulfate, with a balanced complete analysis fertilizer. During the process, two to three supplemental applications of a high analysis potassium source is also beneficial for good root system development. Until the height of cut of the putting surfaces is reduced below 0.25 inch, there is really no benefit from the use of putting green grade fertilizers. An every-4- to 5-days application frequency produces a better turf growth response than an every-7-days fertilization program. Furthermore, if a fertigation system is available, it can also be of assistance in the grow-in process.

An environmental note: A thin, immature turf cover combined with high fertilization rates and heavy irrigation is the ideal condition for possible nitrate leaching. Thus, especially when soluble nitrogen materials are being used, no more than 0.5 pound of actual N per 1,000 square feet should be applied at a time. This should be the maximum soluble nitrogen application rate in the management of established turf areas as well.

Implementation of a mowing program shortly after shoot growth begins is important for encouraging good lateral turf spread, along with smoothing and firming of the surface. Typically, a walk-behind mower is used until sufficient firmness is developed to support the use of a triplex unit. Initially, a ⅜- to ½-inch height of cut should be maintained and the putting surfaces mowed two to three days a week. As turf density and coverage increase, so should mowing frequency. At the same time, height of cut should be gradually worked down to ¼ inch and maintained until essentially full turf coverage has been established.

Approximately six weeks prior to opening the greens for play, the height of cut should be worked down to ⅛ inch or slightly lower. This is useful in identifying any remaining surface irregularities so that they can be corrected. It is recommended that mowing height then be raised to ⁵⁄₃₂ to ³⁄₁₆ inch for the rest of the grow-in period.

In the past, regular verticutting of bermudagrass putting greens was a fairly common practice during grow-in. Although verticutting can help increase density, it can exert additional stress on the turf and actually slow growth. An initial verticutting is recommended to assist in thinning out clumps of sprigging material and smoothing the surface. The verticutting blades should be set to operate just above the soil surface. Then, until turf coverage is developed, verticutting operations should be discontinued. A good alternative practice for increasing turf density and coverage is regular spiking or slicing replications. A weekly or even biweekly program can be established.

Although some surface rolling during the grow-in process is a usual practice, it should be kept to a minimum. A few rollings with a 1- to 2-ton unit does not cause excessive compaction and definitely helps in the development of a smoother surface. Top dressing treatments are also extremely important in developing a smooth and true putting surface. Typically, four to six weeks after sprigging sufficient turf coverage has developed to initiate a top dressing program. A couple of medium to heavy applications are then made to help fill in depressions and improve smoothness. Then, light top dressings every 7 to 14 days are suggested. For the first one to two years, exactly the same material used for the root zone mix should be used for all top dressing treatments. Once a mature profile character has been developed, a straight sand top dressing program is typically established for bermudagrass putting greens.

Under ideal growing conditions, with hot days and warm nights, full turf coverage and an acceptable playing surface can be developed in approximately 90 days from the time of sprigging. However, allowing at least 120 days for grow-in is recommended. We also stress that one to two full growing seasons are required for the development of a truly mature character after any type of putting green construction/reconstruction work. A primary aspect of this maturing process is the development of a slight amount of organic matter (thatch) accumulation in the upper root zone area. This organic accumulation is needed for nutrient and moisture retention as well as proper surface resilience. Typically, the first winter after construction/renovation, there may be complaints about the greens not "holding" approach shots. Moreover, the turf surface is not as tolerant to traffic and wear. Thus, some patience and education of the golfers are needed to minimize problems. Time is an important basic ingredient in the maturing process of new greens.

If time is available during grow-in, a small-diameter tine coring replication approximately six weeks prior to opening the greens to play is suggested. Coring is helpful in further smoothing of the surface, breaking up and incorporating any organic grow-in layers, and maintaining better resiliency through the first winter. We recommend the use of ¼-inch-diameter hollow-core tines. The cores generated should be broken up and worked back into the turf surface. Sufficient top dressing should be applied (if necessary) and worked in to backfill the holes to 90 to 95% of their capacity. Then a rolling replication is usually conducted to reestablish good surface smoothness. During the winter months, water injection cultivation and spiking replications are also beneficial for maintaining a degree of surface resiliency.

Special Note

Throughout the grow-in process, it is important to closely monitor putting surfaces and collar areas for the development of any "off-type" bermudagrasses. Contaminants should immediately be removed. If necessary, two to three spot applications of glyphosate (Roundup) should be made. Then the area of contamination is dug out and sod plugs are installed. Mechanical removal of any weeds that develop is also worthwhile. I cannot overemphasize the importance of early contamination/encroachment control efforts for maintaining a monostand turf cover and ensuring optimum performance over the long term.

Bermudagrass Fairways: Establishment and Grow-in

by James Francis Moore
DIRECTOR, CONSTRUCTION EDUCATION PROGRAMS
USGA GREEN SECTION

Thanks to the aggressive nature of bermudagrass, fairway establishment is a relatively fast and simple process. However, as is the case for every area of the golf course to be planted, a combination of good preplant preparation, good planting materials, and good postplant care will result in a top-quality product.

Preplant Considerations

As basic as it may seem, one of the most often overlooked—yet most important—considerations in planting bermudagrass is light. Hybrid bermudagrass is a remarkably adaptive plant. However, it is not shade tolerant. Full sun conditions must be provided for at least eight hours a day for bermudagrass to flourish, especially under traffic. Once this most basic requirement is met, hybrid bermudagrass can provide what many believe to be the best fairway playing surface in golf.

Chemical soil analysis should be conducted for the areas to be planted. It is important to test each area of the course that has a significantly different soil type. For example, many of today's golf courses are built on reclaimed sites and/or sites that are covered with soil of widely varying quality. Test each area, since the amendments necessary to promote good turfgrass growth in each area may well be different.

Soil reaction (pH) should be adjusted to 6.0, or to 7.0 if possible. The addition of sulfur or lime may be needed to meet these requirements. These are ideal reactions and do not imply that bermudagrass cannot be grown in soils of higher or lower pH. In fact, bermudagrass is one of the most forgiving grasses when it comes to soil reaction. However, because the application of amendments to provide more favorable growing conditions is usually an inexpensive process and can improve the plant's ability to extract nutrients from the soil, the cost and effort are justifiable.

The same soil tests provide insight as to the nutrient status of the soil. As a general rule, a starter analysis fertilizer (usually on a 1:2:1 ratio such as 10-20-10) should be applied at a rate to provide 50 pounds of nitrogen, 100 pounds of phosphorus, and 50 pounds of potassium per acre. Keep in mind that this is a general rule, because, in many parts of the country, phosphorus and potassium are in abundance in native soils. Occasionally, micronutrient deficiencies will also be identified by the soil tests.

The application of a micronutrient fertilizer package will help to correct such deficiencies.

The next step to accomplish prior to planting is to ensure good soil moisture. Note that good soil moisture does not mean that the surface has to be wet. In fact, wet surface soil will make sprigging of the bermudagrass nearly impossible. During the construction of a new course, the soil is often moved numerous times and in the process becomes extremely dry even as deep as 12 inches. It is a good idea to irrigate lightly (so as not to cause erosion) numerous times prior to planting. Allow the surface to dry before planting, and resume irrigation immediately after the sprigs are laid down.

Although it is sometimes very difficult to obtain a smooth surface (depending on the amount of clay or rock in the soil), a smooth surface at planting time will be rewarded with top-quality playing conditions much more quickly. A smooth planting bed reduces the scalping that occurs during mowing, particularly in the first few weeks following planting.

Planting dates must also be carefully considered. In most parts of the country where bermudagrass fairways are used, typical planting dates range from April through September. Although earlier and later planting dates are sometimes successful, they result in greater risk to the turf. Planting before soil and air temperatures have risen to the point at which the bermudagrass will grow rapidly will result in extended exposure of the immature sprigs. This increases the chances of desiccation as well as insect and disease pathogen injury. On the other hand, a late planting date predisposes the turf to a much greater chance of winter injury. A mature stand of bermudagrass turf has an insulating mat of organic matter (thatch) that helps protect the crown of the plant from low temperatures and winter traffic while the turf is dormant. Mature bermudagrass develops rhizomes beneath the soil surface, which are also better protected by thatch from low temperatures and physical wear and tear. And, even though bermudagrass is a warm-season turf, the extreme heat of midsummer can slow establishment rates. The ideal planting date, if possible, is in early summer when temperatures have risen to the point at which bermudagrass is actively spreading horizontally.

Planting Rates and Procedures

Planting rates for bermudagrass sprigs, usually measured in bushels, vary a great deal depending on the desired speed of establishment. Rates as low as 300 bushels (Industry Standard Bushel, or ISB) per acre will result in good coverage in as little as 10 to 12 weeks. In contrast, rates as high as 750 (ISB) bushels per acre are sometimes used to achieve complete coverage in 6 to 8 weeks. The normal establishment rate is approximately 450 bushels per acre for Tifway 419 bermudagrass sprigs.

Although the bushels-per-acre measurement may seem a reasonable method of determining planting rates, in practice this is confusing and unreliable in the field. Technically, a bushel holds 1.24 cubic feet of bermudagrass sprigs. However, over the years, the sod industry has used two measurements, namely, the Georgia and the Texas bushel. The industry standard bushel (ISB) or Georgia bushel measures .04 bushel or ⅓ of the standard U.S. measurement (the Texas bushel). Therefore, it is important to be careful in specifying planting rates to ensure that all parties are using the same measurement technique. The majority of the industry uses the ISB measurement.

Even with agreement to make the ISB measurement the standard, additional problems arise concerning how the grass is harvested and planted. Some producers maintain that 1 square yard of sod will yield 1 bushel. However, different harvesting techniques can change the yield significantly. There is also the problem of whether or not the sprigs are moist and/or compressed in the delivery truck.

For the reasons cited, most bermudagrass planting rates are based on the density of the sprigs laid on the soil. Terms such as light, medium, or heavy, referring to a planting rate, are growing more common. A light rate (typically 300 bushels per acre) results in a sprig laid every 2 to 3 inches. A medium rate places sprigs much closer, about every inch or so, and approximates the 450-bushel-per-acre rate, whereas a heavy rate, 750 bushels per acre, literally covers the fairway with sprigs.

Once the sprigs are laid down, it is best to press them lightly into the soil. There are several types of machines for accomplishing this task, including specialized bermudagrass planting machines. All use a variation of the straight agricultural disk or coulter set on 2- to 4-inch centers to press the sprigs into the soil.

Grow-in

Once sprigs are planted, irrigation must begin immediately. Light and frequent irrigation is needed to ensure that the sprigs do not dry out. Depending on conditions (particularly wind), the sprigs may have to be irrigated as often as every two hours. However, this irrigation must be extremely light (usually one or two turns of the sprinkler) to keep sprigs moist without eroding the underlying soil.

As the turf begins to put down new roots, irrigation should be tapered back. Tapering back should occur within 10 to 14 days. As roots elongate, irrigation continues to be reduced in frequency and increased in duration. Within three to four weeks following planting, irrigation is cut back to once per day. The key is to maintain a moist (not wet) soil in the upper 3 to 4 inches of the profile.

Fertilizing is necessary every 10 to 14 days at a rate that provides approximately 45 to 50 pounds of nitrogen per acre (1 to 1¼ pounds of N per 1,000 square feet). Occasionally, heavier rates are used; sometimes as much as 50 pounds of N per acre are applied on a weekly basis. Applications of this proportion are discouraged, however, because of the increased likelihood of environmental damage should soil erosion occur. Fertigation is an excellent supplement to granular applications and has the significant advantages of very light and nearly constant feeding of the new turf and the complete elimination of the need for application equipment (which often causes rutting on wet soils). A combination of both fertilizer techniques seems to work best. Granular applications are made prior to planting and when the stand is established well enough that spreading equipment can traverse the fairways without damage. These applications apply nutrients in larger amounts, typically between ½ and 1 pound of an element per 1,000 square feet. Fertigation is used thoughout the entire grow-in process and typically applies elements in rates approximating ⅒ of a pound per 1,000 square feet or less.

Mowing begins as soon as the turf can be clipped without being pulled from the soil. Under ideal growing conditions, mowing can begin in as little as three weeks. Mowing equipment must be extremely sharp and should utilize hydraulically driven reels instead of the ground wheel driven type. Initial mowing heights depend largely on the smoothness of the planting surface and the condition of the sprigging material. As a general rule, mowers should be set at about 1 inch for the first cutting. The fairway should be mowed three times a week to encourage lateral spreading of the turf. Some scalping is unavoidable and, in fact, is a key part of the smoothing process. Cutting heights are gradually lowered to the final ½-inch setting over the next eight to ten weeks.

Under ideal conditions, a fairway will be completely covered with Tifway 419 bermudagrass within 8 to 10 weeks following planting. However, this does not mean it is ready to withstand the passage of carts or heavy traffic. Although the fairways may be played, all vehicle traffic (except mowers) must be kept to the paths or in the roughs. This rule should be enforced for the entire first season. Only after the turf has developed an extensive rhizome system and the cushioning organic pad discussed earlier is it ready to take vehicle traffic.

Once mature, a hybrid bermudagrass fairway requires regular mowing (usually, the more often the better), vertical mowing to prevent thatch, and routine fertilization. Hybrid bermudagrasses are remarkably tolerant of traffic, disease, and insect pests and recover quickly from injury. However, they do not tolerate shade. As stressed earlier, the full sun requirements of bermudagrass must be given the highest priority.

Draft Specification — USGA and Similar Greens

by Norman W. Hummel, Jr.
HUMMEL & CO., INC. SOIL SCIENTISTS

Phase One: Materials Selection and Definition Prior to Construction

Gravel Drainage Materials

The gravel shall be a washed pea stone or crushed stone that meets the following criteria: gravel materials shall not have an LA abrasion test (ASTM C-131) value exceeding 40, and a loss not exceeding 12% using the sulfate soundness test (ASTM C-88). In addition, the underdrainage stone must meet the following particle size criteria:

100% passing a ½ inch sieve.
No more than 10% passing a 2 mm (No. 10) sieve.
No more than 5% passing a 1 mm (No. 18) sieve.
A uniformity coefficient (D90/D15) of less than or equal to 2.5.
The D15 of the gravel must be less than or equal to 5 × D85 of the root zone mix.
The D15 of the gravel must be greater than 5 × D15 of the root zone mix.

Root Zone Mix

The root zone will be defined in this section and shall be selected as such. The root zone mixture will consist of a sand, processed peat or compost, and a topsoil (if the owner or architect desires). The root zone mix will be evaluated using the ASTM Test Methods for putting green root zones by the Owner's Testing Agent. A sand sample, a processed peat or compost, and, if desired, a topsoil shall be submitted to the Owner's Testing Agent, and tested for adherence to the specifications.

Processed Sand

The sand shall meet the following particle size criteria:

	Sieve Mesh	Diameter of Sieve (mm)	Allowable Range % Retained
Gravel	10	2.00	0–3%
Very coarse sand	18	1.00	0–10% Combined with gravel
Coarse sand	35	0.50	At least 60% in this range
Medium sand	60	0.25	
Fine sand	100	0.15	20% maximum
Very fine sand	270	0.05	5% maximum
Silt		0.002	5% maximum
Clay		Less than 0.002	3% maximum

In addition, there should be 100% passing the No. 5 screen (4 mm), but the sand should contain no more than 10% very fine sand, silt, and clay combined.

Topsoil

The topsoil shall be friable, productive, agricultural soil free from stones, debris, or soil clumps ¼ inch or larger, free of rhizomes of quackgrass or any other noxious weeds, and free of any herbicide residue.

Processed Peat and Compost

Peat and compost shall be free of sticks, stones, and other debris and comply with the following: Peat shall have a total ash content of less than or equal to 15% and a moisture content of 40 to 70%. A compost shall have a total ash content of no more than 40%, should be proven to be nonphytotoxic, and has preferably been aged for one year.

Upon approval of these three components, the Owner's Testing Agent shall blend the components as deemed most appropriate and then define the ratio of the sand, peat, or compost, and topsoil (if desired), used to create the root zone mix. The ratio of sand, topsoil, and peat or compost shall be based on laboratory testing and performance criteria defined in these specifications.

The test results on the approved root zone mix will establish the specifications for approval or rejection of all subsequent quality control submittals during construction. (The specifier should place here—who bears the cost of testing.)

Root Zone Mixture Performance Testing

ASTM Test Methods for sand-based putting greens shall be used for the performance testing. Water retention shall be done at 30 cm tension. Tests shall determine compliance with the specified mixing ratio and provide calibration data for the quality control program. Tests shall comply with the following criteria on a core compacted at 14.3 ft-lb/square inch.

Saturated hydraulic conductivity (inches per hour)	6 to 24 inches per hour
Bulk density (gm/cc)	1.3–1.65
Total Porosity (percent)	35%–55%
Aeration porosity*	15%–30%
Capillary porosity*	15%–25%
Saturation percentage*	40%–55%

The root zone mixture shall have an organic matter content of 0.7 to 3% on a dry weight basis, as determined by Method 1 of ASTM F-1647. The sand-soil-peat or compost shall be mixed off-site to a uniform consistency.

Phase Two—Quality Control During Construction

All gravel drainage materials and root zone mix shall be tested and approved prior to delivery or to placement on the greens site.

*Determined at 30 cm tension.

Gravel Drainage Material

A 1-gallon sample from each 500-cubic-yard lot of gravel shall be tested. Upon approval of each of the materials, the gravel shall be released for placement on the greens site.

Root Zone Mix

After approval of the root zone components and mix, a 1-gallon sample of the blended mix for every 500 tons of mix shall be submitted for testing, to include particle size analysis and organic matter content. Physical performance testing may be required if the Owner's Testing Agent determines that there are discrepancies in the samples. Upon approval of the blended root zone mix, the material shall be released for placement on the green.

Inspection Costs

The owner shall bear all costs for first submittals, including the testing of gravel or root zone mix. The contractor shall pay for subsequent testing and shipping of rejected samples.

Sample Authentication

An owner's representative must be present during the sampling and packaging of gravel and root zone mix. The sample shall consist of a subsample taken from a composite of samples taken from cross sections from the top, bottom, and sides of the stockpile. A 1-gallon sample in a sealed plastic bag or container shall be packaged and sent to the Owner's Testing Agent.

Owner's Testing Agent: Hummel & Co., Inc.
61 Cayuga Street
Trumansburg, NY 14886
(607) 387-5694
Dr. Norman W. Hummell, Jr.

Fertilizer

The final root zone blend as determined by the testing agent will be tested for soil fertility, and a complete fertilization program will be recommended by the Owner's Agent for the installation maintenance period.

Draft Specification—California Green

by Norman W. Hummel, Jr.
HUMMEL & CO., INC. SOIL SCIENTISTS

Phase One—Materials Selection and Definition Prior to Construction

Gravel Draingage Materials

The gravel shall be a washed pea stone or crushed stone that meets the following criteria: Gravel materials shall not have an LA abrasion test (ASTM C-131) value exceeding 40 and a loss not exceeding 12% using the sulfate soundness test (ASTM C-88). In addition, the underdrainage stone must meet the following particle size criteria:

100% passing a ½ inch sieve.
No more than 10% passing a 2 mm (No. 10) sieve.
No more than 5% passing a 1 mm (No. 18) sieve.
A uniformity coefficient (D90/D15) of less than or equal to 2.5.
The D15 of the gravel must be less than or equal to 5 × D85 of the root zone mix.
The D15 of the gravel must be greater than 5 × D15 of the root zone mix.

Root Zone Sand

The root zone sand will be defined in this section and shall be selected as such. The root zone sand will be evaluated using the ASTM Test Methods for putting green root zones by the Owner's Testing Agent. A sand sample shall be submitted to the Owner's Testing Agent and tested for adherence to the specifications.

Processed Sand

The sand shall meet the following particle size criteria:

	Sieve Mesh	Diameter of Sieve (mm)	Allowable Range % Retained
Gravel	10	2.00 ⎫	⎧ 0%–10%
Very coarse sand	18	1.00 ⎭	⎩ Combined
Coarse sand	35	0.50	82%–100%
Medium sand	60	0.25	50%–70%
Fine sand	140	0.15	
Very fine sand	270	0.05 ⎫	⎧ 0%–8%
Silt		0.002 ⎭	⎩ in this range
Clay		less than 0.002	

In addition, there should be 100% passing the No. 5 screen (4 mm) and no more than 30% fine sand. In addition, the sand shall have a uniformity coefficient (D60/D10) of between 2.0 and 3.5.

The test results on the approved root zone sand will establish the specifications for approval or rejection of all subsequent quality control submittals during construction.

(The specifier should place here—who bears the cost of testing.)

Root Zone Sand Performance Testing

ASTM Test Methods for sand-based putting greens shall be used for performance testing. Water retention shall be done at 40 cm tension. Tests shall comply with the following criteria on a core compacted at 14.3 ft-lb/square inch.

Saturated hydraulic conductivity: (inches per hour)	15–50 in/hr
Total porosity (percentage)	35%–55%
Aeration porosity*	15%–30%
Capillary porosity*	10%–20%
Saturation percentage*	25%–55%

Phase Two—Quality Control During Construction

All gravel drainage materials and root zone sand shall be tested and approved prior to delivery to or placement on the greens site.

Gravel Drainage Material

A 1-gallon sample from each 500-cubic-yard lot of gravel shall be tested. Upon approval of each of the materials, the gravel shall be released for placement on the greens site.

Root Zone Sand

After approval of the root zone sand, a 1-gallon sample of the sand for every 500 tons of sand shall be submitted for testing, to include particle size analysis. Physical performance testing may be required if the Owner's Testing Agent determines that there are discrepancies in the samples. Upon approval of the root zone sand, the material shall be released for placement on the green.

Inspection Costs

The owner shall bear all costs for first submittals, including testing and shipping of gravel or root zone mix. The contractor shall pay for subsequent testing and shipping of rejected samples.

Sample Verification

An owner's representative must be present during the sampling and packaging of gravel and root zone sand. The sample shall consist of a subsample taken from a composite of

*Determined at 40 cm tension.

samples taken from cross sections from top, bottom, and sides of the stockpile. A 1-gallon sample in a sealed plastic bag or container shall be packaged and sent to the Owner's Testing Agent.

Owner's Testing Agent: Hummel & Co. Inc.
61 Cayuga Street
Trumansburg, NY 14886
(607) 387-5694
Dr. Norman W. Hummel, Jr.

Fertilizer

The final root zone sand, as determined by the testing agent, will be tested for soil fertility, and a complete fertilization program will be recommended by the Owner's Agent for the installation maintenance period.

Notes

1. Alister Mackenzie, *The Spirit of St. Andrews* (Chelsea, Mich.: Sleeping Bear Press, 1995).
2. A 100-pound bag of 10-6-4 commercial fertilizer contains 10 pounds of nitrogen (N), 6 pounds of available phosphoric acid (P_2O_5) and 4 pounds of soluble potash (K_2O). To apply 1 pound of N per 1,000 square feet, one divides the first figure of the ratio into 100; 10 is therefore the amount to apply. The fertilizer would also provide 6 pounds of P_2O_5 and 4 pounds of K_2O.
3. D. N. Austin and J. Driver (*Erosion Control,* January/February 1995) classified erosion control materials: conventional mulches, loose or anchored; hydraulic mulches, loose or anchored; rolled erosion control products (RECPs), including nets rolled over loose mulches, staked and stapled; open-weave geotextile meshes; erosion control blankets (biodegradeable materials, including straw, wood, and coconut textiles) rolled onto the area and anchored with staples or stakes; and geosynthetic mattings as an alternative to riprapping.
4. The USGA 1993 recommendations for putting green construction are described in *The Green Section Record* (March/April 1993). Appendices A and B in this chapter provide draft specifications for USGA and California greens, prepared by Norman W. Hummel.
5. According to Norman Hummel in an address to the annual meeting of the American Society of Golf Course Architects, March 1996, the architect should consider such greens in deciding the method to specify.

Turfgrass Selection
for Golf Course Construction

by James T. Snow, National Director
USGA GREEN SECTION

The course should be equally good during winter and summer, the texture of greens and fairways should be perfect, and the approaches should have the same consistency as the greens.

From *Golf Architecture,* 1920, by Alister Mackenzie (1870–1934)

Ever since the first golf courses were constructed in the United States in the late 1800s, significant amounts of time and money have been spent in the selection, evaluation, and propagation of grasses for use as playing surfaces for the game of golf. Each decade brought with it progress and success in the evolution of such grasses. Together with improved technologies and the increased capabilities of golf course superintendents, maintenance standards and playing conditions have improved steadily. In the early 1930s, John Montieth, director of the USGA Green Section, stated, "The turf on today's fairways is as good as that on greens at the turn of the century." This statement could have been repeated in the intervening years.

Since World War II, the game of golf has grown tremendously in popularity, and the number of turfgrass cultivars has grown along with it. It is estimated that there are nearly 400 named turfgrass cultivars today, most of them representing about a dozen of the most popular turfgrass species. The large number of grasses and the genetic diversity they represent are good from the standpoint of finding grasses well suited to a particular location. On the other hand, taking advantage of these resources requires a broad understanding of the capabilities and weaknesses of the various species and cultivars.

There are many factors that must be considered in selecting the best grasses for a particular site. In addition to the ability of a grass to survive and to provide an attractive, good playing surface for the game of golf, a factor that continues to grow in importance is how well a grass contributes to the environmental stewardship required of the game of golf today. It is not enough to select a grass based only on its appearance and play characteristics; more and more, grasses are being selected with reduced water and pesticide needs. This is a trend that unquestionably will grow.

Many of the factors that must be considered in selecting grasses for new course construction and renovation are described in this chapter. They have been categorized under several headings: (1) General Adaptability Factors, (2) Species/Cultivar Adaptability Factors, and (3) Golfer Preference Factors.

General Adaptability Factors

The first screen applied in selecting a grass is obvious and simple: Can the grass survive as a perennial in the region of the country where it is proposed for use? In this respect, there are several factors to consider.

Climatic Adaptation

Grasses can be divided into two broad categories: warm-season grasses and cool-season grasses. Warm-season grasses have an optimum growing range of 80 to 95°F and, therefore, are generally grown in the southern United States. Although they tend to be more drought, heat, and wear tolerant than most cool-season species, warm-season grasses are less tolerant of cold winter temperatures and suffer killing damage when grown too far north. Warm-season grasses are used on golf courses in the tropical, warm temperate, and transition zone areas of the country (see Figure 13.1), although some are not dependably winter hardy in the transition zone.

Cool-season grasses grow best within a temperature range of 60° to 75°F, making them best adapted to the cool temperate region of the country. They also are used extensively in the northern portion of the transition zone, and some are used in the warm temperate and upper tropical zone to a limited degree. The limiting factors in the use of

FIGURE 13.1   This latest version of Major Zones of Turfgrass Adaptation in the United States includes the often referred to, but seldom identified, "transition zone."

cool-season grasses in the South are high summer temperatures and relative humidity, which disrupt growth of the turf plant and enhance disease activity. Thus, temperature is arguably the single most important factor in determining the adaptability of grasses to a particular area, although relative humidity can have a profound effect in some climatic zones because of its influence on disease incidence. For example, some cool-season grasses are better able to flourish in the southerly latitudes of the drier Southwest than in the more humid Southeast.

Another climatic factor that can be important in grass selection is rainfall. In arid climates, golf courses with weak irrigation systems or lack of adequate water supplies must rely on drought-tolerant grasses. Lack of rainfall also affects soil factors that can influence grass selection. Yet, some grasses do not respond well in areas of high rainfall.

Still another factor to consider is seasonal cloudiness. In cool marine climates, for example, low light levels and heavy golfer traffic during the winter months favor *Poa annua* over creeping bent grass. Kentucky bluegrass is another species that does not thrive or compete well when light levels are low. In general, most warm-season turf species are not tolerant of low light levels.

Soil Factors

A site's soil characteristics can have a significant influence on turfgrass selection. Soil texture (e.g., sandy versus clayey) is an important feature that can affect soil moisture, soil fertility, compaction proneness, and other factors. In more arid parts of the country, and in other areas where recycled water or degraded water sources are used, soil salinity is an important consideration in grass selection. The use of salinity-tolerant species and cultivars is recommended on these soils (see Table 13.1).

Table 13.1
*Relative Salt Resistance of Several Turfgrass Species**

Cool Season	Warm Season	Relative Ranking
	Seashore paspalum	Superior
Alkaligrass	Zoysiagrass	Excellent
	St. Augustinegrass	
Creeping bentgrass	Bermudagrass hybrids	Good
	Bermudagrass	
Tall fescue	Bahiagrass	Fair
Perennial ryegrass	Centipedegrass	
Fine fescues	Carpetgrass	Poor
Kentucky bluegrass	Buffalograss	

*Based on the most widely used cultivars of each species; there is significant variability among cultivars within most species.

Source: Adapted from M. P. Kenna and G. L. Horst, "Turfgrass Water Conservation and Quality." In *International Turfgrass Research Journal*, vol. 7, edited by R. N. Carrow et al. (Overland Park, Kans.: Intertec Publishing, 1993), 99–113.

Soil pH is another important characteristic, with extremes below 5.7 or above 7.5 likely to reduce nutrient availability or cause other problems for certain species (see Table 13.2).

Table 13.2
Relative Soil Acidity Tolerance
*of Turfgrasses Used on Golf Courses**

Cool Season	Warm Season	Relative Ranking
		High
Tall fescue	Seashore paspalum	
Fine fescues	Carpetgrass	
Colonial bentgrass	Centipedegrass	
Creeping bentgrass	Bermudagrass	
Perennial ryegrass	Zoysiagrass	
Kentucky bluegrass	Buffalograss	
Annual bluegrass	St. Augustinegrass	
	Bahiagrass	
		Low

*Comparisons are made only within columns and not between columns.

Source: Turfgrass Management, 3rd ed. by A. J. Turgeon, © 1991. Adapted by permission of Prentice-Hall, Inc., Upper Saddle River, NJ..

Species/Cultivar Adaptability Factors

After climatic and soil characteristics have been accounted for, there are many species- and cultivar-related factors that must be considered in selecting grasses for golf course construction.

Disease Resistance

Some turfgrasses require regular applications of fungicides. This treatment can add significantly to the cost of course maintenance and can pose a threat to the environment. Whenever possible, disease-resistant species should be selected (see Table 13.3). Within some species, there is significant variability among cultivars, so check with local authorities when selecting cultivars.

The disease susceptibility of a particular species depends to some degree on the part of the country where it is grown. For example, cool-season grasses being grown in the transition zone often require greater fungicide use than in northern or more arid areas. From the standpoint of minimizing disease problems, warm-season species should be used in the transition zone instead of cool-season grasses.

Table 13.3
Relative Disease Potential
of Turfgrasses Used on Golf Courses*

Cool Season	Warm Season	Relative Ranking
		High
Annual bluegrass	St. Augustinegrass	
Creeping bentgrass	Bermudagrass	
Colonial bentgrass	Zoysiagrass	
Fine fescues	Carpetgrass	
Kentucky bluegrass	Bahiagrass	
Perennial ryegrass	Buffalograss	
Tall fescue	Centipedegrass	
		Low

*Comparisons are made only within columns and not between columns.

Source: Turfgrass Management, 3rd ed. by A. J. Turgeon, © 1991. Adapted by permission of Prentice-Hall, Inc., Upper Saddle River, NJ..

Insect Resistance

Insects can be significant pests in many grass species, requiring use of expensive pesticides that have potential to harm other wildlife. There is significant variability with respect to insect resistance among the cultivars of some species, so check with local authorities. In the case of perennial ryegrass, fine fescues, and tall fescue, be sure to select cultivars that contain endophytes, which discourage the feeding of chewing and sucking surface insects. Also note that buffalograss cultivars with greater pubescence on the leaves are less prone to mealybug damage.

Heat Tolerance

When using cool-season grasses in the South and in the transition zone (e.g., creeping bentgrass on greens), use cultivars that exhibit heat tolerance. These cultivars often have the capacity to maintain a good root system during hot weather and high soil temperatures. Mid-Atlantic Kentucky bluegrass types generally are superior to other Kentucky bluegrasses in areas of summer heat and humidity (see Table 13.4).

Cold Tolerance

Cold tolerance is an important characteristic for warm-season grasses used in the transition zone. There are cold-tolerant cultivars of most warm-season species, and turfgrass breeders are introducing more each year. The label "Cold tolerant" is not an absolute guarantee, however, and factors such as shade, poor drainage, close cutting height, and other cultural management practices can increase susceptibility to cold damage (see Table 13.5).

Table 13.4
Relative Heat Tolerance
of Turfgrasses Used on Golf Courses*

Cool Season	Warm Season	Relative Ranking
		High
Tall fescue	Buffalograss	
Creeping bentgrass	Zoysiagrass	
Kentucky bluegrass	Bermudagrass	
Colonial bentgrass	Carpetgrass	
Fine fescues	Centipedegrass	
Perennial ryegrass	St. Augustinegrass	
Annual bluegrass	Bahiagrass	
		Low

*Comparisons are made only within columns and not between columns.

Source: Turfgrass Management, 3rd ed. by A. J. Turgeon, © 1991. Adapted by permission of Prentice-Hall, Inc., Upper Saddle River, NJ..

Table 13.5
Relative Cold Tolerance
of Turfgrasses Used on Golf Courses*

Cool Season	Warm Season	Relative Ranking
		High
Creeping bentgrass	Buffalograss	
Kentucky bluegrass	Zoysiagrass	
Colonial bentgrass	Bermudagrass	
Fine fescues	Bahiagrass	
Tall fescue	Centipedegrass	
Perennial ryegrass	Carpetgrass	
Annual bluegrass	St. Augustinegrass	
		Low

*Comparisons are made only within columns and not between columns.

Source: Turfgrass Management, 3rd ed. by A. J. Turgeon, © 1991. Adapted by permission of Prentice-Hall, Inc., Upper Saddle River, NJ..

Although cold tolerance itself is not a major concern with most cool-season species in the United States, ice sheet damage can be devastating to perennial ryegrass and to *Poa annua*.

Drought Tolerance/Water Use Rates

The ability to survive drought conditions can be an important factor in selecting grasses for areas of a course that receive infrequent irrigation, such as roughs in both cold-season and warm-season areas. Drought-tolerant grasses, however, are not necessarily low water users. For example, tall fescue is drought tolerant but has a high water use rate. Selecting grasses with low water use rates is important where water consumption is closely regulated. In the transition zone, the use of warm-season grasses can result in water savings of 50%, as compared with the use of cool-season grasses (see Tables 13.6 and 13.7).

Table 13.6
Relative Drought Resistance of Turfgrasses in Region of Climatic Adaptation and Preferred Cultural Regime

Turfgrass Species[1,2] Cool Season	Warm Season	Relative Ranking
	Bermudagrass[2] Bermudagrass hybrids[2]	Superior
	Buffalograss Seashore paspalum[2] Zoysiagrass Bahiagrass	Excellent
Fairway wheatgrass	St. Augustinegrass[2] Centipedegrass Carpetgrass	Good
Tall fescue		Moderate
Perennial ryegrass[2] Kentucky bluegrass[2] Creeping bentgrass[2] Hard fescue Chewings fescue Red fescue		Fair
Colonial bentgrass Annual bluegrass		Poor
Rough bluegrass		Very poor

[1]Based on the most used cultivars of each species.

[2]Variable among cultivars within species.

Source: Adapted from M. P. Kenna and G. L. Horst, "Turfgrass Water Conservation and Quality." In *International Turfgrass Research Journal*, vol. 7, edited by R. N. Carrow et al. (Overland Park, Kans.: Intertec Publishing, 1993), 99–113.

Table 13.7
Summary of Mean Rates of Turfgrass
Evapotranspiration of Several Turfgrasses

Turfgrass Species* Cool Season	Warm Season	Relative Ranking
	Buffalograss	Very low
	Bermudagrass hybrids Centipedegrass Bermudagrass Zoysiagrass	Low
Hard fescue Chewings fescue Red fescue	Bahiagrass Seashore paspalum St. Augustinegrass	Medium
Perennial ryegrass	Carpetgrass Kikuyugrass	
Tall fescue Creeping bentgrass Annual bluegrass Kentucky bluegrass Italian ryegrass		High

*Based on the most used cultivars of each species; there is significant variability among cultivars within most species.

Source: Adapted from M. P. Kenna and G. L. Horst, "Turfgrass Water Conservation and Quality." In *International Turfgrass Research Journal,* vol. 7, edited by R. N. Carrow et al. (Overland Park, Kans.: Intertec Publishing, 1993), 99–113.

Establishment Rate

Establishment rate can be an important factor in course construction from the standpoint of avoiding erosion and opening the course for play as quickly as possible. Some grasses are very quick to establish from seed, and others are quite slow. Desirable grasses that are slow to establish often are mixed in the seedbed with grasses with a quick establishment rate to gain the benefits of both. Sod is frequently used for erosion control on slopes; it is also used on greens, tees, and fairways on some courses where fast establishment is needed. Sprigging and/or sodding are common means of establishing many of the warm-season species, since many of the best cultivars are propagated vegetatively (see Table 13.8).

Wear Resistance

Selection of wear-resistant species can be important for turf areas that will receive heavy foot or golf car traffic. For example, perennial ryegrass is a better choice for small, heavily trafficked tees than creeping bentgrass. Likewise, a Kentucky bluegrass/perennial ryegrass mix is a better choice than bent grass for fairways that are expected to receive heavy golf car use (see Table 13.9).

Table 13.8
Relative Establishment Vigor of Turfgrasses Used on Golf Courses*

Cool Season	Warm Season	Relative Ranking
		High
Perennial ryegrass	Bermudagrass	
Tall fescue	St. Augustinegrass	
Fine fescues	Bahiagrass	
Annual bluegrass	Centipedegrass	
Creeping bentgrass	Carpetgrass	
Colonial bentgrass	Buffalograss	
Kentucky bluegrass	Zoysiagrass	
		Low

*Comparisons are made only within columns and not between columns.

Source: *Turfgrass Management*, 3rd ed. by A. J. Turgeon, © 1991. Adapted by permission of Prentice-Hall, Inc., Upper Saddle River, NJ.

Table 13.9
Relative Wear Resistance of Turfgrasses Used on Golf Courses*

Cool Season	Warm Season	Relative Ranking
		High
Tall fescue	Zoysiagrass	
Perennial ryegrass	Bermudagrass	
Kentucky bluegrass	Bahiagrass	
Fine fescues	Buffalograss	
Creeping bentgrass	St. Augustinegrass	
Colonial bentgrass	Carpetgrass	
Annual bluegrass	Centipedegrass	
		Low

*Comparisons are made only within columns and not between columns.

Source: *Turfgrass Management*, 3rd ed. by A. J. Turgeon, © 1991. Adapted by permission of Prentice-Hall, Inc., Upper Saddle River, NJ.

Recuperative Ability

Although creeping bentgrass is not particularly wear resistant, it has excellent recuperative ability. In other words, it can recover quickly from divots and other types of damage. Perennial ryegrass, on the other hand, is wear resistant but does not recover well from injury. Kentucky bluegrass has both good wear resistance and recuperative ability. In the warm-season species, bermudagrass is rated highly for both characteristics and zoysiagrass has excellent wear resistance but poor ability to recover from damage (see Table 13.10).

Table 13.10
Relative Recuperative Capacity of Turfgrasses Used on Golf Courses*

Cool Season	Warm Season	Relative Ranking
		High
Creeping bentgrass	Bermudagrass	
Kentucky bluegrass	St. Augustinegrass	
Tall fescue	Bahiagrass	
Perennial ryegrass	Carpetgrass	
Annual bluegrass	Centipedegrass	
Fine fescues	Buffalograss	
Colonial bentgrass	Zoysiagrass	
		Low

*Comparisons are made only within columns and not between columns.

Source: Turfgrass Management, 3rd ed. by A. J. Turgeon, © 1991. Adapted by permission of Prentice-Hall, Inc., Upper Saddle River, NJ..

Shade Tolerance

Most golf courses in the United States have large numbers of trees. Therefore, the ability of grasses to tolerate shade can be an important consideration. Generally, cool-season species have significantly better shade tolerance than warm-season species. In fact, among the warm-season grasses used on primary golf course areas, only zoysiagrass has some tolerance of shade. Tall fescue, a heat-tolerant cool-season species, is often used for shaded rough areas in the transition zone and in the South (see Table 13.11).

Fertility Requirement

Golf course fertilization, which can be an expensive item in the budget, has the potential to affect groundwater and/or surface water supplies. Therefore, selection of grasses that have a lower fertilizer requirement can save money and reduce the potential for environmental impacts. Among the commonly planted cool-season grasses, there is little difference in fertility needs. Among the warm-season grasses, bermudagrass requires significantly more fertilizer than zoysiagrass and buffalograss; however, it has much better recuperative ability. Bermudagrasses with lower fertility requirements (e.g., Floratex) are available (see Table 13.12).

Table 13.11
Relative Shade Tolerance
of Turfgrasses Used on Golf Courses *

Cool Season	Warm Season	Relative Ranking
		High
Fine fescues	St. Augustinegrass	
Annual bluegrass	Centipedegrass	
Colonial bentgrass	Zoysiagrass	
Tall fescue	Carpetgrass	
Creeping bentgrass	Bahiagrass	
Kentucky bluegrass	Bermudagrass	
Perennial ryegrass	Buffalograss	
		Low

*Comparisons are made only within columns and not between columns.

Source: Turfgrass Management, 3rd ed. by A. J. Turgeon, © 1991. Adapted by permission of Prentice-Hall, Inc., Upper Saddle River, NJ.

Table 13.12
Relative Fertility Requirement Range
of Turfgrasses Used on Golf Courses *

Cool Season	Warm Season	Relative Ranking
		High
Annual bluegrass	Bermudagrass	
Kentucky bluegrass	St. Augustinegrass	
Perennial ryegrass	Zoysiagrass	
Tall fescue	Centipedegrass	
Creeping bentgrass	Carpetgrass	
Colonial bentgrass	Bahiagrass	
Fine fescues	Buffalograss	
		Low

*Comparisons are made only within columns and not between columns.

Source: Turfgrass Management, 3rd ed. by A. J. Turgeon, © 1991. Adapted by permission of Prentice-Hall, Inc., Upper Saddle River, NJ.

Golfer Preference Factors

Cutting Height

Requirements for the game of golf place great demands on grasses in respect to cutting heights, and species of both warm-season and cool-season grasses have distinct limitations. In the dilemma concerning selection of bentgrass versus Kentucky bluegrass for fairways in the North, cutting height is a major consideration. Bentgrass should be cut at ½ inch or less, whereas Kentucky bluegrass should not be cut to less than ¾ inch. For those who require the most dense, closely cut turf, bentgrass is the choice. On the other hand, for public courses or other facilities where most golfers are less skilled, Kentucky bluegrass or perennial ryegrass may be preferable (see Table 13.13).

Table 13.13
*Relative Mowing Height Adaptation of Turfgrasses Used on Golf Courses**

Cool Season	Warm Season	Relative Ranking (mowing height)
		High
Tall fescue	Bahiagrass	
Fine fescues	St. Augustinegrass	
Perennial ryegrass	Carpetgrass	
Kentucky bluegrass	Centipedegrass	
Colonial bentgrass	Buffalograss	
Creeping bentgrass	Zoysiagrass	
Annual bluegrass	Bermudagrass	
		Low

*Comparisons are made only within columns and not between columns.

Source: Turfgrass Management, 3rd ed. by A. J. Turgeon, © 1991. Adapted by permission of Prentice-Hall, Inc., Upper Saddle River, NJ.

Golfer demands for ultrafast greens, combined with the introduction of many new creeping bentgrass cultivars during the past decade, pose a challenge as to which bentgrass to select for greens. Some bentgrasses are more tolerant of very close cutting heights than others, but this is just one factor to consider in this important decision.

Turfgrass Density

High-density turf (with many shoots per unit area) is a requisite for putting greens, and most golfers consider it important for tees and fairways, where grass blades should not interfere when the club face strikes the ball. Yet many golfers prefer turf that is less dense in roughs. There are choices of species and cultivars that vary in density for each of these areas. For example, there are new creeping bentgrasses for greens that have significantly greater densities than those of cultivars available in the past. Generally speaking, grasses with greater density require more intensive management and are more costly to maintain (see Table 13.14).

Table 13.14
Relative Shoot Density
of Turfgrasses Used on Golf Courses**

Cool Season	Warm Season	Relative Ranking
		High
Creeping bentgrass	Bermudagrass	
Colonial bentgrass	Zoysiagrass	
Fine fescues	Buffalograss	
Annual bluegrass	St. Augustinegrass	
Kentucky bluegrass	Centipedegrass	
Perennial ryegrass	Carpetgrass	
Tall fescue	Bahiagrass	
		Low

*Comparisons are made only within columns and not between columns.

Source: Turfgrass Management, 3rd ed. by A. J. Turgeon, © 1991. Adapted by permission of Prentice-Hall, Inc., Upper Saddle River, NJ.

Aesthetic Factors

Many golfers consider the aesthetic appeal of a golf course to be an important factor in their enjoyment of the game. In fact, most golfers consider the appearance of the course more important than the playability of the turf. They want the turf to be attractive year-round and to be as dark green as possible. Cool-season grasses generally provide a dark green, pleasing color, whereas most of the warm-season grasses have a lighter, duller green color. Moreover, most warm-season grasses go off-color or completely dormant during the winter season.

The problem is particularly striking in the transition zone, where cool-season grasses are preferred even though warm-season grasses would provide a better playing surface (on fairways), use less water, require less pesticide use, and cost less to maintain. Unfortunately, warm-season grasses in the transition zone have a long dormancy period, from mid-fall to mid-spring, and golfers are quick to abandon the benefits of these grasses (bermudagrass, zoysiagrass, and buffalograss) for the nice appearance of the cool-season grasses (Kentucky bluegrass, perennial ryegrass, and creeping bentgrass).

Golfers also prefer grasses with a fine texture, particularly on greens, tees, and fairways. Thus, they prefer bentgrass to bermudagrass on greens. They dislike fine-textured turf in the roughs and prefer cool-season grasses to bermudagrass, when possible (see Table 13.15).

Table 13.15
Relative Leaf Texture
*of Turfgrasses Used on Golf Courses** *

Cool Season	Warm Season	Relative Ranking
		Coarse
Tall fescue	Carpetgrass	
Perennial ryegrass	St. Augustinegrass	
Kentucky bluegrass	Bahiagrass	
Colonial bentgrass	Centipedegrass	
Creeping bentgrass	Zoysiagrass	
Annual bluegrass	Bermudagrass	
Fine fescues	Buffalograss	
		Fine

*Comparisons are made only within columns and not between columns.

Source: Turfgrass Management, 3rd ed. by A. J. Turgeon, © 1991. Adapted by permission of Prentice-Hall, Inc., Upper Saddle River, NJ.

Budget Considerations

The budget level expected at a new course is a significant factor in determining which turfgrass species to plant. If an adequate budget is anticipated, golfers will generally opt for the best grasses from the perspective of playability and/or aesthetics. These grasses are not necessarily the best adapted for the area and require more work and greater expense (e.g., bentgrass for greens in the warm, humid South; bentgrass or perennial ryegrass on fairways in the transition zone; and cool-season grasses in roughs in the transition zone and in warm, arid areas).

As noted previously, temperature is perhaps the single most important factor in determining the ability of a grass to survive or thrive in a particular location, in viewing the nation from north to south. The map of the United States in Figure 13.1 shows four temperature zones that help define which grass species are adapted to those areas. Within each zone, there are many other factors to consider in selecting the most desirable grass species and cultivars for a site, including those mentioned earlier.

In viewing the country from east to west, another significant factor in selecting the best grasses is evident—precipitation. Just as temperatures increase from north to south, precipitation generally declines from east to west. Precipitation can affect many of the decision factors mentioned earlier, including soil chemistry, disease activity, susceptibility to drought and salt stress, and so forth. This east-to-west precipitation gradient has a distinct effect on grass selection, occasionally at the species level but particularly at the cultivar level.

The following sections discuss the commonly used turfgrass species in each of the four major temperature zones defined in Figure 13.1. It is beyond the scope of this discussion to address issues of cultivar selection, although sources of information are provided later.

Selecting Grasses for the Cool Temperate Zone

Nearly all of the turfgrasses used in the cool temperate zone are cool-season grasses, as might be expected. Following is a breakdown by play area on the golf course.

Greens

Creeping bentgrass is the grass of choice for new construction throughout the cool temperate zone. Until the 1980s, the cultivar Penncross had a near monopoly for greens use, but now there are a dozen or more new cultivars that are significantly better than Penncross in many characteristics. These new grasses provide opportunities for better putting surfaces, but often their performance is superior only in certain parts of the country. Check with local authorities for information about the best cultivars for a specific area.

Although practically all golf courses plant bentgrass on newly constructed greens, most golf courses find that *Poa annua* shares or dominates the turf stand after five to ten years. In areas of the zone where ice sheet damage is not common, many superintendents actually prefer this grass and would plant it on newly constructed greens if seed were available. Today there are two active breeding programs with the goal of producing superior *Poa annua* cultivars, and seed should be available by the end of the 1990s. On old golf courses that are renovating one or several greens, these new annual bluegrass cultivars will probably be used, either alone or in mixtures with creeping bentgrass, to reflect more accurately the composition of the greens on the rest of the course.

Tees

The selection of grasses for tees is generally based on three factors: (1) tee size, (2) predominance of shade, and (3) anticipated maintenance budget. For tees that are large (at least 100 square feet of useable teeing area for 1,000 anticipated rounds of golf per year), receive little or no shade, and can experience intensive management, creeping bentgrass is the preferred species. For tees that are relatively small, receive significant shade, and/or cannot be maintained intensively, perennial ryegrass or a combination of ryegrass and Kentucky bluegrass is often used. In more arid areas, Kentucky bluegrass can be used alone. If possible, perennial ryegrass should not be used in the northern part of the cool temperature zone, as it is susceptible to ice sheet damage. Where shade is dense, however, neither bentgrass nor Kentucky bluegrass will persist.

Fairways

The preferred grass for fairways throughout much of the cool temperate zone is creeping bentgrass, but this grass requires more intensive management and generally a larger budget than the alternatives. In the more southern part of the zone, perennial ryegrass is commonly used on high traffic, lower-budget courses. In the more northern parts of the zone, Kentucky bluegrass is used on lower-budget courses, either by itself or in combination with fine fescues and/or perennial ryegrass. Kentucky bluegrass does particularly well in the more arid and higher-altitude areas as a lower-cost alternative to creeping bentgrass.

Roughs

A 60-30-10 (or similar) mixture, by weight, of Kentucky bluegrass, fine fescues, and perennial ryegrass is an excellent choice for roughs in much of the cool temperate zone. One or two species will dominate each area of the course, depending on shade, soil characteristics, traffic effects, and other factors. In areas known to be shady, the amount of fine fescue should be increased and Kentucky bluegrass decreased. In more arid areas, buffalograss can be used effectively to reduce water use and maintenance costs.

Selecting Grasses for the Transition Zone

The transition zone is the most challenging area for which to select turfgrasses. It is called the *transition zone* because it is the transition area between the cool temperate zone, where cool-season grasses thrive and dominate, and the warm temperate zone, where warm-season grasses thrive and dominate. In this zone, cool-season grasses are particularly prone to summer disease and heat stress pressure, whereas the warm-season grasses experience a long season of dormancy and are prone to winter injury.

Greens

Despite occasional problems with midsummer performance, creeping bentgrass is used throughout the transition zone. Bentgrass cultivars that exhibit heat stress tolerance and good midsummer rooting should be selected, especially in the southern portion of the zone. Local authorities should be consulted for recommendations.

Tees

In the northern portion of the transition zone, cool-season grasses such as perennial ryegrass and creeping bentgrass are utilized for tees. In the southern part of the zone, zoysiagrass and bermudagrass are generally used. In the more arid and higher-elevation areas of the zone, Kentucky bluegrass may be used alone or in combination with perennial ryegrass.

Fairways

Selecting grasses for fairways in this zone can present a dilemma, as there is no grass ideally suited to the area. In the more northern areas, creeping bentgrass and perennial ryegrass are commonly used, although zoysiagrass has its supporters, too. In the southern portions of the zone, zoysiagrass and winter-hardy common bermudagrasses (*Cynodon dactylon* cultivars) are most frequently used. In the higher-elevation, arid parts of the zone, Kentucky bluegrass can also be used. Consult with local authorities for the pros and cons of using each species and cultivar.

Roughs

In the northern parts of the transition zone, cool-season grasses such as Kentucky bluegrass, fine fescues, and perennial ryegrass are commonly used, either alone or in mixtures with each other. If shade is a problem, tall fescue is added to the mixture. In the more southern areas, common-type bermudagrasses are used in sunny areas and tall fescue is often used in shady areas. In the more arid parts of the Central Plains and the West, buffalograss can be used to good advantage.

Selecting Grasses for the Warm Temperate Zone

Grass selection in the warm temperate zone is more straightforward, with warm-season grasses predominating in most areas. Winter overseeding with cool-season grasses is common in this zone, to provide golfers with an attractive playing surface in the winter months.

Greens

Because of the superior putting surfaces it produces, as compared with bermudagrass hybrids, creeping bentgrass is by far the most common species used for greens in the warm temperate zone. Selecting the bentgrass cultivars that are best adapted to the hot, humid summer weather of this zone is essential. Check with local authorities for information about these selections.

In the more southern parts of the region, Tifdwarf hybrid bermudagass (*Cynodon dactylon X.C. transvaalensis*) is occasionally used, especially on lower-budget courses. Tifgreen is still used on some courses in the more western part of the zone.

Tees

In the more western parts of the zone, tees are often planted to common bermudagrasses, zoysiagrass (particularly in semishade), and, at higher-budget courses, hybrid bermudagrass (usually Tifway). In the Southeast, Tifway is the standard for nearly all courses.

Fairways

Bermudagrass dominates fairways in the warm temperate zone. In the Southeast, Tifway is the standard grass for fairways. Farther west, common bermudagrass selections often are used on lower-budget courses, whereas Tifway is widely used at courses with greater budgets. Along the northern fringe of the zone, some courses use zoysiagrass or one of the cold-hardy bermudagrasses (e.g., Vamont, Quickstand). In the more arid western parts of the zone, perennial ryegrass is used occasionally.

Roughs

Hybrid bermudagrasses dominate rough areas in the Southeast, whereas common bermudagrasses are generally utilized farther west in sunny areas of the roughs. In the more northern sections, tall fescue can be used to advantage in shady rough areas. In the drier parts of the Midwest and the West, buffalograss can be successfully used, while in the higher-elevation areas, some courses use perennial ryegrass and Kentucky bluegrass.

Selecting Grasses for the Tropical Zone

Grass selection for the tropical zone is relatively straightforward. Winter overseeding of cool-season grasses is used on many courses in the northern portion of this zone.

Greens

Tifdwarf hybrid bermudagrass dominates greens in this zone. Tifgreen is sometimes used at lower-budget courses, but it cannot tolerate mowing lower than ⁵⁄₁₆ inch. Many courses have tried to grow creeping bentgrass in this zone, but most have abandoned the effort and have replanted with bermudagrass.

More recently, Tifdwarf bermudagrass has experienced severe problems with contamination and genetic mutation. Sources of stolons should be carefully checked. Sod certification is being considered in areas where it does not presently exist, and university researchers are investigating new methods of identifying cultivars and genetic variants.

Tees

Tifway, Tifgreen, and, occasionally, Tifdwarf hybrid bermudagrasses most often are used on tees, with the latter two generally found at higher-budget courses. Common-type seeded and vegetative bermudagrasses are also utilized in some areas.

Fairways

Tifway hybrid bermudagrass is the most commonly used fairway grass in the tropical zone. Improved common-type seeded bermudagrass also is being used to a greater extent, especially in the more western parts of the zone.

Roughs

Tifway bermudagrass is the most commonly used grass in the Southeast. Farther west, improved common seeded bermudagrass is often used in roughs, though Tifway bermudagrass is generally used adjacent to Tifway fairways to avoid encroachment of the common type into the Tifway on the fairways. In the more southern parts of the zone, St. Augustinegrass, centipedegrass, and bahiagrass (particularly on unirrigated areas) are sometimes utilized. In the more arid Western areas, buffalograss can be used effectively.

The Benefits of Using Cultivar Blends

As noted previously, turfgrass breeders have introduced hundreds of cultivars that exhibit one or more improved traits as compared with cultivars used in years past. Some of these new cultivars, for example, may be superior in terms of heat tolerance or low water use rates, yet they may be very susceptible to certain diseases. By using blends of cultivars with different traits within a species, some studies have shown that the broader genetic diversity in the turf stand can reduce the potential for severe epidemics or damage to the stand.

For many years, Penncross creeping bentgrass was the primary grass used in establishing new greens. Today, many new cultivars exhibit traits superior to Penncross, yet most are effective in only limited climatic zones within the country. Moreover, these new grasses have not been established for a long period of time, and there is concern that some previously unseen weakness may eventually show up and cause a significant problem if a single cultivar is planted. Consequently, many new greens are being planted to blends of several bentgrass cultivars that appear best suited to the area and show differences in susceptibility to certain diseases or other problems. Blends should consist of cultivars that are similar in color, texture, and vigor, thereby minimizing the possibility of unsightly segregation problems within the first few years.

Experts do not agree on the advisability of blending multiclone varieties of bentgrass. Opponents believe that blending is a step toward mediocrity and that the best approach is to characterize all the varieties and select the very best one for a particular area. Until this information is available, however, blending may be a good insurance policy.

Blending of cultivars also is recommended in using Kentucky bluegrass or perennial ryegrass on fairways, roughs, and tees.

Sources of Information

During the past 20 years, turfgrass breeders have introduced hundreds of new cultivars and several nontraditional turfgrass species to the market, providing grasses that clearly are superior to many of those used previously. This trend is likely to continue for the foreseeable future. Nevertheless, these new grasses often are less widely adapted than their forebears and are best suited to specific regions. This places a burden on the golf course architect or the owner's representative to obtain the latest information about the performance of these grasses before making a decision. The following paragraphs present several important sources of information.

The USGA Green Section

Each of the 15 regional agronomists of the United States Golf Association Green Section consults at more than 120 golf courses annually and is exposed to the merits and faults of grasses as they are established and maintained under golf course conditions. Representing a nonprofit service organization with no commercial ties, these regional agronomists constitute an excellent source of information about which species and cultivars are best adapted to the various parts of their regions and how these grasses perform under various course conditions and maintenance practices. For more information, contact the United States Golf Association, P. O. Box 708, Far Hills, NJ 07931. Phone: (908) 234-2300.

The National Turfgrass Evaluation Program

The National Turfgrass Evaluation Program (NTEP) is a self-supporting nonprofit program sponsored by the United States Department of Agriculture (USDA) and the

National Turfgrass Federation. It is designed to develop and coordinate uniform evaluation trials of turfgrass cultivars and promising selections throughout the United States and Canada. Most of the field trials are conducted at land grant universities, and reports of the evaluations are published annually for each of the species investigated. The reports, which are available for a nominal fee, show results from each university participating in the evaluation, including information about several growth, appearance, and adaptation characteristics. For additional information, contact

> Kevin Morris, National Program Coordinator
> National Turfgrass Evaluation Program
> Beltsville Agricultural Research Center — West
> Building 002, Room 013
> Beltsville, MD 20705
> Phone: (301) 504-5125

University Turfgrass Extension Specialists

Many land grant universities employ turfgrass extension specialists who coordinate turfgrass interests state-wide, including NTEP trials. These specialists can provide information about how grass species and cultivars perform in their particular states and can supply the names of other contacts who are able to provide information on a local level. Contact the USGA Green Section for the names of these specialists.

Turfgrass Seed Companies

The major turf seed companies employ representatives who can provide specific information about the turf species and cultivars they produce, including the blends and mixtures they market. They also can refer you to golf courses that have used their grasses.

Golf Course Superintendents

Today an increasing number of superintendents are planting demonstration plots of new turf varieties in nurseries or practice areas. If you are fortunate enough to find such a superintendent nearby, this can be yet another source of information on how new varieties perform locally.

Construction Methods, Equipment, and Commodities: The Constructor's Viewpoint*

The one aim of inventors is to reduce the skill required for golf. Golf architects must wage a battle against inventors by designing courses that emphasize golfing skills over equipment.

From *Concerning Golf,* 1903, by John Laing Low (1869–1929)

Construction Methods and Equipment

by Gary Paumen
CROWN GOLF CONSTRUCTION CORPORATION

Construction methods have changed dramatically in this century, especially since World War II, as have seed and other commodities that golf architects specify and contractors purchase.

No longer are we building golf courses with drag boxes and mules along with hand labor and farm equipment; nor are we hand-raking large areas and removing stones by hand as we did in the 1970s. Today a contractor may have millions of dollars' worth of equipment on-site, including huge bulldozers, pans, and scrapers for earth moving and lighter specialized equipment for installing irrigation and drainage and preparing seed beds and seeding.

Still, the dominant objective of the contractor is to create a golf course as envisaged by the architect who has been retained by the owner to convert his or her ideas to reality. Yet costs have spiraled, and budgets can be in the multimillion dollar range. This is one reason contractors want to know about the owner's financing.

The contractor hopes that owner and architect have selected a tract of land satisfactory for developing a golf course. Yet we realize that many a site may be far from ideal. In turn, we trust owner and architect to realize that costs will then be greater.

Whatever the site, we need a route plan for the course shown on a topographical map, plus detailed plans and specifications from the architect. Together, these constitute the blueprint for the future course, similar to an architect's plans for a building. Therefore, in order to satisfy the owner, we look to the architect for the final plan.

Erosion and Sediment Control

Once our proposal has been accepted and we have been notified to proceed, the first step is to implement the Erosion and Sediment Control Plan prepared by the architect

*Compiled by the Golf Course Builders Association of America, Executive Vice President: Philip Arnold.

and/or environmental specialist in accordance with federal (including Army Corps of Engineers), state, and local regulations. A decade and a half ago, the approval process took a few weeks. Today it may take years. During that time, costs will have increased. Owners may then wish to recover some of that time by accelerating the construction process.

Contractors have no argument with the objectives of the sediment and erosion control processes. We are good citizens and have all heard the shocking statistic that the amount of sediment traveling down the Mississippi in a single year equals the amount of material mined in the entire nation in the last hundred years.

The straw or hay bale technique long used for controlling sediment is no longer always deemed adequate. Contemporary specifications may include sediment traps, retention and detention ponds, diversion channels, dikes, and sedimentation separators. These are generally installed during the period immediately before construction. We also need specifications to prevent erosion as the work proceeds.

Because our work is no longer confined to one area of the country, contractors are often licensed as general contractors in one or more states. This alone implies that we are intensely aware of local, state, and federal laws and regulations.

Prior to starting execution of the erosion control plan, we expect the routing of the course to be adequately staked. As a minimum, we expect flags to mark tee areas, pivot points, and centers of greens. We are responsible for maintaining these center lines throughout construction.

When clearing today, we may not open up the entire course—or even a very large portion of it—and then bring in earth-moving equipment to work on every hole. We are more likely to proceed painstakingly on a few holes at a time so as not to create an immense area that will be devoid of vegetation for many months.

Clearing and Grubbing

This is the start of the "third dimension,"—contractors' shoptalk for the creation of the golf course on the ground as envisioned by the architect. Everything is to be cleared eventually to the edges of the vegetation that is to remain. Clearing is performed in increments to save as much native vegetation as possible. The cleared area for a hole is known to us as "the box." Clearing is completed as described in Chapter 8.

Earth Moving

The first step in the earth-moving process is stripping and stockpiling topsoil, taking care to site stockpiles where they will not interfere with later work, including shaping and installing irrigation and cart paths. Generally, we strip topsoil, whether it is sand, gumbo (a fine, very sticky soil), or something in between. Topsoil of almost all qualities is worth saving.

For stripping we use paddlewheel scrapers, which can stockpile the material as large mounds. Depth of stripping depends on depth of topsoil, which can be several feet but is often only a few inches. That topsoil must be returned to fairways and some rough areas, and more may be added. Still, the architect and the contractor yearn to save every cubic yard of the original soil, because a golf course under construction never seems to have enough.

We prefer paddlewheel scrapers for stripping and returning topsoil because they produce uniformity in both stripping and replating, and we believe they exert a beneficial influence on the soil by fluffing it so that it is more workable in preparing seed beds.

A major effort should be made to have cuts and fills balance wherever possible. Depending on the arrangement between owner and architect, the architect or an outside engineer may be brought in to calculate the cuts and fills. Sometimes calculations are left to the contractor; no doubt he or she will carefully check those provided by others.

Distance determines the type of equipment to be used to move earth. For a short distance of 200 feet or less, Caterpillar D-8s or D-9s or equivalent makes are used. For distances of 500 to 1,000 feet, the preferred equipment is 627s or 631s or the equivalent, or paddlewheel scrapers that can put down the material accurately.

If the distance is 1,500 feet or more, the contractor may "top-load." This involves the use of large excavators, 3 to 3½ cubic yards or larger, loading into off-road vehicles, such as 50-ton quarry trucks; or the material can be loaded directly into scrapers such as 627s or 637s. As cuts and fills progress and material is put in place, it is rough-shaped, often with large dozers such as D-8s, D-9s, and D-10s, or the equivalent. Size depends on the type and amount of material, the time frame, and how fast the material is brought to the site.

Note the gaps in the aforementioned distances—for example, between 1,000 and 1,500 feet. In these areas the contractor decides what to use, as, in fact, he or she does in all areas designated earlier. A contractor may wish to use items of equipment far different from those discussed here, which are put forward as examples only.

All work described in the preceding paragraphs follows the "critical path" (Figure 14.1). In practice, many a contractor builds the course on paper before he or she starts clearing or earth moving. The contractor realizes that this is needed to keep the project on time and on budget.

Clearing, earth moving, and shaping may progress simultaneously. The contractor and his or her people must stay on top of these operations and keep the owner and the architect informed. In fact, the architect or an architect's representive must be involved, because the course bears the architect's signature. As contractors say, the product is a "150-acre business card" for both architect and contractor.

Like all construction projects, a golf course must start off on the right foot. An effective pre-contract signing meeting, with owner, architect, and contractor present, is very important, as is having the architect or his or her representative on the job site as often as possible. For example, during clearing it would be easy to destroy trees the architect wants left, and in earth moving the more the architect is involved the less likely it is that earth must be moved twice—a major reason that costs soar.

One can see why owner and architect seek a contractor with extensive golf course experience to create the "third dimension." It is apparent, too, that constant communication between all parties is of intrinsic importance.

Architects become accustomed to working with certain contractors, arriving at a certain comfort level in their relationship in regard to interpretation of plans and specifications, frequency of the architect's periodic visits of inspection, and a host of other important matters. Although the architect can seldom be on the project daily, as the comfort level increases the two can be in contact frequently by telephone, fax, and written correspondence.

The greatest cost in any course building project is nearly always earth moving. Huge pieces of equipment are in use to move an immense volume of earth each hour. This is achieved by experienced operators working under an experienced construction superintendent. The superintendent relies on the operators to carry out the instructions he or she gives at the beginning of the day even though the superintendent may not see them for hours at a time.

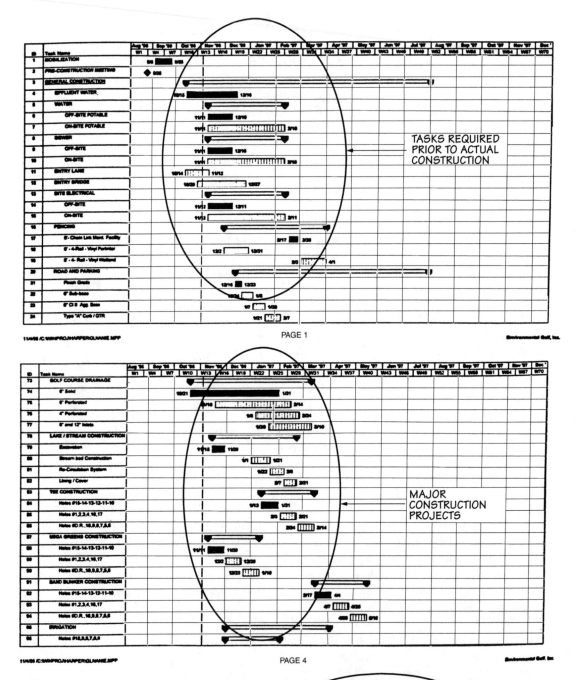

FIGURE 14.1 Here are reproductions of the first, fourth, and last pages of a seven-page critical path diagram. Although task names and dates are unreadable due to the reduction process, you can get a "picture" of how the system works. Major categories and tasks are noted, as are the start and stop dates. The bars can designate work by either the prime contractor, subcontractor, or others.

The first page organizes tasks required prior to actual golf course construction, including a preconstruction meeting, estimate of the total time to completion, utility work, and mobilization.

By the fourth page, the course is into major construction projects such as lakes and streams, tees, greens, bunkers, and irrigation.

Page seven completes the work with turfgrass installation and maturation.

Shaping

During rough shaping, there is a tendency to downgrade the size of equipment. Yet talented shapers have the ability to rough shape with a Caterpillar D-8 or its equivalent. Following rough shaping, further shaping may be required to execute the architect's critical shapes. This is achieved by an operator, known as the shaper, using even smaller equipment. In recent years, talented shapers and their work have become critical to shaping greens, bunkers, and other features.

During all this time, the contractor and his or her superintendent are following the critical path (see Figure 14.1) but may have to make changes in case of bad weather or late deliveries. Although such changes have been anticipated and embodied in the path in at least a general way, the construction superintendent must still make changes on virtually a daily basis. As golf architects say, contracting and construction supervising are not for the faint of heart. The only constant in construction sequences is that they are always changing, requiring flexibility. For example, if the soil in one area is wet on a particular day, it would be better to change to another operation or to a drier area.

We believe that a contractor should run a clean-looking job, one that is well maintained and neat. This makes the owner proud of the project and reduces problems with inspectors. Furthermore, the work in progress is then attractive to potential members, future players, those considering purchase of fairway lots, and the media, including photographers who turn up unexpectedly.

As shaping proceeds, the contractor is constantly aware that surface drainage is critical. At this time, or earlier, large-diameter storm drain pipe, 24 inches or larger, may be installed. The contractor may also install pipe of other specified sizes at this time to keep the site as dry as possible throughout construction so that equipment can return as soon as possible following a storm or, in early spring, following snowmelt.

We classify golf drainage as either major (storm drainage), which is often but not always water entering from off-site, or minor (interior drainage), which is installed for greens, tees, bunkers, depressions, and other interior features. The major drainage, which may require a cover of several feet, is most likely installed prior to heavy earth moving.

For minor drainage, requiring less cover, we look to the architect for gradient and outfalls (outlets). Regarding outfalls, there are five common but troublesome problems that can arise if they have not been given adequate thought at the time of installation.

1. Water from an outfall runs across the surface of a playing area.
2. Puddles are created at the outfall. Even in out-of-play areas these are objectionable.
3. Worst of all, when the outfall is a sump in a playing area and reaches capacity in wet periods, it backs up onto playing areas.

4. Water is puddled behind a golf car path that was installed late in the critical path.
5. No longer are we allowed to use ponds and streams and other open water as out-falls.

Irrigation

Irrigation is discussed in Chapter 10. Therefore, we do not include a detailed description here, but emphasize the following points:

1. The irrigation system should be installed under direction of the contractor. He or she has tens of thousands of dollars riding on the availability of water at planting time.
2. Despite written agreements, the permanent power source may not be in place when it is needed. In practice, there can be a lag time of weeks. Therefore, an alternative source of power, such as a generator, must be considered by the owner, architect, and contractor at or before signing the contract.
3. There is often a problem with controls to be hooked into a maintenance building that is still under construction, or not even started.
4. Delivery dates of irrigation equipment can be delayed for weeks. Therefore, many contractors order materials as soon as contracts are signed.

We emphasize that if irrigation water is not available at planting time, this is a major problem. Its availability must be thought through as the critical path (see Figure 14.1) is formulated.

Preparation of Seed Beds: The USGA Green Method of Construction

Contractors respect the fact that greens are the most important part of the golf course in regard to setting, style, shape, size, and conditioning. Contemporary green construction is so precise that laboratories with special equipment have been established to analyze the materials used on greens.

The architect gives the closest attention to the contractor's work on the green complex, and the architect may specify that his or her approval is required, step by step, throughout construction. The architect may require his or her approval for the shaping of the green (and surrounds), its elevation together with the approach, the view the green presents to the oncoming golfer, and, probably, the view from future surrounding residences. Most architects want the green to look as though it had been there forever. Green contruction demands the use of surveying instruments as contrasted with doing it all by eye. This in turn calls for the architect's approval at every step.

In regard to the cavity (the basin that contains the USGA layers, namely, gravel, sand, and topmix), many architects insist that the subgrade be parallel to the finished surface, although the USGA has stated that this is not a requirement if the grade of the gravel layer conforms to surface grade.

The architect will no doubt be involved with the drainage patterns. Rules of thumb are that laterals should not be more than 20 feet apart and that there should be 100 linear feet of subdrainage for each 1,000 square feet of putting surface. These are minimums; often more tile is needed. Again, instruments are necessary to ensure correct levels as the drainage is installed.

Once tile is in the ground, the gravel, coarse sand (if used), and topmix are installed. We spread layers with tracked bulldozers such as wide-track Caterpillar D-3s,

D-4s, or the equivalent, working from the sides and always moving over the spread materials. We do not permit wheeled vehicles in the cavity once tile is installed.

The D-3 or D-4 compacts the material, but some architects specify additional compacting by rolling, as well as keeping the material wet to assist in this compacting. For minor grading within the cavity, such as to correct the subgrade gravel and surface grades, some architects permit a small finishing tractor with a box blade or front-end loader. Still, this equipment must work carefully. Some architects specify that no machines at all be let inside the cavity. This, of course, means placing the material by hand followed by special attention to rolling or other forms of compacting.

While work on the greens is under way, other operations are starting: preparation of seed beds, seeding, planting, and/or sprigging. Here again, contractors refer to the critical path (see Figure 14.1) and constantly study the flowcharts to check progress. Although a flowchart runs left to right, many contractors think in terms of a diamond, in that construction starts at a point with erosion control and grows to its widest point, which is about halfway through construction when nearly all aspects are going on concurrently. The pace of construction then gradually diminishes to the point at which all items are complete.

As finish shaping progresses, smaller pieces of finishing equipment, including rock rakes and stone pickers, are brought on-site, along with rock pickers if the course is located in a stoney area. Seed beds are finished to the ultimate degree of perfection, which depends on the area of the course (e.g., putting surface or roughs) being seeded.

Seed beds must be free of roots, rock, and debris and "fluffed," as contrasted with a compacted surface, to ensure that they are amenable to seed and seedlings. If the seedbeds are not already a prepared mix, soil conditioners and starter fertilizers are added and mixed to a 2- to 4-inch depth, depending on specifications.

As a result of rainfall or other factors, seedbeds may have to be "refluffed" several times. A hard, compacted surface inevitably leads to a sparse stand of grass.

The next procedure is seeding, unless the area is planted vegetatively. Many contractors prefer to seed early in the morning before the wind comes up. Wind blows fairway seed into the rough, or vice versa, or onto greens. Two types of dry seeders are commonly used: the cultipacker type, which sows the seed, covers it, and rolls it all in one operation; and the broadcast-type seeder. The cultipacker type requires a dry seed bed, whereas the broadcast type can be used on a wet one. A third type, the hydroseeder, is becoming increasingly popular.

Whatever the type of seeder used, it is important the the seed be sown on the intended area. This can be a problem with both broadcast and hydroseeders, but it can be mastered through close supervision. Seeding depth may also be a problem—for example, with bentgrass, which can easily be covered too deeply.

The contractor must carefully plan as little traffic as possible across newly seeded areas, but access to these areas may be required. For instance, if bunker walls are to be sodded, the sod may need hand watering. The problem of access may be less critical today than in the past because of contemporary irrigation systems, but these are by no means all state-of-the-art systems. Therefore, access for irrigating some areas must be carefully considered.

Grow-in may be included in the contractor's agreement, or it may be handled by the owner and the superintendent. Sometimes grow-in is the period from seeding until turf reaches an acceptable stand; sometimes it includes the period needed to produce a stand of playable grass. Whatever the period, contemporary irrigation systems that carry fertilizer and amendments have revolutionized grow-in. This level of sophistication, however, has not yet been reached nationwide, much less globally.

Paths and Crossings

Today many paths and crossings provide access for golf machinery and, perhaps, wheeled road vehicles, including loaded trucks. Therefore, they require sturdy construction and an adequate width of 10 to 12 feet.

Because culverting is seldom permitted, bridges may have to be installed. Regulations often call for free spans, with no pilings or endwalls in wetlands. These free spans can be reinforced section bridges, installed with cranes or poured in place.

A Contractor's Observations

Contractors and others involved in constructing brand new courses observe that the work that has been executed has constituted major surgery on the land. Its root mass has been disturbed, and air circulation and the angle of sun rays have been changed, as has the soil profile. It can be years before the area restabilizes. During that period, trees may die, unforeseen drainage problems may arise, and there may be settling regardless of the best efforts in compacting during construction.

Purchasing Fertilizers, Seed, and Soil Amendments

by Richard Elyea
THE TEE 2 GREEN CORPORATION

Virgil Meir and Dean Mosdell
THE SCOTT COMPANY

A well-planned program is as important in preparing seedbeds and planting as it is in maintaining the stand. A program superificially thought out produces poorly colored, sparse turf susceptible to damage of many types. On the other hand, a stand achieved by overmanagement with fertilizers and water can be susceptible to still other problems.

Fertilizers and soil amendments do not in themselves produce quality turf. That is achieved through a balance of nutrients, plant protection products, water, and maintenance practices, following the physical creation of an ideal environment involving such factors as correct soil depth, adequate tree-clearing widths, and extensive drainage. Choices of turfgrass species and the specific variety or varieties within each species are also critical for the long-term success of the plan (these have been dealt with in Chapter 13).

Chemical Testing and Sampling

In addition to physical tests needed to establish a root zone mix, chemical testing of the soil and water is called for early in the project. Indeed, soil testing is recognized as the most effective method for determining nutrient reserves in a soil. In addition to indicating the status of the soil, it can also assist in diagnosing problems that may occur in the future.

Soil samples for a new project should seldom be collected until excavation and grading of an area are complete. Samples taken previously may not reflect the nutrient value of the seedbed, although some early testing is desirable.

For chemical analysis, the recommended depth for systematic sampling is often from 0 to 3 or 6 inches because 80% of the future fibrous root system will be in those top inches. But this depth is not a universal specification. There are authorities that recommend even deeper sampling, with the objective of favoring deeper roots by satisfying nutrient deficiencies, often phosphorus, at lower levels, although the efficiency of grass roots in mining nutrients at these depths is very low.

Analyses of root zone mixes acquired from a vendor are usually available. If not, or if a mix has been prepared in-house or locally, it is mandatory to establish what it contains in the way of nutrients, even though these are minimum in contemporary sand-based mixtures.

For fairways, roughs, and all areas where special root zone mixes have not been used, additional samples are recommended to determine the need for lime or sulfur, the former to raise pH and the latter to reduce it. During construction is the time to apply these amendments, rather than after the grass has grown, when it may be difficult or impossible to do so.

Water quality tests, coupled with nutrient tests, are advisable; if effluent water is to be used, they are mandatory. Major problems encountered with effluent water are alkalinity, salinity, high sodium content, and the presence of heavy metals and, possibly, solids. Because all of these conditions can destroy soil structure and be directly toxic to plants, their detection and assesment are needed. They can also cause wilt, chlorosis, and loss of turf vigor.

Complete Fertilizers and the Salt Index

Complete fertilizers contain the primary nutrients, nitrogen (N), phosphorus (P), and potassium (K). Fertilizers are salts, which can cause extensive damage if applied too heavily or improperly to seedling grass, or even before seeding if readily available and the weather is ideal for rapid germination. It is therefore important to note the salt index of a fertilizer. The higher the index, the greater the potential for damage if overapplied.

Ideally, a fertilizer for preseeding and grow-in is chosen to accomplish the following objectives, although one may be more important in selecting the preseeding application than the application at grow-in:

1. Ease and economy of application
2. Minimum caustic or toxic effect
3. Efficient plant utilization
4. Environmental sustainability

To accomplish these, the fertilizer will have these characteristics:

1. Small particles
2. A minimum bulk density
3. Easy spreadability
4. Homogeneity
5. Cost-effectiveness
6. A good margin of safety, at least three to four times the required rate

There are three categories of fertilizers, each with advantages and disadvantages, as described in the following paragraphs.

1. *Inorganics.* These are highly soluble fertilizers with a high burn potential unless encapsulated with a water insoluble coating. Nutrients in inorganics are readily available to plants and therefore produce a surge of growth, probably at the expense of root growth. They are susceptible to both leaching and volatilization. Frequent light applications are needed to satisfy plant demands. Coated fertilizers vary in nutrient release characteristics depending on the type and thickness of the coating. Rate of release depends on temperature. Coated products extend the period when plants can avail themselves of their nutrients. Accordingly, higher ratios and fewer applications are feasible.

2. *Natural Organics.* These are by-products from the processing of animal, plant, and municipal wastes. Common sources are processed sewage sludge, composted poultry manures, hydrolyzed feathers, dried blood, and bone meal. Natural organics have a low content of nutrients, but many contain micronutrients. Natural organics are slow to release and are broken down in the soil into available plant food by soil organisms requiring warm soil temperatures.

3. *Synthetic Organics.* These are manufactured materials with characteristics similar to those of both inorganics and natural organics, including quick greening effects, long residual effects, efficiency, and relative safety. Examples are urea and polymer-coated urea, methylene ureas, and ureaformaldehyde materials. Synthetics produce healthy top growth but not at the expense of the root system. They are frequently considered to be ideal for the grow-in period.

Generally speaking, nitrogen, phosphorus, and potash are needed prior to seeding and throughout the grow-in period. Phosphorus is very important at these times because it is an element that assists in establishment and root growth but tends to stay where it is put in the soil. Emerging roots must be in close proximity to absorb soil-available phosphorus.

A ratio of a starter fertilizer often used is 3-4-1 (3% nitrogen, 4% phosphoric acid, and 1% potash) with micronutrients. Yet such generalities must be modified according to test results, soil types, and preferences of the architect and superintendent.

Seed

A wide variety of warm-season and cool-season grasses are available for production of turf. The choice of the ideal species and the preferred variety or mixture of varieties within the species is a critical factor in the long-term success of the plan. Turfgrass species and their selection are discussed in Chapter 13 by the national director of the USGA Green Section. Still, we must emphasize that there is a growing trend to select varieties that contain endophytes, organisms that enhance the plant's resistance to surface feeding, chewing, and sucking insects and, possibly, to fungus diseases. Species ensuring even more impressive turf varieties with improved resistance to specific herbicides and higher levels of stable resistance to a broad range of diseases and insects, will probably become commercially available starting at about the year 2005, as a result of genetic engineering.

The current standard in the industry is "blue tag" certification. This quality standard ensures that the variety named on the label is indeed the variety in the bag and that it has met a set of specified minimum standards for germination and purity, which include maximum levels of other crop seeds, weed seeds, and inert matter. Certification standards differ for each turf species and may vary according to the state where the seed is produced. These purity standards are based on a minimum specified seed sample size.

Species	Sample Size (gm)	Noxious Weeds
Kentucky bluegrass	1.0	10.0
Perennial ryegrass	5.0	50.0
Tall fescue	5.0	50.0
Fine fescue	3.0	30.0
Bentgrass	0.25	2.5

Noxious weeds are plant species that are defined in each state's seed laws as problem species for that state's agricultural industry; therefore, the list of noxious weeds varies according to the state. The noxious weed list for certification purposes is generally the list for the state in which the seed is grown. The following is a typical standard for certified "blue tag" Kentucky bluegrass, based on a 1-gram test.

	% by Weight
Pure seed minimum	95.00
Other crop seed, maximum	0.25
Inert matter, maximum	5.00
Weed seed, maximum	0.30
Germination, minimum	85.00
Canada bluegrass, maximum	0.25
Poa annua	2.00

Based on a 10-gram examination, no seeds from the production state's noxious weed list are allowed. These standards appear to be quite extensive, but they can frequently be misleading, because other crop seeds are not listed as noxious.

A more comprehensive test, such as the Gold Tag test, which notes *both crop and weed seeds* in the test size of the noxious weed examination, is performed when a larger test is more desirable or demanded. The need for a larger test noting all crop and weed seeds is that the most troublesome and difficult to control "weeds" in turf are generally other turf species and perennial forage grass species (officially designated as "other crop seeds" on the label). These contaminant species are a serious problem in fine turf even if the label indicates 0.00% "other crop seeds"!

High-quality bermudagrass and St. Augustinegrass in the South are established largely from sprigs or sod, although there is seed available for bermudagrass, most often used for roughs and medium-quality fairways. However, there is growing interest in developing seeded bermudagrass with the high quality of the cultivar tifway 419 with its increased adaptability to low water and fertilizer use, a relative tolerance to alkaline soils, and resistance to certain insects. Earlier spring green-up is being sought as well. These new-seeded bermudagrasses are also intended to be finer in texture and more cold tolerant. Although they look promising, time will tell.

In the meantime, a wonderful array of grass species are already available for cool and warm regions of the nation. Yet in the interest of quality, correct grass selection is all-important to construction. It is common practice for the architect to specify the seed and for the contractor to purchase it. In specifying and purchasing seed materials, Tables 14.1 and 14.2 are profoundly significant.

Table 14.1
Dissecting a Seed Mixture by Converting Seed Weight Percentages to Seed Count Percentages

Step 1: Multiply (a) purity percentage by (b) number of seeds per pound to find (c) the number of seeds per pound in the mixture.

Seed Mixture

(a) % Purity		(b) Total Seeds per Pound		(c) Seeds per Pound in Mixture
11.10 Chewings fescue	×	448,640	=	49,799
8.50 Kentucky bluegrass	×	1,390,253	=	118,172
5.20 Highland bent grass	×	6,130,270	=	318,774
46.50 Annual ryegrass	×	190,508	=	88,586
26.00 Perennial ryegrass	×	240,403	=	62,505
				637,836

Step 2: Add all seeds of each variety to find the total number of seeds per pound in the mixture. In this example, this equals 637,836.

Step 3: Divide the number of seeds per pound of each variety by the total number of seeds per pound in the mixture. This determines seed count percentages.

Variety	Seeds/Pound		Mixture		Seed Count %
Chewings fescue	49,799	÷	637,836	=	7.8%
Kentucky bluegrass	118,172	÷	637,836	=	18.5%
Highland bentgrass	318,774	÷	637,836	=	50.0%
Annual ryegrass	88,586	÷	637,836	=	13.9%
Perennial ryegrass	62,505%	÷	637,836	=	9.8%
					100.0%

Notes
1. The mixture used in this table as an example may have little merit on a contemporary golf course. Prior to introduction of state-of-the-art irrigation and lightweight mowing, fairways and roughs were sometimes sown to similar mixtures. The species best adapted then asserted itself.
2. Under conditions ideal for colonial bentgrass, the resulting stand from this mixture could be close to 100% highland bentgrass.
3. Ryegrasses were included for quick cover. Yet the high percentage in this mixture under certain conditions could result in a pure ryegrass stand.
4. To dissect a mixture further, one can determine the viable seeds per pound by multiplying the number of seeds per pound in each species by the germination rate.

Table 14.2
Seeds per Pound of Turfgrass Species
(Seed Weight Varies by Cultivars)

Cool-Season Grasses	Seeds per Pound
Bentgrass (Agrostis family)	
Creeping (*Agrostis stolonifera*)	6,130,270
Colonial (*Agrostis capillaris*)	6,130,270
Redtop (*Agrostis giganta*)	4,851,200
Bluegrass (Poa family)	
Kentucky (*Poa pratensis*)	1,390,253
Rough (*Poa trivialis*)	2,091,050
Annual (*Poa annua*)	1,195,680
Fine Fescue (Festuca family)	
Red or Creeping Red (*festuca rubra*)	365,120
Chewings (*Festuca commutata*)	448,640
Hard (*Festuca brevipila*)	591,920
Coarse Fescue (Festuca family)	
Tall (*Festuca arundinacea*)	206,383
Meadow (*Festuca pratensis*)	225,440
Ryegrass (Lolium family)	
Annual (*Lolium multiflorum*)	190,508
Perennial (*Lolium perenne*)	240,403
Timothy (*Phleum pratense*)	**1,163,458**
Warm-Season Grasses	*Seeds per Pound*
Bermuda (*Cynodon dactylon*)	
Hulled	2,070,638
Unhulled	1,585,297
Buffalograss (*Buchloe dactyloides*)	
Burs	49,895
Caryopses	335,657
Bahiagrass	**272,154**

Selecting the Root Zone Mix

by Christine Faulks
GREENSMIX DIVISION, A DIVISION OF FAULKS BROTHERS CONSTRUCTION, INC.

Because of documented success, choice of a growing medium for greens and tees is based on *USGA Recommendations for Putting Green Construction*. These recommendations were revised in 1993; copies are available from the Green Section and its regional agronomists. Only by studying them can one comprehend their scope and integrity. The reader's attention is drawn to Appendices A and B of Chapter 12 by Norman W. Hummel, who played a major role in the 1993 revision.

All materials used must be tested and approved by a laboratory recognized by the USGA. That laboratory can then design a root zone mix combining sand with organic matter and, sometimes, soil. There are also commercial blenders located in many states supplying these mixtures already approved by the USGA.

The organic matter used by many golf course builders in the United States and Canada is sphagnum peat moss obtained in the continental United States and Canada. Combined with the specified sand, it meets the criteria of physical properties shown in USGA specifications. When soil is used, other organic materials, if approved by a recognized laboratory, can be used. The USGA requests the minimum sand content of the soil be 60% with a clay content of 5 to 20%.

The USGA recommends that the root zone mix be blended off the green or other feature where it is to be used. As mentioned earlier, a mix already tested is obtainable from professional soil blending companies, as indeed are mixes prepared to order. These companies may also provide professional custom soil blending on-site with mobile blenders or at the sand plant location. This permits use of local materials if they reach specifications.

During the blending process, the mixture is tested periodically to ensure it is meeting requirements for specified properties. We recommend that these field-quality control checks be coordinated with independent laboratory checks, even though the quality control technician in the field is proficient in the test method. Testing and approval are mandatory before the material is placed in the cavity.

Part III

The Business of Golf Course Design

Golf Course Financing

by Richard L. Norton, Vice President
NATIONAL GOLF FOUNDATION

The course should be so interesting that even the plus man is constantly stimulated to improve his game in attempting shots he has hitherto been unable to play.

From *Golf Architecture*, 1920, by Alister Mackenzie (1870–1934)

The golf course architect plays an important role in helping to guide a client and his or her development team through the planning, design, permitting/approvals, and construction of new, expanded, or renovated golf courses. Obtaining development funding, from both debt and equity sources, remains the number one challenge and principal obstacle to successful development. Too many golf course development projects fail to get financing because the developer and his or her team of "experts" did not complete the appropriate research and planning needed to assess the risk, attract the necessary funds, and secure success.

This chapter on golf course financing covers the following topics:

- General Types of Debt and Equity Sources
- Overview of Requirements for Obtaining Debt and Equity Financing
- Putting Together a Package to Raise Debt and Equity Capital
- The Feasibility Study
- Physical Analysis/Site Overview
- The Business Plan
- Sources of Funds

General Types of Debt and Equity Sources

To get started, most projects need a combination of equity (ownership interest in the golf course) and debt (loans that must be repaid). Equity is typically obtained from owners, investors, and corporations. Debt financing is usually obtained from banks and other institutions.

The way funding is obtained depends on the type of course being planned for development. This section discusses financing for three different types of courses: daily fee courses, private membership courses, and municipal courses. There are other variations, such as semiprivate courses and driving ranges, but, for the purposes of financing, the focus is on the funding *generally* used for each of the three main types.

Daily fee courses can be funded by

Personal savings or corporate funding (equity)
General and limited partnerships (equity)

Real estate investment trusts or REIT (equity)
Friendly leases (equity)
Conventional loans (debt)
Seller financing (debt)

Private membership courses may be financed in the same way as daily fee courses. In addition, they may also obtain

Cash from members' initiation
Equity shares
Member deposits as debt

Municipal courses may be either entirely publicly owned or private/joint ventures. Municipal courses may be financed by

General obligation bonds
Revenue bonds
Sale/leaseback (turnkey development)
Private donor contributions
Land leases
Lease purchases
Conventional loans

Of course, most courses are developed using combinations and variations of these methods. The right combination depends on the project's unique circumstances.

Overview Requirements for Obtaining Debt and Equity

Currently, daily fee courses and semiprivate courses that are generated on a for-profit basis are most popular among investors and lenders, but, no matter what type of course is being planned, certain aspects have to appeal to the people with the money.

It may be surprising to learn that, as different as these sources are, they are all looking for *basically* the same type of information and they are all evaluating proposed projects according to very similar criteria.

Current Trends and Requirements in Golf Course Capitalization

In 1994, the National Golf Foundation (NGF) conducted a survey of golf course owners/operators and golf course lenders. Although the results of this survey may not reflect what is occurring at all golf course developments, they do provide insights into certain realities that are present in new golf course financing today.

From the developers/operators of golf courses under construction we learned a number of things. First, equity is important. Golf course loans typically require equity of at least 40 to 50%. Equity comes from different sources. Limited partnerships, corporations, and personal wealth are the most important sources of equity. Other sources of more limited availability and use include REITs, pension funds, and syndications.

Second, a track record helps. Loan terms and equity requirements are relaxed somewhat if the borrower has a track record of developing/operating successful golf courses.

Third, an established relationship with a lender also helps. Such a relationship is often key to obtaining a loan. Understandably, loans are most often made by a "local" institution.

Finally, land is not the ideal collateral. Lending institutions prefer personal property and income from unrelated businesses over land as collateral.

From informed lenders we learned that both debt and equity sources of financing are conservative in light of S&L and banking woes and real estate overbuilding. Lenders have several concerns with new golf course loans.

- Golf course improvements have a low residual value. The lender has no fallback position if the golf course operation fails.
- Golf is a service business. The success of the loan is a function of projected, uncertain cash flows, not underlying real estate value.
- It is easier to lend on an existing golf course with a cash flow track record than on a new golf course with an uncertain cash flow.
- Federal regulators/bank examiners become very anxious if golf course loans do not perform according to projections the first year.
- Golf courses are not large investments. Institutional investors indicate that golf course "deals" are not big enough to attract institutional attention.
- The FDIC has no specific underwriting guidelines for golf course credits. Golf courses are treated as conventional real estate credits. Creditors are concerned that bank examiners will not look upon golf course loans favorably; therefore, they are reluctant to lend. Bank examiners look primarily for cash flow from property and borrower cash reserves, and, secondarily, at the auction value of the property.
- Investors are concerned about the principal of their investment. Golf courses are unfamiliar to them in terms of proven resale value, liquidity of the market, growth rate in greens fees, and future profitability. These concerns must be addressed directly in the business plan.

Experienced golf course lenders are eager and willing to lend on golf courses and have overcome obstacles by

- Creating loan structures that acknowledge potential negative cash flows in the early years of operation; that is, they capitalize working capital requirements/ shortfalls.
- Requiring sufficient cash reserves to cover all contingencies.
- Increasingly offering equity participation in order to decrease borrower equity requirements and lower effective interest rates on debt.

Documentation Typically Required by Lenders and Investors

Lenders and investors looking at new developments say that successful "requests for financing" typically include

Detailed cost of development budget
Detailed estimated operating budget

Credible market potential (rounds and fees)
Qualified management team
Source documents for cash flow projections
Comparable project profile
Borrower's credit history
Cash equity investment by the developer
Loan-to-value ratios and debt coverage ratios that are within the lender's acceptable guidelines
Evidence of ability to fund shortfalls
Evidence of permits

Lender and investor requirements for financing the purchase of an existing golf course, a renovation, or a refinancing petition include

Detailed operating history and facilities
History of course ownership
Detailed description of the existing facility
Audited tax returns
Rounds and fee history at comparable golf facilities
Amount of equity invested
Management team qualifications
Borrower's credit history
Reasonable expectations
Identified market niche
Plan for use of capital
Realistic project completion dates (with a clear time line)
Skilled operations team
Description of permits secured
Good records from previous projects
Loan-to-value ratios and debt coverage ratios that are within the lender's acceptable guidelines
Water study
A clear plan to turn around a poorly managed existing course

Putting Together a Package to Raise Debt and Equity Capital

This section discusses in detail the requirements for raising debt and equity capital. It describes the different types of documents that must be completed.

First Things First: Putting Together a Team

When asked the question, "What factors determine whether a project will be successful?" lenders and investors alike look at two main criteria: solid numbers and an experienced team. This does not mean assembling as many experts as possible, with attorneys and accountants lined up on one side of the room and operations managers on the other. Each project is unique and has its own requirements for expertise. However, there are two general rules to follow.

1. Involve people only as needed.
2. Include people with good track records in their fields of expertise.

Generally, for new courses, both a planning team and an operations team may be desirable (see Chapter 16).

Planning Team The planning team should be very business oriented. It must decide whether the project is economically feasible and must be able to substantiate its claims. The planning team will probably change as the project moves from predevelopment to construction.

Predevelopment Although each project has specific needs, the predevelopment team should probably include the following:

Golf course architect. The golf course architect may be asked to propose an approximate cost range to construct the proposed facility based on the specific characteristics of the property and the type of facility desired by the client. Later, the architect designs the course within a target budget level.

Feasibility consultant. A feasibility study is a vital step in every project. It should be conducted by an independent consultant or firm that has no vested interest in its outcome. This objectivity is important, because the feasibility study will be viewed as credible by potential lenders and equity partners only if the information is determined to be impartial and objective.

Engineer. An engineer is needed to complete physical site studies. The engineer should have experience in the type of project being planned.

Environmental consultant. This is typically a specialist who can help identify any environmental issues (wetlands, habitat, hazardous materials, etc.) that might affect the cost or feasibility of the project.

An accountant (or finance expert). This should be someone who is familiar with the business objectives and can use standard accounting procedures. Following completion of the feasibility and market studies, the project's finance expert develops projected financials for the entire business plan.

Construction The construction team should probably include the following members, as applicable.

Superintendent. During the construction phase, the superintendent supervises grow-in and irrigation.

Architect. The architect ensures that the course is completed according to plan.

Contractor/builders. The contractor constructs the course and supervises all subcontractors.

Operations Team Once the planning phase is completed, an operations team is needed. The operations team should consist of business people who are interested in golf business, not golf enthusiasts who dabble in business. The following members should be considered:

- Operations director/manager.
- Club manager (for private clubs only). This may be the same person as the operations manager.
- Marketing team. Marketing must be considered before the course opens.
- Superintendent.
- Golf professional.
- Food and beverage manager.

All these people should ideally have experience in running a facility similar to that which is being planned.

The Need for a Business Perspective

Anyone who has ever had a home built for him or her knows how costs can skyrocket. The same thing can happen with a golf course if business perspective is lost. Wouldn't it be great to put a water hazard here or a bunker there? Maybe it would be great, but, if the budget calls for a certain amount to be spent on the course, it is essential to keep to the budget. The same is true for expensive clubhouses. Where are the hard numbers to support the project revenue needed to make such an investment profitable? Again, to get the necessary financing, remember to be a practical business person rather than a romantic visionary.

Package—What Package?

Golf is not just an investment in real estate. It is a business venture and must be treated like one. Even though the land may be valuable, investors and lenders know that once improvements have been made to the golf course, it will not be easily converted to other uses. Therefore, lenders want to know whether the golf *business* can succeed, not how much the land is worth. Golf, like the recreation and entertainment industry in general, does not enjoy the benefits of as many "rules of thumb" as some other industries. Thus, a businesslike package must be presented.

You have heard people talking of needing a "package." In this case, the package is a set of documents that lenders and investors use to decide whether to lend money or invest in a proposed or existing golf course.

In a typical project, an independent feasibility study comes first. It tells, from an objective viewpoint, whether the project is feasible. Before someone invests in the project or lends money (and before spending a lot of investment time and money), a feasibility study should be undertaken. A feasibility study indicates whether the project has a good chance of succeeding.

If the answer is "yes," then the next step is to put together a business plan. The business plan guides the process through the completion of the project and beyond.

When all this information is put together, along with any other documentation required by the lender or investor, you have a *package*. Essentially, it is the combination of a vision for the project and the compilation of expert opinion that justifies investing in or lending on the project.

The sections that follow describe each of the necessary documents. Although the focus is on new courses, the criteria are essentially the same for the purchase of an existing course. See "For Existing Courses," later in this chapter, for special requirements.

The Feasibility Study

A feasibility study is conducted to determine whether a project has a strong probability of economic self-sufficiency. More specifically, a feasibility study is conducted:

- When preparing to purchase a specific parcel of land for a golf development
- When preparing to purchase a specific existing facility
- When considering a specific market or region for golf development or acquisition

- When considering upgrading an existing course, which would shift its market potential
- When seeking a credible examination of a project, market, or facility's potential for the purpose of obtaining financing through a partnership or commercial lenders

Using an Independent Consultant

A feasibility study is a vital step in every project to help determine the need for a particular golf course in the market and its potential for financial success. The feasibility process involves participation by project planners, developers, marketing staff, and an independent consultant or firm that has no vested interest in the outcome of the study. This independence is important, inasmuch as the feasibility study will be viewed as credible by potential lenders and equity partners only if the information is determined to be impartial and objective. There are a number of credible consulting firms in the golf industry that can provide this vital service.

For a new project, a feasibility study should be one of the first steps a development team takes to assist in the planning of the project. For an existing course, the analysis should take place prior to the implementation of any major operational changes or purchase agreements.

A feasibility study can result in major changes to any envisioned development.

A Good Example: Using a Feasibility Study to Identify a Market Niche

Sunrise Developers hired XYZ Associates of Raleigh, North Carolina, to conduct a feasibility study of a golf course it planned to develop near Cincinnati, Ohio. The study cost Sunrise about $18,000, but its results had a major impact on the development. The study indicated that a new daily fee golf course was needed within a 15-mile radius of the site and that such a course could support 50,000 rounds. Unfortunately, two other golf developments were being proposed in the area. The study analyzed the plans for the other two courses and determined that Sunrise should develop an upscale course to distinguish itself from the other two. The demographics of the area supported an upscale development. That course is now operating very successfully.

Steps to the Feasibility Study

Certain data must be obtained to gain an estimate of the number of golf rounds currently being provided within the market area. To this end, the following steps are taken:
- *Overview of the community.* An overview section should report on recent trends in real estate development, employment, and changes in the population of the area. These factors and others provide a picture of the economic strength in the immediate region and significant trends that can affect a proposed golf project.
- *Defining the market.* The market area for the proposed development is determined by the density of the existing commercial and residential real estate in the area, the quality of the roadways providing access to the site, and the distribution of golf courses that would compete with the proposed facility. Generally, the report includes a map of the area indicating what falls within a three-, five-, and ten-mile radius or whatever distances are appropriate for that particular market.
- *Competitive course survey.* A competitive course survey examines those courses that are considered to be competition for the proposed facility, whether they are existing, under construction, or planned for development in the near future. This is a

critical component of the feasibility study. The planned structure of the proposed course (daily fee, private membership, or municipal) has a strong influence on which courses are competitive within the market area. The study team should visit each comparable existing course and describe it.

Demographic Structure of the Area   Once the market area is determined, the demographic characteristics of the market area residents are used to determine their potential demand for golf. The age and income distribution of the residents are examined in relation to the distribution of the demographic characteristics of golfers within the same region of the country to estimate the number of potential golfers and the number of potential rounds demanded on an annual basis.

NGF statistics can help in determining the potential number of rounds, but investigators must be careful to consider the specifics of the local community.

Charts can be used to show age and income data for the particular market. Then one can apply participation data to demographic data to project demand. This helps in knowing where to target the course.

Note that, although demographic information is important, it is not as important (and often not as accurate) as a competitive course survey.

Market Share   The estimated potential demand for rounds of golf within the market area is compared with the current number of rounds being supplied by competitive facilities. This comparison determines the status of the market area as undersupplied, oversupplied, or at equilibrium for annual rounds of golf. Utilizing local weather trends, the study should project the number of potentially playable days and estimate the maximum number of rounds of golf a facility in that area of the country could provide. Based on the type of facility proposed and the anticipated quality of the course, the anticipated rounds of play for the first five years of operation can be estimated, expressed as a percentage of maxiumum capacity for the area.

Architectural Analysis   The planning team should include a golf course architect, typically one who knows the geographic region of the proposed course so that he or she is familiar with factors such as soil conditions, topography, drainage, and area construction costs. The role of this team member is to provide an approximate cost range to construct the proposed facility based on the specific characteristics of the property and the type of facility desired by the client. This portion of the report details the various elements and considerations for the site involved, as well as for the anticipated course, expressed within a range.

A site analysis should also answer the following questions:

- Is there adequate acreage?
- Are soils appropriate?
- Are there any special environmental concerns?
- Are there protected wetlands on the site?
- What is the topography?

At this point, this is just a preliminary study. These issues should be explored in more detail in the physical analysis.

Financial Overview   Projected green fee levels and/or membership fees are determined for the proposed facility based on the anticipated quality of the course, the type and price level of competitive facilities in the market area, and the anticipated target market of the new facility. Other sources of revenue are also examined, including golf cars, pro shop, driving range, and food and beverage service for golfers. With these projections and the performance projections derived from the Market Share section of the study, estimated revenues over the first five years of operation can be provided. The estimated operating budget for the proposed facility is developed, based on anticipated staffing levels and the quality of course maintenance envisioned. The resulting estimate of net operating income indicates the potential fiscal success for the proposed development. In addition, these financial projections address the question of how much can be spent to develop the facility to adequately retire that amount of debt.

The Financial Overview section of the report should include a cash flow (revenues less expenses less debt service) analysis. Each of the following items should be included:

Operating Revenues

- Green fees (broken into distinct categories such as 18-hole, nonresident, weekday, winter)
- Season passes
- Membership fees and dues (described by categories of membership, if applicable)
- Golf cars
- Range fees (if applicable)
- Food and beverages
- Merchandise
- Other (lockers, bag storage, etc.)
- Pro shop and lessons (typically part of the pro's compensation package)

Operating Expenses

- Labor (including benefits and taxes)
- Maintenance costs (supplies, chemicals, fertilizer, seed, fuel, etc.)
- Utilities (electricity, gas, and water)
- Insurance (liability, structural, fire, equipment, etc.)
- Legal and accounting services
- Taxes and licenses
- Administrative supplies (telephone and office)
- Marketing
- Costs of goods sold (merchandise, food, and beverages)

When cash flow is projected over five to seven years and the amount of debt service each year is subtracted (showing the cumulative cash flow), you have completed a *pro forma,* which is an important part of the overall package.

Summary of Findings and Recommendations   The report should include a brief summary of pertinent information relative to the proposed facility and the market area. Finally, the report should make a go/no go recommendation or suggestions on how to make the project viable.

What About Feasibility Studies for Existing Courses?

For appraisals of the market and financial strength of existing courses, the preceding categories are valid, expect that less emphasis is placed on the architectural aspects and the future financial projections. More information on the existing facility and existing financial strengths is needed to focus on the current operation. Only after a full accounting of the market and the facility's operation can projections be made into the future for financial performance, taking into account any planned operational or physical changes to the facility.

Physical Analysis/Site Overview

A physical analysis (which includes both an environmental and an engineering report) should be done in conjuction with the feasibility study or shortly thereafter.

Often golf projects come to a grinding halt when problems involving permitting, site planning, water issues, or soil quality arise. One of the most difficult aspects of this stage in planning is that thousands of dollars may be required to evaluate the site's viability. This investment does not constitute a visible improvement to the property that will be appreciated by customers. Rather, these aspects of planning have become a price of entry into the business of golf course development as a result of increased legislation in the areas of water use, soil protection, drainage, wetlands management, and so forth. Planning fees in this phase of a course's construction can range from less than $100,000 to more than $1 million. Each site is unique and requires individual analysis.

The physical analysis should be conducted with knowledge of what type of golf facility will be built. Because site issues can have an impact on a design, developers must have a clear idea as to what level of difficulty they wish to offer. Changes to a design plan to accommodate environmental and engineering requirements can ultimately affect the quality of the course, which can make the course more or less successful in the marketplace.

Time is another factor that must be considered. Site evaluation and permitting can take years, so a project's viability may have to be checked and rechecked a number of times as it relates to the changing market conditions. Developers of projects that require many years in the permitting process can find that a one-time strong golf market or strong local economy has disappeared owing to a number of circumstances. Hence, careful planning in the area of site permitting and engineering are key to a project's success.

The physical analysis should be completed by experienced professionals. It should examine the following factors and their implications for the development of a golf course.

> *Topography.* How much must the land be modified?
>
> *Hydrology.* What water is available, how will it get here, what is the quality, and how much will it cost?
>
> *Geology.* What is the underlying soil?
>
> *Climate.* How many days of golf will be available each year? How many hours of golf are there daily during each month of the year?
>
> *Environmental factors.* Are any wetlands or endangered plants or animals affected by the proposed course?
>
> *Utilities.* Is there easy access to existing utilities?
>
> *Zoning and regulation.* How will zoning affect the proposed course?
>
> *Legal permits.* What permits are needed, and how hard are they to get? What are the costs associated with various permits?

The Business Plan

Following a positive feasibility analysis and physical site analysis, the purchaser/developer must compile detailed project information to incorporate into a business plan. The business plan uses feasibility findings but expands on the development/permitting costs involved and highlights the project's financial potential in greater detail. The business plan will be part of the package that presented to lenders and investors. *Note:* The financing for the golf course should be separate from the financing of any accompanying real estate project.

Components of a Business Plan*

Business Overview

- Report summary
- Overview/history of the project

The Project

- Introduction (overview, what's in the plan)
- Summary of the feasibility study (noting that the complete feasibility study is available upon request)
- Logo and photographs
- Development overview
- Operations overview
- Site plan layout
- Course design
- Media releases on the course

Location

- Statistical summary
- Multistate map
- State map
- County area map
- Local map
- Area description
- City officials
- Description of the town
- Description of the county

The Site

- Aerial photographs
- Summary data
- Description
- Survey of the site
- Legal description
- Environmental analysis

---

*Adapted from Benjamin R. Jones, "Financing for the Recreation Industry," *Putting Around* (January /February 1993).

Construction

- Introduction
- Project cost summary
- Critical path schedule

Start-up Budget

- Funds to start up inventory
- Publicity
- Training costs
- Uniform costs
- Office supplies

Forecasts

- Introduction
- Five-year forecast (pro forma)
- Notes and assumptions
- Debt coverage projection
- Source and application of funds
- Notes to application of funds
- Capital improvement program
- Working capital requirements

Management

- Operational plan
- Detailed development budgets
- Marketing/promotion
- Individuals involved/qualifications
- Resumes

Developer
Your company

- Profile
- References

Personnel

- Profile
- References
- Other key individuals involved (partners)

Exhibits

- Market Analysis
- Your other developments (names, photos, brochures, financial statements)

The Package

A full package is the business plan. However, investors and lenders may say, "I don't need the full package. Could you please send me . . ." Therefore, the package becomes whatever the investor or lender requests.

Various presentations of the information should be prepared. These can range from a media presentation to a two-page summary, thus allowing any potential requests to be addressed.

For Existing Courses

When the plan involves the purchase or refinancing of an existing course, the course's track record as well as any plans for improvement must be shown. In the business plan, actual performance records should be highlighted, including the following:

- Audited financial statements (going back five years, if possible)
- Water study
- Credit history
- Personal guarantee, if available
- Title report
- Environmental studies
- Planning permits
- Project approval requirements
- Adequacy of existing utilities

If you are planning improvements to the course, you might consider describing your plans to

- Improve the grounds
- Improve the signage
- Eliminate excess inventories
- Increase rounds
- Improve collections
- Increase league play
- Increase pro shop sales
- Reduce expenses

Sources of Funds

Most projects are funded using a combination of equity and debt capital. Typically, to obtain debt financing, a certain amount of equity is required. Thus, strategies for generating equity are often critical to the success of a project.

Raising Equity

Equity is typically generated from the following sources:

Use of personal savings/assets or corporate funding
Limited partnerships
Private club-member equity
Real estate investment trusts (REITs)

Among these sources, personal savings, limited partnerships, and member equity are by far the most common.

REITs have become a "hot topic" since National Golf Properties was successful in raising large amounts of capital this way in 1993. The organization's success in raising new capital for continued purchases of more courses has made it an even bigger player in the golf industry. However, REITs are complicated and security laws are strict, so they are not for everyone.

Many upscale private clubs begin with the establishment of a nonprofit organization that solicits membership fees, which are put into an escrow account that will be used to develop a golf course. Projects of this type are usually targeted at the well-to-do golfer who is seeking an exclusive membership at a private club. Although membership fees may be very high, the memberships are not always viewed as investments.

Other membership alternatives include

- Offering the buyer of membership and related real estate interest a limited partnership
- Giving the buyer a preferred membership structure that allows him or her to keep a membership and eventually sell an additional membership
- Waiving dues or golf car fees for a year or two

Sources of Traditional Debt Financing

There are an increasing variety of debt financing vehicles available for golf course development, acquisition, and expansion.

Banks and S&Ls (construction and takeout)
Golf capital companies (GATX Golf Capital, Textron Financial, Nations Capital)
Insurance companies
Pension funds
Investment banks

Of those listed here, local banks and golf capital companies represent the dominant sources.

Conventional Loans

Conventional loan patterns often feature three phases. First is the construction loan, for perhaps one to three years. The lending institution typically requires a takeout guarantee of the lower-rate construction loan at the end of that time.

In a second phase, the takeout loan may be from another lender, or even from the same institution, probably at a higher rate (perhaps 2% higher) for about five years.

The third phase of a conventional loan pattern is the long-term loan for the ongoing project from a bank or insurance company. It is also possible that the long-term lending institution will ask for some equity in the project.

Other Debt Vehicles

Although conventional loans are the most popular sources of financing, there are other options.

Two-stage financing. Two-stage financing includes taking out two completely different loans from two different lenders. The advantage to having two loans is that some lenders are set up to do construction financing and some are not; therefore, allowing two-stage financing broadens the financing available. However, two loans are usually more expensive than one, considering that the recipient of the loan pay two sets of loan fees.

Seller financing. If a buyer is purchasing an existing course, the seller may agree to finance the sale. In these cases, the seller is acting as the bank. If the buyer defaults on the loan, the seller can take back the course (paying for the share the buyer has acquired over time). Sellers who can afford these deals like them because they provide income. Buyers like these deals because they can save money by negotiating terms and fees.

Funding for Municipal Courses   A number of financing alternatives are available today for new municipal golf facilities. With the creation of financing vehicles such as revenue bonds, cities and counties have been able to raise funds at low interest rates for a variety of projects, including golf courses. In addition, a number of new companies have formed to assist municipalities in the planning, construction, and operations of golf courses. The combination of low-interest-rate financing and private section expertise has been a primary reason for the rapid development of municipally owned golf courses.

Municipalities have several development, financing, and operational options. Operationally, municipalities must consider whether they wish to operate their golf courses themselves or have a professional management company operate their facilities.

The structure of financing projects can vary a great deal and depends on the community's bonding resources, its desire to accept debt responsibilities, and its skills in organizing the development of a large-scale project such as a golf course.

Municipal funding alternatives include the following:

General budget allocation. Golf course capital requirements are funded out of budget surpluses. (Not many public entities are in a situation permitting such allocation.)

Sale of general obligation or revenue bonds. General obligation bonds require voter approval and are backed by all income sources to the public entity. Revenue bonds are backed by the city's credit rating and revenues from designated sources, including the golf course itself. Revenue bonds may not require voter approval.

Such sales are great potential sources, provided that the city or county is willing to use them.

Certificates of participation (COPs). The city or county is required to establish a public development corporation, which contracts with a private developer for design and construction of the facility. The contract calls for a turnkey complex to be delivered at a guaranteed fixed price. The public development corporation uses its financing powers to sell tax-exempt COPs or similar financing vehicles. Debt service is funded from the golf course positive cash flow. In the event of a revenue shortfall, the public agency's general fund provides additional security. A golf course management company is typically retained to operate the course. In 20 to 30 years, when the bonds are fully repaid, the golf course reverts to the city or county.

Lease/Purchase Financing   Lease/purchase financing requires a leasehold contract between a municipality and a lease/purchase finance entity. The contract calls for a turnkey complex to be delivered at a guaranteed fixed price to the municipality. However, the municipality may elect to competitively bid the construction contract.

Other Lease/Purchase Characteristics

* The municipality agrees to make lease or installment payments on the golf course until the golf course improvements are paid off (usually 20 to 22 years).

- Installment or lease payments are funded from golf course net revenues. The city and its general fund remain the ultimate guarantor for any operating shortfalls.
- The course is developed, and in some cases managed, by a private company. The municipality retains control over the property through the leasehold interest.
- At the end of the 20 to 22 years, the golf course is sold to the municipality for $1.
- The advantages of this financing vehicle are that no debt will appear on the municipality's balance sheet, the bonding capacity of the city is not affected, and, when the lease expires in 20 to 22 years, the municipality will own the golf course free and clear.

16

Utilizing a Team Approach to Permitting and Construction Monitoring

by S. Jeffrey Anthony, Barbara B. Beall, and Kevin J. Franke
THE LA GROUP, P.C.
SARATOGA SPRINGS, NEW YORK

Committees should leave well enough alone, especially when they have a really fine course.

From *Concerning Golf,* 1903, by John Laing Low (1869–1929)

Playing fields of golf vary widely from course to course and from location to location. Given each course's unique nature, it is reasonable to expect that project management for developing new golf facilities would also be highly variable. However, there are common trends and lessons that can be gained from past experiences in project management and applied to new projects.

The benefits of using a team approach to project management and how it can be implemented are the lessons presented here. Written from the perspective of the environmental consulting firm with experience working on a variety of golf course and other development teams in New York State, this chapter examines when and how a team approach can be used to ensure that the client's and architect's dreams are realized.

Project Initiation, Program Development, and Issues Identification

Project Initiation

A golf development project is often initiated by an owner of a property who wants to build a golf course. A project may also be commenced by a developer looking for a piece of property on which to locate a golf course and, perhaps, housing or other commercial development. In these situations, the owner or developer (the client) assembles a project team to begin the review of the project.

Less often, a municipality or other governmental agency may decide to renovate, expand, or build a golf course facility and publishes a "request for proposal," which is circulated within the consulting community. In this case, consultants take the lead in building a project team in hope of being awarded the contract for the work.

In any of these situations, a core project team is assembled to assist the client in determining whether the development concept is feasible. Evaluating the feasibility of the development concept is typically referred to as the "Preliminary Feasibility Analysis" phase. The core team typically consists of the developer or owner, the golf course architect, and two or three other individuals, depending on the nature of the course.

An environmental attorney may be included in the core team when the course is located in a highly regulated environment, because this professional can play an important role as strategist and facilitator during the permitting process. When a site appears to have physical or regulatory constraints, it is appropriate for a land-use planning professional with skills in environmental sciences and landscape architecture to be included on the core team. In the development of a resort course, or if there are potential marketing or financial concerns, a marketing professional may have a leadership role.

Members of this core team are usually chosen based on an established relationship with the client, such as through a law or engineering firm, or through referrals from golf industry personnel or a personal attorney. If the client has a working relationship with an environmental consulting firm, that firm may be selected before other team members. A golf course architect may be chosen based on a relationship established during previous projects or by his or her response to a letter of interest circulated by the client.

Even though potential members of the core team may have been referred to the client by a trusted individual, it is still important to conduct interviews and check references to ensure a good fit between team members and that the potential members are all suitably qualified for the proposed project. This need for reference checks and an interview applies to the selection of all team members.

Program Development

After assembling the core team, the client usually takes the lead in setting goals, with core team members assisting in developing details, identifying the type of golf course that the client is envisaging, and evaluating associated programs (i.e., clubhouse, housing, recreational facilities).

Issues Identification

During this preliminary phase, relevant issues are identified and a budget, including the minimum acceptable development necessary to support the project, is assessed. Preliminary information gathering may also be conducted, including the following:

- A marketing study may be conducted to assess existing golf facilities and the economic and demographic characteristics of the region to determine whether the goals and type of project proposed are economically realistic. (The previous chapter emphasized an independent consultant). We consider him or her to be on the team, unless retained initially only to determine if the golf course will be profitable.
- A site assessment, sometimes at a preliminary level (i.e., review of available maps, site walk), and more often with additional detail (i.e., topographic surveys), is necessary to determine whether site conditions have the potential to support the proposed development. Potential issues to be resolved are identified, and a list of necessary permits is compiled.

After program elements and issues have been identified, the core team should assess the situation to determine what other consultants may be needed. The project now can move toward building and organizing the rest of the project team. The additional team members assist in completing the preliminary feasibility analysis and will have input throughout the ensuing project phases.

Building the Project Team

Additional consultants are not always needed for golf course developments; sometimes a project can proceed with just a few specialized professionals. In regions with limited environmental regulations, sites with limited sensitivity, or projects with substantial public approval or local support, a project team may simply consist of core team members, provided they have adequate experience to prepare all necessary plans and obtain the limited number of required permits.

In the majority of cases, however, new golf course projects require a larger project management team. This is especially true when there are site constraints (i.e., limited size, sensitive environmental resources), when regulations are numerous or multilayered, when special issues must be addressed, or when public controversy (i.e., a group opposed to the project) is a potential threat.

The client's philosophy plays a major role in hiring consultants, developing a qualified project team, and gathering information for the project. A project progresses smoothly when a client thoughtfully weighs the team's advice in making decisions and assists whenever possible. Open communication between core team members early in the process can help all to comprehend the intrinsic value of a quality project team and the paramount need for it to gather all necessary data and define how the project will proceed.

Available Services

A diverse consulting community has developed throughout the United States and elsewhere. Table 16.1 outlines the responsibilities of these consultants: landscape architects, environmental scientists, community planners, engineers, specialty consultants (in agronomy, archaeology, irrigation, traffic), and public relations/marketing professionals and accountants. Clubhouse architects and golf course superintendents, unique but necessary for golf course developments, are also included.

Table 16.1
Responsibilities of Project Team Members

Owner/Developer or Representative

Responsible for initiating and financing the project, along with setting and maintaining the goals of the project, final decisions, and compliance with permits.

Golf Course Architect

Responsible for advising the owner regarding the goals of the project, the suitability of the site, creation of the golf course and specifications for its construction, and ensuring that accessory program elements fit the design concept.

Environmental or Land Use Attorney

Responsible for researching, designing, and facilitating the regulatory strategy, with input from the environmental consultants and others on site condition issues and coordination with the owner and architect. Often takes the lead on zoning and wetland permit issues.

Table 16.1 (cont'∂)

Accountant or Financial Expert

Responsible for examining the market conditions and advising on the most suitable type of course development, and for advising the owner on the cost/benefit of various proposed actions in the overall financing of the project.

Landscape Architect

Responsible for providing detailed layouts for all site components, including grading and drainage, planting, lighting, parking areas, roads, walkways, storm water runoff, and the location and design of enhancement plantings. This professional may also serve as project coordinator for the team.

Land Planners

Responsible for providing information on demographics and zoning during the feasibility analysis and gathering information on the political landscape. May also assist in obtaining grants for development or renovations of municipal courses.

Environmental Scientist

Responsible for providing detailed information regarding site conditions, analyzing project impacts, and proposing mitigation measures. This professional works with the environmental attorney to develop permit applications and environmental documents, may assist in permit processing, and may provide construction monitoring services.

Engineer

Responsible for the design of utility systems (water distribution and sewage collection) and oversight for technical details of site design plans. An engineer's stamp is often required on plans submitted to county or state regulatory agencies. Often oversees construction of utility systems.

Specialty Consultants (Agronomists, Archaeologists, Traffic Consultants)

Responsible for data collection, impact assessment, development of mitigation measures, report preparation and coordination for their areas of expertise, and may conduct coordination with the regulatory agencies involved in their areas of concern. Reports can be used on their own or appended for reference in other environmental planning documents with recommendations incorporated into the project design.

Public Relations/Marketing Professional

Responsible for providing market research and analysis to assess the best marketing niche for the course, given the economic and demographic conditions. Works with project team to ensure that presentations and materials will be well received by the public and reviewing agencies and will reflect the marketing of the course. Reviews program elements for consistency with the marketing plan and implements marketing plan in attracting members or customers.

Building Architect

Responsible for clubhouse design, as well as design of other buildings (maintenance, recreational), to assure that the design is compatible with other program elements and the needs of the project and is in compliance with applicable regulations.

Table 16.1 (cont'd)

Irrigation Consultant

Responsible for the design of the irrigation utility system, including assessing capacity requirements, and the design of the intake, pump house, lines, heads, and control facilities. This consultant is responsible for design, construction, and technical support during operation.

Golf Course Superintendent

Responsible for initiating the operation and maintenance of the golf course as well as listing and specifying maintenance equipment. Because the superintendent will assume responsibility for maintenance of the facility, his or her input into final design plans, especially utility systems and access, is valuable to ensure that the facility will be easy to maintain and operate. The superintendent may be responsible for grow-in alone or with the contractor and constantly observes the operation, advising the person to whom he or she reports. Such observations by the person responsible for maintaining and enhancing the layout far into the future afford the owners and players innumerable benefits.

It is important to identify the responsibilities of all team members at the beginning of the project to avoid confusion and duplication of efforts during the planning phases when areas of involvement may not yet be well defined.

Developing a table, such as that shown in Table 16.2, is useful in organizing the core team's findings, identifying the consultants that are required and their areas and levels of responsibility. It is another way to assign responsibility for handling particular issues and to ensure that all issues have been identified and considered in the planning phase.

Factors in Consultant Selection

Several factors are taken into consideration during the project team selection process. One is whether the project would be better served by a firm with regional or national recognition or a local firm with connection to the municipal and county government where the project is located. This factor is best evaluated by determining which approvals will be the most difficult to obtain, which consulting firm is best qualified to represent the project in those negotiations, and whether there is a firm that can conduct negotiations at a variety of governmental levels.

A second consideration is whether the project would benefit more by a multidisciplinary consulting firm that can supply expertise in a variety of the needed disciplines or by a number of smaller consulting firms. Although a multidisciplinary firm is generally organized around a primary profession, typically either landscape architecture or engineering, the firm may also employ individuals with other areas of professional expertise. The primary focus of the firm will shape the approach taken during work on the project. For projects with sensitive aesthetic issues, a landscape architecture firm may provide the best focus, whereas sites with difficult engineering issues, such as steep slopes or poor soils, may benefit from the capabilities of an engineering firm.

An advantage of using a multidisciplinary firm is that coordination among a majority of the professionals involved in the project occurs in one place with individuals who have previously worked together. The drawbacks are that one company holds significant responsibility for the success of the project, the character of the project may be

Table 16.2
Mosaic of Program/Issues and Expertise

Program Elements	Golf Course Architect	Environmental Attorney	Financial Advisor	Landscape Architect Land Planner	Environmental Scientists	Engineers	Specialty Consultants*	Public Relations Marketing	Building Architect	Golf Consultants**
Golf Course Design	●									
Clubhouse	○		○	○	○				●	
Master Plan	○			●	○	○		○		
Housing			○	●	○	○	●	○		
Maintenance Facility	○			○	○	○			●	○
Traffic Circulation				○		●	●			
Irrigation	○			○	○	○				●
Landscaping	○			●				○		○

Client's Project Team

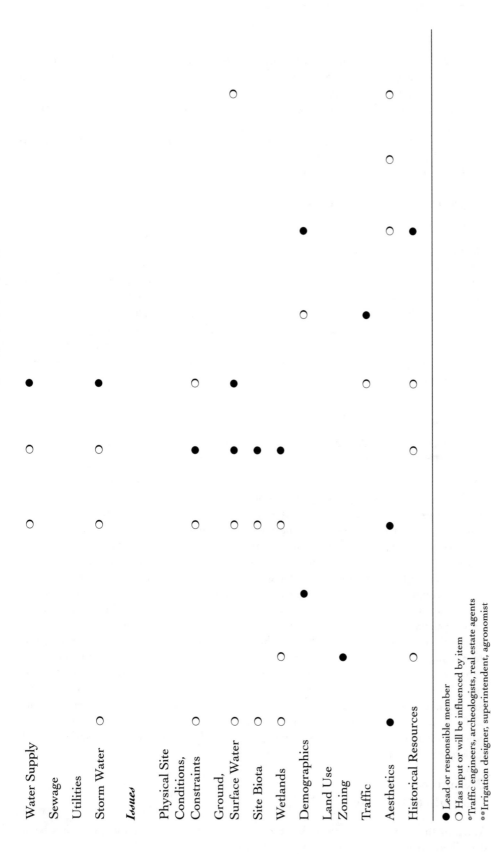

influenced by the focus or philosophies of the firm, and a project with limited scope may not require engaging such a large firm.

The need for other support services and their availability from various firms may also influence the selection of consultants. These services include geographic information systems (GIS) analysis/mapping, and computer-assisted design and drafting (CADD). Some firms may even provide chemical fate modeling (nutrients and pesticides), integrated pest management, and turf management planning and may have individuals on staff with a strong agronomy background.

Organization of Team Lines and Communication

Communication between team members is professional common sense, with lines of communication usually evolving with a project. Still, an organizational chart and expectations regarding formal and informal communications (progress memos, decision items, change work orders) should be included in contract language and discussed at the start-up meeting. Project team meetings at the commencement of each phase should also be included in the scope of work. These meetings are valuable for summarizing the findings of the previous phase, consensus building, setting goals, and assigning responsibilities and time frames for the next phase of work. This agenda ensures that everyone is working in concert.

The Phases of Project Design Development

The phases of project design development are intertwined, not necessarily linear, and tend to occur concurrently. For purposes of this discussion, the preconstruction component is presented in three main phases: preliminary feasibility analysis, detailed site assessment, and project design and permitting. Some land use planners and architects develop a "critical path" of design and permitting actions that must be taken to reach the goals of the project. Other consultants prepare "best and worst case scenarios," recognizing some of the uncertainty associated with the permitting process time frame.

Throughout the design process, especially on smaller sites with environmental constraints, the golf course architect and consultants must work together to balance the course design and permitting issues. Consultants on a project team are typically directed by the client and golf course architect. The latter works with the owner in defining and developing the course's character, and the consultants provide the background work and information necessary to implement these concepts. Sometimes, however, the environmental resources of the site or another permitting issue may require direction from the consultant on those issues or locations. Fostering an atmosphere of respect for the focus of the various members, together with an open sharing and "give and take" of information and ideas among team members, will encourage development of the best design and permitting solutions.

Preliminary Feasibility Analysis

Much of the work associated with the preliminary feasibility analysis phase has been described earlier. At this stage, the goals are to

- Build the complete project team
- Develop the project's goals and programs
- Determine, based on a preliminary review, the site's feasibility

As the rest of the project team is assembled, members identify other issues or information that must be addressed or incorporated into the project, develop additional information regarding feasibility of the site, and examine the need for obtaining additional land.

The Detailed Site Assessment Stage

The second phase of project design development is detailed site assessment. The goals of this phase are to

- Develop complete information regarding site conditions
- Understand the political landscape
- Develop a master plan and alternatives that illustrate the golf course routing and other program areas
- Develop a detailed permitting strategy
- Receive preliminary feedback from all permitting agencies
- Develop a high confidence level regarding the feasibility of the proposed project

To meet these goals, a number of work items, including those discussed in the following paragraphs, must be completed. This is not a comprehensive list. Variations in site conditions and situations will require modifications and additions.

- Develop surveys and reports of site conditions (boundaries, site features, topography—preferably at 2-foot contour intervals, groundwater, soils, wetlands and surface waters, vegetation, wildlife habitats, historical and archaeological features, roads, zoning, past land uses, hazardous materials, scenic views and aesthetic resources).
- Develop surveys of off-site conditions (adjacent land uses, regional landscape, demographics, zoning practices, traffic, and utilities capacities).
- Gather information (endangered species, water source analysis for potable and irrigation water, potential impacts of the proposed project on the areas of study).
- Survey the political landscape and attitudes about the project. Meet with active environmental groups, adjacent landowners, property owners willing to sell land, local and county governments, economic development corporations. Anticipate any unusual informational requests that may arise during the approval process (e.g., chemical modeling) and initiate a response.
- Develop multiple alternative layouts of the golf course and support facilities. Using these various layouts, conduct preliminary assessments of potential impacts, identify mitigation measures and permit requirements. Alternative layouts need not be drastically different, and all alternatives developed should be saved in case it should become necessary to demonstrate avoidance of impacts during permitting.
- Reach a consensus among the project team members on the preferred alternative, along with the benefits and drawbacks of all layouts. Determine the significant issues for each alternative and whether changes can be made to each alternative to resolve those issues yet maintain the integrity of the design and permitting process.

- Develop a comprehensive regulatory strategy that discusses all necessary permits, including informational requirements of the submittal, the review processes, and time lines. The strategy should include a format for organizing the information (perhaps around a central regulatory document such as an environmental impact statement) and determine which processes will be conducted concurrently. Table 16.3 lists many of the permits that may be required for a new golf course development in New York State. (Permits and regulations vary across the county and are also dependent upon the nature of the site and the golf course proposed. Identifying what permits may be required and developing a strategy for obtaining those permits should be conducted early in the project.) Similar permits, although not identical, will be needed in other states. There may also be additional permits needed, for items such as water withdrawals, tree or vegetation removal, and chemical storage and usage on-site together with equipment washing facilities. These items are not regulated by permit in New York State but are usually reviewed during the process mandated by the State Environmental Quality Review Act.
- Hold preapplication meetings with various regulatory agencies to determine permitting feasibility, requirements, and time frames.

Table 16.3
Potential Permits and Reviews
for a Golf Project in New York State

Federal	
U.S. Army Corps of Engineers	Permits for impacts to wetlands and waters Coordination with federal resource agencies
U.S. Fish and Wildlife Service	Review for federal endangered species
State	
Environmental Conservation	Freshwater Wetlands Permit Stream Disturbance Permit Section 401 Water Quality Certificate State Pollutant Discharge Elimination System (SPDES) permit for storm water and sewage point source outfalls

Project Design and Permitting Phase

The goals of the project design and permitting phase are to

- Develop, as needed, preliminary or final plans used to resolve design issues or for permitting
- Prepare plans adequate to complete the construction activities on the site as needed, given regulatory involvement and construction style of the architect and client
- Obtain all necessary permits with the least expenditure of time and effort

Permitting is continued in this phase after the preapplication meetings. Applications are submitted and necessary documents are developed in anticipation of information requests of the various agencies. The permitting process should follow the strategy and time frames developed earlier unless there are situations that cause a reevaluation of the strategy.

Drawings and Plans   Some architects still prefer to work in the field from preliminary plans, using their own construction crews for final shaping. This method, almost universal prior to the present regulatory age, is feasible if the architect has control over the construction crew. However, use of preliminary plans may not be acceptable to regulatory agencies if extensive tree clearing is called for, significant volumes of earth are to be moved, extensive surface and subsurface drainage is needed, work is to be performed near environmentally sensitive areas, or permits for accessory facilities are required. Detailed plans will probably be needed for such work, and invariably for water systems, sewage treatment systems, and driveway curb cuts. Construction level drawings for all of the foregoing can often be developed concurrently with the permitting review and are reviewed by local agencies as a special condition to permits.

Switching Gears from Permitting to Construction

Sometimes projects have difficulty in making the transition from the design phase to the construction phase.

Moving into construction involves bringing in a construction team, which may include a contractor and/or a superintendent. If these individuals were not involved in the permitting and design processes, they will not have much background knowledge regarding the project, nor the same emotional and professional investment as other project team members. Yet, for economic savings, the client may look to reduce the involvement of the earlier members of the project team who are invested in the project. Some contractors work to get the project team out of the picture so as to lessen scrutiny onsite, thus providing the potential to short-cut or save money. There is also a natural push to "get on with it" and jump right into construction.

To assure a smooth transition between the permit/design phase and the construction phase, it is important to have a period of interaction between the construction group and the project team. It is equally important for the client and project team to actively encourage compliance with the design drawings and permits, both prior to and during the construction phase.

Design drawings and permits should not be perceived as obstacles to construction, but rather as opportunities to implement the aesthetic features of the design and to avoid adverse financial consequences that can result from permit noncompliance.

There are a number of steps that can be taken to minimize construction difficulties. First, establish a positive attitude regarding permits and design drawings, which will be reflected throughout the construction project management. Double-check that all approvals have been received prior to releasing the construction bid package or awarding the contract.

Incorporate permits and design drawings into the bidding package, construction documents, and/or contract as compliance items, and discuss permits, design drawings, and consequences of noncompliance in prebid and preconstruction meetings. It is important to provide opportunities for the project team and the contractors to get to know one another at meetings. Members of the project team should be available during the construction start-up phase to answer any questions and monitor work.

Mark all construction limits and sensitive resource areas in the field prior to mobilization of equipment. Tour these areas with the construction chief.

Install silt fences and other soil erosion control devices in compliance with permits, preferably prior to large equipment mobilization on-site, at the earliest possible time, or in compliance with the Erosion Control Plan. Be sure to document maintenance of silt fences and erosion control devices.

Establish formal lines of communication for construction project management. Maintain a monitor or owner's representative on-site; establish inspection procedures for resource agency representatives, and review them with the contractor.

Smaller Projects at Existing Facilities

Some projects are limited in scope to alterations or upgrades of an existing facility rather than construction of a completely new golf course. Projects of this type may require retaining consulting services because of the permitting, monitoring, or technical issues involved. For example, consulting services may be required in the following instances:

- Meetings with regulatory personnel, especially those involving potential violations
- Activities in wetland areas or bodies of water
- Construction of ponds for irrigation, playing interest, or aesthetics
- Issues regarding pesticide/herbicide use, including additions to chemical storage buildings or equipment washing areas
- Extensive tree removal
- Habitat preservation or restoration
- Construction of drainage projects with collection systems
- Major irrigation system renovations
- Retaining wall design and construction
- Repair of major soil erosion problem areas
- Placement of residential development next to existing golf course
- Aesthetic changes to amenities, including ponds, swales, and fountains
- Construction of new buildings

The same steps followed in larger projects are necessary for smaller projects at existing facilities. The owner/developer identifies the issues and the appropriate type of assistance needed for the project, assembles the project team, assesses site conditions, and develops and implements a regulatory and design strategy.

Minisceongo Golf Club: A Case Study

The Minisceongo Golf Club is located in the town of Ramapo in Rockland County, New York. The following describes the team approach taken to design, permit, and construct a private "high-end" 18-hole golf course with a number of amenities.

The project was initiated in early 1991 by a developer, Bergstol Enterprises, which had purchased an option to buy a 145-acre site previously used as a boarding school. The developer retained a golf course architect, Roy Case of the Case Golf Company, and an environmental law firm, Whiteman, Osterman and Hanna, located in Albany, New York.

This law firm had significant project experience with the LA Group, a multidisciplinary consulting firm offering services in the fields of landscape architecture, civil engineering, environmental sciences, and planning, and suggested their services to the client. The LA Group was retained to conduct environmental site analysis, assist the attorney through the state and federal wetland permitting process, complete permitting at the local level, engineer utility systems, and complete site plan layouts and landscape amenities for the golf course. A clubhouse architect, Alesker, Reiff and Dundon of Philadelphia, Pennsylvania, was also brought onto the project team.

Prior to the environmental consultant's involvement, federal and state wetland delineations had already been completed for the site and a number of alternative routing plans had been developed by the golf course architect and the developer.

One of the first steps taken by the environmental attorney was to initiate preapplication meetings with the New York State Department of Environmental Conservation (NYSDEC) and the U.S. Army Corps of Engineers (ACOE) to make sure that it would be feasible to obtain state and federal wetland permits and to determine whether alternative layouts or lands would have to be considered. Figures 16.1, "State Wetlands," and 16.2, "Federal Wetlands," illustrate the layout of the course and its relationship to these resources.

It became obvious that the project layout would require additional lands in order to have the desired course length (7,000+ yards) and to ensure a project that was "permittable." Additional lands were obtained from Rockland County in exchange for lands from the golf course and monetary contributions. This exchange of lands required the approval of Rockland County and the New York State legislature, which were obtained by the developer, the local assemblyman, and the developer's general practice attorney. Figure 16.3 illustrates the scope of this exchange.

During the spring and summer, the environmental consultant completed a detailed assessment of all project site characteristics, along with federal and state wetland delineations on the county property obtained in the land exchange.

During this same time period, two archaeological consultants were hired to complete archaeological and historical assessments on the property, including prehistoric sites, an eighteenth-century cemetery, and a chapel-like building eligible for listing on the National Register of Historic Places. As it turned out, this building was rehabilitated and used as the clubhouse. A traffic consultant was also hired to coordinate and resolve traffic issues and concerns.

The organizational chart for the project team is illustrated in Figure 16.4. In this case, the LA Group, P.C., managed the various team members involved in the project. There are a variety of ways to organize a project team depending upon the management strengths of the different team members.

In September 1991, the project team initiated conceptual site plan review with the town of Ramapo. An Expanded Environmental Assessment Form (EEAF) had been prepared, but shortly thereafter the town determined that the project would require the preparation of a more detailed Environmental Impact Statement (EIS). Scoping of the EIS occurred in January 1991. Scoping is the process of developing a list of issues to be examined in the environmental review and involves the input of the public, agencies with a concern related to the project, and the lead agency responsible for the project.

Anticipating that the town would require the preparation of an EIS for the project, the consultant formatted the information obtained during the site assessment so that it

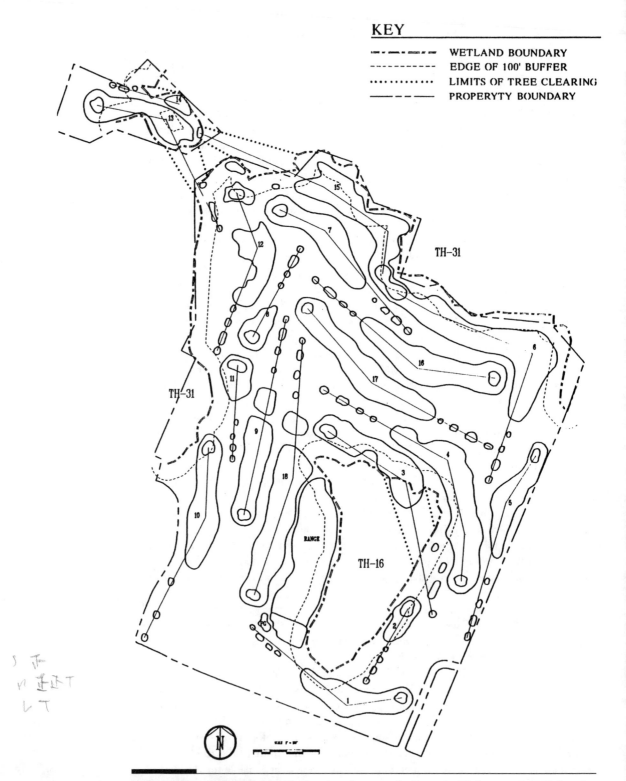

— · — · — · —	WETLAND BOUNDARY
— — — — —	EDGE OF 100' BUFFER
· · · · · · · · · ·	LIMITS OF TREE CLEARING
— — — — —	PROPERYTY BOUNDARY

FIGURE 16.1   *State wetlands. The location of state wetlands on the Minisceongo Golf Club project site. (Courtesy the LA Group, P.C.)*

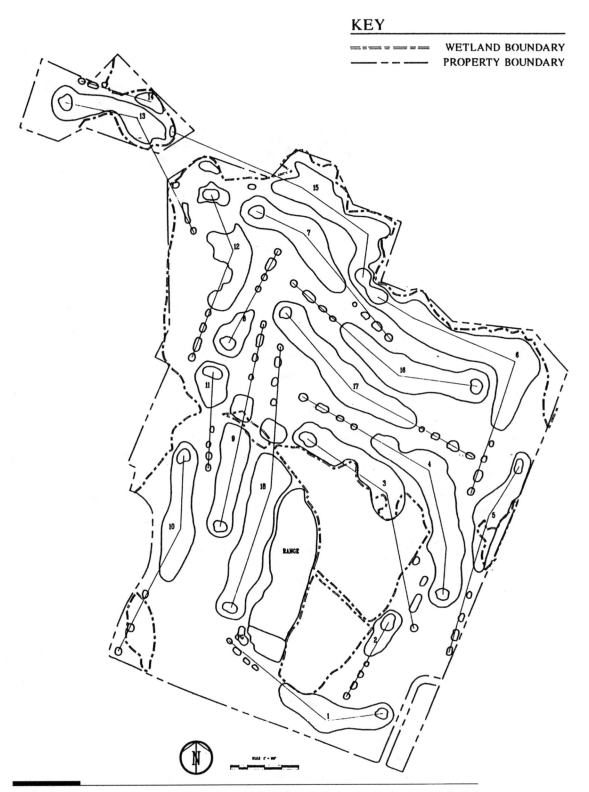

KEY

═ ═ ═ ═ ═ ═   WETLAND BOUNDARY

─── ─ ── ─   PROPERTY BOUNDARY

FIGURE 16.2   *Federal wetlands. The location of federal wetlands on the Minisceongo Golf Club project site. (Courtesy the LA Group, P.C.)*

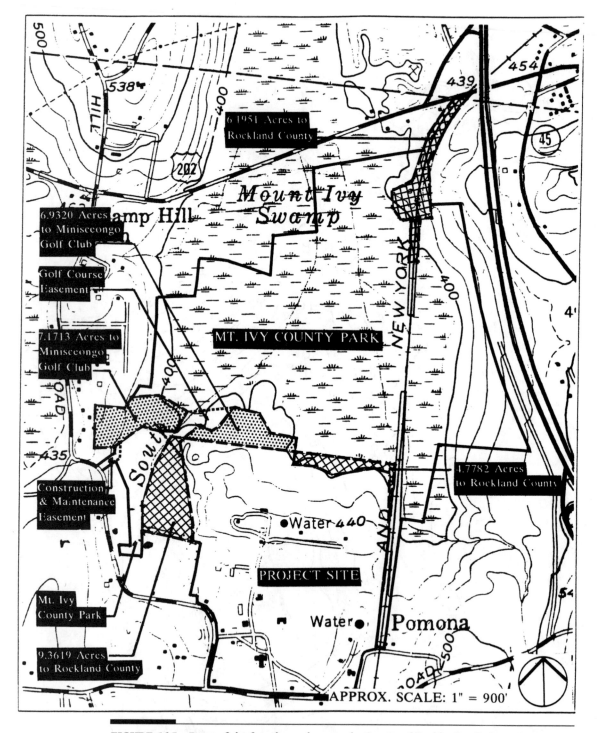

FIGURE 16.3   *Proposed land exchange between the County of Rockland and the project sponsor, Minisceongo Golf Club. In order to create a project site that would be large enough and configured properly to allow for a golf course of a desired length, additional lands were needed. The project sponsor obtained lands from Rockland County in exchange for golf course lands on the golf course parcel and monetary contributions. (Courtesy the LA Group, P.C.)*

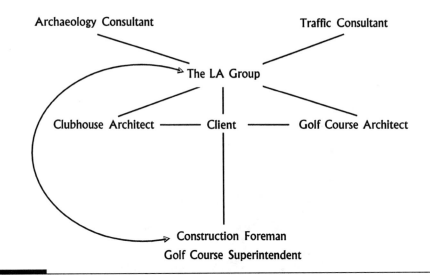

FIGURE 16.4   Team organization chart for the Minisceongo Golf Club project. In this case, the LA Group, P.C., managed the various team members involved in the project. There are a variety of ways to organize a project team, depending upon the management strengths of the different team members.

could be quickly reorganized into an EIS. The issues that would be identified during scoping were also anticipated, and together these actions taken by the consultant resulted in a one-month turnaround from the completion of the scoping to submittal of the Draft Environmental Impact Statement (DEIS).

Four specific issues raised during scoping received extra attention:

- Length of the construction period and area of grading
- Potential for wetland impacts
- Adverse impacts to water resources from chemical use, including fertilizers
- Potential for traffic impacts

The LA Group addressed these issues openly, with as much documentation and detail as possible, in an effort to eliminate concerns regarding those issues or at least to focus discussion. Full disclosure of information usually results in a more expeditious review and approval process. The DEIS contained as appendices:

Stormwater Management Report
Irrigation Pond Study
Integrated Pest Management Plan, including chemical fate modeling and analysis
Soil and Erosion Control Plan
U.S. Army Corps of Engineers' Wetland Delineation
Traffic Impact Study
Archaeological reports

The body of the DEIS also thoroughly discussed these issues and others, including the basis of the course and site layout. Preliminary-level site plan drawings were mainly used, although particulars of the project, such as the parking and clubhouse layout, were much more detailed. This approach can be seen by comparing Figure 16.5 with Figure 16.6, which shows the details for the area around the clubhouse, and Figure 16.7.

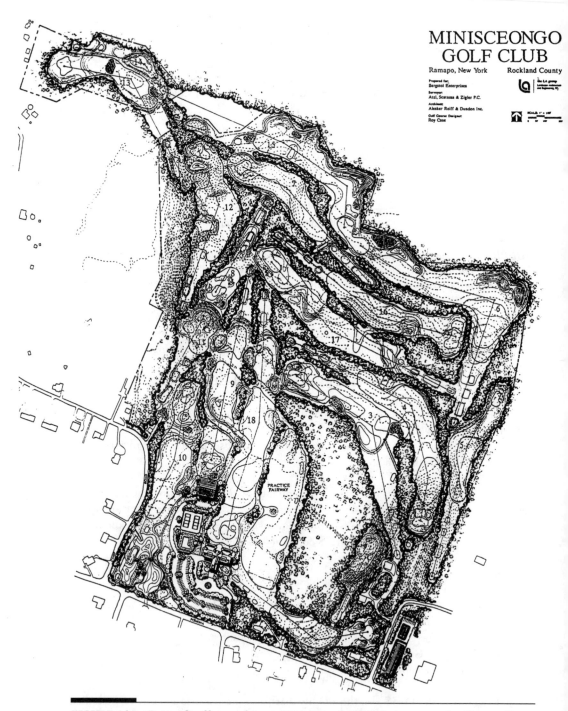

MINISCEONGO
GOLF CLUB
Ramapo, New York   Rockland County

Prepared for:
Bergstol Enterprises
Surveyor:
Atzl, Scatassa & Zigler P.C.
Architect:
Alesker Reiff & Dundon Inc.
Golf Course Designer:
Roy Case

FIGURE 16.5   *Proposed golf course layout, Minisceongo Golf Club. A conceptual golf course layout design was included in the DEIS for the Minisceongo Golf Club. Providing conceptual level drawings in the DEIS allowed for flexibility in the review and permitting process with resource agencies on issues such as wetlands, since significant funds had not been spent developing construction level drawings. (Courtesy the LA Group, P.C.)*

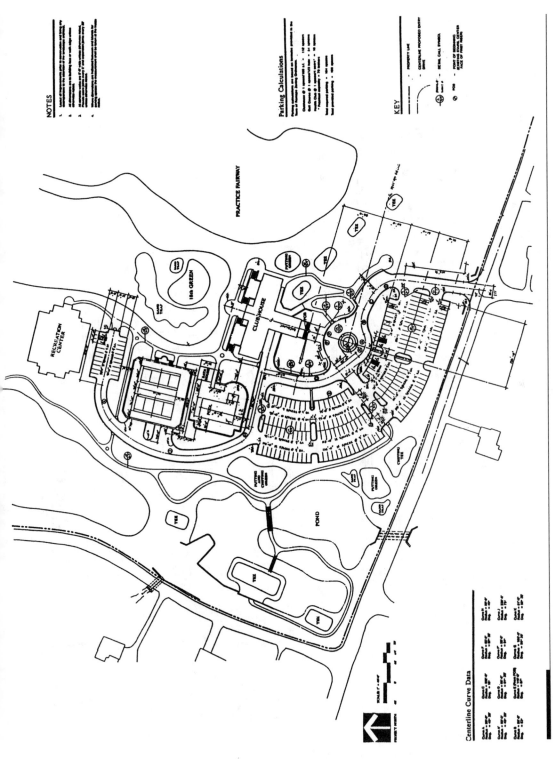

FIGURE 16.6 Area around clubhouse, Miniseeongo Golf Club. In contrast to the conceptual golf course layout design, more detailed design was provided for the area around the clubhouse. This detailed design allowed the local planning and review agencies to closely examine the issues, such as parking and access, associated with site plan review. (Courtesy the LA Group, P.C.)

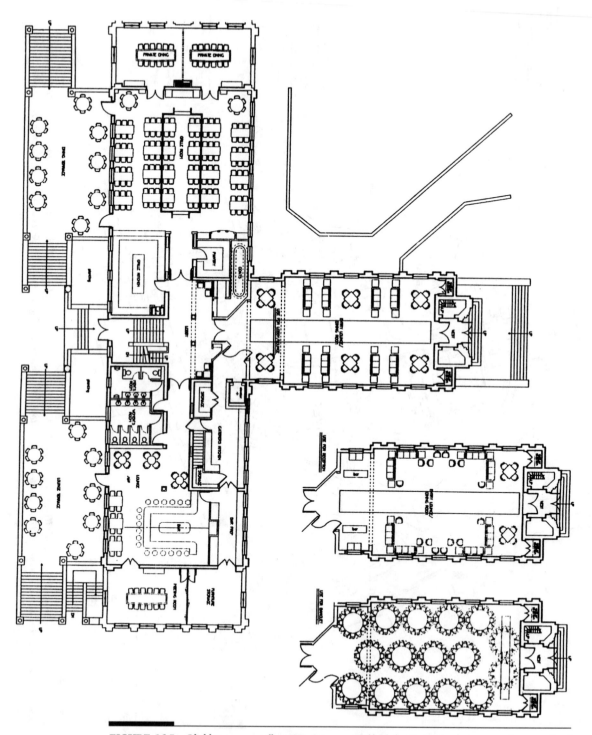

FIGURE 16.7   *Clubhouse upper floor, Minisceongo Golf Club. Again, in contrast to the conceptual golf course layout design, more detailed design was provided for the interior of the clubhouse. This allowed architectural and historic/cultural issues to be discussed, since the clubhouse was eligible for listing on the National Register of Historic Places. (Courtesy Aleisker, Reiff & Dundon Inc.)*

The state and federal wetland permits were processed separately, but concurrently with the town's review of the project. The approvals, all of which were in place by the end of 1992, included the following:

Federal

- U.S. Army Corps of Engineers, Nationwide Permit 26 for wetlands

State

- Department of Environmental Conservation
    - Article 24 State Wetlands Permit
    - Dam Safety Permit
    - SPDES Permit for stormwater discharge points
    - 401 Water Quality Certificate
- New York State Legislature
- Approval of Land Exchange
- State Parks, Recreation and Historic Preservation Consultation

County

- Legislature Approval of Land Exchange
- Parks and Recreation Approval of Land Exchange
- Planning Board, General Municipal Advisory Review of Site Plan
- Drainage Agency, Review of Soil Erosion Control Plan
- Department of Health, Review of Swimming Pool, Restaurants

Town

- State Environmental Quality Review Act (DEIS, FEIS)
- Site Plan Approval
- Demolition and Building Permits

Site work began in the winter of 1992–1993 with a significant amount of demolition. Vegetation clearing began in the spring of 1993, with site construction work completed in the fall of 1993. The developer's construction team was utilized for the majority of the site construction. Shapers familiar with the golf course architect's work were brought in for grading under direction of the architect, who visited the site regularly during construction. Grow-in continued until the course was opened for limited play in July 1994.

The developer retained the environmental consultant as an environmental monitor. The reponsibilities of that role included making bimonthly site inspections, assuring that construction was conducted in compliance with permits, and identifying and resolving problems. The environmental consultant also participated in on-site inspections by the state and federal resource agencies. The environmental attorney had a more limited role in this phase of the project and mainly assisted in the resolution of resource agency concerns.

The environmental consultant continues to participate in the postconstruction monitoring of the site's wetland mitigation planting required as part of the state wetland permit.

Approximately 3½ years passed between project initiation and the commencement of play on the course. This project moved smoothly and relatively quickly through the design, permitting, and construction phases for the following reasons:

- Tasks and responsibilities were clearly delineated by the project team, and there was effective coordination among team members.
- The client understood the need for spending money up front to obtain good information and accomplish his goals.
- The client and members of the project team respected one another's particular focus during the design, permitting, and construction process. The project team made a good faith effort to comply with permit and design drawings.
- The environmental consultant anticipated the information needs of the regulatory agencies and the public and provided materials to defuse concerns and issues.
- The client worked with a trusted construction crew who did not have a different agenda of "build it quick and dirty." As a double check, the construction was monitored.

17

The Business of
Building a Golf Course

Glaring artificiality of any kind detracts from the fascination of the game.

Adapted from *Scotland's Gift GOLF,* 1928, by Charles Blair Macdonald (1856–1939)

Following World War II, the golf architect was often called upon for assistance in promoting, organizing, and locating funds for a new course. Specialists now undertake these early steps. *The Directory of Golf,* published annually by the National Golf Foundation, lists them.

Still, golf architects must be knowledgeable about these subjects, because specialists and owners will seek their advice. In practice, architects provide valuable information by outlining the experiences of others with whom they have worked, unless, of course, this information is confidential. Indeed, the advice of an architect with a long and respected track record is sometimes essential.

The Critical Path

Once the concept for creating a golf facility is reasonably firm, there are many steps involved along the "critical path" in bringing the project to a successful conclusion. Flexibility is paramount, with the owner, architect, and specialists arranging the plan of action according to circumstances.

Step I: The Architect's Preliminary Site Visit

The architect's preliminary visit to a site is mandatory to determine whether the tract is suitable for golf or can be converted without excessive monetary outlay. This visit is followed by an outline report, based in part on the architect's experience with similar projects, in regard to a number of issues.

- Site desirability
- Preliminary and general estimated cost ranges
- Problems the owner may encounter
- Estimate of revenue (truly, this is a guesstimate)
- The value of the golf course as an adjunct to a resort, real estate development, or other business

At this stage, the list of pitfalls encountered by others may also be put forward to emphasize that costly mistakes can be made along the critical path. This initial report is a "first impression" and is subject to later painstaking study and review by the owner and the specialists involved.

Costs incurred by the owner for the architect's preliminary visit and report are probably limited to the latter's fee, unless background plans and other data are acquired at this time.

Step II: Feasibility Study

The feasibility study (described in Chapter 15) may require a second visit to the site by the architect or by another designer to provide a second opinion. The architect may also assist the feasibility specialist in preparing development costs along with the monetary flow during construction.

Costs incurred by the owner for this step may include

1. A second site visit by the architect
2. The study by the feasibility specialist. This study may embrace the following additional costs:
    a. Acquiring a topographic map, wetlands plan, and other background plans
    b. Hydrological services to ascertain whether irrigation water and drinking water are available
    c. Ascertaining the presence or absence of three-phase electricity or another power source and the cost of bringing it to the site, which can be determined merely by contacting the appropriate power company
3. The architect's preparation of preliminary route plans
4. Preliminary studies of available financing

Step III: Early Action

Acknowledging the need for flexibility, this step in the critical path may involve costs for

1. Placing an option or equivalent on the real estate.
2. Completing financial arrangements.
3. Acquiring permits. The preliminary plan may be all that is called for by permit grantors. Yet, at this point, the final route plan can be helpful and may be requested by the regulatory bodies. Sometimes (fortunately, rarely) detailed plans and specifications may be requested by permit grantors.

Step IV: Final Acquisition of Real Estate

In addition to the cost of real estate, expenses include

1. Closing costs
2. Broker's fees
3. Outlays involving environmentalists, engineers, soil scientists, and other members of the team described in Chapters 15 and 16

Step V: Construction of the Golf Course

For construction of a golf course (described in Chapter 8), costs include

1. Nine, 18, or more holes, plus practice areas
2. Golf course architect's fees for working drawings (plans and specifications) and periodic site visits

3. Irrigation planning and installation, including piping, heads, wiring, and controls, along with pumps and pump house, bringing power to the site, and developing the water source
4. Salaries for the future course superintendent if he or she is on-site during construction, and salaries for the construction superintendent or other construction management service
5. Maintenance equipment and course furnishings (benches, ballwashers, hole cups, tee markers, flags, and other items)
6. Maintenance (grow-in) from seeding until opening
7. Construction of an equipment building, separate chemical storage building, equipment washing facilities, and installation of fuel storage
8. Construction of golf car paths
9. Construction of shelters, bridges, and other structures
10. Providing drinking water on the course
11. Purchasing golf cars, if they are not leased
12. A contingency of 15 to 20% for numerous unforeseen outlays

Step VI: Construction of Clubhouse and/or Pro Shop

Costs for construction of a clubhouse and/or a pro shop include

1. Clubhouse architect's fees
2. The buildings—clubhouse, including pro shop, and golf car storage
3. Furnishings
4. Utilities: electricity, drinking water, and telephone
5. Sewerage (which can be a major item)

Step VII: Clubhouse Grounds

Costs for the clubhouse grounds include

1. Landscape architect's fees
2. Landscaping
3. Entrance road, including curb cuts
4. Parking lot
5. Swimming pool
6. Other facilities, such as tennis

Step VIII: Other Outlays

In the construction of any golf course, there may be additional outlays, which can include

1. Fencing
2. Highway signs
3. Initial advertising and public relations
4. Legal fees in addition to permit acquisitions
5. Debt service before opening
6. Real estate taxes before opening
7. Owner's insurance

Step IX: Contingency

Numerous unforeseen expenses will be encountered in building a golf course. A large contingency is therefore recommended, probably 15 to 20% or more of the estimated cost of all the aforementioned items. This contingency does not include inflation, although the prudent developer will allow for that unknown. Inflation in golf course construction is higher than prevailing national inflation, because course construction involves ever higher standards as demanded by golfers. Furthermore, new products are available but at higher prices. Yet lenders may object to too large a contingency and demand refinement of the estimates.

Once the contract for the work has been let, or if the work is to be executed by a method other than contracting, the steps involved are as outlined in Chapter 8.

Appendix A (at the end of this chapter) serves as a method for estimating the cost of a course, as well as the basis for partial payments to contractors and changes in the contract price for items added or deleted. Appendix B by the Golf Course Builders Association of America provides a more abbreviated list.

Golf Course Financing

The golf architect should be familiar with the various aspects of golf course financing. (Chapter 15 describes acquisition of funds).

Notwithstanding difficulties in arranging financing, the last two decades of the twentieth century have seen more adequate funding for golf course construction as contrasted with earlier decades when funds were inadequate and the ultimate in quality could not be achieved initially.

Overseas funding for golf course development is sometimes available, and some golf architects know private investors who are looking for opportunities to invest in a profit-motive golf course in the United States on an equity basis if the owner and project appear to the architect to be sound in all ways. Understandably, an architect cherishes such access to these sources and recommends them only to trusted clients with whom he or she has worked previously.

In the period following the Korean War, private member-owned clubs were sometimes organized, with potential members purchasing memberships that included equity in the club's facilities. Membership sale was the major source of financing. Yet traditional sources also contributed once a large percentage of the memberships had been received.

Some groups contemplate profit-motive private clubs with members holding no equity. These groups endeavor to promote and sell memberships in order to finance their projects. Their efforts seldom produce the needed funds unless the promotor provides a sufficiently large share of the funds him- or herself. Moreover, an immense amount of time and effort is needed to find members. Yet, this can be a successful type of financing.

Pitfalls in Golf Course Development

Golf and golf real estate projects often are not owned by the developer who took the early risks. This fact has an impact on golf course financing, making it more difficult to acquire. There are a number of reasons that golf courses and golf real estate development projects have failed for initial investors but flourished for those who succeeded them:

1. Careful fiscal management was not practiced.
2. Owners become land poor by purchasing too much land and overlooking future real estate taxes.
3. Real estate was purchased outright without options before the extent of environmental (e.g., wetlands), archaelogical, and other limitations were ascertained and permits acquired.
4. Debt service (principal and interest) was overlooked.
5. A too large and elaborate clubhouse was constructed.
6. Opening as a strictly private facility delayed the day when the profit-motive course operated in the black. Several years may be needed to reach full membership, whereas a daily fee or semiprivate layout tends to bring in more revenue in early years.
7. Small outlays were overlooked in construction and maintenance budgeting.
8. Guidelines for setbacks of residences were overlooked.
9. The fact that the golf real estate market is cyclical, with deep valleys and high peaks, was forgotten, with real estate arriving on the market during a valley.
10. The owner was overoptimistic as to development costs and revenue.
11. The owner never acquired adequate financing in the first place and started construction with insufficient commitments from lenders.
12. Lending institutions were forced to withdraw.

How Capital Outlays Can Be Postponed, "Work in Progress"

The celebrated Alister Mackenzie has observed in *"The Spirit of St Andrews"*, "On several occasions we have made the skeleton of a course which has subsequently become of championship rank. . . . Even in the early days the members got a great deal of pleasure out of playing it and watching it improve year by year." Yet Mackenzie emphasized "finality," pointing out that it can be achieved eventually even if funds are not available initially.

Successful courses have indeed been developed by individuals with minimum funds who were able to postpone work.

One of the success stories of golf has been "work-in-progress" family-operated courses that provided occupations for parents and children alike, while the value of the real estate also appreciated. In the present era of high real estate costs, immense sophistication in the playing fields of the game, and contemporary golfers expecting perfection on opening day, this is a more difficult road to follow. But for years following the Korean War, when course construction flourished after a long hiatus, the practice was fairly common. It is still possible, however, particularly on privately owned daily fee layouts and at private clubs that are adding holes.

The owner's ultimate goal must be to build a course that eventually satisfies golfers' yearnings for perfection. To reach this goal, initial compromises will be needed. Yet each item of work has to be performed in accordance with the highest standards.

First the architect prepares a plan, along with specifications and directions explaining the work required to attain a quality layout in years to come, although the course will be open for play in the meantime.

Items that may be left in abeyance include back tees, if separate from the main tees, and if female players concur, mowing merely a portion of fairway or rough to tee height for them. Perhaps all or part of bunker construction can be postponed. One practice has been to form bunker mounds and hollows, including surface drainage, but omit sand and tile until funds are available.

Although extensive drainage is often required, this may be achieved by installing open drains, as a first step, without tile and pipe until funds are available. Open drains cause problems for play and maintenance, but delaying completion can result in large initial savings.

Selective clearing can be limited to those roughs where many balls are likely to land, and car paths can be built with a stone preparation and/or stone dust, leaving paving to the future. In practice, some owners have found that these unpaved paths are preferred to paved paths. And one hopes that the architect has followed existing contours in order to reduce the quantity of earth to be moved. Historically, such simplicity has produced intensely interesting layouts and was inherent in the philosophy of Donald Ross, considered to be the grand master of our art form.

There may be on-site or nearby resources that should not be overlooked. A sandy loam or a sandy topsoil found locally may be ideal for the green and tee root zone mix. Moreover, the USGA Green Section now permits modification in its method for green construction, allowing the coarse sand layer to be omitted and crushed stone to be substituted for expensive pea gravel in the drainage blanket. These modifications can result in immense savings, and the less costly method of green construction that involves topmix on a tiled subbase with no gravel blanket has produced excellent greens along with large savings.

The owner can also install a partial irrigation and pump system. Working with the irrigation designer, the owner then makes plans to augment it over the years until he or she eventually achieves a state-of-the-art system.

If work is postponed at any point, it is important that players be aware that the current course is a work in progress, already planned and in a stage of implementation. By all means, let players see the final plans. Feeling that they are in on the ground floor of what will someday be a fabulous layout is certainly an incentive for players to regard the "inadequacies" of the unfinished course in a positive light. Several renowned layouts did not start out as they are today. Yet if players are not made aware of the situation, the reputations of the owner, the course, and the architect may be compromised.

Historically, one significant postponement of expenditures entails leaving construction of the clubhouse for the future, with a temporary building or trailer provided in early years, or a clubhouse constructed with basic facilities only and added to in the future.

Timing and Scheduling the Critical Path

The feasibility study can be completed within a few weeks. Arranging financing and acquiring permits may take months or years. Once these have become realities and all other arrangements are in place, we have found the most satisfactory procedure is to bid the work and let the contract, allowing the successful bidder to start at once regardless of the season, unless ordinances preclude breaking ground in certain months.

In the Boston, Massachusetts, area, for example, it is ideal to clear trees over winter. This allows wind and sun to reach cleared areas and soil to dry so that grubbing, boulder removal, and earthwork can be under way by late April or earlier and so that seeding can be substantially completed by mid or late September. With an effective grow-in, it may then be possible to open the course in the period from Memorial Day to July 4, eight or nine months after completion of seeding. Seeding in less ideal periods requires a longer grow-in period—sometimes months longer.

In more southern areas, the time frame is wider, and in more northern areas narrower. Yet, when everything is in place and the soil workable, the best policy—north or south—is to start regardless of season. We have seen owners postponing work until "ideal" months, only to encounter adverse weather despite their expectations.

Contracts

Agreement Between Owner and Golf Course Architect   Because course design is comprehensive and is affected by the work of those in other professions, a written agreement is needed.

Some course architects use standard forms—for example, the American Institute of Architects (AIA) or the American Society of Golf Course Architects (ASGCA) document. Many have developed their own forms with legal advice. Still others record an agreement with a client in a final letter arising from an exchange of letters and verbal discussion.

Because course design is an expanding profession, the architect who is working with a team may believe that, in addition to the contract document, a letter is necessary to clarify several items the owner may wrongly assume to be part of the golf architect's services. Among these is the degree of the architect's responsibility for

> Structures such as bridges and shelters
> Siting and construction of golf car paths
> Procurement of permits
> Storm drainage (including water entering and leaving the site), dams, and all impoundments
> Pollution of waterways
> Staking
> Contractors' insurance (Many golf course architects believe that the owner is more qualified than they to determine what is required, although the architect may advise the types and amounts of insurance others have used.)

Contract Between Owner and Contractor   Contract systems between an owner and a contractor include the following:

1. *A lump-sum contract.* This type of contract covers the entire work, with the contractor's price including his or her profit. Because they are rigid, lump-sum contracts may limit the artistry of the designer. Moreover, the designer may not be able to convey in drawings the shapes of features as he or she envisages them, or may need to change them as the work evolves. This limitation may be overcome in part, and fairly so for both parties, by requiring a number of hours of equipment use at set rates added to the final contract sum. The contractor is entitled to know the range of these changes, just as the owner and architect need to know total costs.

2. *Subcontracting ("subbing").* Subbing is a method whereby items of the total work are contracted separately by the owner. For example, separate contracts may be let for clearing, earth moving, preparing seed beds, and seeding. Irrigation and drainage installation may also be separate items. Final shaping of features may also be separate. When subbing, the owner is acting as his or her own general contractor. This sometimes results

in a lower total cost for the entire job, because it permits contractors other than golf course specialists to provide proposals for some phases. In practice, subbing generally extends the time needed to complete the entire job, because each successive contractor needs to know whether the preceding contractor completed his or her work in a satisfactory manner. When the contractor can only guess at what the predecessor will do, he or she may submit a higher proposal or bid.

3.   *A cost-plus contract.* Under this type of contract, the contractor provides the work at cost plus a fee based on a percentage of the total actual cost, or the fee is predetermined as a lump sum of estimated cost. For example, on a $2 million project: final cost plus 10%, or estimated cost plus a predetermined firm $200,000 regardless of final cost.

4.   *A unit-price contract.* The contractor completes the work, charging unit prices for work at figures agreed upon. These unit prices could be charged according to length, area, cubic yardage, or another measurement. Because there are many unknowns in building a golf course, this method has proved to be fair for both owner and contractor on occasions, but not invariably so.

5.   *A cost-minus contract.* This method, used before World War II when British golf course architects and contractors roamed the globe, is probably no longer practiced. It involved the architect (sometimes a design-and-build firm) providing an outside estimate for building the course. If the work was executed for less than this estimate, the owner and contractor divided the difference. But if the architect's outside estimate was exceeded, the contractor was responsible for the difference.

6.   *Force account.* In this system, combinations of the aforementioned methods are used, and owners on occasion build courses themselves, acting as their own contractors, hiring equipment and labor on an hourly basis, and purchasing materials themselves. This method is perilous; strict budgeting is needed.

The Contract Documents

Owner and Contractor   There are differences between public and private contracts, including but not limited to affirmative action and other rules and regulations required in public contracts. Furthermore, legally, but with exceptions, no changes are permitted in public contracts without bidding, even if they lead to improvements.

A set of contract documents includes

1.   Notice to Contractors, Invitation to Bidders, or Requests for Proposals.
2.   The agreement or contract form.
3.   *The general conditions:* Most municipal jurisdictions have standard forms, as do many large corporations, which contain the general conditions of a contract. The AIA and other professional societies also have their own. These general conditions include a host of items not catalogued in this book, such as contract administration, changes in the work, payments, termination of the contract, and many others.
4.   *Special conditions:* These include bonds and insurance. Bond requirements often comprise a bid bond and a performance, labor, and materials bond. Although the architect may include insurance and bond requirements in the bid package, the owner is responsible for specifying actual requirements. An acceptance or guarantee bond warranting the work, or parts of it, for a year of more is also a requirement.
5.   Addenda covering amendments, additions, and deletions since the documents were first prepared.

6. The contractor's unit prices for his or her work (see Appendices A and B at the end of this chapter). These prices become the basis for monthly payments and for change orders.
7. *Drawings:* Most often these appear on separate sheets. Yet some architects consolidate them into one or two sheets. They include
    a. The route plan (see Chapter 3)
    b. The clearing plan
    c. The grading plan
    d. The drainage plan
    e. The irrigation plan, usually including an electrical plan
    f. The seeding plan, showing areas to be seeded to different species
    g. Individual green and tee plans
    h. Individual drawings showing a typical green, tee, and bunker, and grades and construction of pond banks
    i. Soil profiles showing construction of all grass areas, including drainage, subsoil, and root zone mix
    j. A plan showing all environmental requirements

Written Specifications   In addition to drawings, a detailed narrative, known as the specifications, is needed to cover

1. A list of work items included in the contract
2. Finish date and requirements for acceptance
3. Materials including but not limited to seed, fertilizer, soil amendments, drainage and irrigation pipe, sand for bunkers and root zone mix, topsoil, subsoil, and paths
4. Staking
5. Clearing specifications
    a. Clearcutting
    b. Selective clearing of treed roughs
    c. Additional work by an aborist on trees that are to remain
6. Specifications for general grading of fairways, greens, tees, roughs, and other features
7. Specifications for shaping
8. Ledge removal; this is often included as an extra at a predetermined unit price
9. Pond specifications
10. Irrigation specifications
11. Drainage specifications
12. Smoothing, preparation of seed beds and seeding
13. Contractor's maintenance requirements for grow-in
14. Cleanup, along with removal of sediment and erosion structures, unless these are to remain
15. Finish dates for substantial completion of planting, completion of contract, and date contractors' equipment is to be off the site
16. Acceptance

Acceptance, item 16 in the preceding list, can be controversial. Some architects accept the work upon completion of seeding. Yet until there is a catch of grass, the area is subject to heavy erosion and also delayed settling of filled areas. Architects may therefore require a satisfactory stand of grass following a minimum of 30 days' maintenance provided by the contractor or owner.

Some contracts specify maintenance by the contractor until the course is playable. Unless the contractor's staff includes a qualified golf course superintendent, this can prove unsatisfactory and unduly expensive.

The definition of a satisfactory stand of grass (not a playable one) can be ambiguous. Here is one sometimes used:

Acceptance on behalf of the owner will be made by the architect at the end of the 30-day period.

It will be made on the basis of a uniform stand of specified grass. A uniform stand of grass does not, however, imply that the contractor is responsible for maintaining the grass until it is playable.

Acceptance is based on the following, provided all work has been executed in accordance with the contract documents.

1. No barren areas larger than 1 square foot on greens, aprons, or tees
2. No barren areas larger than 12 square feet on fairway and grassed rough areas
3. One hundred percent of all stones larger than softball size and 90% of all stones larger than golfball size, together with all debris, shall have been removed from all playing areas.

Acceptance requirements may also include specifications for hand-picking, or the equivalent, of stones and debris on all areas in the period after seeding and prior to final acceptance.

Quantity Cost Estimates Including Labor, Equipment and Material

Item #	Item	Unit	Unit Price	Quantity	Extended Price
1	*Mobilization*				
	a. Equipment On-site	LS			
	b. Insurance	LS			
	c. Bonding Not Including Guarantee Bond	LS			
	d. Field Office, Sanitary Facilities, and Employee Parking	LS			
2	*Erosion and Sediment Control*				
	a. Silt Fence	LF			
	b. Straw Bales	Bale			
	c. Detention Pond#1	LS			
	#2, etc.	LS			
	d. Retention Pond #1	LS			
	#2, etc.	LS			
	e. Other Structures #1	LS			
	#2, etc.	LS			
3	*Staking*	*LS*			
4	*Clearing*				
	a. Clearcut	Acre			
	b. Selective				
	(1) Treed Areas (Forest)	Acre			
	(2) Individual Trees (Park)	Tree			
5	*Arboricultural Work*	*Tree*			
6	*Tree Planting*				
	Species 1	Tree			
	Species 2, etc.	Tree			
7	*Grubbing and Disposal*				

Item #	Item	Unit	Unit Price	Quantity	Extended Price
	a. Clearcuts	Acre			
	b. Selectively Cleared	Acre			
8	*Stripping and Stockpiling Topsoil*	*Acre*			
9	*Major Grading of Greens, Tees, Fairways, Rough, Bunkers, Mounds, Ponds*	*Cubic Yd.*			
10	*Shaping Subbase of Greens, Including Greenside Bunkers and Other Surrounds*	*Green*			
11	*Shaping Subbase of Tees*	*Tee*			
12	*Shaping Fairway and Rough Mounds*	*Mound*			
13	*Shaping Fairway and Rough Bunkers, Including Surrounds and Drainage*	*Bunker*			
14	*Shaping Ponds*				
	Pond #1	LS			
	Pond #2, etc.	LS			
15	*Lining Ponds*	*SF*			
16	*Storm Drainage*				
	a. 1-Foot Pipe	LF			
	b. 2-Foot Pipe, etc.	LF			
	c. Catch Basin Type 1	LS			
	d. Catch Basin Type 2, etc.	LS			
17	*Interior Subdrainage*				
	Catch Basins Type 1	LS			
	Type 2, etc.				
	Sumps	LS			
	Manholes Type 1	LS			
	Type 2, etc.	LS			
	Tile 4-inch	LF			
	6-inch, etc.	LF			
18	*Stream Diversions*				
	Earth Moving	LF			
	Bank Protection				

Item #	Item	Unit	Unit Price	Quantity	Extended Price
	a. Seeding	SF			
	b. Sodding	SF			
	c. Wooden Bulkheads	LF			
	d. Stone Bulkheads	LF			
	e. Riprap	LF			
	f. Bioengineering	LF			
19	*Irrigation*				
	Pump House	LS			
	Pumps	LS			
	Pipe				
	1-inch	LF			
	2-inch, etc.	LF			
	Heads Type 1 and Wiring	LS			
	Type 2, etc., and Wiring	LS			
	Drains	Drain			
20	*Constructing Putting Surfaces, Including Collars, Practice Putting Green, but Not Target Greens*				
	Gravel Layer in Place	SF			
	Coarse Sand Layer in Place	SF			
	Topmix in Place	SF			
	Prep of Seedbed and Planting	SF			
21	*Surrounds*				
	Topsoiling	LS			
	Preparation and Planting				
	Seeding	SF			
	Sprigging	SF			
	Sodding	SF			
22	*Pitching and Chipping Green*	*LS*			
23	*Tee Construction, Not Including Practice Tee*				
	Gravel Layer	CY			
	Topmix	CY			
	Prep of Seedbed and Planting				
	Seed				
	Sprigs				
	Sod				

Item #	Item	Unit	Unit Price	Quantity	Extended Price
24	*Tee Banks*				
	Topsoiling	Tee			
	Prep and Planting				
	Seeding	SF			
	Sprigging	SF			
	Sodding	SF			
25	*Fairways, Not Including Practice*				
	Topsoiling	CY			
	Prep and Planting				
	Seeding	Acre			
	Sprigging	Acre			
	Sodding	SF			
26	*Grassed Roughs*				
	Topsoiling	CY			
	Prep and Planting				
	Seeding	Acre			
	Sprigging	Acre			
	Sodding	SF			
27	*Treed Roughs*				
	Topsoiling	CY			
	Prep and Planting	Acre			
28	*a. Additional Sod Laid*	*SF*			
	b. Additional Topsoil Provided	*CY*			
29	*Bunker Completion*				
	a. Lining	SF			
	b. Sand in Place	CY			
	c. Preparing and Planting Surrounds	SF			
30	*Grow-in All Areas*	*LS*			
31	*a. Golf Car Paths*	*LF*			
	b. Golf Car Paths with Curbs	*LF*			
32	*Drinking Water to Tees*	*LS*			
33	*Culverts*				

Item #	Item	Unit	Unit Price	Quantity	Extended Price
	a. Culvert Size 1	LF			
	b. Culvert Size 2, etc.	LF			
34	*Bridges*				
	a. Type 1	Bridge			
	b. Type 2, etc.	Bridge			
35	*The Practice Fairway*				
	a. Clearing and Grubbing	Acre			
	b. Grading	CY			
	c. Practice Tee Complete	LS			
	d. Practice Bunker at Tee	LS			
	e. Strip of All-Weather Surface	SF			
	f. Target Green Complete with Bunkers	Green			
	g. The Fairway Complete	LS			
	h. Irrigation	LS			
	i. Grow-in	LS			
36	*Additional Items Sometimes Required*				
	1. Ledge Rock				
	a. Ledge Rock Dynamited	CY			
	b. Ledge Rock Ripped	CY			
	c. Boulders Larger Than ?	CY			
	d. Trench Rock Dynamited	CY			
	e. Trench Rock Ripped	LF			
	f. Boulders Larger Than ?	CY			
	2. Guarantee Bond	LS			
37	*Items Added or Subtracted Since Contract Documents Were Completed*				
	a.				
	b.				
38	*Total of Extended Prices = Lump-Sum Price for Completion of the Golf Course in Accordance with the Plans and Specifications*				

CY = Cubic Yard
LS = Lump Sum
LF = Linear Feet
SF = Square Feet

Quantity Cost Estimates Including Labor, Equipment and Material

The Golf Course Builders Association of America lists the following items as an abbreviated basis for estimating construction costs.

Item #	Item	Unit	Unit Price	Quantity	Extended Price
	Mobilization	LS			
	Layout/Stake	LS			
	Erosion Control	LS			
	Clearing	Acre			
	Selective Clearing	Acre			
	On-site Topsoil	CY			
	Off-site Topsoil	CY			
	Excavation — Conventional	CY			
	Excavation — Topload	CY			
	Excavation — Rock	CY			
	Rough Shaping	LS			
	Storm Drainage	LS			
	Golf Drainage	LS			
	Irrigation/Pump Station	LS			
	Greens	SF			
	Tees	SF			
	Bunkers	SF			
	Bridges	LF			
	Bulkheading	LF			
	Car Paths	LF			
	Fine Grading	LS			
	Seedbed Prep	ACRE			
	Grassing Seed/Sprigs	ACRE			
	Grassing Sod	SF			
	Bonding	LS			

Chapter

18

Training of the Golf Course Architect

A course should never pretend to be, nor is it intended to be, an infallible tribunal of skill alone. The element of chance is the very essence of the game, part of the fun of the game.

From *Concerning Golf*, 1903, by John Laing Low (1869–1929)

Course design is part art form, part skilled craft, and part engineering, according to golf architect Michael J. Hurdzan. Robert Trent Jones has often stated that golf architects provide the cornerstone of the game.

The primary role of the golf architect is to create exciting, memorable, and functional layouts. Yet that role also includes preliminary investigations, reports and estimates, assistance in obtaining necessary permits, provision of plans and specifications, critical assistance in selecting the contractor, periodic visits to the site to observe progress and to see whether the work is proceeding in accordance with plans and specifications, along with consultation on grow-in and achieving a playable greensward.

Indeed, the golf architect may be retained well into the future of a course to advise on changes and problems. More often than not the architect is the "captain of the ship," whether the project is a brand new course or a major alteration. The architect is the creator.

Like building architects and engineers, the golf course architect is called upon, before, during, and after construction, to make decisions often involving interpretation of his or her drawings and specifications. Although employed by the owner, the architect makes these judgments in the spirit of absolute fairness.

A course architect may also be asked to advise on, and perhaps appear in court as an expert witness on, environmental issues, land taking, safety issues, and identification of the original designer in cases involving historical significance and preservation. Sometimes, too, he or she is asked to provide a second opinion on issues such as site selection and the type of course that is needed.

In an era of expanding golf course development, the knowledge and skill of course architects have become ever more evident in the scores of new courses they have designed and the numerous established layouts they have remodeled. Following the end of the Korean War, a profession that had almost become a lost art during the Depression and World War II was given a new and vigorous lease on life.

Academic Training

In recent years, golf has become a way of life for many. Because of their golfing skills and deep attachment to the game, many young people are contemplating or being attracted to course design as a career. It has been a worthwhile and rewarding one for some.

Love of the game and the ability to play it are essential. Still, they are not enough. Academic and practical training are also needed, as is the study of available literature.

We believe the preferred route for the aspiring golf architect is to first obtain a degree in Landscape Architecture and Environmental Design, with additional emphasis on agronomic and civil engineering subjects.

Yet the profession of golf course architecture requires a broad background. Robert Trent Jones, the dean of the profession, while pursuing a course of studies at Cornell University in the early Depression years, audited courses in the classics. A generation later, one of his sons, Robert Jr., studied law, and another son, Rees, majored in history. Both went on to landscape architecture before becoming golf architects of signature rank.

Using a more traveled path, Howard Maurer, a practicing golf architect, obtained an associate degree in ornamental horticulture and attended the Winter School for turfgrass managers at the University of Massachusetts before obtaining a bachelor's degree in landscape architecture at Syracuse University.

History shows that to excel, a golf course architect must be a well rounded and knowledgeable person. Perhaps this is because development of the playing fields for this ancient game requires the combined efforts of many people and professions, while golf courses and the game appear to be exerting an impact on our way of life during a period of profound change in society.

Basic disciplines such as literature, history, foreign languages, and mathematics are part of a golf architect's education, as are the less basic but still important subjects of law and computer literacy.

In an effort to ascertain what studies, in addition to their majors and the basics, have been useful in their careers, we queried practicing golf architects. Listed alphabetically, their answers were: architecture; art—its history, appreciation, and its creative techniques in various media, including sketching and watercolors; agronomy—soil and plant studies, including turfgrass science; agricultural engineering—particularly drainage and irrigation; horticulture—plant materials; photogrammetry—involving new techniques arising from space exploration; public speaking and oral communication; and visual arts—such as photography, use of projectors, and other aids.

In 1991, a breakdown in percentages of degrees held by all members of the American Society of Golf Course Architects was developed. The trend to landscape architecture as the preferred background continues (Figure 18.1).

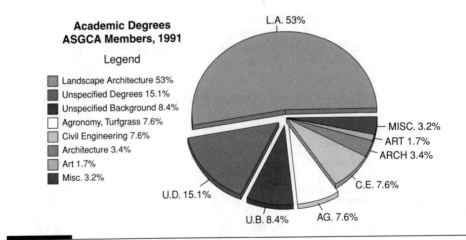

FIGURE 18.1   *Although the percentage has varied over the past several decades, landscape architecture continues to offer the best curriculum for the aspirant in golf course architecture. It is, indeed, golf course architecture without the golf.*

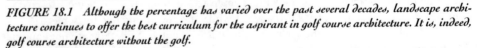

Practical Training

Apprenticing. Most in the profession have held entry-level positions with a golf course architect before entering private practice. Through the association of generations, the lore of the profession grows and the knowledge of its members widens. To this end, entry-level positions and summer employment in design offices are highly desirable, but they can be difficult or impossible to find because the number of design offices is limited. Probably next best is to work, for a summer or more, for a course builder or contractor. By doing so, aspiring course architects, with the cooperation of the contractor, can study plans and their execution on the ground even though they may be employed as equipment operators or laborers.

Golf course maintenance. A golf architect's work can be functional only if future maintenance aspects have been considered and embodied in his or her plans and specifications. Working a season or more on an established course under direction of the maintenance superintendent, in addition to apprenticing under someone in the field of course design or construction, an aspiring designer can evaluate the superintendent's problems and become familiar with maintenance practices, techniques, and machinery and learn how a golf course operates.

Travel. Training sooner or later includes travel to study famous layouts and the work of designers, past and present, on this continent and abroad. Above all, it is necessary to visit the ancient links of Scotland.

Although maintenance standards of British layouts vary from those in North America, in that the greenswards of American courses are more lush and refined, it has been said that the nearest thing to an enduring text on golf course design is the Scottish linksland. Certainly no architect, experienced or beginner, can overlook the centuries of golf played in Scotland. There it evolved into the game we know today, and from there the earliest course designers have hailed. Canadian golf architect Stanley Thompson, who started many in the field, was heard to say, "Practicing golf course architecture without studying the links of Scotland is like a divinity student not reading the Bible." We also recommend that the aspiring architect be familiar with the design codes as prepared long ago by J. L. Low, C. B. Macdonald, and Alister Mackenzie. They are included at the back of this book.

The end result of bringing a golf course into play is a work of art—the creation of an artist who, when he or she deems it best to do so, overlooks guidelines. David Earl in *Golf Journal* (October 1994) quotes golf architect Rees Jones' answer to the question, "What does it take to be a golf architect?"

> Golf course designing is a craft—you learn by doing and by seeing other golf courses. . . . Working on U.S. Open venues has helped me a lot, because I had to study the original designs and why they were revered. You need to have some references.

Experience also shows that the time needed to prepare oneself for a career in course design equals that for a doctor of medicine.

Should civil engineering rather than landscape architecture be the preferred academic background for a career in course architecture? Golf course architect Mark Mungeam, who prepared himself from an early age to enter the profession, selected the engineering discipline and explores that route.

Civil Engineering as the Academic Background for Golf Course Design

by Mark A. Mungeam
GOLF COURSE ARCHITECT
CORNISH, SILVA AND MUNGEAM, INC.

"Architecture is the application of art to engineering construction," according to Daniel W. Mead and J. R. Ackerman in their book, *Contract Specifications and Engineering Relations*.

Although not always recognized, there has been a strong link between course design and civil engineering since landmark American courses first appeared at about the turn of the century. Within a few years, architects were retaining civil engineers as construction superintendents to convert their concepts to reality.

In practice, some of these early engineers traveled from site to site to execute the designer's plans, and in doing so soon became the field architects. The best known was Seth Raynor, a Princeton University graduate hired by Charles Blair Macdonald in 1908 to survey the property that became the National Golf Links of America, a landmark course that revolutionized golf architecture. Raynor stayed on with Macdonald to assist in supervising its construction, along with a dozen other Macdonald layouts, before going on his own to become a widely respected golf architect.

Another of the engineer/architects, J. B. McGovern, was A. W. Tillinghast's supervisor in construction of Winged Foot. He later entered into a long association, in a similar role, with Donald Ross, whom he subsequently assisted in establishing the American Society of Golf Course Architects (ASGCA). Still another was Roger Rulewich, a past-president of the Society, who was principal designer for more than 30 years for Robert Trent Jones, the architect who is said to have influenced course design more than anyone in history.

No doubt technical-minded persons are the perfect fit with visionaries who conceive the playing fields of the game. Yet some civil engineers are or become visionaries themselves. Examples among current members of the ASGCA are Brian T. Ault, Michael Dasher, Jeff D. Hardin, Gary and Ronald L. Kern, Tom Pearson, Gerald W. Pirkl, and Algie M. Pulley, Jr.

It is said that the preferred academic background for course design is landscape architecture. Yet as the number of issues that concern the golf architect increase in this era of regulation and rapid expansion of golf, the value of an academic background in civil engineering has been enhanced.

The aforementioned D. W. Mead and J. R. Ackerman also state in their book:

> The essential aim of engineering education is not so much to impart technical knowledge to the students as to furnish the training which will enable them to understand and investigate the conditions which surround a problem, to determine the fundamental principles on which its successful solution depends, to ascertain and analyze the elements which influence and modify it, to design the structures or superintend the proper construction of such structures or works and carry them to successful and economical completion.

Training in civil engineering applicable to golf architecture includes but is by no means limited to the following:

- Facility with contemporary information technology
- Environmental planning

- Hydraulics, including irrigation
- Planning and resource management, including mapping of soils, vegetation, slopes, wildlife habitat, floodplains, property lines, and all other site constructions
- Surveying
- Soil mechanics
- Structural design
- Contract law
- Development of plans, specifications, and contract documents
- Construction project management

A civil engineer in practice becomes a team member, and a critical one in planning, permitting, and constructing a golf course, even if not the architect. In that capacity the civil engineer is still called upon to comment on the feasibility of the architect's concepts and may be involved as early as site selection. Several other specific roles for the engineer are to

1. Review the architect's grading plans in regard to runoff, balance of cut and fill, along with sediment and erosion control
2. Plan pond construction, stream diversions, and storm drainage
3. Consult regarding the irrigation system
4. Stake the architect's course on the ground and check finished grades before and after their execution
5. Play a major part in obtaining permits
6. Assist in construction supervision, particularly any work the engineer him- or herself has planned (now seldom the day-to-day supervision some engineers once provided)

Obviously, golf course architecture and civil engineering are interrelated. No doubt a degree in the latter discipline provides a superb academic background. Yet as a golf architect who holds such a degree and finds the discipline immensely valuable, I still hesitate to make a firm recommendation for engineering over landscape architecture as the preferred background for course design. Still, civil engineering contributes substantially and is worthy of consideration by those contemplating such a career.

The Literature of Golf Course Design

Five instructive books authored by golf architects and published in Great Britain or the United States in the 1920s are available in handsome facsimiles. They include works by H. S. Colt and C. H. Alison, Alister Mackenzie, Robert Hunter, George C. Thomas, and Tom Simpson, who collaborated with golfer and writer H. N. Wethered. All are included in the bibliography of this book. All are required reading for a student of course design.

In 1981, following a hiatus of more than a half century, *The Golf Course* by Geoffrey S. Cornish and Ronald E. Whitten appeared. It was the first definitive text on the history of golf architecture and architects and was followed by several significant books on course design by other architects and writers, including Fred. W. Hawtree, Robert Trent Jones with Larry Dennis, John Strawn, Tom Doak, Robert Trent Jones, Jr., Desmond Muirhead and master planner G. L. Rando, who updated previous separate works by Rees L. Jones and Patrick Phillips. These were followed by Pete Dye's autobiography, prepared with Mark Shaw, and a handsome definitive book by Michael Hurdzan. In the meantime, two manuscripts prepared by architects long gone, namely Alister Mackenzie and Donald Ross, came to light and were published, as were many articles and photographs by golf architect A. W. Tillinghast in still another book.

Informative passages or chapters on course design are also included in books devoted primarily to other aspects of the game. For example, insights into design are included in turn-of-the-century writings by Willie Park, Jr., Horace G. Hutchinson, and others. These were followed in 1903 by John L. Low's *Concerning Golf* and in 1928 by Charles Blair Macdonald's *Scotland's Gift: Golf.* These are also listed in the bibliography of this book along with others that have a profound bearing on course design.

In recent years, golf periodicals have given increasing space to the subject of course design. For example, *Executive Golfer* features a series on design and redesign by architect Desmond Muirhead, and *Golf Magazine* ran a series of articles by golf architect Tom Doak, who has been involved in that magazine's ratings of golf courses.

Bradley S. Klein, professor of government and a former PGA tour caddy before and after receiving his doctorate, has been a prolific writer on design for a number of publications, including *Golfweek* and *Links Magazine.* Klein is also a contributing editor to America Online's *Golf* on the Internet and author of a significant book of essays on course design and controversies relating to it.

Yet it is Ronald E. Whitten, architectural writer for *Golf Digest,* who has continued the traditions established by Herbert Warren Wind in the *New Yorker* and equally famous British authors such as Bernard Darwin and Donald Steel.

By the late 1980s, Whitten was recognized as the voice of golf course architects and architecture. Tom Doak called him "the most qualified non-architect in the world." While continuing to write features for *Golf Digest* and *Golf World,* Whitten has coordinated the selection of golf courses included in listings such as *America's 100 Greatest . . .* and the best courses opened in the current year. Although the influence of these ratings on design itself has not been fully evaluated, their impact on architects is apparent.

Whitten also introduced "The Armchair Architect," a competition sponsored by *Golf Digest* open to non-architects for the design of a hole. Attracting thousands of entries, it is reminiscent of competitions run in British publications before World War I. Winning one of those contributed to the early fame of Alister Mackenzie. Whitten is also responsible for editing the Donald Ross manuscript "Golf Has Never Failed Me."

Literature of Related Disciplines

The complete library of required reading for a golf course architect includes books on related subjects. Among the most important is turfgrass science. The bibliography of this book cites ten texts on turfgrass.

Because it is the basis for the fundamental considerations of design, publications concerning the environment are of paramount importance. Such publications are also contained in the bibliography.

Other Resources

Architects Associations

- The American Society of Golf Course Architects (ASGCA), 221 North LaSalle Street, Chicago, IL 6060

Incorporated in 1947, this is the first and only organization in North America of those who create the playing fields of the game. Under direction of its presidents, their boards, and Paul Fullmer, the first and only executive secretary to date, this group has become increasingly influential in the world of golf. Many of its contributions have arisen from the efforts of dynamic committees coordinated by Fullmer. Committee work has been productive, possibly because members are skilled and experienced in meeting with committees.

The writers, one of whom is among the oldest members, have observed the yearning of the new generation of members to excel individually while contributing to the profession, its art form, and the environment. Entry standards are precise and exacting.

The questions "What is a golf course architect?" and "What is the ASGCA?" are answered by the Society's own definition:

> The American Society of Golf Course Architects is comprised of leading golf course designers in the United States and Canada. These golf course architects, who are involved in the design of new courses and renovation of older courses, bring many years of experience to every project.
>
> Members of the American Society of Golf Course Architects by virtue of their knowledge of the game, training, experience, vision and inherent ability are in all ways qualified to design and prepare specifications for a course of functional and aesthetic perfection.
>
> ASGCA members are further qualified to execute and oversee the implementation of plans and specifications to create an enjoyable layout that challenges golfers of all abilities and exemplifies the highest standards and traditions of golf. ASGCA members will counsel in all phases of the work to protect the best interests of the client.
>
> Each member of the American Society of Golf Course Architects is engaged primarily in the practice of golf course architecture and his/her qualifications have satisfied the ASGCA Board of Governors in all respects.

- The British Institute of Golf Course Architects (BIGCA), Merrist Wood House, Worplesdon, Guildford, Surrey, England GU3 3PE

This group, based in Great Britain, has similar aims and objectives to those of the American organization. A major objective has been furthering education in course design and the role of the profession in society. Until recent years this group was known as the British Association of Golf Course Architects, an organization formed after the American Society but probably related to the International Society of Golf Course Architects, an unincorporated group based in London before World War II, which no longer exists.

Australia, France, Japan, and several other countries now have organizations, and the European Society of Golf Course Architects has become active on that continent. British, French, and European societies have formed a Council of European Architects to collaborate on aspects such as education, ecology, the environment, and safety.

Seminars and Other Formal Studies

- The Harvard Graduate School of Design, Office of External Relations Professional Development, 48 Quincy Street, Cambridge, MA 02138

This school conducts annual seminars on golf course design and development. These are arranged so one can attend a single two-day seminar on design or one- and two-day sessions on environmental issues, golf course development, and planning of adjoining real estate. The entire program extends over a week.

- The Golf Course Superintendents Association of America (GCSAA), 1421 Research Park Drive, Lawrence, KS 66049

This organization periodically and regionally conducts similar seminars on course design, construction, and environmental issues related to course development. The GCSAA was, in fact, the pioneer in education in these subjects and is largely responsible for its impact on its own profession and those of others.

- The Professional Golfers Association of America, 100 Avenue of the Champions, P.O. Box 109601, Palm Beach Gardens, FL 33410

This group also conducts well-attended seminars covering a variety of subjects, with sessions on design presented by leading course architects.

In addition to the aforementioned nonprofit seminars, several for-profit courses are available.

Many, perhaps the majority, of schools or departments of landscape architecture conduct lectures and drawing board exercises on the subject of course design. One university provides a more comprehensive course, the University of Guelph, Guelph, Ontario, Canada N1G 2W1. Its Independent Study curriculum offers a correspondence course, "Golf Course Design and Construction." An authoritative and informative illustrated loose-leaf textbook by golf architect Robert Kains is provided to students.

Responsibilities of the Architect

Who Was the Golf Course Designer?

The golf industry is forever faced with the problem of deciding who, indeed, did design a particular golf course. The decision is further complicated when the golf course architect, planner, engineer, contractor, shaper, golf course construction superintendent, owner or developer, or all of these declare that they "built the golf course." All may well have participated to a considerable degree.

As for the actual design, there are a number of tasks that must be accomplished in order to complete a golf course, ready for play. We can weigh these responsibilities in terms of their effect on the character, integrity, and playability of the final product.

Responsibilities of the Golf Course Designer

1. *Preliminary Planning, Including*
   a. Thorough study of all data relating to the project and the program for golf course development
   b. The final routing of each golf hole and overall circulation pattern
   c. Determination of the general character of each golf hole
   d. Location of clubhouse/golf shop/starter's position and other ancillary buildings and features
   e. Location of maintenance center

    f. Initial construction cost estimate

    g. Consultation and design as required for permit approval process

2. *Design Development, Including*

    a. Expanding the aforementioned "general character" of each hole with more detail, usually in sketch format with or without a written description

    b. Preparation of a more precise version of the construction cost estimate

    c. Development of schedule and budget for construction

3. *Preparation of Construction Documents*

    Specific determination of the detailed characteristics of each feature of each golf hole by on-site decision or by producing

    a. Layout plans, usually covering staking, clearing, rough grading, drainage, irrigation, turf, and trees.

    b. Detail drawings covering construction of golf course features, drainage, irrigation, tree planting, car paths, water features, and other hardscapes

    c. Written specifications for construction work, usually including general conditions, special conditions, the basic specifications (may also include documents to be used during the bid/negotiation process and for supplier and contractor contracts)

4. *Contractor/Supplier Selection, Including*

    a. Preparation of a bidder list and bidder qualifications

    b. Prebid conference

    c. Consultation during the bid period

    d. Analysis of bids and aid in selection of successful bidder (s) and suppliers (s)

5. *Periodic Observation of Construction, Including*

    a. Preconstruction conference

    b. Periodic site visits during construction

    c. Preparation of observation visit reports

    d. Consultation and redesign service to accommodate new problems or opportunities discovered during construction

    e. Analysis of and recommendation to the client regarding contractor/supplier requests for payment

    f. Determination of substantial completion or actual completion of the construction work

    g. Consultation during grow-in period up to opening of the golf course

We have considered the two general ways that most golf course designers function in the design process.

1. Traditional Architect/Project Relationship

Project Responsibility	Average Time Allotment
Route/General Character	20%
Design Development	15%
Construction Documents	35%
Contractor Selection	3%
Periodic Observation	27%
	100%

2. Design/Build Relationship

Project Responsibility	Average Time Allotment
Route/General Character	12%
Design Development	8%
Construction Documents	20%
Contractor Selection	2%
Periodic Observation	58%
	100%

The categories and weighted percentages in the preceding table are quite arbitrary, although based on study, research, and past experience. There is no reason that any individual, golf course design office, golf publication, or any other jurisdiction or authority cannot develop its own categories and numbers.

When the question arises as to who should get major credit for the design, then one can determine what percentage of each individuals' time was spent on each responsibility. A multiplication exercise, then adding up the total, will tell who should get the kudos. Some states require that, at least in building construction, there be an "Architect of Record." We are not trying to establish any legal format for possible liability but rather to determine, as fairly and authentically as possible, who was the golf course designer.

In this day and age, it is no longer realistic to think that "eighteen stakes on a Sunday afternoon" or a quick sketch routing plan on an envelope or napkin constitutes the "design" of a golf course. There are too many additional people involved and functions performed that are as critical, or more so, to the outcome of the golf course design process.

Note: If a portion of the design work is not actually done (such as preparation of construction documents or preparation of a tree planting plan), then that portion cannot be credited to anyone.

Inasmuch as staking plans can be done by a surveyor or civil engineer; clearing, grading, and drainage plans by a civil engineer; irrigation plans by a supplier or irrigation designer; and tree and turf plans by a landscape architect; then obviously none of these could be credited to the potential designer unless he or she did some portion of the document preparation or made substantial design decisions in the field.

An examination of dozens of examples seems to indicate that a total of 61% of the work would constitute a substantial contribution to the design process. That percentage is only a suggestion. In the final analysis, the golf course architect is the person who conceived of and successfully combined the 18 compositions and assured that his or her concepts were faithfully executed on the land.

The Design Codes

In accepting the presidency of the American Society of Golf Course Architects in 1994, Donald Knott said, "Architects should expand the envelope of accepted standards. Great courses call for courage, skill, strategy, self control, a test of temper, and they reveal integrity."

As early as 1903, John Laing Low, a golf writer who had dabbled in design, prepared guidelines for planning golf courses. In 1920, Alister Mackenzie listed his own, as did Charles Blair Macdonald in 1928. These guidelines, once referred to as "The Codes," remain recommended reading for all involved in this art form. Because of their enduring timeliness, they should be read before embarking on the exercises that follow in Appendix B.

From Concerning Golf, *1903, by John Laing Low (1869–1929)*

1. "A golf course should provide entertainment for the high and medium handicapper while at the same time present a searching and difficult test for the accomplished golfer."
2. "The one aim of inventors is to reduce the skill required for golf. Golf architects must wage a battle against inventors by designing courses that emphasize golfing skills over equipment."
3. "The shortest, most direct line to the hole, even if it be the center of the fairway, should be fraught with danger."
4. "The architect must allow the ground to dictate play. The good architect sees that there is a special interest for the accomplished golfer in each stroke, just as the billiard player always has in mind the next stroke or strokes."
5. "The fairway must be oriented to both the tee and the green, thereby stressing the importance of placing the teeshot in a position from which the green can be approached with safety."
6. "Bunkers should be used sparingly by the architect. Except on one-shot holes they should never be placed within 200 yards of the tee. Ridges and depressions are the best way of controlling the entrance to the green. The best hazard on a course is a fairway bunker 200 to 235 yards from the tee, placed 5 to 10 yards off the accomplished player's most favorable line to the green."
7. "Whenever possible putting greens should be of the low, narrow plateau type, with the plateau tilting away, not toward the player. No green should be higher at the back than it is in front, for that gives a player confidence. Only half the flagstick should be seen from where the approach shot should be played."
8. "A course should never pretend to be, nor is it intended to be, an infallible tribunal of skill alone. The element of chance is the very essence of the game, part of the fun of the game."
9. "All really great golf holes involve a contest of wits and risks. No one should attempt to copy a great hole because so much may depend on its surroundings as

well as some feature miles away in the background which influences and affects the play of the hole. If the terrain is suitable, some of the character of the original might be incorporated elsewhere."

10. "Inequalities of putting green surfaces should not be exaggerated. A tilt from front to back or left to right or vice versa is sufficient. There should always be a special position for the flagstick on important days."

11. "Committees should leave well enough alone, especially when they have a really fine course."

From Golf Architecture, *1920,* *by Alister Mackenzie (1870–1934)*

1. "The course, where possible, should be arranged in two loops of nine holes."
2. "There should be a large proportion of good two-shot holes, two or three drive-and-pitch holes, and at least four one-shot holes."
3. "There should be little walking between greens and tees, and the course should be arranged so that in the first instance there is always a slight walk forward from the green to the next tee. Then the holes are sufficiently elastic to be lengthened in the future, if necessary."
4. "The greens and fairways should be sufficiently undulating, but there should be no hill climbing."
5. "Every hole should have a different character."
6. "There should be a minimum of blindness for the approach shots."
7. "The course should have beautiful surroundings, and all the artificial features should have so natural an appearance that a stranger is unable to distinguish them from nature itself."
8. "There should be a sufficient number of heroic carries from the tee, but the course should be arranged so that the weaker player with the loss of a stroke or a portion of a stroke shall always have an alternate route open to him."
9. "There should be infinite variety in the strokes required to play the various holes—interesting brassy shots, iron shots, pitch and run-up shots."
10. "There should be a complete absence of the annoyance and irritation caused by the necessity of searching for lost balls."
11. "The course should be so interesting that even the plus man is constantly stimulated to improve his game in attempting shots he has hitherto been unable to play."
12. "The course should be so arranged that the long handicap player or even the absolute beginner should be able to enjoy his round in spite of the fact that he is piling up a big score."
13. "The course should be equally good during winter and summer, the texture of greens and fairways should be perfect, and the approaches should have the same consistency as the greens."

Adapted from Scotland's Gift GOLF, *1928,* *by Charles Blair Macdonald (1856–1939)*

1. "There can be no really first-class golf course without good material to work with. The best material is a sandy loam in gentle undulation, breaking into hillocks in a

few places. Securing such land is really more than half the battle. Having such material at hand to work on, the completion of an ideal course becomes a matter of experience, gardening, and mathematics."

2. "The courses of Great Britain abound in classic and notable holes, and one has to study them and adopt their best and boldest features. Yet in most of their best holes there is always room for improvement."

3. "Nothing induces more to the charm of the game than perfect putting greens. Some should be large, but the majority would be of moderate size, some flat, some hillocky, one or two at an angle, but the great majority should have natural undulations, some more and others less undulating. It is absolutely essential that the turf be very fine so that the ball will run perfectly true."

4. "Whether this or that bunker is well-placed has caused more intensely heated arguments (outside the realm of religion) than has ever been my lot to listen to. Rest assured, however, when a controversy is hotly contested over several years as to whether this or that hazard is fair, it is the kind of hazard you want and it has real merit. When there is unanimous opinion that such and such a hazard is perfect, one finds it commonplace. I know of no classic hole that does not have its decriers."

5. "To my mind, an ideal course should have at least six bold bunkers, at the end of two-shot holes or very long carries from the tee. Further, I believe such holes would be improved by opening the fair green to one side or the other, giving short or timid players an opportunity to play around the hazards if so desired, but of course properly penalized by loss of distance for so playing. Other than these bold bunkers, no other hazards should stretch directly across a hole."

6. "What a golfer most desires is variety in the one-, two-, and three-shot holes, calling for accuracy in placing the ball not alone in the approach but also from the tee. Let the first shot be played in relation to the second shot in accordance with the run of the ground and the wind. Holes so designed permit the player to, if he so wishes, take risks commensurate to the gravity of the situation."

7. "Tees should be in close proximity to previous greens. This walking 50 to 150 yards to the next tee mars the course and delays the game. Between the hole and next teeing ground people sometimes forget and commence playing some other game."

8. "Hills on a golf course are a detriment. Mountain climbing is a sport in itself and has no place on a golf course. Trees in the courses are also a serious defect, and even when in close proximity prove a detriment."

9. "Glaring artificiality of any kind detracts from the fascination of the game."

Note to the Reader About Appendix B

The plans printed in Appendix B are available in AutoCAD format and can be downloaded from the John Wiley & Sons FTP server. If you have Internet access and would like to download the AutoCAD files, please follow these instructions:

1. Launch your Internet browser or FTP software.
2. Connect to the following FTP address: **ftp.wiley.com**
3. If requested, under User Name/ID, type: **anonymous**
4. If requested, under User Password, type: **[your email address]**
5. Select the following subdirectory: **public/products/subject/architecture/graves**
6. Select the files you want to download.
7. Download and read the README.TXT file for more information.

If you have any questions about downloading the files, call Wiley Technical Support at (212) 850-6753 or email techhelp@wiley.com.

If you have any questions about the files or need information about future updates, please contact the author at (925) 939-6300 or email teeitup@netvista.net.

CUSTOMER NOTE:

Please read the following before downloading and using the files.

This software contains files to help you utilize the models described in the accompanying book. By downloading the files, you are agreeing to be bound by the following agreement:

This software product is protected by copyright and all rights are reserved by the author, John Wiley & Sons, Inc., or their licensors. You are licensed to use the software on a single computer. Copying the software to another medium or format for use on a single computer does not violate the U.S. Copyright Law. Copying the software for any other purpose is a violation of the U.S. Copyright Law.

This software product is sold without warranty of any kind, either express or implied, including but not limited to the implied warranty of merchantability and fitness for a particular purpose. Neither Wiley nor its dealers or distributors assumes any liability for any alleged or actual damages arising from the use of or the inability to use this software. (Some states do not allow the exclusion of implied warranties, so the exclusion may not apply to you.)

Design Exercises

Background information and ancillary plans of La Purisma Golf Course, designed by coauthor Robert Muir Graves in the Santa Barbara, California, area are included in the text. After reading Chapter 3 and reviewing the design codes, begin with Exercise 1.

Do not examine Plans B, C, and D1, D2, and D3 in detail until the appropriate exercise is complete.

The Site

The site consists of 300 acres of former pasture land, ranging from flat to rolling, with some steep slopes. The soils are deep sandy loam. Although water was impounded when the aerial survey map was flown, wet lands are not an issue. The climate is warm-temperate with little rain. Winds predominate from southwest to northwest. All utilities are available in the clubhouse/maintenance center area. There are seven archeological sites shown that are potential Native American burial grounds. Fill is acceptable on the sites, but excavation is limited to a 2-foot depth.

The Program

This is to be an 18-hole (two 9-hole loops) golf course, par 72, at least 6,500 yards long from the men's regular tee. The course must be playable and enjoyable for all types of golfers but strong enough to host a national pro-tour tournament. A full-sized practice range is required, including areas to work on all the short game shots.

Exercise 1

After you read Chapter 3, use Plan A, the base map, to

a. Study contours and other features.
b. Outline 18 holes and practice fairway with centerlines for fairways, squares for tees, and circles for greens.
c. Compare your routing with Plan B as executed after you complete b above. Remember that every person who has ever designed a golf course has had his or her own ideas as to how it should be done.

Caution: A golf architect regards the land, not the base map, as the canvas. Therefore, in practice he or she may not put pencil to paper until days, or even weeks, have been spent examining the site and surroundings. Such study is of intrinsic importance, to "get the feel of what nature has provided" and to reveal distant vistas, wind effects, and subtle contours not shown on the topo.

Nevertheless, for this "paper exercise," we require you to put pencil to paper after studying only the topographical plan. Little will be accomplished until pencil is, in fact, put to paper.

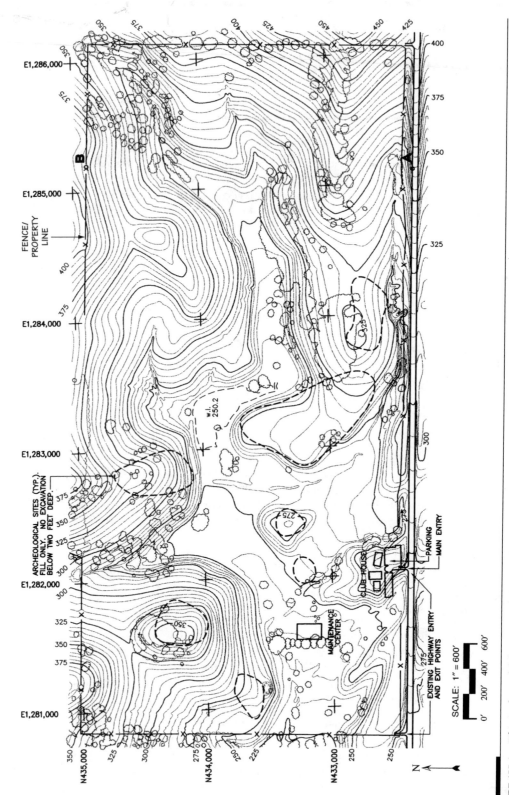

E1,286,000

E1,285,000

E1,284,000

E1,283,000

E1,282,000

E1,281,000

FENCE/
PROPERTY
LINE

ARCHEOLOGICAL SITES (TYP.)
FILL ONLY, NO EXCAVATION
BELOW TWO FEET DEEP.

w.l.
250.2

CLUB HOUSE

PARKING

MAIN ENTRY

EXISTING HIGHWAY ENTRY
AND EXIT POINTS

MAINTENANCE
CENTER

SCALE: 1" = 600'

0'   200' 400' 600'

N

PLAN A   This is the scaled base map of the site. It is also referred to as the topographical (topo) or background plan. The contour interval is 5 feet. The clubhouse and entrance road are shown as actually sited and close to actual scale. (See page 380 for instructions on downloading AutoCAD files.)

382

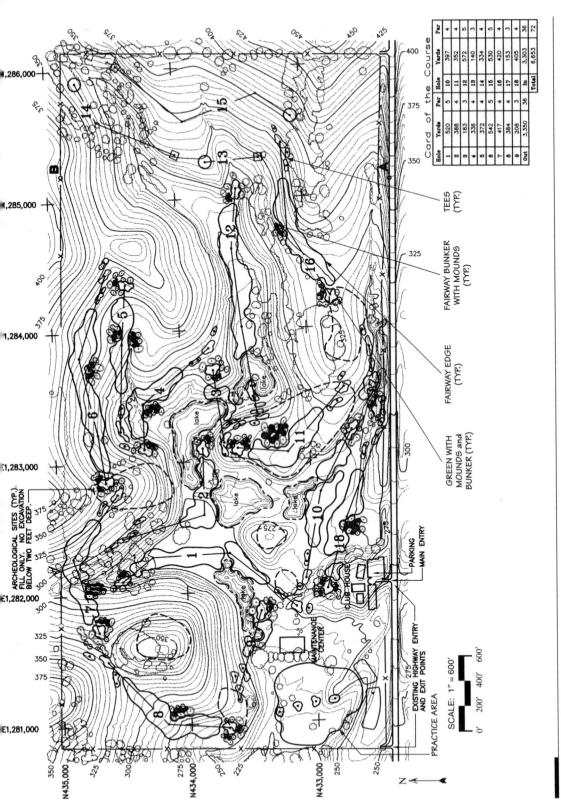

Card of the Course

Hole	Yards	Par	Hole	Yards	Par
1	520	5	10	397	4
2	388	4	11	352	4
3	183	3	12	572	5
4	336	4	13	140	3
5	372	4	14	334	4
6	542	5	15	530	5
7	417	4	16	420	4
8	384	4	17	153	3
9	208	3	18	405	4
Out	3,350	36	In	3,303	36
			Total	6,653	72

TEES (TYP.)

FAIRWAY BUNKER WITH MOUNDS (TYP.)

FAIRWAY EDGE (TYP.)

GREEN WITH MOUNDS and BUNKER (TYP.)

SCALE: 1" = 600'

0'   200'   400'   600'

N

PRACTICE AREA

ARCHEOLOGICAL SITES (TYP.). FILL ONLY. NO EXCAVATION BELOW TWO FEET DEEP.

PARKING

MAIN ENTRY

EXISTING HIGHWAY ENTRY AND EXIT POINTS

CLUB HOUSE

MAINTENANCE CENTER

PLAN B   This is a plan of the 18 holes, practice fairway, and other features as executed and now in play. However, bunkering and other features on a par 3, a par 4, and a par 5 hole—numbers 13, 14, and 15, respectively—are not shown. (See page 380 for instructions on downloading AutoCAD files.)

383

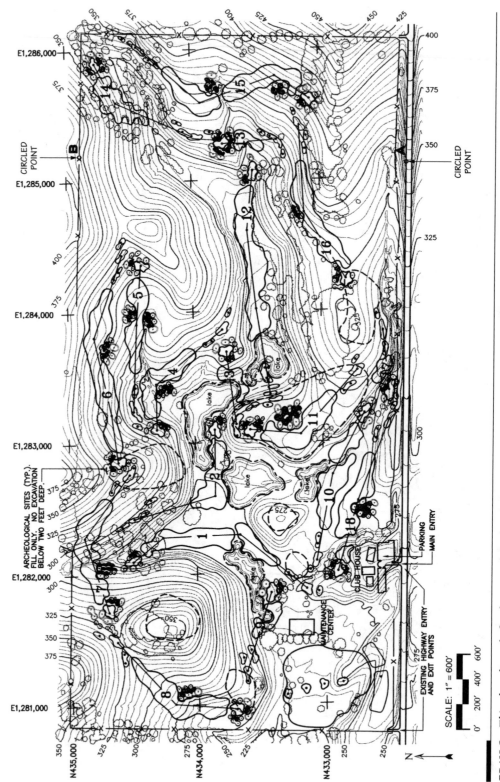

PLAN C   *This plan shows the development of the three holes referred to in Plan B. (See page 380 for instructions on downloading AutoCAD files.)*

384

Exercise 2

After you have completed Exercise 1 and have read Chapter 4,

a. Using squared or plain tracing paper, add greens, tees, fairways, bunkers, mounds, and other features to each of the three centerline only holes from Plan B (holes 13, 14, and 15).

  You may wish to refer to Appendix C at the back of the book, which contains many symbols that will help you to show the characteristics of the golf hole features, such as greens and bunkers. You may also wish to use color for lines and/or shading to make the drawings read more clearly.

b. Compare your plans with the three holes as actually executed and shown on Plan C. Again, do not overlook the fact that your plans will be different from those actually executed at La Purisima.

Exercise 3

After completing Exercise 2, use the centerline plan prepared in Exercise 1 to complete each hole as in Exercise 2, and add a continuous golf car path tee to green. Also show areas for golf car staging, golf car storage, and shelters (this is the route plan).

  Compare your plan to Plan C prepared by the co-author. Remember that on 300 acres, almost all of which is usable, there are many dozens, if not a hundred, different golf holes that could be developed sucessfully.

Exercise 4

Three holes, 13, 14, and 15 and tee 16 on Plan C, are eliminated through eminent domain. Note on Plan C two circled points: "A" on the highway and "B" on the north property line. Connect "A" and "B." All land east of line A-B are taken from the golf course. Show how remaining holes can be rerouted to compensate for this loss. The objective is to change as few holes as possible and not lose any total yardage or strokes to par. Again, there are numerous ways to accomplish this, even without touching the front nine. Compare with the author's solutions, Plans D1, D2, and D3.

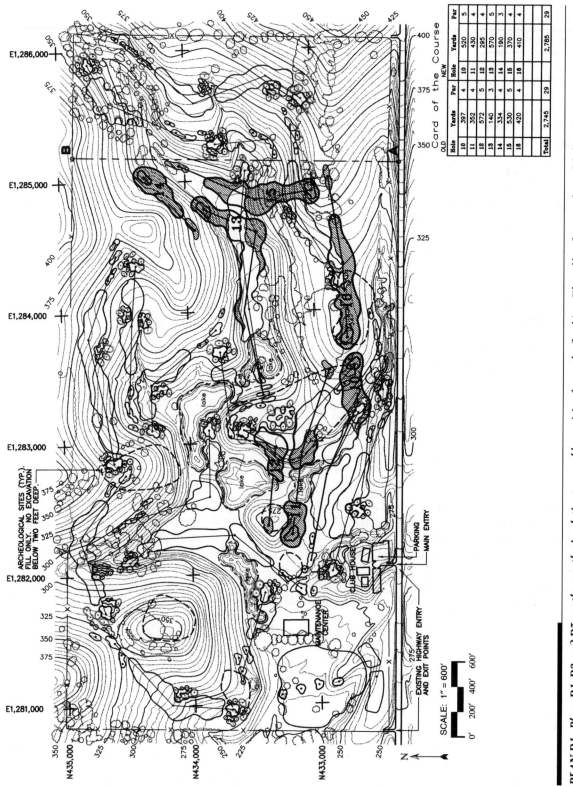

Card of the Course

OLD			NEW		
Hole	Yards	Par	Hole	Yards	Par
10	397	4	10	520	5
11	352	4	11	430	4
12	572	5	12	295	4
13	140	3	13	570	5
14	334	4	14	190	3
15	530	5	15	370	4
16	420	4	16	410	4
Total	2,745	29	Total	2,785	29

PLAN D1 Plans D1, D2, and D3 are the coauthor's solution to a problem arising from a land taking. The golf card covers changed holes only, as a comparison. (See page 380 for instructions on downloading AutoCAD files.)

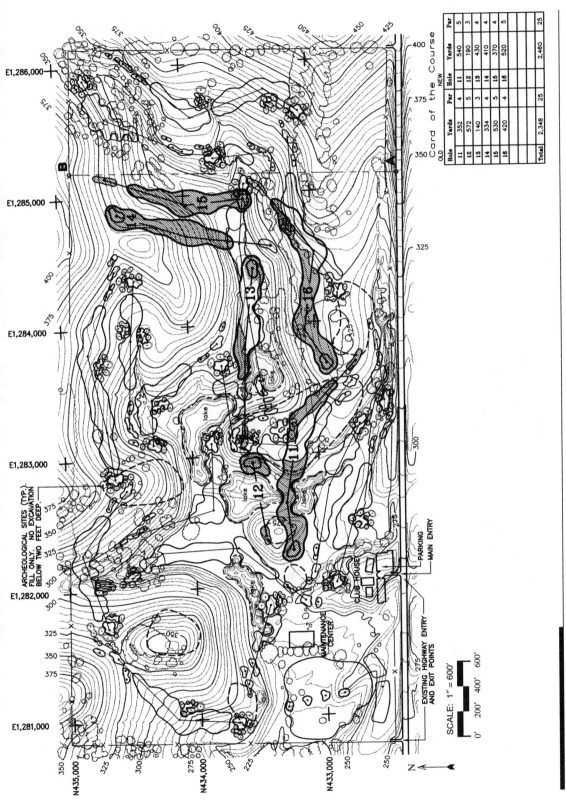

Card of the Course

	OLD				NEW		
Hole	Yards	Par	Hole	Hole	Yards	Par
11	352	4	11	11	540	5
12	572	5	12	12	190	3
13	140	3	13	13	430	4
14	530	5	14	14	410	4
15	420	4	15	15	370	4
16			16	16	520	5
Total	2,348	25		Total	2,460	25

PLAN D1 Plans D1, D2, and D3 are the coauthor's solution to a problem arising from a land taking. The golf card covers changed holes only, as a comparison. (See page 380 for instructions on downloading AutoCAD files.)

387

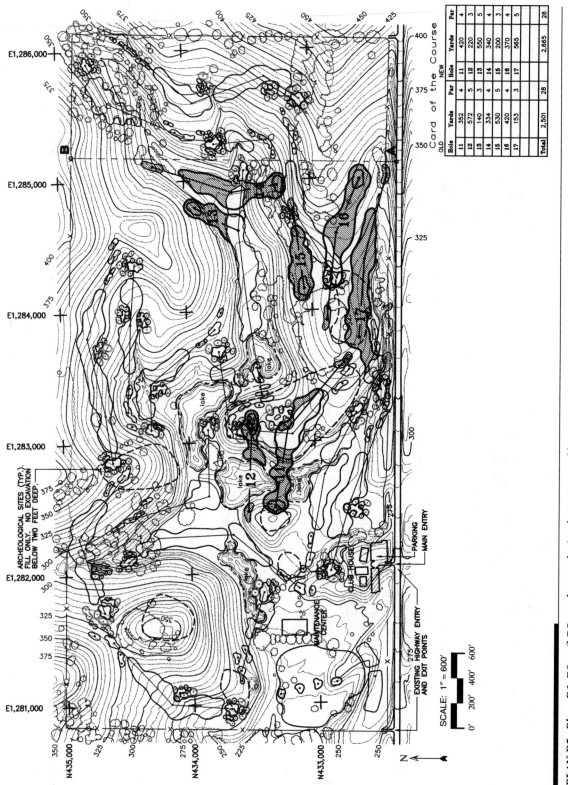

Card of the Course

	OLD			NEW	
Hole	Yards	Par	Hole	Yards	Par
11	352	4	11	420	4
12	572	5	12	220	3
13	140	3	13	550	5
14	334	4	14	340	4
15	530	5	15	200	3
16	420	4	16	370	4
17	153	3	17	565	5
Total	2,501	28		2,665	28

PLAN D3 Plans D1, D2, and D3 are the coauthor's solution to a problem arising from a land taking. The golf card covers changed holes only, as a comparison. (See page 380 for instructions on downloading AutoCAD files.)

388

Exercise 5

Using paper squared in tenths, plan a working drawing at scale 1″ = 40′ or greater for a minimum of three of the greens added in Exercise 4 (a working drawing is one the contractor can follow to produce final grades). Compare with plans of those greens as executed by the coauthors.

The green grading studies shown below are for holes 13, 14, and 15 as actually developed for La Purisima. Since your holes will be different, your solution to green design will be different as well.

The grid lines shown on the plans are 40 feet apart.

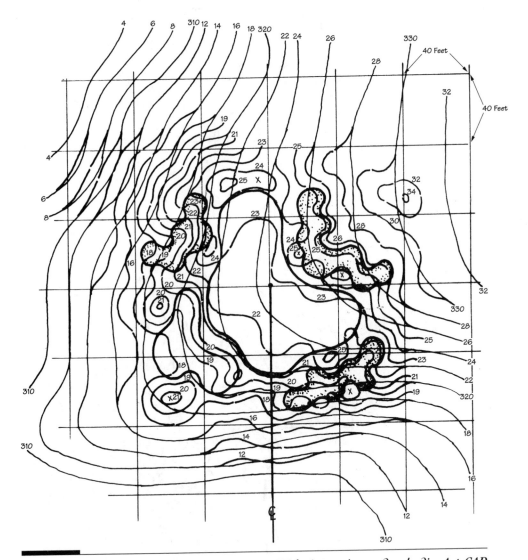

La Purisma: Green No. 13, Grading Study. (See page 380 for instructions on downloading AutoCAD files.)

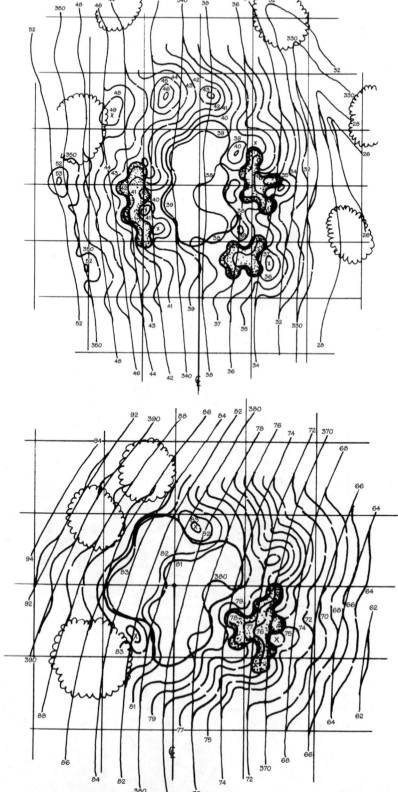

*La Purisma: Green No. 14,
Grading Study. (See page 380 for
in-structions   on   downloading
Auto- CAD files.)*

*La Purisma: Green No. 15,
Grading Study. (See page 380 for
in-structions on downloading Auto-
CAD files.)*

Symbols for Golf Course Design

Many design offices and individual designers have their own favorite symbols that they will want to retain. The following symbols are suggestions that can be helpful, particularly during the design development stage, when the golf course character and playability will evolve. These symbols can also be helpful during production of construction documents, at which time the designer may want to elaborate on and/or expand the list to suit the project.

Name of Feature   *Symbol*

(Examples are given solely for their subject physical characteristic.)

I. **Special Golf Course Features**
   A. Centerline with Turning Point

   B. Tee

   C. Fairway (or practice range) Edge

   D. Sand Bunker

   E. Grass Bunker

   F. Lake/Pond

   G. Creek/Stream

   H. Green

   I. Green Perimeter Chip/Putt Swale

   J. Mound

   K. Hollow

391

Name of Feature   *Symbol*

II. **Vegetation**
    A. *Turf*
        1. Green

        2. Tee

        3. Fairway

        4. Light Rough

        5. Heavy Rough

    B. *Trees*
        1. *Conifer*
            a. Light Foliage
                (example: *Pinus canariensis*)

            b. Dense Foliage
                (example: *Thuja plicata*)

        2. *Deciduous*
            a. Light Foliage
                (example: *Gleditsia triacanthus*)

            b. Dense Foliage
                (example: *Ulmus americana*)

        3. *Broadleaf Evergreen*
            a. Light Foliage
                (example: *Eucalyptus nicholii*)

            b. Dense Foliage
                (example: *Quercus agrifolia*)

    C. *Ground Covers*

        1. Heavy Texture
            (example: *Hedera canariensis*)

        2. Light Texture
            (example: *Fragaria chiloensis*)

Name of Feature   *Symbol*

III. **Hardscapes**

    A. Golf Car Path

    B. Service/Maintenance Road

    C. Curb

    D. Retaining Wall
       (vertical or sloping)

       1. Masonry

       2. Concrete

       3. Metal

       4. Wood

    E. Golf Car Parking

    F. Auto Parking

IV. **Drainage**

    A. Underground Drainpipe
       1. Solid

       2. Perforated

    B. Drainage Inlet/Outlet
       1. Masonry

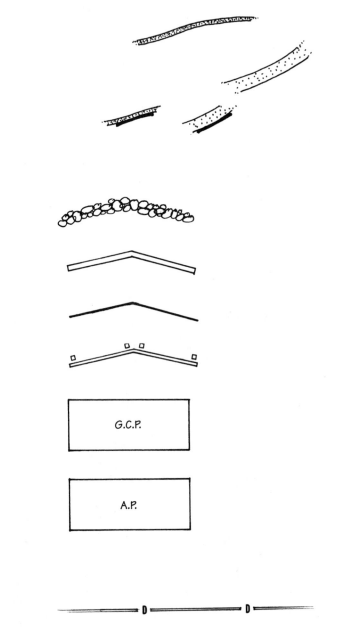

Name of Feature   *Symbol*

2. Concrete

3. Metal

4. Wood

C. Catch Basin

D. Drain Swale

E. Berm

V. **Irrigation**
   A. *Pipe*
       1. Lateral

       2. Mainline

   B. *Irrigation Heads*
       1. Full Circle

       2. Part Circle

   C. *Valves*
       1. Quick-Coupler

       2. Remote Control

       3. Section/Isolation

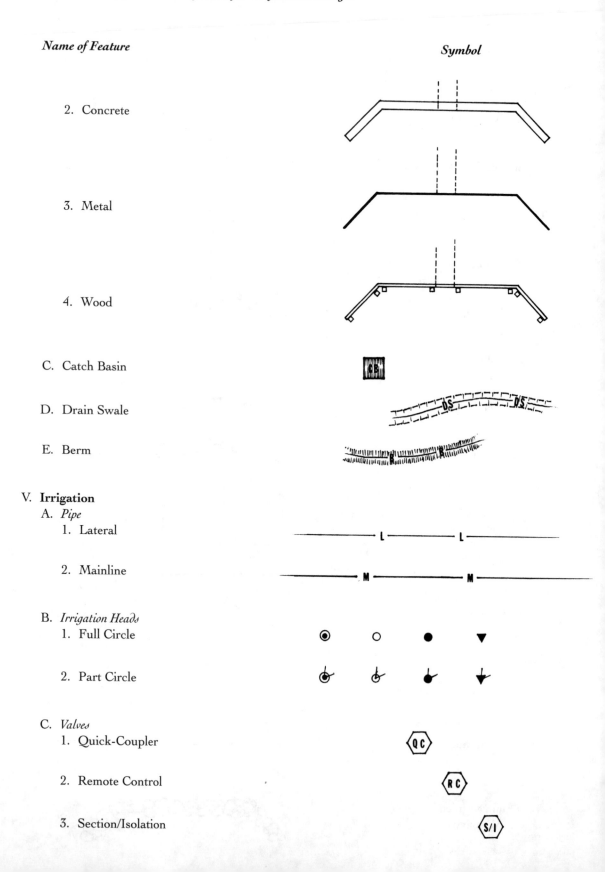

Name of Feature   *Symbol*

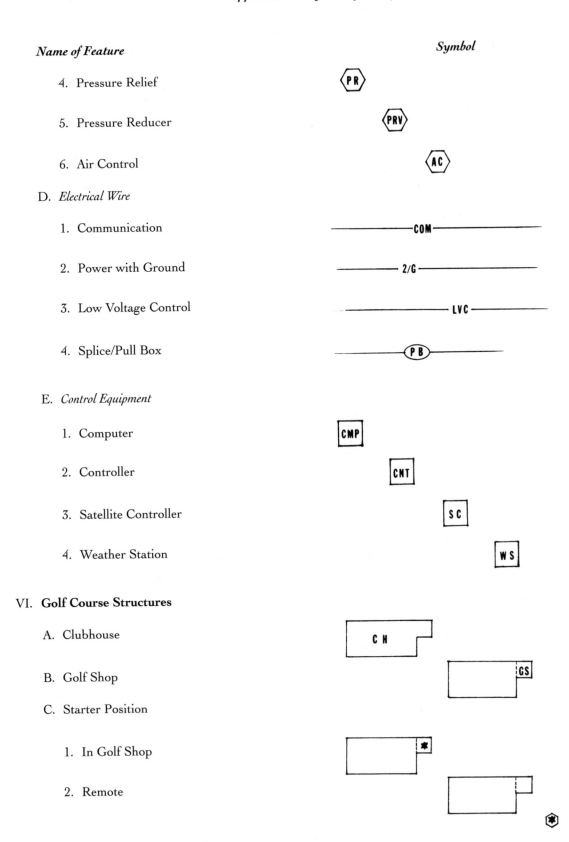

    4. Pressure Relief

    5. Pressure Reducer

    6. Air Control

D. *Electrical Wire*

    1. Communication

    2. Power with Ground

    3. Low Voltage Control

    4. Splice/Pull Box

E. *Control Equipment*

    1. Computer

    2. Controller

    3. Satellite Controller

    4. Weather Station

VI. **Golf Course Structures**

    A. Clubhouse

    B. Golf Shop

    C. Starter Position

        1. In Golf Shop

        2. Remote

Name of Feature   *Symbol*

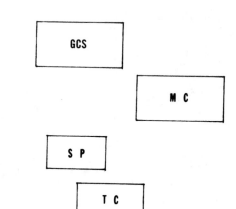

D. Golf Car Storage

E. Maintenance Center

F. *Recreation Facilities*
    1. Swimming Pool

    2. Tennis Court

Resources

Hard-to-Find Book Sources

Facsimiles of several out-of-print books on course design are available from the following:

Classics of Golf, P. O. Box 10285, Stamford, CT 06923-0001

Grant Books, Victoria Square, Droitwich, Worcestershire, England WR9 8DC

George Lewis/Golfiana, P. O. Box 291, Mamaroneck, N.Y. 10543

The Old Golf Shop, Inc., 325 West Fifth Street, Cincinnati, OH 45202

USGA Rare Book Collection, Golf House, P. O. Box 3000, Far Hills, NJ 07931-3000

Turfgrass Science Textbooks

Beard, James B. *Turfgrass Management for Golf Courses*. 2d ed. Chelsea, Mich.: Sleeping Bear Press, 1997.

———. *Turfgrass Science and Culture*. Englewood Cliffs, N.J.: Prentice-Hall, 1973.

———. *Turf Management for Golf Courses*. Minneapolis: Burgess Publishing, 1982.

Daniel, W. H., and R. P. Freeborg. *Turf Managers Handbook*. Cleveland, OH: Harvest Publishing, 1979.

Emmons, R. D. *Turfgrass Science and Management*. Albany, N.Y.: Delmar Publishers, 1984.

Hanson, A. A., and F. W. Juska, eds. *Turfgrass Science*. Madison, Wis.: American Society of Agronomy, 1969.

Karnok, Keith. *Turfgrass Management Information Directory*. Chelsea, Mich.: Ann Arbor Press, 1997. Brings together sources of turfgrass information.

Madison, John H. *Practical Turfgrass Management*. New York: Van Nostrand-Reinhold, 1971.

———. *Principles of Turfgrass Culture*. New York: Van Nostrand-Reinhold, 1971.

Musser, Burton H. *Turf Management*. 2d ed. New York: McGraw-Hill, 1962.

Piper, C. V., and R. A. Oakley. *Turf for Golf Courses*. 2d ed. New York: Macmillan, 1929.

Soil Science Society of America. *Glossary of Soil Science Terms*. Madison, WI, 1997.

Turgeon, A. J. *Turfgrass Management*. Englewood Cliffs, N.J.: Prentice-Hall Regents, 1991.

Allied Organizations and Libraries

For a complete list of organizations and libraries, refer to the *1998 NGF International Directory of Golf.*

American Society of Golf Course Architects (ASGCA), Paul Fullmer, Executive Secretary, 221 North LaSalle Street, Chicago, IL 60601. *Entry standards are rigid. Yet involved in creating the playing fields of golf, it serves the interests of all in the profession, the game of golf, and the environment.*

Audubon Society of New York State, 45 Rarick Road, Selkirk, NY 12158. *Ronald G. Dodson, President, maintains that everyone is responsible for taking care of the earth. The Society's cooperative sanctuary system includes a program directed to golf courses.*

Club Managers Association of America, 1733 King Street, Alexandria, VA 22314.

Donald Ross Society, P. O. Box 403, Bloomfield, CT 06002 (For historic data, contact W. P. Jones, P. O. Box 9774, 5315 Collingwood Road, Raleigh, NC 27624).

Givens Memorial Library, Pinehurst, NC 28374.

Golf Course Builders Association of America (GCBAA), Phillip Arnold, Executive Vice President, 920 Airport Road, Suite 210, Chapel Hill, NC 27514. *The organization includes golf course construction contractors and two categories of associate memberships: one for manufacturers, dealers and others connected to course products; the other for members of the allied associations of golf.*

Golf Course Superintendents Association of America (GCSAA), 1421 Research Park Drive, Lawrence, KS 66049. *Since 1926 this organization of professional course superintendents, now numbering more than 16,000, who manage and maintain golf facilities in the United States and worldwide, has been widely recognized for its vitality, along with the depth and variety of its shows, educational programs, and publications. Its membership has made a profound contribution to the perfection of contemporary golf courses and the joy of playing the game and has had a beneficial impact on the environment and society.*

Ladies Professional Golf Association (LPGA), 2570 W. International Speedway Boulevard, Suite B, Daytona Beach, FL 32114-1118

National Club Association, 3050 K Street N.W., Suite 330, Washington, DC 20007

National Golf Course Owners Association (NGCOA), 14 Exchange Street, P. O. Box 1061, Charleston, SC 29402. *A professional society of course owners dedicated to communicating knowledge to its membership.*

National Golf Foundation (NGF), 1150 South U.S. Highway 1, Jupiter, FL 33477. *This organization serves as a clearinghouse for golf data and publishes the most complete set of studies and other literature related to the business of golf. It has prepared and researched many subjects of collateral value to the course architect, including organizing, promoting, financing, and operating golf courses. Under direction of President and CEO Joseph F. Beditz, the Foundation plays an enormous role in the business of golf. A catalog of publications is available.*

Professional Golfers Association of America (PGA), Palm Beach Gardens, FL 33418-9601. *One of the most influential organizations in golf. It provides a catalog of its publications.*

PGA Tour, Sawgrass, 112 TPC Boulevard, Ponte Vedra Beach, FL 32082.

PGA World Golf Hall of Fame, 100 TPC Boulevard, Ponte Vedra Beach, FL 32082.

Ralph W. Miller Golf Library One Industry Hills Parkway City of Industry, CA 91744.

The Royal Canadian Golf Association, Golf House, 1333 Dorval Drive R.R.#2, Oakville, Ontario, Canada L6J423. *This is the ruling body of golf in Canada. It maintains an extensive museum of Canadian golf history and the Canadian Golf Hall of Fame.*

Tufts Archives, Pinehurst, NC 28374.

United States Golf Association (USGA), Golf House, P. O. Box 2000, Far Hills, NJ 07931. *This is the governing body of golf in the United States. It owns the world's largest golf library and distributes golf books, facsimiles, and its own magazine,* Golf Journal, *nine times annually. The Green Section of the USGA is also active in sponsoring books related to turfgrass science, the environment, and the management of golf courses. It sponsors research and maintains regional offices throughout the United States to provide the most extensive technical turfgrass services offered in the history of golf. The* Green Section Record *is published six times annually. Catalogs of USGA and Green Section publications are available.*

Pamphlets and Videotapes

Cornish, G. S., and W. G. Robinson. *Golf Course Design: An Introduction.* Reprinted by GCSAA, 1989.

Golf Course Superintendents Association of America. *Golf and Environment Series* (Videotape).

Hurdzan, Michael. *Evolution of the Modern Green.* ASGCA, reprinted 1990.

Robert, E., and B. Roberts. *Lawn and Sports Turf Benefits.* Pleasant Hill, Tenn.: The Lawn Institute, 1990.

USGA Recommendations for Putting Green Construction. Published by the *USGA Green Section Record*, March-April 1993.

Electronic Resources

Television

"Par for the Course." A 30-minute TV program produced by the Golf Course Superintendents Association of America is aired Sunday mornings on ESPN. A variety of episodes includes design, the benefits of a golf course to the community, environmental profiles, and others. The role of the key person, namely the golf course superintendent, in maintaining and enhancing the playing fields of the game is paramount.

Videos and Disks

Golf Course Superintendents Association of America. This organization provides videos and disks on golf course subjects together with tapes of "Par for the Course" episodes.

National Golf Foundation. This organization has indexed over 1,500 golf industry related topics on disk and describes this service as "the largest directory to literature about the business of golf. . . ."

The Golf Course Superintendents Association of America. The Center for Resource Management. This organization has created a video called "Environmental Principles for Golf Courses in the U.S."—a joint effort by environmental groups and the golf industry.

Web Sites

The American Society of Golf Course Architects. This organization provides "The Architect's Corner" weekly on the Web Site: http://www. golfdesign.org. It describes favorite holes of members and the extensive knowledge of the behind-the-scene planning and processes linking the hole from tee to green.

Other Web Sites that describe golf courses include but are by no means limited to—

golf.com URL: http://golf.com
Golf Course Database URL: http://www.traveller.com/golf
GolfData Web URL: http:www.gdol.com
Golf Online URL: http://www.golfonline.com/
Golf World URL: http://golf.com/golfworld/
GolfWeb URL: http://www.golfweb.com/cgi-bin/disp3.cgi?.

Organizations

www.gcsaa.org
National Golf Foundation URL: http://www.gate.net/-ngf/ngf.html
Professional Golfers' Association of America: www pga.com
Royal Canadian Golf Association URL: www.rcga.org
United States Golf Association URL: www.usga.org
PGA TOUR URL: www pgatour.com
IGOLF URL: www igolf.com

Note: There are new web sites coming online every day using a search engine such as Yahoo. Lycos, Infoseek, and so on will get the user the latest and greatest golf related web sites.

Bibliography

Adams, John. *The Parks of Musselburgh*. Droitwich, Worcestershire, England: Grant Books, 1991.

Bahto, George. *The National School of Design*. Chelsea, Mich.: Sleeping Bear Press, 1997. *The definitive work on Charles Blair Macdonald and his associates Seth Raynor and Charles Banks.*

Balogh, James C., and William J. Walker. *Golf Course Management: Environmental Issues*. Chelsea, Mich.: Lewis Publishers, 1993. *An informative book on environmental issues.*

Barclay, James A. *Golf in Canada: A History*. Toronto: McLelland and Stewart, 1992. *A reference book of intense interest, including passages on Canadian designers, with golf architect Stanley Thompson, a giant in the profession, featured.*

Bartlett, Michael, and Tony Roberts. *The Golf Book*. New York: Arbor House, 1980.

Bauer, Alek. *Hazards: Those Essential Elements in a Golf Course Without Which the Game Would Be Tame and Uninteresting*. Chicago: Tony Rubovitis, 1913, and Droitwich, Worcestershire, England: Grant Books, 1993.

Beall, Barbara B. "Bringing in the Hired Guns, How to Choose an Environmental Consultant." *USGA Green Section Record*. United States Golf Association (March/April 1995).

Braid, James. *Advanced Golf*. London: Metheun, 1908.

Browning, Robert. *A History of Golf*. New York: E. P. Dutton, 1955, and Classics of Golf, 1985.

Choate, Richard S. *Turf Irrigation Manual*, 5th ed. Dallas, Texas: Telasco Industries, 1994. (Available through the Irrigation Association, Fairfax, Virginia)

Clark, Robert. *Golf: A Royal and Ancient Game*. London: Macmillan, 1899.

Colt, H. S., and C. H. Alison. *Some Essays on Golf Course Architecture*. New York: Charles Scribners Sons, 1920, and Droitwich, Worcestershire, England: Grant Books, 1993.

Colville, George M. *Five Open Champions and the Musselburgh Golf Story*. Musselburgh, Scotland: Colville Books, 1980.

Cornish, Geoffrey, and Ronald E. Whitten. *The Golf Course*. New York: Rutledge Press, 1981, 1982, 1984, 1987, and Stamford, CT: Classics of Golf, 1989. *The seminal text on course designers, this book includes profiles of those who have practiced the art form since its inception, as well as lists of their courses.*

— — —. *The Architects of Golf*. New York: Harper Collins, 1993. *A complete update of* The Golf Course *with photographs of each profiled architect. Additional illustrations are arranged chronologically to outline the history of the profession.*

Cousins, Geoffrey. *Golf in Britain.* London: Routledge and Kegan Paul, 1975. *A historical, societal, and economic background of golf in Great Britain, much of which is applicable to golf in North America.*

Darwin, Bernard. *The Golf Courses of the British Isles.* London: Duckworth & Co., 1910, and Stamford, CT: Classics of Golf, 1988. *Illustrated by Harry Rowntree with evocative watercolors, this is said to be golf's first "coffee table book."*

Darwin, Bernard. *James Braid.* London: Hodder and Stoughton, 1952.

Darwin, Bernard, Sir Guy Campbell, et al. *A History of Golf in Britain.* London: Cassel and Co., 1952. *A chapter on golf architecture in Britain by Sir Guy Campbell is "required" reading for golf architects.*

Davis, William H. *The World's Best Golf.* Trumbull, Conn.: Golf Digest, 1991. *This illustrated work followed a series by Davis and the editors of* Golf Digest *starting in 1974. Great golf courses worldwide are described. Apparently, Bill Davis and his researcher Topsy Siderowf did not believe that a course had to be an extravaganza to make a contribution, although they admired outstanding layouts.*

Doak, Thomas. *The Confidential Guide to Golf Courses.* Chelsea, Mich.: Sleeping Bear Press, 1996. *One golf architect's opinions of nearly a thousand links and courses he visited around the globe. Interesting for all golfers; it is even more interesting for designers who like to know what others think of their work.*

———. *The Anatomy of a Golf Course.* New York: Lyons and Burford, 1992. *Written by a youthful golf architect belonging to a generation of newcomers to the profession, with diagrams by Gilbert Hanse, another young architect, this book should be read by all in design or involved in master planning of projects that include golf.*

Dobereiner, Peter. *The Glorious World of Golf.* New York: McGraw Hill, 1973.

Dye, Pete, with Mark Shaw. *Bury Me in a Pot Bunker.* New York: Addison-Wesley, 1995. *A remarkable autobiography of a remarkable person and his remarkable wife, golf architect Alice Dye.*

Gimmy, A. E., and M. E. Benson. *Golf Courses and Country Clubs: A Guide to Appraisal, Market Analysis, Development and Financing.* Chicago: Appraisal Institute, 1992. *An important text for the golf architect's library.*

Gordon, John. *The Great Golf Courses of Canada.* Willowdale, Ontario, Canada: Firefly Books, 1993. With photography by Michael French. *This work portrays the greatness of golf architecture in Canada.*

Graffis, Herb. *The PGA.* New York: Thomas Y. Crowell, 1975.

Grant, Donald. *Donald Ross of Pinehurst and Royal Dornoch.* Golspie, Scotland: The Sutherland Press, 1973.

Grant, H. R. J., and J. F. Moreton. *Aspects of Collecting Golf Books.* Droitwich, Worcestershire, England: Grant Books, 1996.

Grimsley, Will. *Golf: Its History, People, and Events.* Englewood Cliffs, N.J.: Prentice-Hall, 1966.

Harker, D., S. Evans, M. Evans, and K. Harker. *Landscape Restoration Handbook.* Boca Raton, Fla.: Lewis Publishers, not dated. *Described as an ecological call to arms, this is an impressive reference work.*

Hawtree, Fred W. *Triple Bauge*, Woodstock, Oxford, England: Cambuc Archive, 1996. *An account of the evolution of medieval games into golf.*

———. *The Golf Course: Planning, Design, Construction and Maintenance*. London: E. and F. S. Spon, 1983; reprinted 1985, 1989, 1990, 1992, and completely revised in 1996 in collaboration with golf architect Martin Hawtree. *This work is by a renowned course architect whose father was, and son is, also distinguished in the profession.*

———. *Colt & Co. Golf Course Architects*. Woodstock, Oxford, England: Cambuc Archive, 1991. *A biographical study of H. S. Colt, one of the most influential course designers in history, and his partners C. H. Alison, J. S. F. Morrison, and A. Mackenzie—a foursome whose work is found in many countries and is pervasive to our art form.*

Henderson, J. T., and D. I. Stirk. *Golf in the Making*. London: Henderson and Stirk, 1979. *A comprehensive illustrated history of playing equipment and golf ball technology.*

Hunter, Robert. *The Links*. New York: Charles Scribners Sons, 1926, and USGA Rare Book Collection, Far Hills, N.J. 1994. *The first known American book on course design, its contents remain timely. Author John Strawn edited the facsimile edition.*

Hurdzan, Michael J. *Golf Course Architecture: Design, Construction and Restoration*. Chelsea, Mich.: Sleeping Bear Press, 1996. *Magnificent and educational are two words appropriate to a description of this work.*

Hurdzan, Michael J. "Minimizing Environmental Impact by Golf Course Development: A Method and Some Case Studies." In *Handbook of Integrated Pest Management for Turf and Ornamentals*, edited by Anne R. Leslie. Chelsea, Mich.: CRS Press, 1994.

Irrigation Systems Design Manual. Fresno, Calif.: Buckner, 1988.

Jenkins, Dan. *The Best 18 Holes in America*. New York: Delacorte Press, 1966.

Jones, Rees L., and Guy L. Rando. *Golf Course Developments*. Technical Bulletin 70. Washington D.C.: Urban Land Institute, 1974. *This seminal and influential work on integration of golf and residences was later updated by others. See Muirhead and Rando (1994) and Phillips (1986).*

Jones, Robert Trent, with Larry Dennis. *Golf's Magnificent Challenge*. New York: McGraw-Hill, 1989. *A spectacularly illustrated autobiography by the architect who has influenced his art form probably more than any other designer in history.*

Jones, Robert Trent, Jr. *Golf by Design*. Boston: Little Brown, 1993. *Written to assist the player in comprehending course design and how doing so may save him or her a stroke., this book adds another dimension to golf and is instructive for the course architect as well.*

Jones, Robert Tyre. *Golf Is My Game*. Garden City, N.Y.: Doubleday, 1960.

Kains, Robert. *Golf Course Design and Construction*. Guelph, Ont.: University of Guelph, 1993. *This study, with abundant illustrations, is the text for a correspondence course provided by the University of Guelph.*

Klein, Bradley S. *Rough Meditations*. Chelsea, Mich.: Sleeping Bear Press, 1997. *Essays on the principles of course architecture that explore tensions between classical style and modern aspects of business, technology, and public perceptions. As a respected student of golf, Klein does not hold back on judgments that are both sharp and entertaining.*

Klemme, Mike. *A View from the Rough.* Chelsea, Mich.: Sleeping Bear Press, 1995. *This work and its outstanding photography are a tribute to golf architects, contractors, superintendents, and environmentalists who strive for favorable environments for many species.*

Kroeger, Robert. *The Golf Courses of Old Tom Morris.* Cincinnati, Ohio: Heritage Communications, 1995. *Abundant data of immense interest concerning "Old Tom" and his layouts are included.*

Love, William R. *An Environmental Approach to Golf Course Architecture.* Chicago: The American Society of Golf Course Architects, 1992. *Aspects of course design and their significance to the environment are put forward in text and convenient checklist form by an accomplished architect.*

Low, John L. *Concerning Golf.* London: Hodder and Stoughton, 1903, and Far Hills, NJ: USGA Rare Book Collection, 1987.

Macdonald, Charles Blair. *Scotland's Gift GOLF.* New York: Charles Scribners Sons, 1928, and Stamford, CT: Classics of Golf, 1985.

Mackenzie, Alister. *The Spirit of St. Andrews.* Chelsea, Mich.: Sleeping Bear Press, 1995. *Written in 1933 but not published, this manuscript was brought to light in 1995 by the author's stepgrandson, Raymond A. Haddock. It soon became a classic.*

———. *Golf Architecture.* London: Simpkin, Marshall, Hamilton, Kent & Co., 1920, and Stamford, CT: Classics of Golf, 1988 and Droitwich, Worcestershire, England: Grant Books, 1982. *This little book holds a mighty message for golf architects.*

Mahoney, Jack. *The Golf History of New England.* Weston, Mass.: New England Golf, 1995.

Martin, H. B. *Fifty Years of American Golf.* New York: Dodd, Mead & Co., 1936.

Mead, Daniel W., and Joseph Reid Akerman. *Contract Specifications and Engineering Relations.* New York: McGraw Hill, 1956.

Muirhead, Desmond, and Guy L. Rando. *Golf Course Development and Real Estate.* Washington, D.C.: Urban Land Institute, 1994. *Prepared in the tradition of Rees Jones and Guy Rando's first ULI book on the subject, this is a valuable reference for all involved in the integration of golf and residences.*

Mulvoy, Mark, and Art Spander. *Golf: The Passion and the Challenge.* New York: Rutledge Books, 1977.

National Golf Foundation. "Golf Course Design and Construction." Jupiter, Fla.: National Golf Foundation, 1990.

Park, Willie, Jr. *The Game of Golf.* London: Longmans Green and Co., 1896. *This work contains a chapter on course design, one of the first ever written. Park is considered to be the doyen of contemporary golf architecture.*

Peper, George. *Golf Courses of the PGA Tour.* New York: Harry F. Abrams, 1986.

Phillips, Patrick L. *Developing with Recreational Amenities: Golf, Tennis, Skiing, Marinas.* Washington D.C.: Urban Land Institute, 1986.

Pira, Edward. *A Guide to Golf Course Irrigation System Design and Drainage.* Chelsea, Mich.: Ann Arbor Press, 1997.

Price, Charles. *The American Golfer*. New York: Random House, 1964, and Stamford, CT: Classics of Golf, 1987.

———. *The World of Golf*. New York: Random House, 1962.

Price, Robert. *Scotland's Golf Courses*. Aberdeen, Scotland: Aberdeen University Press, 1989. *Addressing the geology of their landforms, this book describes courses in the homeland of golf. With the playing fields of the game occupying expanding acreage worldwide, along with our increasing ability to modify land forms by moving earth, this book is "required reading."*

Robertson, James K. *St. Andrews—Home of Golf*. St. Andrews, Fife, Scotland: J & G Innes, 1967.

Rochester, Eugene W. *Landscape Irrigation Design*. St. Joseph, Mich.: American Society of Agricultural Engineers (ASAE), 1995.

Ross, Donald A. *Golf Has Never Failed Me*. Chelsea, Mich.: Sleeping Bear Press, 1996. *Written long ago by one who hailed from the Scottish links to become the preeminent course architect in the United States, the manuscript was located by golf architect David Gordon, who gave it to the ASGCA, which in turn undertook to sponsor its publication with Ronald E. Whitten as editor.*

Ryde, Peter, D. M. A. Steele, and H. W. Wind. *Encyclopedia of Golf*. New York: Viking Press, 1975.

Shackelford, Geoff. *The Captain*. Chelsea, Mich.: Sleeping Bear Press, 1997. *The definitive work concerning George C. Thomas, golf course architect, rose breeder, and author of* Golf Architecture in America. *It is another of those valuable books that outline careers of distinguished golf architects.*

———. *Masters of the Links*. Chelsea, Mich.: Sleeping Bear Press, 1997. Essays by golf architects Mackenzie, Tillinghast, Hunter, Macdonald, Crenshaw, Dye, and Doak.

Sheehan, Lawrence. *A Passion for Golf*. New York: Clarkson Potter, 1994.

Steel, Donald. *Classic Golf Links of England, Scotland, Wales and Ireland*. Gretna, La: Pelican Publishing, 1993. *Written by a prominent golf architect and writer, this work is significant to the art form.*

Strawn, John. *Driving the Green*. New York: Harper Collins, 1991. *A descriptive non-fiction work detailing the trials and tribulations of an owner and his architect, the celebrated Arthur Hills, in bringing the development of Iron Horse Golf and Country Club in Florida to a successful conclusion. Having spent months on the project before and during construction, Strawn, a historian and former Reed College professor, produced a realistic, stranger-than-fiction account of what is involved in course planning, permit acquisition, and construction.*

Sutton, Martin H. F. (ed.). *Golf Course Design, Construction and Upkeep*. Reading, England: Sutton & Sons, 1950.

Sutton, Martin H. F., ed. *The Book of the Links*. London: W. H. Smith & Sons, 1912.

Taylor, Dawson. *St. Andrews, Cradle of Golf*. London: A. S. Barnes & Co., 1976.

Tillinghast, A. W. *The Course Beautiful*. Warren, N.J.: Treewolf Productions, 1995. Compiled, designed, and edited by R. C. Wolffe, Jr., and R. S. Treebus, with a foreword by Rees Jones and research by A. F. Wolffe, *this informative book includes Tillinghast's articles and letters together with photography of his golf holes and plans.*

Thomas, George C. *Golf Architecture in America.* Chelsea, Mich.: Sleeping Bear Press, 1997. *A beautiful reprint of the original work.*

———. *Golf Architecture in America: Its Strategy and Construction.* Los Angeles: Times-Mirror Press, 1927, and Far Hills, N.J.: USGA Rare Book Collection, 1990. *Regarded as the American classic on course design, this book has inspired generations of designers and writers.*

Tufts, Richard S. *The Scottish Invasion.* Pinehurst, N.C.: Pinehurst Publishers, 1962.

Tulloch, W. W. *The Life of Old Tom Morris.* London: Werner, Laurie, 1908, and Far Hills, N.J.: USGA Rare Book Collection, 1992.

United States Golf Association. *Golf: The Greatest Game.* New York: Harper Collins, 1994. *An anthology by persons widely known in the world of golf, this book celebrates the first 100 years of the game in the United States. "The Architects Vision," by Tom Doak, must rank among the most visionary works on design. Another chapter, by John Strawn, outlines the history of the USGA, an important subject for those practicing course architecture.*

Ward-Thomas, Pat, Herbert Warren Wind, Charles Price, and Peter Thomson. *The World Atlas of Golf.* New York: Random House, 1976. *With a foreword by Alistair Cooke, written by a team of acclaimed golf writers, and superbly illustrated, this book ranks among the most beautiful and informative writings related to course design.*

Wethered, H. N., and T. Simpson. *The Architectural Side of Golf.* London: Longmans Green & Co., 1929; second edition, titled *Design for Golf,* London, 1952, and Grant Books, Droitwich, Worcestershire, England: 1995. *Regarded by some as the British classic on the subject, this work is now available as a handsome facsimile with an introduction by renowned American designer Arthur Hills. The facsimile includes several of Simpson's famous ink sketches with color washes, and some black-and-white sketches of individual greens, so detailed that a golfer might say "I can read that green."*

Wind, Herbert Warren. *Following Through.* New York: Tickner & Fields, 1985.

———. *The Story of American Golf,* 3d ed. New York: Alfred A. Knopf, 1975.

———. *Herbert Warren Wind's Golf Book.* New York: Simon and Schuster, 1971.

Wind, Herbert Warren, ed. *The Complete Golfer.* New York: Simon and Schuster, 1954.

Glossary

With the apparently limitless expansion of golf, the vocabulary related to the design, development, and construction of its playing fields continues to expand. This glossary includes words, terms, and shoptalk that developers, designers, constructors, and others in the allied professions encounter. Publications referred to are listed in the bibliography.

Abutment The support on the ends of a bridge or its arches.

Accessibility rate The total population in a defined area expressed as the number of persons per 18-hole course. (*Authority:* Gimmy and Benson, 1992.)

Acid fertilizers Fertilizers with acid residues that cause increasingly acid soils.

Acid soil A soil that is acid in the uppermost or A horizon. Strictly speaking, this is a soil with a pH of less than 7. In shoptalk it refers to a soil pH of 6 or lower.

Acre foot A volume with an area of 1 acre and a depth of 1 foot. An acre inch equals 27,225 gallons.

Aeration of soil (1) The exchange of soil and atmospheric air, or the process that reduces carbon dioxide in soil and raises its oxygen content. (2) The practice of punching holes in turf to enhance this exchange.

Aerial golf Playing the ball through the air as contrasted with bump-and-run golf, which involves bouncing the ball off topographical features in an effort to direct it.

Aggregate Sand, gravel, soil, or stone screened or washed to attain a specific particle size.

Aggregation (soil) The binding of soil particles into a granule.

Agronomy The science of soil management and crop production. Turfgrass science is a branch, with turfgrass the crop.

Agrostologist A botanist who specializes in grasses. Until World War II, "turfgrass science" was often called agrostology.

Alkali soil A soil containing sodium (exchangeable) in sufficient quantities to inhibit plant growth. An alkali soil has a pH of 8.5 or higher.

Alps A classic golf hole, namely the 17th at Prestwick Golf Club in Scotland, that has been widely adapted. One such adaptation is the 3rd at the National Golf Links of America.

Amendment (soil) Material such as organic matter, added to soil to change its physical properties, as contrasted with fertilizer, added to change it chemically.

Angle of repose The angle between the horizontal and the slope where soil has reached equilibrium following downward and outward settlement.

Anion A negatively charged soil particle.

Approach The area from which a medium to short shot to the green is possible.

Approach courses   Par 3 layouts with no tees. This allows golfers to select their own teeing positions.

Apron (or collar)   The area, a mower's width or wider, around a putting surface.

Aquascaping   The landscaping of shorelines with aquatic vegetation, or the creation of wetlands in which aquatic vegetation is introduced. Objectives include enhancement of water quality and aesthetics, as well as creation of habitats for numerous species.

Artificial turf   Artificial materials simulating turfgrass.

Backfill   Soil or other material used to refill excavated areas.

Background plan   *See* Base map.

Bail-out area   An area provided to receive the ball if a golfer decides not to try for the primary target.

Balance   A word used in regard to nines of equal playing interest, or to the distribution of holes in regard to difficulty.

Balls (golf)   The feather or featherie was the first widely used golf ball, although less widely used boxwood balls were in existence before it. The featherie was replaced by the gutta percha around 1850. In turn, it was replaced by the Haskell or rubber-cored ball around 1900. Scores of changes have occurred since then.

Bank run gravel or sand   A mixture of gravel, sand, and fines existing in a bank.

Bank yardage   The volume of undisturbed material in a bank or pit, as contrasted with the volume of loose materials after loading.

Base exchange capacity   *See* Cation exchange capacity (CEC).

Base map   A scaled topographical map or background plan showing existing features.

Basin or cavity   The rimmed depression made to hold gravel, sand, and root zone mix layers required to satisfy USGA specifications for green construction.

Bay and cape   *See* Bunker.

Bench mark (B.M.)   A designated geographic point usually located by coordinate system or GPS (Global Positioning System) to which other measurements, such as elevations, refer.

Bench terrace   A flat area existing on or notched into a hillside.

Bend (or pivot)   The point at which a hole turns right or left.

Bents   Fine-textured grasses of the *Agrostis* species, widely used on golf courses. On the links of Scotland caddies refer to coarse grasses of several species in the rough as bents.

Bentonite   A plastic clay that swells when wet; used to seal ponds.

Berm   A ridge of earth, as contrasted with a mound.

Bid   A firm price provided by a bidder, not subject to negotiation. *See* Proposal

Bioengineering   The combining of engineering concepts with biology. An example is protection of stream banks with both vegetation and structures.

Bite-off hole   *See* Heroic design.

Black layer   A black-colored layer that develops in the upper inches of a putting surface under anaerobic conditions.

Blade   (1) The part of an excavator, often a bulldozer, that excavates and pushes earth. (2) The cutting blade of a lawn mower. (3) The flat portion of a grass leaf.

Blend (seed)   Two or more cultivars of the same species mixed together, as contrasted with a mixture, which contains two or more species.

Blender   A machine used to mix soil, sand, and organic materials.

Blind hole or shot   If players cannot see the landing area or green from where they are playing, the hole is considered blind. It is partially blind when only the flagstick is visible.

Borrow area or pit   An area from which topsoil or fill is generated for usage elsewhere.

Boulder   A rock that cannot be easily lifted by one person. When extra charges for ledge and boulder removal are called for, the extra charges are defined by measurement.

(The) Box   A contractor's term to describe the cleared area of a hole, while the corridor or envelope is the entire area of the hole, cleared or uncleared.

Breaking the back   Stabilizing a peat soil by adding fill to a depth beyond which the peat compresses no further.

Breather   An easy hole, provided to reduce pressure on the golfer.

Broom (Scotch)   *See* Links plants.

Bulk Density   The mass of dry soil in relation to the bulk volume. One study found it irrelevant in predicting performance of root zone mixes.

Bulkhead   A wooden, concrete, or stone structure erected to stabilize embankments or for aesthetic purposes.

Bump and run   *See* Aerial golf.

Bunker   According to the rules of golf a bunker is a hazard with a prepared area, often a hollow, with sand or grass. (The word *trap* is not officially recognized.) The following terms are used in relation to *bunker*.

> **Bay**   Sand between the capes of grass on sides or faces of bunkers
> **Cape**   Grass tongues between bays
> **Face**   The bay of sand on the greenside of the bunker
> **Fan wall or fan-faced bunker**   One with railroad tie walls or equivalent
> **Flash**   A narrow bay or face of sand protruding upward
> **Grass wall or grass-faced bunker**   One with grass walls
> **Sand wall or sand-faced bunker**   One with sand walls

Burn   Scottish word for *stream.*

Butts   *See* Land tile.

Calcarious soil   A soil containing sufficient calcium carbonate to be detected by hydrochloric acid (fizzing).

Calcined clays and aggregates   Stable granular minerals prepared at high temperature for use as soil amendments.

Capacity (course)   The number of rounds a course can comfortably accommodate in a day.

Capacity utilization of a course   The number of rounds played on a course divided by the number projected. A private club may express this by the number of members divided by the desired number.

Cape Hole   A par 4 or 5 with a "bite-off" tee shot and an approach to a green perched above an intimidating hazard. The 18th at Pebble Beach or the 5th at the Mid-Ocean.

Capes and bays   *See* Bunker.

Capillary water   Water held in small pores of a soil under tension. The water can move upward.

Carbon-nitrogen ratio   The ratio by weight of organic carbon to total nitrogen. Materials with a high C-N ratio reduce availability of nitrogen.

"Cardiac" hole   A steeply graded hole that is strenuous to walk.

Carry   The distance a ball flies in the air. Carry is used as a noun or a verb.

Casual water   The Rules of Golf define this as "any temporary accumulation of water on the course visible before or after the player takes his stance, and is not in a water hazard."

Catch basin   A structure into which surface and subsurface drainage is led, and from where it is piped away. May also include a sieve device to catch bulky materials.

Cations   Positively charged soil particles, including calcium, magnesium, sodium, potassium, ammonium, and hydrogen.

Cation exchange capacity (CEC)   The total quantity of cations a soil can adsorb, or the total exchangeable cations a soil can adsorb expressed as milliequivalents per 100 grams of soil.

Cavity   *See* Basin.

CC&Rs   The abbreviation for Covenants, Conditions, and Restrictions agreed to in a formal agreement.

Channels   Drainage ditches, swales, and other depressions through which surface water flows.

Check dam   A small dam constructed in a stream to reduce energy and velocity and to enhance deposition of sediment.

Chemigation   The application of chemicals through the irrigation system.

Chip   A short run-up or aerial shot.

Chipping or fringe swale   An area adjoining the putting surface, often in a depression. Mowed to collar height, it permits a putt or chip.

Chiseling   Loosening topsoil or subsoil with a chisel plow without turning the soil.

Chocolate drop   A mound rounded in the form of a chocolate drop.

Choker layer   Shoptalk for the coarse sand layer between gravel and root zone mix in the USGA green.

Classic golf hole   A term used to describe any renowned hole, but restricted in design circles to famous holes that have been widely adapted to other courses. Examples are Redan, Alps, Cape, and Eden.

Clay   Mineral soil with particle size less than 0.002 mm.

Clear cutting   The removal of all or nearly all trees, as contrasted with selective clearing, which implies leaving most trees.

Clerk of the works   The person on a construction site responsible for records. The term is also used to describe the person on-site responsible for the project.

Clubs   Traditional names and comparisons to present-day clubs. *Note:* The jigger could be compared to the modern 3 iron, although it was not exactly a mid-mashie. A baffy (not listed) was a wooden club used in the gutta percha era that flattened grass as it swept the ball off the turf.

1 Wood	Driver or bulger
2 Wood	Brassie
3 Wood	Spoon
4 Wood	Cleek
1 Iron	Driving iron
2 Iron	Mid-iron
3 Iron	Mid-mashie or jigger
4 Iron	Mashie iron
5 Iron	Mashie
6 Iron	Spade mashie
7 Iron	Mashie niblick
8 Iron	Lofter
9 Iron	Niblick
Putter	Putter

Coffer dam   A temporary wall placed in a wet area to prevent water entering the area as work proceeds.

Collar   *See* Apron.

Con Docs   An abbreviation for Construction Documents.

Conform line   The edge of grading operations.

Constructor   The contractor or other person building the course or feature.

Contour interval   The difference in elevation between adjacent contour lines.

Contour line   A line joining an accumulation of points all at the same elevation about a given datum, bench mark, or elevation.

Contour mowing   An undulating line between rough and fairway, as contrasted with a straight line.

Cool-season grasses   Grasses that thrive in cool regions. Major golf course species include bluegrass, bentgrass, fescues, and ryegrass.

Corduroy Logs placed under fill to prevent settling. Geotextiles are more commonly used today.

Coring (1) Aeration of established turf by removing soil cores. (2) The removal of 12 to 18 inches of soil from a green, in order to replace it with USGA-specific layers or other soils.

Corridor or envelope The total area in which the golf hole is planned and placed. Unlike "the box," it includes treed roughs and buffer zones.

Cost plus A contract whereby the contractor is reimbursed for the cost of his or her work plus a set percentage or set fee.

Country club A club providing facilities such as swimming and tennis in addition to golf, whereas a golf club is restricted to golf.

Course rating (USGA) The evaluation of the playing difficulty of a course for scratch golfers under normal course and weather conditions. It is expressed as strokes taken to one decimal point and is based on yardage and other obstacles to the extent that they affect the scoring ability of the scratch golfer.

Cover crop A temporary vegetative cover, planted to protect soil from erosion in the period before a permanent cover is established. *See* Green manure crop.

Critical path The sequencing of the entire project. It is usually determined before work starts on the ground.

Cross bunker A bunker running at almost right angles across a hole.

Crowned green or tee A green or tee with grades pitching off the surface and downward in at least two directions.

Cultivar (variety) A variety of a species that retains its distinguishing features when reproduced by seed or vegetatively.

Culvert A conduit to carry water.

Cup or hole According to the Rules of Golf, the hole shall be 4¼ inches (108 mm) in diameter and at least 4 inches (100 mm) deep, and if lined, the lining shall be at least 1 inch (25 mm) below the putting surface, with an outside diameter not exceeding 4½ inches (108 mm).

Curtain drain An open or subsurface drain installed to intercept surface or subsurface water before it reaches lower areas.

Cut and fill Lowering a hill and filling adjacent depressions with the soil. May also refer to removing material from one area to fill another at a greater distance.

Daily fee course A privately owned facility open to the public for a green fee. When memberships are also available, the facility is termed **semiprivate.** If the course is owned by a public entity, it is termed **municipal,** although it is still a daily fee course.

Datum A point of reference from which other elevations on a site are measured.

Dead-air green A green hemmed in by trees or hills that inhibit air circulation.

Desalinization The removal of salts from soil or water.

Desiccation The complete drying of plants following wilting.

Detention pond   A pond structured to detain water and then release it under control, as contrasted with a retention pond, which retains water for a period and then releases it by overflow.

Dewatering   Removal of water by pumping, channeling, or evaporation from an area to be worked.

Divot   A piece of turf dislodged by a golfer's club.

Dogleg   An obvious bend, right or left, on a golf hole.

Dormant seeding   The sowing of seed late in autumn, with the intention that it not germinate until the following spring.

Double green   A green played from two different holes.

Double penalty   Most often this refers to a situation in which a player recovering from a bunker also has a tree to contend with.

Dragline   An excavator with a bucket attached by cable, allowing the bucket to be pulled toward the operator.

Draw   A controlled right-to-left golf shot; unlike a hook or pull because it is made deliberately.

Dredge   Equipment used to excavate or deepen a pond.

Driving range   A floodlit, commercial venture with artificial teeing surfaces. *See* Practice fairway.

Dugout pond (dug pond)   A pond constructed by excavating, as contrasted with one created by damming.

Eagle   The score of two strokes less than par for a hole.

Eden Hole   The par 3 eleventh or High Hole (Home) on the Old Course. Playing into a headwind off the Eden River across Hill or Strath Bunkers, one tries to stop short of the pin at the elevated green to avoid a treacherous downhill putt.

"Eighteen stakes on a Sunday afternoon"   A facetious expression used in the early years of golf in America to describe laying out a golf course.

Electrical conductivity   A measurement used to gauge the degree of salinity of water or soil.

Elephant's nose or mound   A uniquely shaped mound found on layouts of Raynor, Banks, Thompson, and other courses.

Endophitic fungi   Fungi present in some species or varieties that control insects and other fungi.

"English parks"   Treed roughs, grassed and mowed to create the refined look of English parklands.

Entrance   The area between bunkers, mounds, water, or roughs that allows one to run the ball over the ground and onto the putting green.

Envelope   *See* Corridor.

Ephemeral stream   A stream above the water table that erupts as a direct and immediate result of precipitation, as contrasted with a steady-flowing stream from a spring.

Equity or nonequity club   A private club where members own or do not own a share of the facility. The term "**proprietary facility**" is also used.

Erosion   The removal of soil by water, wind or gravity.

Esker   A ridge of gravel or sand deposited by a glacial stream.

Eutrophication   The aging of ponds and lakes as aquatic plants become prolific and reduce the oxygen content of the water. It is accelerated by runoff containing nitrogen and phosphorus.

Evapotranspiration (ET) rate   A measure of the water lost by evaporation from the soil and transpiration from vegetation. *See* Transpiration.

Executive or precision course   A short course, generally less than 5,000 yards in length, with many par 3s and a total par seldom exceeding 60.

Face bunker   *See* Bunker.

Facility   According to the NGF, this is a complex containing one or more golf courses.

Fade   A controlled shot from left to right; unlike a slice or push because it is deliberate.

Fairgreen   A term for fairway and approach; rarely used today.

Fairway   The refined area of turfgrass starting in front of the tee and proceeding to the green.

Fallowing   A practice of leaving ground unvegetated with several objectives, including reduction of weeds. The practice has been abandoned in golf construction because it aggravated erosion.

Feather or featherie   *See* Balls (golf).

Fertigation   The application of fertilizers through the irrigation system.

Fertilizer ratios   The three figures on a fertilizer bag that provide the percentages of nitrogen (N) available, phosphoric acid (P_2O_5), and water soluble potash (K_2O) in the fertilizer. In a 100-pound bag of 10-6-4 fertilizer, there are 10 pounds of nitrogen, 6 pounds of phosphoric acid, and 4 pounds of potash.

Field capacity   The moisture, expressed as percentage, in a soil 48 hours after a drenching by rain or irrigation; expressed as percentage of oven-dried soil.

Fines   Very fine sand, smaller than 0.01 mm plus clay and silt particles.

Finish grade   The final grade as required by plans and specifications.

Finish surface   The finished soil surface, free of stones, debris, sharp humps, and hollows.

Flagstick   According to the Rules of Golf, a moveable, straight indicator with or without bunting, centered in a hole to show its position.

Flash   *See* Bunker.

Floodplain   A level area flooded periodically.

Flow   The movement of players, riding and walking.

Fluffing   Loosening a seedbed to make it suitable for seed germination.

Flume   A channel constructed with wood, asphalt, or concrete to carry flowing water.

Flusher   A device at the upper end of a tile system, permitting water under pressure to be forced through the tile.

Focal spots   A real estate term for areas that command higher prices because of scenery or views of play.

Focus group interview   A market research technique whereby a group of potential customers are questioned on specific subjects (Gimmy and Benson, 1992).

Force account   A method of construction whereby an owner pays for invoiced labor, materials, and equipment directly.

"Form follows function"   An architectural axiom of profound significance to course architecture. With the function dictating the form, for example, a short approach shot may call for a small, severely contoured putting surface.

Fragipan   A compact soil horizon that interferes with water and root penetration.

Freeboard   The vertical distance from the designed high-water level of a pond to the top of the surrounding embankment.

Freeze road   A haul road established for winter construction by removing snow to permit freezing of the soil to a depth sufficient to support heavy equipment.

French drain   Subdrainage with no tile, such as a trench filled with stone, sand, or other porous material. The term varies by region. In Quebec it refers to use of flat stones erected to provide an underground conduit for water.

Frequency of cut   The number of blades in the reel of a mower.

Fresno scraper   *See* Hand scraper.

Fringe swale   *See* Chipping swale.

Front-end loader   A tractor with a loader up front.

Furze   *See* Links plants.

Gabions   Galvanized wire baskets that are filled with stones.

Georgia bushel   *See* Industry Standard Bale (ISB).

Geotextiles (geosynthetics)   A group of widely used polymer products with an increasing role in golf course construction.

Golf car and golf cart   A golf car is a two-seated powered vehicle, whereas a golf cart is a single bag carrier pulled by hand or powered.

Golf and country club (G&CC)   A term used in Canada, and to a limited extent in the United States, for a country club providing golf and other amenities.

Golf club   A club providing golf only.

Golf club   (equipment) *See* Clubs.

Golf Course Superintendents Association of America (GCSAA)   The organization of professional people who maintain and enhance golf courses.

Golfing grounds   Used in reference to a golf course for a short period in history, following the use of "the green," a term that was abandoned in the 1890s.

Golf participation   A National Golf Foundation term for the annual percentage of the population, five years of age or older, that has played golf at least once in the year surveyed.

Golf revenue multiplier (GRM)   This figure equals sales price divided by direct golf revenue from green fees, car rental, and practice fairway (Gimmy and Benson, 1992).

Golf values   Characteristics that attract players to a layout: e.g., playability, beauty, conditioning, and traditions.

Grade stake   A stake indicating a proposed grade.

Gradient, grade, or slope   The relation between the grade line to the horizontal, expressed in percentage or ratio of horizontal measurement to vertical. Thus, 4% equals 1 foot vertical difference in 25 feet horizontal distance. It is also expressed in the angle in degrees between horizontal and grade line.

Grain   The direction in which grass blades lie on a putting surface.

Grass bunker   A depressed grassed area; a hazard only when designated as such.

Grassed waterway   A channel with sides, and the floor, protected from erosion by grass.

Grass-faced bunker   *See* Bunker.

Gravel   Particles of rock 2 mm in size and greater.

Gravel layer   The gravel blanket under the topmix of a USGA green.

Gravitational water   Water that moves into, through, and out of soil under the influence of gravity.

Green   Until the last decade of the nineteenth century the entire course was known as "the green." Hence, *greenkeeper, green chairman,* and *green fees* have no *s.* (*See* Putting green)

Green chairman   The member of a club elected or appointed to chair the committee responsible for the course.

Green fee   The fee charged to play a round. Until World War II it permitted the golfer to play all day.

Green fee multiplier (GFM)   Used in the sales comparison approach. Gimmy and Benson (1992) state that it equals the sales price of the course divided by the annual number of rounds times the average green fee.

Greenkeeper   The term long used for the person responsible for maintenance of a golf course. Today that person is more often called the superintendent or golf course manager. However, the term used in much of the golfing world outside the United States is *head greenkeeper.*

Green manure crop   A crop such as winter rye, buckwheat, or a legume that is plowed under to physically improve the soil. The practice of green manuring golf courses prior to seeding has almost disappeared, although cover crops to control erosion are still widely used prior to seeding permanent grasses.

Green speed   The distance in feet that a ball rolls from a stimpmeter.

Greensward or sward   A grass-covered soil.

Ground covers   Vegetation, not necessarily grass, used to cover unmowable areas that are out of play on a golf course.

Ground under repair   A clearly marked area from which players can pick up and drop balls without penalty.

Grout   A sealing mixture of cement and water, used in construction of earthen dams to increase their strength.

Grow-in   The period from the time seed is sown until the golf course is playable.

Grubbing   Removing roots and stones with a root rake attached to a bulldozer.

Guesstimate   Shop talk for an estimate involving guesswork but often needed in early stages of course development. It is intended to be more accurate than a "ballpark" figure.

Gutta percha ball   The "guttie"; the ball developed around the mid-nineteenth century and used until the end of that century exerted an enormous influence on the increasing popularity of golf because it was more durable and less costly than the feather ball that preceded it, and it often flew farther as well. *See* Balls (golf).

Halfway house   A shelter, sometimes ornate, where refreshments are served and rest room facilities are available.

Hand level   A level held in the hand to ascertain grades.

Hand scraper   A steel box originally pulled by horses or another power source. Handles on the box are manipulated by a person to fill and dump it. Fresno and slip scrapers were hand scrapers.

Hands-on   A shop term for work where execution is closely controlled by the person in charge.

Hardpan   A hard, sometimes impermeable, subsoil.

Hard water   Water that holds mineral matter in solution.

Harrow   An agricultural implement used in preparation of seedbeds to break lumps of soil.

Haskell or hard-cored ball   The successor to the gutta percha. It flew farther and called for longer holes. *See* Balls (golf).

Haul road   A temporary road installed for hauling materials during construction.

Head   The height of water in feet above a specific level. Height can be converted to pounds of pressure per square inch by multiplying by 0.4335. Pounds of pressure can be converted to height by multiplying by 2.30.

Heather   *See* Links plants.

Heaving   The breaking of plant roots by the alternate freezing and thawing of soil.

Heavy metals   Dense metals, including but not limited to cadmium, cobalt, chromium, copper, and zinc. Toxic to turfgrass under certain conditions, they still may be needed by plants as minor elements.

Heroic design   Golf design that provides hazards placed on diagonals to the shots, allowing players to "bite-off" what they choose. The more is bitten off, the more advantage there is for the next shot. Designers point out that this is intrinsically a blend of strategic and penal design.

Highest and best use   A term designating use of land to achieve the highest return.

Hogback   A ridge more or less in the middle of a green or fairway that propels or nurses golf balls right or left.

Holding qualities   The extent to which a green or landing area holds a golf shot.

Hole   (1) The architect's composition including tee, rough, fairway, bunkers, and green. (2) The 4¼ inch-diameter hole in the green to which the ball is targeted.

Hook   A stroke starting right of target and finishing to the left.

Horizons (soil)   (1) Parallel layers of soil arising from soil-forming processes. Often there are three horizons, labeled A, B, and C.

Humic acid and humus   Terms for the end products of organic composition.

Hydraulic fill   Fill moved by water pressure.

Hydro mulching   The application of mulch with a hydroseeder.

Hydroseeding   The sowing of seed by water under pressure.

Hydrosprigging   The sowing of sprigs by water under pressure.

Impervious soil   A soil through which roots, air, and water do not penetrate.

In   *See* Out and In.

Industry Standard Bale (ISB)   Technically, a bushel holds 1.24 cubic feet of Bermuda grass sprigs. The ISB is 0.4 cubic feet, or one third of the standard U.S. measurement. ISB is also referred to as the Georgia bushel. The Texas bushel is the same as the United States bushel.

Infiltration   The flow of liquid *into* a soil or sand, as contrasted with percolation, which is the flow *through or down*.

Integrated Pest Management (IPM)   The use of pesticides in conjunction with management practices. Integrated Management is a broader term involving turfgrass quality with cost benefits, public health, and environmental quality (Balogh and Walker, 1993).

Intercepting drain   *See* Curtain drain.

Intermediate layer   The coarse sand layer placed between gravel and the root zone mix in a USGA green.

Internal Drainage   (1) The drainage by gravity within a soil. (2) Drainage within the course, as contrasted with drainage of water onto and off the course.

Invert   The inside bottom of a pipe that determines the level of a pond.

Iron Byron   A machine for measuring the liveliness of a golf ball. Located at Golf House, Far Hills, N.J. it is used to determine if a ball meets the specifications of the ruling bodies of golf. Frank W. Thomas is the technical director.

Kame   A ridge of gravel or sand deposited by glacial action.

Landform   The natural form of the land; examples include linksland, flat, or mountainous.

Landing area   The area of a golf hole where tee shots land. Two landing areas are needed on par 5s.

Land poor   The financial condition arising from ownership of excess acreage that is not sellable because of the market, its designation as a wetland or an archeological site, or other circumstances, for which taxes are still assessed. Sites with an overabundance of unusable buildings are called building poor.

Land tile   Clay pipe with openings (butts) between its lengths.

Layering in the soil   Undesirable layers arising from construction or maintenance practices.

Lay-up   A shot resulting from a player deliberately playing short of the target.

Leaching   Removal of plant food elements and other materials in solution or suspension from the soil.

Length of a course   The sum of the lengths of the 18 holes.

Length of a hole   The distance measured horizontally from the middle of the tee to the center of the green, with doglegs and bends measured as the architect intended them to be played.

Lie   The stationary position of a ball in play on a course, described in terms of the nature of the ground.

Light soil   A coarse-textured soil.

Links   (1) Undulating land sparsely covered with grazed fescues, broom, and other links plants found along the coastlines of the British Isles. (2) A golf course located in dune country, generally treeless and sometimes with a large body of water nearby. This term has been used by Donald Ross and others in alternate ways, even to describe an inland course.

Links plants   Species identified with the roughs on the links of the British Isles. They include the following, which have been introduced to links courses and other courses far from Scotland.

   Broom (*Cytisus* species)
   Gorse (*Viex europaeus*) Also known as firze or whins
   Heather (*Cerica* species) A low-growing member of the heath family
   Marram or sea reed grass (*Psamma arenaria*)
   Sea lyme grass (*Elynus arenarius*) The word *bent* (no connection to bentgrass) is used in the British Isles, often by caddies, to describe stands of sea lyme and marram grass with fescues growing in or nearby

Lip   (1) The vertical edge surrounding a bunker. (2) The edge of the hole on a green.

Loader, front- or rear-end   A machine that excavates and dumps in front, or at the rear.

Long-Range Plan   A master plan prepared for major work on an established course when the work is to be phased in over several years.

Lysimeter   A device to collect and measure the quantity and quality of leachate draining from a soil.

Macroclimate   The climatic conditions that prevail in the general area. Also *see* Microclimate.

Manhole   A catch basin large enough to permit a person to work in it.

Master plan   A plan prepared for developing a new golf course or altering an existing one.

Matched set of clubs   A set of clubs designated by numbering, a system introduced in 1920 to replace the naming of clubs.

Maxwell rolls   Severe contours designed by Perry Maxwell during the Depression on greens already in existence.

Mechanical rake   A rake pulled by a tractor to remove stones and debris and level the soil.

Microclimate   In agriculture the term may refer to the air space adjoining the soil surface. On golf courses it refers to limited areas where temperature, light, or humidity differs from the prevailing climate of the course. (See macroclimate.)

Micronutrients   *See* Nutrients.

Minimalism   The moving of minimum quantities of earth to shape a golf course.

Minor elements   *See* Nutrients.

Mitigation   (1) The creation of wetlands on drylands to compensate for loss of wetlands elsewhere on-site. (2) Alleviation of the need to use wetlands. (3) Limited use of wetlands, e.g., allowing golfers to play across them.

Mixing   *See* Off-site and on-site mixing.

Mobilization   The assembling of a work crew and equipment on-site to execute construction. Acquiring bonds and insurance is sometimes included, as is establishing the field office, sanitary facilities, and crew parking.

Mole   A bullet- or egg-shaped steel ball pulled behind a subsoiler or other device to create temporary drainage channels in the subsoil.

Mound   A small hill, also referred to as a chocolate drop, hillock, hummock, or mogul.

Movement   The representation of motion achieved by artistic sculpting of mounds, bunkers, and other features.

Muck   *See* Peats.

Mulch   Material placed over seed or seedlings to prevent erosion, retain moisture, and minimize temperature fluctuations.

Municipal facility   A facility owned by a public entity such as a municipality, county, or state.

Nap   *See* Grain.

National Resources Conservation Service (NRCS)   The 1995 successor to the Soil Conservation Service of the USDA, NRCS provides technical soil services to land users.

Ninety Degree Rule   An unofficial rule requiring players in golf cars to cross fairways only at right angles once they leave pathways.

Nutrients (macro and micro)   Nitrogen, phosphorus, and potassium are the macro elements, those most needed by plants. Micronutrients, or trace elements, are those needed by plants less often. They include iron, sulfur, magnesium, calcium, boron, copper, zinc, molybdenum, and others.

Off-site and on-site mixing   The preparation of root zone mixes off or on the green or other feature that is being constructed. Mixing on-site is accomplished with a rotary plow, and off-site mixing involves a blender.

(The) Old Course   In the world of golf this is the Old Course at St. Andrews, Scotland.

Organic matter   The residues of plants and animals in soils in varying degrees of decomposition.

Out and In   Until the 1890s many courses proceeded outward for 9 holes (Out) and then back for 9 holes (In or Home). Out and In now refer to the first and second nines.

Outfalls   A term for drain outlets.

Overseeding   (1) Sowing cool-season grasses on warm-season greenswards to provide green color in winter. (2) Seeding established swards to convert them to another grass. (3) Seeding thin areas of turf without turning the existing sod.

Pan (equipment)   (1) A scraper that transports earth (*see* Scraper). (2) A compacted layer of subsoil.

Parkland   (1) Land located in inland sparsely treed areas and carpeted with grass. (2) A designation for courses built on such land. *See* "English parks".

Particle size   The diameter of particles in soil, sand, or fine gravel.

Pea gravel or pea stone   Gravel with a particle size of ¼ to ⅜ inch.

Peats   Partially decomposed organic material of several types, including

> **Sedimentary peat** — little or no value as a soil conditioner
> **Muck soil** — decomposed peat mixed with mineral soil but with limited value as a soil conditioner
> **Reed sedge peat** — derived from sedges with some value as a soil conditioner
> **Peat humus** — a decomposed peat derived from reed sedge peat
> **Moss peat,** also called **sphagnum moss peat** — a valuable conditioner

Penal design   Golf design characterized by compulsory carries over hazards with no alternative routes provided.

Perched water table   A layer of water above the water table, intrinsic to the USGA method of green construction, where water moving downward stops at a coarser layer. Here it forms a reservoir that is tapped by grass roots. As more head develops following addition of more water, the system dumps, with water proceeding to tile lines.

Percolation   The movement of water downward in soil.

Permeability   The capacity of a soil to transmit water, other fluids, and gases and the ease that roots pass through it.

pH   Degree of acidity, with pH 7 as neutral, lower than 7 acid, and higher than 7 alkaline. Technically, pH is the logarithm of the reciprocal of hydrogen ion concentration. *See* Reaction (soil).

Pitch and run   A short lob shot though the air, followed by a roll along the ground.

Pivot point   *See* Bend.

Plant protection materials   A new term for *pesticides*.

Plant succession   The process whereby an area is covered successively by different plant communities. Succession in turf is influenced by managerial practices.

Plateau green   A green located on a small plateau (natural or constructed).

Plowsole   A compacted layer or pan, often resulting from constant use of aerating equipment that has penetrated to a constant depth.

Plugging   (1) A golf ball becoming imbedded in the soil or sand. (2) A form of aeration.

Point drainage   The leading of underground or surface drainage to centrally located catch basins, from where it is tiled or pumped.

Pore space   The total space between particles in the soil, or the fraction of the soil between particles.

Porosity   The percentage of pore space in the total volume of a soil.

Postage stamp   A very small putting surface. The classic is the 8th green at Troon Golf Course in Scotland.

Practice fairway; practice area   Because driving ranges are not permitted in some jurisdictions, these are more appropriate terms at a golf course. *See* Driving range.

Practice green   A green provided for practice putting.

Prebid or Precontract meeting   A meeting held prior to contractors submitting bids or proposals.

Precision course   *See* Executive course.

Pregermination of seed   Treatment of seed by soaking in water or liquid fertilizer to hasten germination, often achieved by placing seed in a cheesecloth bag and soaking overnight. Hydroseeding contributes to pregermination.

Primary rough   The major grassed rough, not including intermediate and treed roughs.

Principles of art (design)   These include harmony, proportion, balance, rhythm, and emphasis.

Private facility   A facility open only to members.

Professional Golfers Association of America (PGA)   The enormously influential and dynamic association of professional golfers.

Profile (soil)   The vertical section of horizons A, B, and C above the underlying bedrock (D).

Profile grade   A surveyed line on ground or paper indicating cut and fill.

Proposal   A negotiable figure put forward to provide a price or a method for the work, as contrasted with a bid, which is not negotiable.

Proprietary facility   *See* Equity or nonequity club.

Pull   A shot going left of target, but not as far left as a hook.

Punch bowl   A green enclosed on four sides by mounds or berms.

Punch list   Shoptalk for a list prepared by the architect near the finish of construction to itemize unfinished work, or work not completed in accordance with specifications.

Pure live seed (PLS)   The percentage by weight of seed that is living and pure.

Push   A shot going right of the target, but not as far right as a slice.

Push-up greens   Shoptalk for greens constructed by returning unprepared topsoil to their surfaces.

Putting course   A course on which only a putter is used. It may include one large putting surface, or 9 or 18 ribbons of putting surface surrounded by longer grass.

Putting green   (1) According to the Rules of Golf, a putting green is all ground prepared for putting on a hole, or defined as such by the Committee. (2) A reference to the practice green.

Quicksand   An unstable subsoil resulting from upward pressure of water.

Reaction (soil)   The degree of acidity or alkalinity expressed as pH. For example:

Below pH 5.5, strongly to extremely acid
pH 5.6 to 6.0, medium acid
pH 6.1 to 6.5, slightly acid
pH 6.6 to 7.3, neutral
pH 7.4 to 8.4, mildly to moderately alkaline
pH 8.5 to 9, strongly to very strongly alkaline

Rebuilding or reconstructing   Major construction work on an established golf course.

Reclamation   Golf course construction on areas other than those under cultivation. Examples are reclamation of derelict land, the conversion of rocky land, and the removal of excess soluble salts from alkaline soils to allow growth of turfgrass.

Redan   The classic par 3 15th hole at North Berwick in Scotland, perhaps the most widely adapted hole in golf.

Redesign   The planning of major changes on an existing course, often including changes in routing.

Regulation eighteen "Full-length" 18-hole course, often 6,000 yards or longer, with the majority of holes being par 4s. Nowhere is it specifically defined.

Relief (landforms) Elevations and/or depressions on the land.

Relief map A map showing changes in elevation by contours, colors, shading or other means.

Remodeling Effecting moderate to radical changes in an existing golf course.

Remote rough Rough beyond the primary. *See* Rough.

Renovation (1) Includes reconstruction work beyond normal maintenance, but not rebuilding. An example is resodding an existing green. (2) Restoring an existing golf course to its original character. *See* Restoration.

Replating Shoptalk for replacing topsoil.

Restoration Reestablishing a hole to the concept of the original designer.

Retention pond *See* Detention pond.

Reversible course One that can be played in reverse, with greens opening from both directions. The Old Course at St. Andrews is reversible.

Revetment A wall graded backward into a slope, or a stacked sod wall as found on the links of Scotland.

Rhizome An underground stem that sends out roots, as contrasted with a stolon, which is above ground with roots at its nodes.

Riparian rights The rights of a land owner to use water on his or her own property.

Riprap Stones thrown together on pond and stream banks to reduce erosion.

Road hole The classic 17th hole on the Old Course at St. Andrews.

Rock picker A mechanical device for picking stones from seedbeds after boulders have been removed.

Root pruning (trees) Pruning roots that are encroaching on a greensward.

Root zone or topmix Specially prepared soil with specified sand, organic matter, and soil content.

Rough All of the golf course that is not green, fairway, tee, or hazard. It includes the primary rough, the intermediate or step cut rough, and tree or remote rough.

Route plan A graphic layout showing the routing of the 18 holes.

(The) Royal and Ancient Golf Club of St. Andrews, Scotland (R&A) Formed in 1754 as the St. Andrews Society of Golfers, this ruling body works with the USGA to keep the rules of golf simple and uniform, and changes to a minimum.

Rub of the green The Rules of Golf define it as "a ball in motion accidentally deflected or stopped by an outside agency."

Runoff The amount of water that flows over the surface of the soil.

Saline-alkaline soil A soil containing sodium and other soluble salts sufficient to severely damage plant growth.

Saline soil   A soil that is nonalkaline but still contains enough soluble salts to reduce turfgrass quality.

Sand   Mineral material of particle size 0.05 to 2.0 mm in diameter.

Sand-faced bunker   *See* Bunker.

Sand trap   Used in place of the preferred term **sand bunker.**

Schedule-rated pipe   *See* Standard Dimension Ratio.

Scotch broom   *See* Links plants.

Scraper   A machine for excavating, hauling, and placing soil.

Scraper, slip or Fresno   A light scraper widely used for transporting and shaping earth until World War II. It was often a scoop pulled by mules, horses, or early farm tractors and controlled by one or two workers at the handles who dumped the earth at the desired site. *See* Hand scraper.

Sediment ponds and basins   Constructed to trap sediment. A pond holds water year-round, whereas a basin is dry part of the year.

Seeders   Common types are *hydraulic,* which apply seed with water; *broadcast,* which sow seed through the air; *cultipacker,* which sow, cover, and roll the seed in one operation; and *drop,* which drop the seed.

Seed mixtures   Mixtures of two or more species. *See* Blend.

Seed purity   The percentage of seed of a particular species in a mixture.

Semiprivate facility   A facility with nonequity or equity membership permitting green fee play. *See* Daily fee course.

Shale   Layered rock formed by hardening of muds and clays.

Shank   A reference to hitting the ball with the extreme heel of the club, sending it off in an unintended direction.

Sheet erosion   *See* Erosion.

Short game   The game around the green including putting, chipping, pitching, and recoveries from bunkers.

Shotgun mixture   A seed mixture of several species popular for fairways and roughs before lightweight mowing and state-of-the-art irrigation were introduced, which provide a more controlled environment. Before that, nature selected the species most suited to the uncontrolled environment.

Shot values   This is an arbitrary term. Many golf architects define this term as "a reflection of what the hole demands, and the reward or punishment it metes out for good or bad shots," a definition put forward by golf architects Kenneth Killian and Richard Nugent.

Signature course   One designed by an acclaimed architect or one that the architect states is his masterpiece.

(The) Signature hole   The hole on the layout most widely recognized, or the one pictured on the score card. It is important to owner and architect for its public relations value.

Silt   Mineral soil with particle sizes from 0.05 down to 0.002 mm.

Sixty (60) hertz power   Shoptalk for what is known as 60 cycles in referring to electrical requirements.

Slice   A shot proceeding far right of the intended target, even though it may have started left.

Slip scraper   *See* Scraper.

Slope   *See* Gradient.

Slope rating (USGA)   Indicates the measurement of the relative playing difficulty of a course for players who are not scratch golfers. The lowest slope rating is 55, and the highest is 155. A golf course of standard difficulty would have a USGA slope rating of 113.

Snag   (1) Sharp branches, dead or living, that protrude from tree trunks. (2) A dead standing tree.

Soil conditioner   A material added to a soil to improve its physical condition, as contrasted with a fertilizer, which is added to provide mineral elements.

(The) Soil Conservation Service (SCS)   *See* National Resources Conservation Service (NRCS).

Soil horizon   A visible layer of soil with biological, chemical, and physical properties different from those of layers above and below it.

Soil map   A map showing soil types and their boundaries.

Soil profile   *See* Profile.

Soil series   NRCS describes a series as a group of soils similar in profile and horizons, developed from a type of parent material.

Soils, heavy   Inorganic soils with a high content of clays, silt, and very fine sands.

Soils, light   Inorganic soils with a high content of sands and gravel.

Soil structure   The arrangement of soil particles into lumps or granules (aggregates).

Soil texture   The size of particles making up the soil with the relative amounts of sand, silt, and clay particles determining texture.

Sole   *See* Plowsole.

Specifications   A written document describing materials, rates, and methods to be used in construction.

Specimen trees   Impressive trees that contribute to playing interest and beauty.

Spillway   A channel, open or closed, gated or ungated, provided to remove excess water from a pond.

Split fairways   Fairways divided crossways or lengthways by a strip of rough.

Spoil   Soil or rock removed from its original site and available for other purposes.

Sprig   *See* Stolon.

Sprigging   Planting pieces of stems or roots of grass. *See* Stolonizing.

Stadium course One with ample spectator areas, as conceived by golf architect Pete Dye collaborating with PGA Tour Commissioner Deanne Beman.

Standard Dimension Ratio (SDR) A measure for pressure rating of PVC pipe, with the same pressure rating for all sizes; unlike Schedule Rated Pipe, which does not involve the same rating for all sizes.

Starter fertilizer A fertilizer with a high phosphorus content applied prior to planting or soon after germination.

Step cut A strip several feet wide between fairway and rough, mowed higher than the fairway and lower than the rough, but played as rough.

Stimpmeter A device to measure the speed of greens in terms of feet the ball rolls from a wood trough elevated at the upper end to a set height. Invented in 1939 by Edward S. Stimpson, it was refined by the USGA in 1978 under the direction of its technical director, Frank W. Thomas.

Stockpile Fill or topsoil placed in piles for future use.

Stolon or sprig An above-ground stem capable of producing new plants.

Stolonizing Until the advent of Penncross in the 1950s this was the preferred method for establishing greens in cool, humid regions. Stolonizing is a technique seldom used today in establishing cool-season grasses, but widely used to establish warm-season grasses, and is generally known as sprigging. It involves vegetative planting in furrows or small holes. It involves broadcasting stolons over a prepared soil and covering them with topsoil.

Storm drainage The drainage system provided for moving excess water off a course following major storms.

Strategic design Golf design that provides alternate routes from tees to greens with the golfer benefitting from well-placed shots.

Stripping Removing topsoil from areas that are to be cut, filled, or otherwise worked.

Strip sodding Laying of sod in strips across the grade.

Subgrade The grade prior to addition of gravel, sand, or topsoil.

Subirrigation The application of irrigation water below ground level.

Subsoiling The breaking of compact subsoils with deep plows and chisels.

Sump An excavated depression to which water is led and from which it drains or is pumped.

Superintendent (1) The person responsible for maintaining and enhancing the golf course, once known as the greenkeeper. The superintendents' professional organization is the Golf Course Superintendent's Association of America (GCSAA). (2) The person in charge of the project during construction.

Surrounds Areas surrounding a green, including but not limited to bunkers, swales, mounds, and depressions.

Sustainable land management (1) The husbandry of the land to enhance its fertility "forever." (2) Construction and maintenance practices together with selection of plant materials that require reduced use of fertilizers and pesticides.

Swale   A shallow channel, perhaps 1 or 2 feet in depth, created to lead surface water to an outfall.

Sward   *See* Greensward.

Tackifiers   Materials applied as sprays to anchor mulch. Examples include petroleum distillates, latexes, gums, colloidal clays, and tars.

Tanbark   A by-product of the leather tanning industry. It is used for golf car and foot paths as a temporary measure.

Target golf   A reference to separated fairways on a hole.

Tee   (1) The area on which tee markers are placed; was formerly known as the tee box. (2) The peg on which the ball is placed when one is playing from the teeing grounds.

Teeing ground   According to the Rules of Golf, this is the starting place for the hole to be played, a rectangular area two club lengths in depth, with a width defined by tee markers.

Tee markers   Wooden or similar blocks that define the outside limits of the teeing grounds.

Tender   A word used rarely in the United States but widely in other countries to describe the contractors bid or proposal.

Texas Bushel   *See* Industry Standard Bale (ISB).

Texas wedge   A putter used off the putting surface or collar.

Thatch   A layer of organic residue, decomposed and undecomposed, living and dead, on or near the surface of the turf.

Through the green   The entire area of the course except teeing ground, putting green, and hazards.

Tiller   The vegetative stem that grows upward in the leaf sheath of a grass plant.

Tilth   An agricultural term for the condition of the soil in relation to its structure.

Top dressing   The spreading of specified soil or sand over a greensward.

Top-load   Contractor's term for loading trucks with a large excavator.

Topographical plan (or topo)   A plan showing contours. *See* Base map.

Total Revenue Multiplier (TRM)   In the sales comparison approach to golf course valuation, this equals sales price divided by total facility revenue (Gimmy and Benson, 1992).

Total soluble salts   The total water-soluble salts as determined by an electrical conductivity test.

Trace elements   *See* Nutrients.

Track   A term popularly used as a synonym for the *course*.

Transit   A survey instrument used to measure distances.

Transpiration   The process by which water vapor is released by a plant to the atmosphere. *See* Evapotranspiration rate.

Trench rock Ledge rock and boulders greater than a specified size encountered in excavation of trenches.

Trickle drain or tube A vertical overflow pipe in a pond. The top of the pipe determines the level of the pond. However, the pond can be drained by opening a valve at the bottom of the pipe.

Truck yardage *See* Bank yardage.

Turf and tree nursery An area set aside to produce sod to repair the greensward, and to grow trees to plant on the course.

Turnkey project A project whereby an architect, or more often a contractor, undertakes to provide a complete playable golf course.

United States Golf Association (USGA) The governing body of golf in the United States.

United States Golf Association Green Section The section of the USGA that is directed to turfgrass.

Unlimited budget A budget in which money is not an object. In design circles it is said facetiously that there are those who can exceed an unlimited budget.

Untouchable or unreachable Golf architect Tom Doak's terms for long par 5s where even the longest hitters seldom, if ever, reach the green in two strokes.

USGA green A green built to specifications prepared by the Green Section, structured to provide rapid drainage and a perched water table to act as a reservoir in dry periods.

Valuation Approaches Gimmy and Benson (1992) list three; cost, sales comparison and income capitalization.

Variety See Cultivar.

Warm-season grasses Turfgrasses that thrive in warm regions.

Washed sod Sod from which all soil and sand particles have been removed by washing.

Water bars Gently sloping berms, furrows, swales, and combinations thereof placed across steep slopes to divert water.

Water hazard According to the Rules of Golf, any area of open water or water course whether or not it contains water.

Watershed The total area from which water drains into a pool or stream.

Water or moisture retention The amount of water retained in a soil; equals the difference between precipitation, natural and applied, versus runoff, including percolation.

Water table The level below which the soil is saturated.

Wetlands According to Balogh and Walker (1993), wetlands include swamps, bogs, marshes, mires, ponds, potholes, and similar areas. Hydrology, vegetation, and soils are used to identify wetlands.

Wilting (wet and dry) The withering of a plant owing to lack of water. Conversely, in a soil saturated to a point that does not permit uptake of water because of a lack of oxygen, "wet" wilt can occur.

Windows   (1) Areas that provide views of the course. (2) Clearings between trees or structures that provide distant vistas or views of adjoining holes. (3) Areas where spectator views of play are not interrupted.

Windrow   A ridge of earth, stones, stumps, or other material placed in a line for loading and removal.

Wood ash   According to plant physiologist T. T. Koslowski, ash is the solid residue of nonvolatile oxides or salts of metals (e.g., sodium, calcium, potash, magnesium, iron, or nonmetallic atoms such as silica) left after wood is thoroughly burned. Wood ash can be a source of potash, and it is sometimes used to raise soil pH.

Working drawings   Designers drawings prepared for builders to follow.

About the Contributing Authors

In order to present the background and parameters of golf course architecture in depth, experts in related fields, and four of our colleagues, contributed complete or partial chapters. The impressive qualifications of these authorities are outlined below.

William W. Amick, ASGCA

Chapter 7 essay, Cayman Golf, and Chapter 11, Golf Courses on Derelict Land

Daytona Beach, Florida, course architect Bill Amick is a past-president of the ASGCA and an accomplished golfer. After graduation from Ohio Wesleyan University, he became a graduate assistant in turfgrass management at Purdue University. Later he apprenticed under course architects William Diddel and Charles Adams. Since entering private practice in 1959 he has been active in course design in the United States and Europe with many renowned layouts to his credit, including Eagle Landing Country Club in South Carolina, the first course designed for the modified Cayman ball. Always searching for "new frontiers," Amick has led in developing courses on landfills.

James McC. Barrett

Chapter 10, Golf Course Irrigation

A leading golf course irrigation consultant, Jim Barrett was graduated from Brown University in 1965 with an A.B. degree in American Civilization. Following four years' active duty in the U.S. Naval Reserve he was clerk of the works and irrigation foreman for a golf course contractor. From 1972 to 1985 he was an associate and irrigation designer with Robert Trent Jones, involved in projects throughout North America, Europe, and the Caribbean. Since 1985 he has been president of James Barrett Associates, one of the first independent consulting firms specializing exclusively in golf course irrigation. As of 1996 he had been involved in 150 golf projects, including several of the top courses in the country.

Kenneth DeMay, FAIA

Chapter 6, Planning the Adjacent Real Estate

Ken DeMay, a principal of Sasaki Associates of Watertown, Massachusetts, has been principal-in-charge of site planning for numerous golf/residential projects. He has collaborated with golf course architects Palmer, Nicklaus, Fazio, Watson, Hurdzan, Prichard, Cupp, McCumber, Rees Jones, and Cornish, Silva and Mungeam. Sasaki has received 30 awards for projects that DeMay designed. He is a registered architect in 28 states and the Virgin Islands. DeMay studied at the U.S. Coast Guard Academy, earned his Bachelor of Architecture degree with honors from Pratt Institute, and Master of Architecture from Harvard University. He has taught for 30 years at the Harvard Graduate School of Design, where he currently teaches golf/residential site planning at the postgraduate level.

Ronald G. Dodson

Chapter 2 essay, Designing with the Land, Not over It

Ronald Dodson was educated at Indiana State University (M.S. in Natural Resource Management), Oakland City University (B.S. in Wildlife Biology), University of Evansville (postgraduate studies in Statistics and Human Relations), and Western Kentucky University (two-year Waste Management Program). He is currently president of Audubon International and chairman of the board of the Audubon Society of New York State. Dodson is author of numerous publications related to the environment, creator of related educational programs, recipient of many honors, and a tireless and objective leader in determining the impact of golf courses on wildlife and environment. His plea for some information and direction—"Tell me how I can help wildlife and the environment"—serves as an inspiration to course designers.

John H. Foy, Director, Florida USGA Green Section

Chapter 12 essay, Bermudagrass Putting Greens, Establishment and Grow-in

John Foy received both his B.S. in Turf Management and a master's degree in Plant Protection and Pest Management from the University of Georgia. He was graduated cum laude and received the Charlie Danner Scholarship for academic performance in turf management from the Georgia Golf Course Superintendents Association. Before joining the Green Section in 1985, John performed field research and development for a pesticide manufacturer, and he has assisted in many construction and renovation projects.

The Golf Course Builders Association of America

Chapter 14, Construction Methods, Equipment, and Commodities: The Constructor's Viewpoint

Philip Arnold, executive vice president of GCBAA made this chapter possible by assembling the writers. Prior to his work with the GCBAA, Arnold was in-house legal counsel for the National Golf Foundation for three years. He attended Florida State University and received his law degree from the University of Memphis.

W. Gary Paumen

Construction Methods and Equipment

Gary Paumen is a construction superintendent, estimator, and marketer for Crown Golf Properties of Northbrook, Illinois. He is skilled both in directing and operating heavy equipment and in manipulating a laptop computer. His forte is directing a golf course project along the critical path from architectural drawings to opening day.

Richard H. Elyea, Virgil Meier, and Dean Mosdell

Purchasing Fertilizer and Seed

Rick Elyea, formerly with Scotts and now with Tee 2 Green, prepared this chapter in draft form. He is a turfgrass consultant providing domestic and worldwide site-specific recommendations on turfgrass, agronomics, and environmental issues for land planners. His paper was reviewed by Scotts scientists Virgil Meier and Dean Mosdell. Additions were made.

Dr. Meier received a B.S. in Agriculture from the University of Illinois, and an M.S. and Ph.D. in Plant Breeding and Genetics from Purdue University. Since 1971 he has developed products and procedures for enhanced seed germination, seed coatings, and treatments for both the consumer and turfgrass professional.

Dr. Mosdell received his undergraduate and master's degrees from Virginia Polytechnic Institute and State University in Agronomy and completed his doctorate at Purdue with research emphasis on nitrogen availability to turfgrass. He serves as director of New Product Development for Fertilizers and Organics at Scotts.

Christine Faulks

Selecting the Root Zone Mix

Christine Faulks is president of Greensmix International Soil Blenders, a leading provider of root zone mixtures for golf course greens and tees. She has been employed in the bulk aggregate supply business since 1978, with special emphasis on quality control. Faulks holds two degrees from the University of Wisconsin-Milwaukee and has taught seminars throughout the country on sand selection, quality control protocol, and organic putting green amendments. She has written numerous articles and assisted in revision of industry textbooks.

Norman W. Hummel Jr.

Chapter 12 Appendices, Draft Specifications—USGA and Similar Greens, and Draft Specifications—California Greens

A native of Buffalo, New York, Dr. Hummel holds a bachelor's degree from New Mexico State University and a master's and doctorate from Pennsylvania State University. A staff member at Cornell University for more than a decade, he entered private practice in 1992 as a soil scientist, based in Trumansburg, New York. He specializes in soil mixtures for golf greens and other turfgrass areas. In 1991, Dr. Hummel devoted his sabbatical to revising laboratory procedures for testing of soils for USGA Green Section specifications. In cooperation with National Director James T. Snow and the Green Section Advisory Committee and Review Panel, he developed the 1993 standard for testing and the methods for constructing USGA greens as set forward in USGA Recommendations for Putting Green Construction.

The LA Group

Chapter 16, The Team Approach to the Design, Permitting, and Construction Monitoring of Golf Projects

The LA Group, a multidisciplinary firm located in Saratoga Springs, New York, was among the first to acquire and utilize high-tech equipment for all phases of design, as well as preparation of specifications and construction supervision. Skilled in environmental sciences, the company is dedicated to investigating what lies beyond existing field knowledge. Three staff members collaborated in the preparation of this paper.

S. Jeffrey Anthony, ASLA

A founding principal of the LA Group, Anthony has more than 25 years' experience in land analysis, master planning, and design. He has published articles on land use policy and lectured widely on environmental resource analysis. As director of landscape design he has successfully completed numerous large-scale golf courses, housing and golf developments, resort facilities, and parks and recreation projects. He specializes in long-range planning and regulatory compliance.

Barbara B. Beall

Beall is an environmental scientist specializing in projects with complicated wetland and regulatory issues, including golf courses. She serves as a continuing education instructor for the GCSAA, teaching "Wetlands and Golf Courses" at seminars nationwide. Prior to her association with the LA Group, Beall worked for the Army Corps of Engineers, where she reviewed course construction. A certified Professional Wetland Scientist, she has published and lectured widely.

Kevin J. Franke

An environmental biologist, Franke serves as project manager for golf courses. Franke is an expert in the use of LEACHM and CREAMS, computer modeling programs for assessing runoff or leaching potential of chemical applications and their effect on aquatic habitats. His articles on these models have appeared in professional journals, including the March/April 1992 issue of the *USGA Green Section Record*.

Thomas A. Marzolf, ASGCA

Chapter 1 essay, Has the Game Changed Due to Advancements in Course Maintenance, Club Design, and Ball Technology?

A design associate of Fazio Golf Course Designers since 1983, Marzolf is a member of the Board of Governors of the American Society of Golf Course Architects, and chair of the Society's Golf Equipment Committee. A 1982 graduate of Virginia Technical College, Marzolf is also a registered landscape architect. He is a native of Columbus, Ohio, and the fourth generation of a golfing family including professionals, collegiate champions, superintendents, and club designers. Marzolf has played an important role in the design of 20 courses in the past decade for the Fazio group, including completed restoration work at Pine Valley, Winged Foot, and Augusta National.

James Francis Moore

Chapter 12 essay, Bermuda Grass Fairways, Establishment and Grow-in

As Director of the Mid-Continent Region of the USGA Green Section, Moore traveled extensively in the United States, Europe, Jamaica, Guam, and New Zealand. He is now program director for the Green Section's new Construction Education Program. His duties include written, Internet, and multimedia resources for construction information and education presentations to golf-related groups throughout the nation. Moore is a graduate of Texas A & M University with a B.S. in Agronomy and Turfgrass Management. He served for six years in the Air Force as a missile system analyst before a seven-year stint as course superintendent at Ridgewood Country Club in Waco, Texas. He is a past-president of the Texas Turfgrass Association.

Desmond Muirhead

Chapter 4 essay, Symbolism and Course Design

A creator, always on the frontier of his art form, and always ahead of the pioneers, Muirhead is president of his own all-encompassing design firm with offices in Newport Beach, California, Jupiter, Florida, and Tokyo, Japan. During his career he has partnered with Gene Sarazen, Jack Nicklaus, Arnold Palmer, and Nick Faldo. Regarded by some as an iconoclast, he has created a wealth of stimulating courses around the world, including several symbolistic layouts. Born in Norwich, England, and educated at Cambridge University, Muirhead has written six books, lectured at many universities, and authored countless articles on golf, while coining the phrase "golf course community." Recently, his plan for Lippo Village in Jakarta, Indonesia, featured a town of 85,000 with several golf courses.

Mark A. Mungeam, ASGCA

Chapter 18 essay, Civil Engineering and Course Design

A graduate of Worcester (Massachusetts) Polytechnic Institute in civil engineering, Mungeam worked in course maintenance and construction before joining course architects Cornish & Silva in 1987. In less than a decade he was a partner in the firm, with designs and redesigns in the United States, Guatemala, Italy, and Switzerland.

Richard L. Norton

Chapter 15, Golf Course Financing

Richard Norton is a leader in strategic positioning analysis, market/financial feasibility, funding/implementation strategies, membership development plans, and operational audits. His clients in the public sector have included Scottsdale, Arizona, Sunrise, Florida, the U.S. Air Force; in the private sector, Marriott Resorts, Quaker Oats, and Golden Bear International. Currently vice president and general manager of National Golf Foundation Research, Norton holds a B.A. and a master's degree in business administration from Brigham Young University. Under Norton's direction, the NGF information service has expanded more than 20,000 data sources and references.

James T. Snow

Chapter 13, Turfgrass Selection

National director of the United States Golf Association Green Section since 1990, Snow joined the USGA in 1976, serving as agronomist and then as director of the Northeastern Region. He oversees the Turf Advisory Service, consisting of 15 regional agronomists who consult with golf course superintendents and course officials at more than 1,600 golf courses each year. He also serves as chair of the USGA's Turfgrass and Environmental Research Committee, with an annual budget in excess of 1.2 million for research in turfgrass improvement and environmental issues. He is editor of the *Green Section Record*, the USGA's bimonthly journal of turfgrass management. Snow received his B.A. and master of science degrees in horticulture from Cornell University. Since joining the USGA, he has written more than 100 articles for industry publications, spoken at innumerable meetings, and made significant contributions to advances in the playing surfaces of golf.

Catherine Suddarth

Golf Facilities in the United States by Years and Decades

Currently Research Manager for the National Golf Foundation Research Department, Suddarth has spent six years with the organization tracking existing golf course supply and golf course development, as well as implementing research studies for NGF members. She has played golf for 35 years, winning four Tennessee Junior Championship titles and three citywide championships.

Ronald E. Whitten

Foreword

Architecture editor for *Golf Digest*, Whitten holds a B.Sc. degree in education from the University of Nebraska, and a Juris Doctor degree from Washburn University School of Law in Kansas. He worked for 12 years as a practicing trial attorney before becoming a full-time editor. Although prolific British writers Horace G. Hutchinson and Bernard Darwin, together with Americans Herb Graffis and Herbert Warren Wind, were generous in remarks devoted to course design, none compare in the study, depth, and attention Whitten has provided architects and their creations.

Whitten is co-author with Geoffrey Cornish of *The Golf Course* and *The Architects of Golf*, two seminal works on golf course designers.

Subject Index

Index of Golf Courses